Trust, but Verify

INTERNATIONAL HISTORY
PROJECT SERIES

James G. Hershberg
series editor

Jimmy Carter in Africa
Race and the Cold War
By Nancy Mitchell

The Regional Cold Wars in Europe, East Asia, and the Middle East
Crucial Periods and Turning Points
Edited by Lorenz M. Lüthi

The Euromissile Crisis and the End of the Cold War
Edited by Leopoldo Nuti, Frédéric Bozo, Marie-Pierre Rey, and Bernd Rother

Poland's War on Radio Free Europe, 1950–1989
By Paweł Machcewicz
Translated by Maya Latynski

Battleground Africa
Cold War in the Congo, 1960–1965
By Lise Namikas

The Soviet Cuban Missile Crisis
Castro, Mikoyan, Kennedy, Khrushchev, and the Missiles
of November
By Sergo Mikoyan. Edited by Svetlana Savranskaya

Divided Together
The United States and the Soviet Union in the United Nations,
1945–1965
By Ilya V. Gaiduk

Marigold
The Lost Chance for Peace in Vietnam
By James G. Hershberg

After Leaning to One Side
China and Its Allies in the Cold War
By Zhihua Shen and Danhui Li

The Cold War in East Asia 1945–1991
Edited by Tsuyoshi Hasegawa

Stalin and Togliatti
Italy and the Origins of the Cold War
By Elena Agarossi and Victor Zaslavsky

[*continued after index*]

Trust, but Verify

The Politics of Uncertainty and the Transformation of the Cold War Order, 1969–1991

Edited by Martin Klimke, Reinhild Kreis, and Christian F. Ostermann

Woodrow Wilson Center Press
Washington, D.C.

Stanford University Press
Stanford, California

EDITORIAL OFFICES
Woodrow Wilson Center Press
Woodrow Wilson International Center for Scholars
One Woodrow Wilson Plaza
1300 Pennsylvania Avenue, NW
Washington, DC 20004-3027
www.wilsoncenter.org

ORDER FROM
Stanford University Press
Chicago Distribution Center
11030 South Langley Avenue
Chicago, IL 60628
Telephone: 800-621-2736; 773-568-1550

2 4 6 8 9 7 5 3 1

Library of Congress Cataloging-in-Publication Data
Names: Klimke, Martin, editor. | Kreis, Reinhild, editor. | Ostermann, Christian, editor.
Title: Trust, but verify : the politics of uncertainty and the transformation of the Cold War order, 1969–1991 / edited by Martin Klimke, Reinhild Kreis, and Christian Ostermann.
Description: Washington, D.C. : Woodrow Wilson Center Press ; Stanford, California : Stanford University Press, 2016. | Series: Cold War international history project series | Includes bibliographical references and index.
Identifiers: LCCN 2016007777 (print) | LCCN 2016020079 (ebook) | ISBN 9780804798099 (hardcover : alk. paper) | ISBN 9781503600133 (ebook)
Subjects: LCSH: World politics—1965–1975. | World politics—1975–1985. | International relations—Psychological aspects. | Diplomacy—Psychological aspects. | East and West—History—20th century. | Great powers—History—20th century. | Detente—History—20th century. | Trust—Political aspects. | Emotions—Political aspects. | Rhetoric—Political aspects.
Classification: LCC D849 .T78 2016 (print) | LCC D849 (ebook) | DDC 327.09/047—dc23
LC record available at https://lccn.loc.gov/2016007777

Cover image: Gary Hershorn/Reuters
Cover design: Naylor Design

Contents

List of Tables and Figures   ix

Acknowledgments   xi

Introduction   1
    Martin Klimke, Reinhild Kreis, and Christian F. Ostermann

I: The Personal Factor

1. Untrusting and Untrusted: Mao's China at a Crossroads,
    1969   17
    Sergey Radchenko

2. "No Crowing": Reagan, Trust, and Human Rights   42
    Sarah B. Snyder

3. Trust between Adversaries and Allies:
    President George H. W. Bush, Trust,
    and the End of the Cold War   63
    J. Simon Rofe

II: Risk, Commitment, and Verification:
The Blocs at the Negotiating Table

4. Trust and Mistrust and the American Struggle for
    Verification of the Strategic Arms Limitation Talks,
    1969–1979   85
    Arvid Schors

5. Trust and Transparency at the CSCE, 1969–1975   102
    Michael Cotey Morgan

6. Trust or Verification? Accepting Vulnerability
    in the Making of the INF Treaty   121
    Nicholas J. Wheeler, Joshua Baker, and Laura Considine

        III: Between Consolidation and Corrosion:
        Trust inside the Ideological Blocs of East and West

7. Whom Did the East Germans Trust? Popular Opinion
    on Threats of War, Confrontation, and Détente
    in the German Democratic Republic, 1968–1989   143
    Jens Gieseke

8. Not Quite "Brothers in Arms": East Germany
    and People's Poland between Mutual Dependency
    and Mutual Distrust, 1975–1990   167
    Jens Boysen

9. Institutionalizing Trust? Regular Summitry
    (G7s and European Councils) from the Mid-1970s
    until the Mid-1980s   198
    Noël Bonhomme and Emmanuel Mourlon-Druol

10. Trust through Familiarity: Transatlantic Relations
    and Public Diplomacy in the 1980s   218
    Reinhild Kreis

        IV: On the Sidelines or in the Middle?
        Small and Neutral States

11. "Footnotes" as an Expression of Distrust?
    The United States and the NATO "Flanks"
    in the Last Two Decades of the Cold War   237
    Effie G. H. Pedaliu

12. Switzerland and Détente: A Revised Foreign
    Policy Characterized by Distrust   259
    Sandra Bott and Janick Marina Schaufelbuehl

Conclusion   279
    Deborah Welch Larson

List of Contributors   289

Index   295

Tables and Figures

Tables

7.1. Infratest 1972 on the Eastern Treaties   149
7.2. Infratest 1973/74 on East and West German Government Aims
     and Intentions   151
7.3. Infratest 1975 on the Inter-German Relationship   154
7.4. Infratest 1975 on the CSCE   155
7.5. Infratest 1978, 1980, and 1982 on Superpower Armed Conflict   156
7.6. Infratest 1981 on the NATO Double-Track Decision   157
7.7. Infratest 1982 on the International Peace Movement   161

Figures

9.1. General view of The Hague European Council meeting,
     November 30, 1976.   201
9.2. G7 formal dinner at the Imperial Palace in Tokyo, Japan,
     May 6, 1986.   206
9.3. Bilateral meeting between Ronald Reagan and François Mitterrand
     during the G7 economic summit in Williamsburg, Virginia,
     May 28, 1983.   209
9.4. Ronald Reagan and G7 leaders viewing a colonial craft display
     in Williamsburg, Virginia, May 29, 1983.   214

Acknowledgments

Without the generous and persistent support of our two cooperating institutions, we would not have been able to produce this volume, which has its origins in an international conference held at the German Historical Institute and the Woodrow Wilson International Center for Scholars on November 7–9, 2011. Our appreciation, therefore, goes to the GHI, its former director Hartmut Berghoff, deputy directors Uwe Spiekermann and Britta Waldschmidt-Nelson, and former administrative director Sabine Fix, as well as Nicole Kruz and Bärbel Thomas for facilitating our conference and supporting this project.

At the Wilson Center, our thanks go to the History and Public Policy Program, in particular to Emily Malkin, Timothy McDonnell, and Sonya Michel for their work on the original conference. At Woodrow Wilson Center Press, we are grateful to Joe Brinley for his trust and dedication, as well as to Shannon Granville for her careful and thoughtful copyediting and for skillfully guiding the book through its production process. Their comments and questions impelled us to clarify and sharpen our ideas and prose, and the book is a better one for it.

Trust, but Verify

Introduction

Martin Klimke, Reinhild Kreis, and Christian F. Ostermann

Trust and distrust are omnipresent when it comes to media coverage of international relations, the speeches and statements of politicians and diplomats, or their memoirs. At all times, written and oral statements on foreign affairs have drawn heavily on the rhetoric of emotions, referring to fear, hopes, trust, mistrust, and disappointment. Visual media such as photographs, paintings, and political cartoons, as well as historical exhibitions and forms of remembrance, indicate or even highlight the supposedly emotional dimension of international relations. Yet both policy practitioners and scholars have wrestled with understanding this elusive factor in a paradigm dominated by seemingly more tangible categories such as military hardware, "national interest," and structural or systemic forces. Trust and distrust are, as emotions in general, often stated but rarely integrated systematically into analyses of international relations.

This volume seeks to explore the "emotional side" of the Cold War and its connections with foreign policy by focusing on trust and distrust as fundamental categories in international relations.[1] It asks how trust and distrust shaped the Cold War as a rhetorical strategy, a political goal, and an emotion.[2] Within this framework, the contributors seek to analyze questions of trust as part of the dynamic of the various relations in the Cold War world; namely, between the superpowers, within the two ideological blocs, and inside individual countries. By testing the role of trust and mistrust in a variety of scenarios at the end of the Cold War, they advocate for opening a new, previously neglected research agenda on the role of emotions in international relations. Trust and mistrust were by no means the only important emotions, let alone factors, in all of the scenarios examined, yet they are of particular importance for explaining actions, strategies, rhetoric, and institutional settings during the Cold War as a period characterized by multifarious dependencies and insecurities that needed careful balancing.

Trust, confidence, and reliability, but also risk-taking and the search for security, were essential ingredients of this conflict, whose dynamics changed rapidly over time and pervaded the domestic politics and international policies of both the superpowers and the countries in their respective ideological blocs. Taken seriously, employing the concept of trust as a category for analyzing historical processes goes far beyond its use as a "feel-good word" in political statements, speeches, and memoirs of politicians or diplomats.[3] It opens up new perspectives on the dynamics of international relations, the entanglement between international and domestic spheres, and relations between structural and personal aspects. The second half of the Cold War, from the end of the 1960s through 1991, is especially suited for an initial attempt to discern the relative weight of trust and mistrust and how such considerations may affect political dynamics and relationships. The period was characterized by both its efforts for rapprochement and its renewed anxieties over the possibilities of a "hot war" between the superpowers and the prospect of global nuclear annihilation. This complex mixture of insecurity, trust, and fear on international and domestic levels shaped Cold War policy, which grew more flexible and diverse as each side sought to escape the orthodoxy of deterrence and mutual assured destruction. Because these transformations affected relations between the two superpowers and caused uncertainties within both blocs, this period provides a rich reservoir of examples of trust-building and risk-taking efforts, as well as verification strategies.

Yet how can we define trust in this context? Although the concept of trust originally was a philosophical notion used, among other things, to describe interpersonal relations and their psychological dimensions, in recent decades it has been applied widely in the fields of sociology, psychology, economics, media studies, political science, and neurobiology.[4] Therefore, a large number of theories exist on what defines trust and distrust. For the purpose of this volume, which aims at tracing trust and distrust in various national and international constellations, it seems appropriate to not define trust too narrowly but to specify general characteristics broad enough to cover the case studies presented.

Trust generally is defined as "a three-part relation that is grounded in the truster's assessment of the trusted with respect to some action," and therefore as an attitude toward other people or organizations who appear trustworthy.[5] It entails different qualities such as predictability of actions, credibility as a belief in whether an actor will keep its word, and the "expectation that someone has benevolent intentions and will not try to exploit us."[6] Yet it is important to note that trust is more than shared interests. It has an emotional quality, and can best be described as a mixture of calculation and emotion.[7]

Consequently, the risk of being betrayed or disappointed is inherent to trust. It "leaves others an opportunity to harm one when one trusts, and also shows one's confidence that they will not take it. Reasonable trust will require good grounds for such confidence in another's good will, or at least the absence of good grounds for expecting their ill will or indifference. Trust then . . . is accepted vulnerability to another's possible but not expected ill will (or lack of good will) toward one."[8] As Niklas Luhmann has put it, "To show trust is to anticipate the future. It is to behave as though the future were certain."[9] During the Cold War, however, not-knowing was the rule rather than the exception, leaving plenty of room for speculation and for what recently has been called the "the imaginary of the Cold War."[10]

Distrust, by contrast, is more than the mere absence of trust and is not necessarily negatively connoted.[11] Distrust can sharpen the senses and heighten vigilance, thus protecting against harm, as is indicated by the phrase "healthy suspicion." However, trust and distrust are context-bound and conditional; both are not a matter of black and white but are "matters of degree."[12] Both trust and mistrust can function like filters in estimating actions or words, for better or worse.[13] Furthermore, feelings of trust and distrust do not necessarily mirror each other and are not always mutual.

This volume traces specific constellations and the factors which led to the building or erosion of (dis)trust or the evocation of such a development on a rhetorical level. The Cold War as structured by the existence of two systems of alliances is ideally suited for such an approach. The superpowers, as well as their alliance partners, naturally perceived each other's actions and strategies very differently at times, and what enhanced trust with one player could at the same time raise suspicion and mistrust among others. How to balance the differing assessments and interests remained an important and highly debated question both within the blocs and between the superpowers.

Before the Geneva summit on arms reduction with the Soviet Union in November 1985, US president Ronald Reagan famously quipped, "Nations do not distrust each other because they are armed. They are armed because they distrust each other."[14] A few days later, when he and Mikhail Gorbachev met for the first time at the summit—the first such meeting between the leaders of the United States and the Soviet Union in seven years—Gorbachev responded in kind: "Trust is not restored right away. It is a difficult process. We have heeded the U.S. president's assurances that the United States is not seeking superiority and does not want nuclear war. We sincerely want these statements to be confirmed by deeds."[15]

Reagan's and Gorbachev's statements hint at several important questions. First, Gorbachev's statement highlights the temporal dimension and the

3

processual character of trust. Trust is limited and reversible; it can be built or destroyed. This holds true for relations not only between competing powers but also between allies and friends. The presence or absence of trust therefore is a dynamic condition that changes over time.[16] As Martin Hartmann has put it, it is a choice and "an achievement and can never be taken for granted."[17]

Maintaining trust requires permanent dedication and involvement, as do attempts to change distrust into trust or to build trust in the first place. In doing so, the idea of trust or mistrust is closely interrelated with concepts of the past and future. Past experiences affect expectations in future developments and color estimates of someone's trustworthiness, as apparent in historical attributions of countries' characteristics; for example, ideas about "archenemies" or "special relationships" in international relations. In addition, the concept of trust illustrates the connection between international treaties and diplomatic assurances in an age of nuclear technology, one of the key themes of the Cold War. Are technologies and efforts toward mutual agreements a sign of distrust, or are they an expression of cautious trust in one's opponent? Are they, in other words, an exercise in trust-building? Furthermore, by demanding deeds and not merely words, Gorbachev's remarks at the Geneva summit referred to an escape from a situation as tense as that which existed between the superpowers in the early 1980s, and from relations characterized by mistrust in general. To minimize the risks and vulnerabilities inherent in trust, those who seek to trust start to develop verification strategies, resort to monitoring, or enforce certain checks and regulations. Deborah Welch Larson and others have outlined how mistrust can be overcome by actions ranging from symbolic actions, such as smiling or shaking hands over "small agreements," to "costly concessions."

Both costly concessions and verification strategies played an important role during the Cold War. Ronald Reagan, for instance, made the "trust, but verify" strategy one of his signature phrases. Presenting this maxim as a translation of a Russian proverb, Reagan predominantly used it when describing US-Soviet relations. In December 1987, for example, the two countries signed the Intermediate-Range Nuclear Forces (INF) Treaty, which set forth the destruction of all land-based nuclear missiles with a range of 300 to 3,400 miles, a permanent halt in the production of such missiles, and—crucially for Reagan—mutual inspection rights. When Reagan announced at the subsequent press conference in Washington that the spirit of the agreement was in keeping with his aforementioned motto, Gorbachev replied with amusement, "You repeat that at every meeting."[18] A costly concession indeed: the Soviet verification provisions were crucial in dissipating US doubts about Gorbachev's motives.[19]

The idea of costly concessions as a signal of trustworthiness illustrates, therefore, the significance of communication. The processes of developing, maintaining, or destroying trust cannot be isolated from communication. That is why the few existing histories of trust are stories of interactions, relationships, and perceptions, and why trust often is regarded as a form of social capital. Symbolic actions and the effective staging of trust, trustworthiness, distrust, and other such qualities play a major role in such communication processes.

Yet when it comes to communications and symbolic actions, new problems arise. Scholarship has suggested that there are different "cultures of trust" and that societies differ in the scope and character of risks they produce as well as in their reaction towards risks and uncertainties.[20] William Reddy introduced the concept of "emotional regimes" that determine which feelings to show and to communicate based on what is opportune at a given time or social context.[21] What is regarded as trustworthy therefore varies from one society to another, as does the meaning of codes or symbols, which complicates communication. Furthermore, semantic differences can cause misunderstandings, even with regard to the term "trust" itself: Whereas English-speaking countries differentiate between "trust" and "confidence," there is no such distinction in German, French, or most other languages. As Ute Frevert has stated, the communication of trust and mistrust eminently is bound to language and rhetoric.[22] Scholars therefore need to distinguish carefully between cultural contexts, rhetoric strategies, vernacular uses of certain terms, and trust/mistrust as analytical concepts.

Investigating trust and mistrust during the Cold War is part of a larger turn toward the role of emotions in recent historiography. Yet the topic remains highly controversial. How emotions should be defined and how they can be applied in historical analysis are the subjects of vigorous debate.[23] The same holds true for the applications of trust and mistrust as analytical concepts in international relations, since definitions and approaches differ between scholars and disciplines. Whereas historians predominantly try to historicize emotions such as trust, mistrust, fear, hope, and pride, pay attention to their change over time, and analyze their expression by specific individuals, social and political scientists operate with game theoretical approaches, mostly neglecting questions about the temporal dynamics, the origins of trust and mistrust, or internal bloc and domestic developments. Others even claim that trust does not play a role in the field of international relations at all.

Previous scholarship on trust and mistrust during the Cold War has focused mainly on its formative and final phases. The integration of Germany and the relationship between Ronald Reagan and Mikhail Gorbachev in particular have been given a great deal of attention.[24] This volume aims at expanding these priorities by focusing on topics such as the personal factor, the role of smaller states, intrabloc developments, and negotiations between the blocs—factors which shaped the Cold War to a considerable degree but so far have not been analyzed systematically in their emotional dimension. The goal is to explore the relative weight of trust in a variety of scenarios both between and within the two ideological blocs, whether in the form of long-standing personal relations that allowed individuals to earn each other's trust (or mistrust) over time, initial in-person meetings between national leaders and negotiators, situations where good faith was a precondition for advancing negotiations in the first place, or trust and mistrust among a general public that for the most part gained information filtered by the media and had little chance to consider the trustworthiness of foreign representatives themselves.[25]

The first section of this volume examines the personal factor—the role of individuals—in creating or obstructing trust-building during the last phase of the Cold War. Charting the deficit of trust in Sino-Soviet relations throughout the 1960s, Sergey Radchenko's analysis of the border clashes between the People's Republic of China and the Soviet Union in March 1969 exemplifies the significant consequences of mistrust and misperceptions for resolving international conflicts. Radchenko details the development of Chinese leader Mao Zedong's perception of the Soviet Union as a challenge to China's autonomy and the (cultural) revolution, underscoring Mao's failure to understand how the Soviet Union interpreted his actions as a credible threat. Employing his own frame of reference, Mao failed to grasp that the Soviet Union did not see the border conflict as a catalyst for internal mobilization and political control at home and in its satellite states, but as yet another manifestation of the seeming irrationality of Chinese foreign policy. Mao's surprise and feeling of hostile encirclement, as well as the deepening of Soviet distrust, paved the way in turn for China's famous rapprochement with the United States under President Richard Nixon.

Sarah Snyder explores Ronald Reagan's strategy of "quiet diplomacy" toward the Soviet Union with regard to human rights as a trust-building initiative, arguing that the success of that approach was key in the developments that finally brought the Cold War to an end. Snyder examines Reagan's efforts for exit visas on behalf of human rights activists, Jewish refuseniks, and religious dissidents such as Pentecostals, following the trail of his strategy through the 1985 Geneva and 1986 Reykjavik summits until his departure from office. In her view, Reagan's promise not to "crow" about his successes in this area and his decision to limit public pressure on Gorbachev about human rights led to increasing concessions by the Soviet Union, which fostered a rising level of trust in their relationship. Coming to see Gorbachev's commitment to personal agreements on human rights as a litmus test for the status of trust between the superpowers as a whole, Snyder credits Reagan's approach with facilitating the end of the Cold War.

Simon Rofe investigates the central role of trust-building for the George H. W. Bush administration and its crucial significance in navigating the political transformations of 1990–91. Portraying Bush's foreign policy as driven by an effort to establish trust among adversaries to minimize risk and maintain order, Rofe shows how Bush and his key advisers, Secretary of State James A. Baker III and National Security Advisor Brent Scowcroft, crafted a strategy of personal diplomacy and caution. Analyzing in particular the demise of the Soviet Union in late 1991 as well as the 1990–91 Kuwait crisis, Rofe highlights the Bush administration's prioritization of reliability, steadfastness, and personal relationships in fostering a culture of mutual trust as key assets for US foreign policy before, ironically, a lack of trust within the US electorate with regard to his tax policy prevented Bush from winning another term.

The second section of this volume on the blocs at the negotiation table shifts the focus from individuals to the fora of exchange in interstate relations, international agreements, and specific diplomatic initiatives. Arvid Schors explores the "politics of dialogue" put on display during the Strategic Arms Limitation Talks (SALT) from 1969 to 1979 as one of the key components of détente efforts between the superpowers. Concentrating on how these talks were perceived by the American public, Schors demonstrates how new verification technology seemingly compensated for the lack of trust among the negotiation partners and at first successfully redirected a deeply ingrained "distrust narrative" in public discourse. Particular to the American case, faith in the combined forces of superior satellite reconnaissance and human intelligence allowed US policymakers to circumvent the volatile field of Soviet trustworthiness, maintain a posture of realistic mistrust and skepticism, and provide both an intellectual rationale and an emotional reassurance for these talks. However, although the Carter administration's communicative strategy at the end of the 1970s explicitly disavowed any notion of trust with regard to SALT, the question of compliance and the belief in absolute verifiability and invulnerability ultimately became too punctured to retain its persuasiveness, thus contributing to the failure of SALT.

Highlighting another influential international negotiating body, Michael Morgan's essay examines the Conference on Security and Cooperation in Europe (CSCE) from 1969 to 1975. Morgan contends that trust was both a tool and objective of the conference, detailing how, even in the absence of trust, a major international agreement was concluded with the Helsinki Final Act of 1975, the outcome of the CSCE talks. In a clear attempt to advance their respective interests, Warsaw Pact member states focused on state sovereignty and the immutability of post–World War II European borders as a cornerstone of their definition of international security, whereas North Atlantic

Treaty Organization (NATO) member states emphasized transparency, freer movement, and human rights, as well as confidence-building measures. As Morgan argues, the "tangled lines of trust and distrust" at the CSCE among the United States, the Western European countries, the neutral states, and the Soviet Union were incredibly complex, owing to the multitude of national interests that crossed different ideological camps, but they eventually secured the conference's success.

In the third contribution to this section, Nicholas Wheeler, Joshua Baker, and Laura Considine use the INF Treaty as a case study to explore the relationship between trust and verification. They argue that the acceptance of verification measures has to be considered an act of trust, since it implies the acceptance of one's vulnerability as a result of an altered perception of the trustworthiness of one's opponent. More specifically, they illustrate how Gorbachev's notion of trustworthiness toward the United States changed through the influence of his inner circle, his understanding of the dynamics of a security dilemma fed by mutual fear and mistrust, his trusting actions toward the development of a common security on an international level, and his personal relationship with Ronald Reagan. By decoupling INF from the Strategic Defense Initiative in February 1987, agreeing to on-site inspections of INF missile manufacturing and storage sites in June 1987, and proposing a global "Double Zero" option including short-range intermediate nuclear forces systems in Europe and Asia in July 1987, Gorbachev's concessions fundamentally contributed to mutual trust-building and made the INF Treaty possible, thereby paving the way for the end of the Cold War.

The third section investigates intrastate and intrabloc relations and the role of trust inside the different ideological systems. Drawing on reports of the East German Ministry for State Security and West German opinion polls, Jens Gieseke outlines ideological, official, and bottom-up trust regimes within East Germany, examining the attitude of the East German population toward its own government and that of the Federal Republic. Gieseke unearths, for example, how a noticeable sympathy and trustworthiness emerged among East Germans toward West German parties and politicians such as West German chancellor Willy Brandt in the wake of Ostpolitik, in conjunction with increasing mistrust in and criticism of their own government, which alarmed East German intelligence officials during the 1970s. However, Brandt's departure in 1974, the presidency of Ronald Reagan, and the renewed nuclear arms race and NATO's decision to position nuclear weapons in Western Europe helped to offset this asymmetry of trust relations by partially alienating East Germans from Western policies, leading to an increasing fear of war and feeling of helplessness in the face of renewed tension between the superpowers. In the first half of the 1980s, this decline of vertical trust relationships and emotional bonds in East Germany opened the space for the rise of horizontal trust regimes in the form of the independent peace movement, which prepared the ground for successive bottom-up activism to blossom later in the decade.

Illuminating the significance of trust in intrabloc relations within the Warsaw Pact, Jens Boysen assesses the relationship between East Germany and Poland during the last phase of the Cold War. Boysen explains how the historical legacy of German-Polish relations infused the relationship of both countries with mistrust, despite the officially proclaimed brotherhood of a "socialist community" mandated from Moscow. Personal enmity between communist leaders Walter Ulbricht and Władysław Gomułka, conceptual differences of notions of statehood, and rivaling foreign policy goals and ideas about tolerance for domestic opposition since the end of the 1970s only exacerbated these tensions, which not even successful military cooperation under the Warsaw Pact umbrella was able to alleviate. Held together by their relationship to the Soviet hegemon, the officially required "trust" between the two countries fully disintegrated in the second half of the 1980s as Gorbachev's reforms allowed Poland a more flexible interpretation of socialism, which East German officials understood as a direct threat to the very survival of socialism itself.

Directing attention to the Western alliance, Noël Bonhomme and Emmanuel Mourlon-Druol describe how the maintenance and fostering of trust was a crucial element in founding both the G7 summits and the European Council in the mid-1970s. Deeply anchored in the strong friendship between West German chancellor Helmut Schmidt and French president Valéry Giscard d'Estaing, both initiatives sought to deepen interpersonal relations as well as recover systemic trust in the Western (economic) systems in an informal, multilateral setting. The institutionalization and frequency of these meetings not only allowed for the development of a framework of informal coordination even in the absence of trust; it also provided a platform for the socialization of new leaders and a ritualistic display of Western unity, thus addressing potential international and domestic deficits of trust by "formalizing informality."

Reinhild Kreis investigates public diplomacy as an attempt to (re)build trust within the Western alliance during the late 1970s and 1980s. Public diplomacy was supposed to help prevent the alleged "drifting apart" of Western Europe and the United States, and to overcome suspicion of and mistrust in the partners' intentions and capabilities, both of which had been shaken during the 1970s and seemed to threaten the cohesion of the Atlantic alliance. Taking West German–American relations as an example, Kreis shows how increased public diplomacy efforts aimed at creating familiarity as a precondition of trust, trying to build on a societal level what is known from interpersonal contacts: trust through familiarity, generated via interaction and shared experiences.

The final section of the volume focuses on trust regimes among small and neutral states in the Cold War. Effie Pedaliu explores the practice of "footnoting" of joint NATO documents by states such as Denmark and Greece as an expression of disagreement with nuclear policies within the Western defense community. In Pedaliu's view, both Denmark and Greece experienced a profound decline of trust in NATO's ability and willingness to protect their national interests, a decline that was caused by a perceived neglect of the northern and southern flanks in favor of US attention to Southeast Asia during the Vietnam War, a switch from "massive retaliation" to "flexible response" and détente in US nuclear policy, and NATO's inaction toward humanitarian abuses during the Greek dictatorship from 1967 to 1974. In addition, sociocultural and economic change, animosity toward the increasingly bellicose tone of the Reagan administration, and a politically convenient anti-Americanism both forced and allowed the Danish and Greek governments to issue dissenting footnotes to NATO communiqués, criticizing alliance policies. These footnotes therefore can be seen as manifestations of distrust that challenged the operation and harmony of NATO as an effective alliance, even if they could not thwart particular NATO decisions.

Sandra Bott and Janick Marina Schaufelbuehl illustrate how Switzerland aimed to redefine its neutrality in international relations in the first half of the 1970s. On the one hand, Switzerland maintained its traditional Cold War maxims of armed defense, neutrality, and solidarity. On the other hand, in the face of détente and the perception of a new global context, the Swiss Federal Council, inspired by the Federal Political Department, embarked on a more active foreign policy that aimed to rebrand Swiss neutrality by renewing "goodwill" and trust toward it. Initiatives to this effect included seeking participation in the CSCE, considering membership in the United Nations, and increased development aid and diplomatic recognition of the remaining communist states with which Switzerland did not have official relations. The development of this global security policy was also driven by a perceived threat emanating from a domestic New Left (the surveillance of which was raised to a dramatic level), subversive forces in the developing world, and the potential of terrorism. Although this reorientation was not entirely successful, it was driven by a profound distrust of previous alliance systems and the process of détente, which eventually led Switzerland to a more globally oriented and defensive posture in international relations. The volume closes with a comment by Deborah Welch Larson, who sums up the findings and suggests directions for further research.

The chapters in this volume seek to demonstrate the usefulness of "trust" and "distrust" as fundamental categories in explaining the Cold War and its demise from the early 1970s to 1990–91 by looking at specific historical cases. Though the cases given here are highly contextual, preliminary in their findings, and limited in scope, they nonetheless point toward the critical importance of understanding the deep-seated emotional underpinnings of Cold War era foreign policy and politics. They also impress on us the extraordinary challenge and feat of overcoming this multifaceted confrontation. Grasping the personal, cultural, and processual nature of trust as a policy element therefore can be instructive not just for scholars in their efforts to historicize the conflict that dominated the latter half of the twentieth century, but also for policy practitioners as they face new international crises and challenges.

Notes

1. For the booming field of history of emotions, see, e.g., Peter N. Stearns and Jan Lewis, eds., *An Emotional History of the United States* (New York: New York University Press, 1998); William M. Reddy, *The Navigation of Feeling: A Framework for the History of Emotions* (New York: Cambridge University Press, 2001); Barbara H. Rosenwein, *Emotional Communities in the Early Middle Ages* (Ithaca, NY: Cornell University Press, 2006); Ute Frevert, *Emotions in History: Lost and Found* (Budapest: Central European University Press, 2011); Susan J. Matt and Peter N. Stearns, ed., *Doing Emotions History* (Urbana: University of Illinois Press, 2013); and Martin Hartmann, *Die Praxis des Vertrauens* [The practice of trust] (Berlin: Suhrkamp, 2011). For concrete applications of this approach to Cold War history, see, e.g., Barbara Keys, "Henry Kissinger: The Emotional Statesman," *Diplomatic History* 35, no. 4 (2011): 587–609; and Frank Costigliola, *Roosevelt's Lost Alliances: How Personal Politics Helped Start the Cold War* (Princeton, NJ: Princeton University Press, 2012). For the application of this approach to more recent case studies, see Todd H. Hall, *Emotional Diplomacy: Official Emotion on the International Stage* (Ithaca, NY: Cornell University Press, 2015).

2. Reinhild Kreis, "Arbeit am Beziehungsstatus. Vertrauen und Misstrauen in den außenpolitischen Beziehungen der Bundesrepublik Deutschland" [Working on the relationship status: Trust and distrust in the foreign relations of the Federal Republic of Germany], in *"Diplomatie mit Gefühl. Vertrauen, Misstrauen und die Außenpolitik der Bundesrepublik Deutschland* [Diplomacy with emotion: Trust, mistrust, and the foreign policy of the Federal Republic of Germany], ed. Reinhild Kreis (Munich: De Gruyter Oldenbourg, 2015), 13–14.

3. Ute Frevert, "Does Trust Have a History?" (Max Weber Lecture Series 2009-01, European University Institute, Florence, 2009), 5, http://cadmus.eui.eu/bitstream/handle/1814/11258/MWP_LS_2009_01.pdf.

4. For introductions into this topic, see, e.g., Piotr Sztompka, *Trust: A Sociological Theory* (Cambridge, UK: Cambridge University Press, 1999); Ken Booth and Nicholas J. Wheeler, *The Security Dilemma: Fear, Cooperation and Trust in World Politics* (New York: Palgrave Macmillan, 2008); Reinhard Bachmann and Akbar Zaheer, ed., *Handbook of Trust Research* (Cheltenham, UK: Edward Elgar, 2006); Roderick M.

Kramer, ed., *Organizational Trust: A Reader* (Oxford: Oxford University Press, 2006); Ivana Marková and Alex Gillespie, ed. *Trust and Distrust: Sociocultural Perspectives* (Charlotte, NC: Information Age, 2008); and Cristiano Castelfranchi and Rino Falcone, *Trust Theory: A Socio-Cognitive and Computational Model* (Chichester: John Wiley & Sons, 2010). See also the "Trust Initiative" of the Russell Sage Foundation (http://www.russellsage.org/programs/other/trust/) and its comprehensive publication series, including Karen S. Cook, Margaret Levi, and Russell Hardin, eds., *Whom Can We Trust? How Groups, Networks, and Institutions Make Trust Possible* (New York: Russell Sage Foundation, 2009); Karen S. Cook, Russell Hardin, and Margaret Levi, eds., *Cooperation without Trust?* (New York: Russell Sage Foundation, 2005); and Russell Hardin, *Trust and Trustworthiness* (New York: Russell Sage Foundation, 2002); as well as the interdisciplinary work of the "Trust Institute" established in 2006 at Stony Brook University (http://www.stonybrook.edu/trust/).

5. Hardin, *Trust and Trustworthiness*, xx.

6. Deborah Welch Larson, *Anatomy of Mistrust: U.S.-Soviet Relations during the Cold War* (Ithaca, NY: Cornell University Press 1997), 19f.

7. Ute Frevert, *Vertrauensfragen. Eine Obsession der Moderne* [Trust issues: A modern obsession] (Munich: Beck, 2013), 16–17; for a critical approach to the definition of trust as an emotion, see Hartmann, *Die Praxis des Vertrauens*, 151–71.

8. Annette Baier, "Trust and Antitrust," *Ethics* 96, no. 2 (1986), 235.

9. Niklas Luhmann, *Trust and Power: Two Works* (Chichester, UK: Wiley, 1979), 10.

10. David Eugster and Sibylle Marti, "Einleitung. Das Imaginäre des Kalten Krieges" [Introduction: The imaginary of the Cold War], in *Das Imaginäre des Kalten Krieges. Beiträge zu einer Kulturgeschichte des Ost-West-Konfliktes in Europa* [The imaginary of the Cold War: Contributions to a cultural history of the East-West conflict in Europe], eds. David Eugster and Sibylle Marti (Essen: Klartext, 2015), 10–13.

11. Edna Ullmann-Margalit, "Trust, Distrust, and In Between," in *Distrust*, ed. Russell Hardin (New York: Russell Sage Foundation, 2004), 60–61.

12. Russell Hardin, "Distrust: Manifestations and Management," in Hardin, *Distrust*, 3.

13. Deborah Welch Larson, "Distrust: Prudent, If Not Always Wise," in Hardin, *Distrust*, 34–59.

14. Ronald Reagan, "Address to the Nation on the Upcoming Soviet-United States Summit Meeting in Geneva," November 14, 1985, Ronald Reagan Presidential Library and Museum, University of Texas at Austin, http://www.reagan.utexas.edu/archives /speeches/1985/111485d.htm.

15. Quoted in Raymond L. Garthoff, *The Great Transition: American-Soviet Relations and the End of the Cold War* (Washington, DC: Brookings Institution Press, 1994), 241.

16. Frevert, "Does Trust Have a History?"

17. Martin Hartmann, "On the Concept of Basic Trust," *Behemoth: A Journal on Civilisation* 8, no. 1 (2015), 15.

18. Ronald Reagan, "Remarks on Signing the Intermediate-Range Nuclear Forces Treaty," December 8, 1987, The American Presidency Project (ed. John Woolley and Gerhard Peters, University of California, Santa Barbara), http://www.presidency.ucsb .edu/ws/?pid=33795.

19. Larson, *Anatomy of Mistrust*, 216–21.

20. Piotr Sztompka, "Trust, Distrust and Two Paradoxes of Democracy," *European Journal of Social Theory* 1, no. 1 (1998): 19–32; Frevert, "Does Trust Have a History?"; and Francis Fukuyama, *Trust: The Social Virtues and the Creation of Prosperity* (New York: Free Press, 1995).

21. Reddy, *The Navigation of Feeling*, 124–28; and Jan Plamper, "The History of Emotions: An Interview with William Reddy, Barbara Rosenwein, and Peter Stearns," *History and Theory* 49, no. 2 (2010), 243.

22. Frevert, *Vertrauensfragen*, 9.

23. Recently, two debates on this issue have been published: Frank Biess, "Forum: History of Emotions," *German History* 28, no. 1 (2010): 67–80; and Plamper, "The History of Emotions," 237–65.

24. Kreis, *Diplomatie mit Gefühl*; Andrew H. Kydd, *Trust and Mistrust in International Relations* (Princeton, NJ: Princeton University Press, 2005); Larson, *Anatomy of Mistrust*; Thomas Forsberg, "Power, Interests and Trust: Explaining Gorbachev's Choices at the End of the Cold War," *Review of International Studies* 25, no. 4 (1999), 603–21; Fred I. Greenstein, "The Impact of Personality on the End of the Cold War: A Counterfactual Analysis," *Political Psychology* 19, no. 1 (1998): 1–16; and Eva Jobs, "Secrecy, Surveillance, Sabotage: Myth-making and the Misunderstanding of Trust in a Transatlantic Intelligence Relationship," in *Privacy and Power: A Transatlantic Dialogue in the Shadow of the NSA-Affair*, ed. Russell A. Miller (Cambridge, UK: Cambridge University Press, forthcoming 2017).

25. On the relative weight of interpersonal relationships versus international and societal elements that contribute to long-term trust building, see most recently Vincent Charles Keating, "Rethinking Diplomatic Transformation Through Social Theories of Trust" (abstract from 9th Pan-European Conference on International Relations, Giardini Naxos, Italy, September 23–26, 2015), http://findresearcher.sdu.dk/portal/files/116195975/diplomatic_conflict_resolution_EISA_paper_final.pdf.

I. The Personal Factor

1. Untrusting and Untrusted: Mao's China at a Crossroads, 1969

Sergey Radchenko

Introduction

The congress hall roared. "Long live Chairman Mao! Love live Chairman Mao Zedong! Long, long live Chairman Mao!" Hundreds of delegates, in their cotton suits and caps, shouted out in ecstasy, their hands outstretched, clasping the "little red book," as Mao Zedong emerged at the podium flanked by Defense Minister Lin Biao, Premier Zhou Enlai, and a coterie of disciples who had risen to power on the tides of the Cultural Revolution. Speaking in his high-pitched voice, Mao proclaimed the opening of "the congress of unity, congress of victory."

In April 1969, the Ninth National Congress of the Chinese Communist Party (CCP) convened in troubled times. Over the three preceding years, Mao had wrecked the very party he had labored to build up, subjecting the country to youthful radicalism to purify the spirit of the revolution and revive an aging utopia. Consumed by internal strife, China became isolated on the international stage and tottered on the verge of a war with the Soviet Union. A god in the eyes of his fanatical worshippers, Mao faced mortal dangers: unrest on the home front and the prospect of an overseas invasion.

In 1969, the People's Republic of China (PRC) marked twenty years since its founding. Twenty years had passed since Mao proclaimed the triumph of the Chinese revolution in rhetoric ringing with overpowering confidence: "We, the Chinese people, have stood up!" Then, China was in ruins, but the future was bright and clear. That future was in carrying forth the promise of country's socialist transformation in a world where China would stand side by side with its "elder brother," the Soviet Union, under the banners of struggle against reaction and imperialism in the unfolding Cold War. China was a member of a family of nations bound by common destiny.

The next twenty years turned this world upside down. Mao's radical domestic policies—breakneck industrialization, gargantuan public works, and the creation of "people's communes"—were meant to help China make a "great leap" into communism, but they backfired badly. By the late 1950s, China faced famine and economic ruin. Mao had sought a shortcut to communism, but instead he had created a monstrous regime where misery was hailed as progress, where poverty was extolled as virtue, and where hideous crimes were perpetrated for the sake and in the name of the revolution. The failure of the "Great Leap Forward" showed the bankruptcy of Mao's radicalism, and the early 1960s witnessed retreat from utopia as the party leadership struggled to keep the country from utter collapse.

Seeing his revolutionary dreams dissipate before his eyes, Mao accused his party comrades of lacking faith in the masses and of attempting a capitalist restoration in China. In 1966, he launched the Cultural Revolution, calling on China's youth to "bombard the headquarters," that is, to criticize and depose party cadres who had betrayed the revolutionary cause. For three years, the country descended into chaos and anarchy as crowds of these youthful "Red Guards," bent on destruction, attacked party and government institutions, taking over schools, factories, and even ministries, and drowning China in an orgy of violence and terror. Truth and falsehood lost all meaning. The border lines between right and wrong were eroded. Even Mao was appalled. By 1969, he had lost his faith in youthful revolutionaries and in his own utopian visions. "Long live!" extolled the crowds—but Mao the revolutionary had already died.

Several weeks before the Ninth Party Congress, on March 2, 1969, Chinese troops set a trap for the Soviet border guards in the vicinity of Zhenbao Island (known as Damanskii Island to the Soviets) on the Ussuri River. Thirty-one Soviet border guards were killed in the skirmish. Two weeks later, Chinese and Soviet troops fought another, much more serious engagement. The Soviets deployed tanks and resorted to massive bombardment of the Chinese positions with new BM-21 "Grad" rockets, killing (in their estimate) up to a thousand Chinese troops.[1] In the following months, China and the Soviet Union balanced, menacingly, on the brink of war. Although the worst did not come to pass, the prospect of war triggered a policy reassessment in Beijing that within a few years brought about China's rapprochement with the United States, even as relations with Moscow went into a deep freeze that continued until the 1980s.

Historians have discussed this turning point at length.[2] The usual line of argument is that Mao Zedong's fear of Soviet invasion forced him to turn to Washington in an act of triangular diplomacy that would support realist interpretations of international politics. But this explanation presents a number of interesting questions. If Beijing and Washington managed to overcome decades of hostility and begin a fruitful dialogue, then why was it not possible to make progress in Sino-Soviet relations? If neither the Soviets nor the Chinese actually planned to wage war against the other (and the historical records support this interpretation), then how could they have misread each other's intentions so fundamentally? These questions go deeper than the superficial realist framework would allow. They bring out the underlying psychology of decision-making. This approach to the question is not new. There is extensive scholarly literature on the intersections between social psychology and international politics, with several studies investigating Soviet-American relations during the Cold War in terms of trust and mistrust between policymakers.[3] This chapter applies the same interpretative psychological framework to explore 1969 as a turning point in China's foreign relations.

China's Road to 1969

In 1949, China, in Mao's words, leaned to the Soviet side in the Cold War. In the 1950s, the Soviet Union extended massive aid to the Chinese. Those were the years of the Sino-Soviet alliance, the bygone age of fraternal solidarity, when the two sides kept no secrets from one another, when their mutual trust was such that Moscow helped Beijing in the pursuit of nuclear weapons and even agreed at one point to hand over to the Chinese a prototype of the atomic bomb. Yet by the late 1950s, the alliance was plagued by hidden frictions. After Mao unexpectedly ordered the shelling of the Guomindang-held Mazu and Jinmen islands in the Taiwan Strait in August 1958, Soviet premier Nikita Khrushchev (who had not been consulted over the military action) became concerned that Mao would start a global war. Given that Mao had gone on record downplaying the significance of the A-bomb and depicting bright prospects for communism after a nuclear war, Khrushchev felt that he could no longer trust his Chinese friend with atomic weapons.[4] The promised bomb was never delivered, and soon Moscow withdrew its experts from China and canceled cooperation agreements. In the early 1960s, the quarrel became public with a spectacular exchange of polemics, in which the Chinese accused their erstwhile brothers of betraying the revolution and Moscow lambasted Beijing for dogmatism and warmongering.[5]

But although on the surface the Sino-Soviet split was about divergent interpretations of the creed of Marxism-Leninism, there were of course other issues at stake. In particular, Mao deeply resented what he perceived as Soviet efforts to impose control on China. He flew into a rage in July 1958 when he learned of a Soviet proposal to establish a joint submarine fleet, which, he

19

thought, would subordinate the Chinese navy to Soviet command: "You don't trust the Chinese, only the Russians," he told Pavel Yudin, the bewildered Soviet ambassador.[6] In March 1965, the Chinese rejected the Soviet offer to station MiG fighter jets in the Chinese city of Kunming to cover the southern border against possible US raids. The reason, the Soviets were told, was that the offer was an attempt to put China under control. The Soviet leaders could not understand the allegation: "They [the Chinese] are not disturbed by the absurdity of the statement that a several hundred people, stationed in the regions bordering [Vietnam] could 'put China under control' with the population of 650 million people."[7]

Moscow's imperialist ambitions aside, there was another reason why Mao Zedong was apprehensive about his erstwhile Soviet comrades. The Soviet Union and China were linked not only by state-to-state but also by party-to-party relations. Even before the PRC was established, the Soviets exercised considerable influence on the CCP's internal politics. Mao did not forget the challenge posed by Wang Ming, who in the 1930s had served as the key proponent of the "Moscow line" in the Chinese leadership. Sidelined by 1945, Wang Ming eventually moved to Moscow, where he continued to criticize "Mao Zedong's betrayal," urging the Soviet leaders to invade China and topple his rival.[8] Mao also believed that former Defense Minister Peng Dehuai, who had blamed him for the disasters of the Great Leap Forward and had been purged from the leadership in 1959, was covertly supported by the Soviet leadership. Moscow voiced concern over Peng's purge, which did not help alleviate Mao's suspicions. PRC president Liu Shaoqi (the country's second-in-command) and CCP general secretary Deng Xiaoping, who were among the main targets of the Cultural Revolution, were condemned for taking China down the road of "revisionism," in effect for serving as agents of Soviet influence. The Soviet Union was seen as a threat not only to China's independence, but also to China's revolution.

What really heightened Mao's suspicions of Moscow's intentions was the Soviet invasion of Czechoslovakia in August 1968 to put an end to the Prague Spring. The intervention was swift and effective, and, to Beijing's surprise, encountered virtually no resistance.[9] Soviet leader Leonid Brezhnev justified the violation of Czechoslovakia's sovereignty by referring to the imperative of saving socialism from the perils of counterrevolution, a rationale dubbed the "Brezhnev doctrine." Although the Chinese leaders did not share Czechoslovak party leader Alexander Dubček's reformist notions of "socialism with a human face," his fate alerted them to the possibility that Chinese communism, too, might become a victim of the Soviet effort to save socialism from Maoist perversion. "They call themselves socialism," Zhou Enlai noted shortly after the Soviet invasion, "but in reality they are social imperialism, now they have already developed into social fascism. They swallowed entire Czecho[slovakia], set up a puppet regime in the same hideous way as the Fascists did that year in Norway [i.e., 1940]. Now that they have gone down that road, what sort of socialism can they speak of?"[10] Worried that Czechoslovakia would be just the beginning, the Chinese leaders called on Romania and Albania, their friends in Europe, to rebuff Soviet encroachments: "Resist," said Zhou. "If you have need, we'll give you cannons."[11]

In 1969, Mao spoke of two possibilities: "Either war will cause revolution or revolution will prevent war."[12] The Soviet invasion of Czechoslovakia was seen as an act of war, but it also had the positive effect as a catalyst of a coming revolution. "There will be a day in the Soviet Union when their people will revolt," Mao concluded when discussing the consequences of the invasion. From this perspective, further Soviet expansionism would only hasten the arrival of another revolution in the Soviet Union. But what if the Soviets chose China as the target? Mao saw a number of benefits in this possibility. First, this would "exercise the masses." Because the last major war China was directly involved in—the 1949 civil war—had ended nearly twenty years earlier, many Chinese did not know how to make weapons: "It's just generally not good when one has not touched a knife or a gun," Mao thought. Second, a war would "expose bad elements," something that Mao was thoroughly preoccupied with in the Cultural Revolution.[13]

Nevertheless, China's internal weakness and backwardness moderated Mao's revolutionary vigor. He did not want a big war. With the escalation of the American involvement in Vietnam throughout the 1960s, the Chinese quietly signaled via various nonofficial channels that Washington should avoid bringing China into the war. Mao skillfully used the Vietnam War to achieve a high degree of domestic mobilization. While he urged the Vietnamese to continue fighting, Mao wanted a limited conflict: something that would trap and exhaust the Americans, inflame revolutionary passions throughout the world, but fall short of an all-out, ruinous war. By the late 1960s, the threat of a spillover from Vietnam no longer appeared as acute. The United States, in Mao's estimate, faced difficulties not only domestically but also in both Europe and in Asia. Its European allies were dissatisfied with the drain of the Asian quagmire, its capitalists were "at odds with each other," and its forces were scattered unhelpfully all over the world. The morale of the American soldiers was low; they did not want to fight. The war, Mao believed, could not last, because the United States "cannot stand wars."[14]

The Soviet situation was in many respects similar. In the Chinese leaders' estimates, Soviet troops, although well equipped, were weak in spirit.

General Nie Rongzhen spoke to the issue in a meeting on March 8, 1969: in the past, he said, the Soviet troops had shouted "Long live Stalin!," but what would motivate them now?[15] Mao put it even in starker terms: Soviet soldiers were like the Guomindang. All they wanted was "face" (i.e., personal glory), loot, and women.[16] More important, perhaps, was the Chinese assessment of the Soviet strategic focus as being in Europe and to some extent in the Middle East. For the Soviets, as for Americans, Asia was just a sideshow. Even when strong Soviet response to the Zhenbao Island shootout challenged this assumption, the Chinese continued to believe that Moscow was "feigning an attack in the East to attack in the West." In this interpretation—which probably would have appeared to Brezhnev as rather strange—the border conflict with China helped the Soviets consolidate their control over Eastern Europe.[17] In 1968, the invasion of Czechoslovakia and Albanian information on a covert Soviet troop buildup in Bulgaria all suggested to Mao that the Albanians, the Yugoslavs, or the Romanians had more reasons to worry about a potential Soviet aggression than China did.[18]

But Mao was worried. He was especially concerned that unlike Nikita Khrushchev, who famously had argued in his day against the thesis that war was inevitable, the new Soviet leadership appeared to take a more ambiguous position. "In recent years they no longer mention this issue. Isn't [it] that they seldom touch upon this issue?" Mao wondered in his conversation with visiting Australian communist Edward Hill in November 1968, and his questioning betrayed a tinge of uncertainty about Soviet intentions. Unlike the Americans, who practically had been beaten in Korea and in Vietnam, the Soviets had experienced no such setbacks in recent memory, so their intentions could not be taken for granted. The buildup of Soviet forces in Siberia and the Far East—already in full swing by 1968—with the introduction of Soviet troops to Mongolia and increasingly assertive Soviet behavior in frequent standoffs with Chinese troops in the border regions, could all be construed as signs that the Soviet Union, as Mao put it, was "preparing to spread the war."[19]

The situation along the Sino-Soviet border gradually deteriorated throughout the 1960s; between 1965 and 1968, the Soviets registered 8,690 "incidents" involving 35,000 Chinese citizens, including 3,000 troops.[20] Most of these incidents were relatively peaceful, with both sides resorting to sticks and rifle butts to reinforce their arguments concerning the disputed border, but Chinese numbers suggest that scores were injured and, in one incident on January 5, 1968, five were killed on the Chinese side.[21] Tensions came to a head between December 1968 and January 1969 in the area of Zhenbao Island, as the Soviet use of armored personnel carriers and helicopters in these encounters increased Chinese perception of military threat. In January 1969, the Chinese

Central Military Commission considered reacting to the tougher Soviet posture. Although detailed records of these discussions are not yet available, the existing information indicates that the Chinese leadership proposed to adopt a "tit-for-tat" response, making good preparations and counterattacking "for the purpose of self-defense." Acting on these instructions, the Heilongjiang Military Region prepared a plan for an ambush of Soviet troops at Zhenbao Island, and on February 19, 1969, the Chinese General Staff and the Foreign Ministry approved the plan, paving the way for the violent border clash on March 2.[22]

The slide from Sino-Soviet alliance to ideological hostility to border confrontation poses a difficult question of interpretation. On the one hand, one can clearly trace the general trajectory of this relationship: from the late 1950s, it was already deteriorating, and in the early 1960s it entered a deep crisis. On the other hand, it was not until the late 1960s that China and the Soviet Union encountered what international relations theorists term the "security dilemma," when each eyed the other as a threat to its very survival and took military countermeasures, which only worsened mutual suspicions. It was not as if Sino-Soviet relations suddenly dropped from the heights of friendship and cooperation into the abyss of a security dilemma. Instead, they descended gradually along the spiral of mistrust.

For the Chinese, this mistrust had complex historical roots. It was certainly in part a projection of the bitter experience of foreign domination: China's century of humiliation, from the Opium Wars of the mid-1800s to the 1949 revolution. The Russians, too, had shared in the imperialist scramble for China, and this legacy continued to plague Sino-Soviet relations. The alliance was inherently unequal—Moscow was in a clear position of leadership—which increased the Chinese sense of vulnerability. Locked into a bilateral relationship as the underdog, Beijing interpreted every Soviet failure of consultation, every slight or oversight, as an attempt to exploit China's weaknesses. So, even when a given situation allowed a variety of interpretations, as with the joint fleet plan or the Soviet proposal to station MiGs in China, Beijing tended to expect the worst: the Soviet Union would take advantage of China because it could and because it had in the past.

But this mistrust was not a constant quantity in Sino-Soviet relations. For instance, Mao had greater reasons to mistrust Joseph Stalin (and vice versa) than he did to mistrust Khrushchev. In fact, after Stalin's death in 1953, the alliance appeared stronger and more durable than ever before. Did Mao ever trust Khrushchev, or did he just mask his feelings? It is interesting that in retrospect, Khrushchev believed the latter possibility to be true, recalling that already in 1954, during his first trip to China, "despite Mao's external friendliness, one could sense his arrogance and some nationalistic manifestations."[23]

This idea that there were two Maos—one "external" and one real—underscored Khrushchev's lack of trust in the Chinese leader. By the same token, Mao did not take Soviet pronouncements at face value and likely mistrusted Khrushchev. Both leaders were willing to put their reservations to the side and engage in a productive relationship—for a time. After a while, however, the balance of mistrust in Sino-Soviet relations exceeded the balance of trust and the alliance began its inexorable slide toward ruin. This point came in 1958. For Mao, the key event was Khrushchev's efforts to establish a joint fleet. For Khrushchev, the turning point was China's unexpected attack on the Mazu and Jinmen islands. Once the balance of trust and mistrust was breached, both sides interpreted each subsequent event in the worst possible light: the spiral of mistrust was fully in place. Ten years later, China and the Soviet Union were shooting at each other.

Mao's Response to the Zhenbao Island Clashes

It is likely that Mao Zedong personally approved the preemptive Chinese attack at Zhenbao Island in March 1969. This seemingly irrational action becomes more understandable, given Mao's assessment of the international situation as favoring world revolution over world war. A trial of strength would not only dissuade the Soviet Union from invading, but also add to revolutionary tides around the world, including China. What Mao had in mind was a limited war, of the kind he had repeatedly (and successfully) waged: most successfully, perhaps, during his shelling of the Taiwan Strait islands in 1958. On that occasion, the Soviets briefly thought him mad, but Khrushchev had a different frame of reference and did not understand how Mao whipped up the revolutionary spirit through careful and controlled military action. Soviet assessments of China's domestic and foreign policies in the run-up to the Zhenbao confrontation once again failed to take Mao for a revolutionary, with the result that Beijing's actions appeared irrational, illogical, and therefore immensely dangerous.

The Soviets were not alone in their misperceptions. The Chinese, too, completely misread the situation and failed to anticipate the Soviet response to the border clashes. The assumption was that it was sufficiently clear that China was in no position to unleash a major war because it was preoccupied with internal matters.[24] It was far behind the two superpowers in military technologies, and its nuclear deterrent was so weak as to be practically unusable. The Chinese leaders had also emphasized that China had no troops stationed overseas, in contrast to the superpowers. Finally, in the excitement of the Zhenbao Island confrontation, Mao Zedong resorted to one argument which, if the Soviet leadership had known about it, would have struck them as rather absurd: "The Soviets know that we will not invade their country as it is so cold there."[25]

When the carefully engineered demonstration of force at Zhenbao deteriorated into full-fledged confrontation on March 15 and 17, with heavy use of artillery by the Soviet side, Mao was bewildered and alarmed. His state of mind is reflected in rambling and contradictory comments at a Politburo meeting on March 15. He declared that the Soviet action was an effort to get "face." In applying this famous Chinese concept to Soviet decision-making, Mao characteristically misread Soviet intentions. He then sarcastically proposed to give the Soviets "face" by retreating into the "countryside" and letting them capture the cities of Harbin, Shenyang, and Changchun, at which point China would "eat them up little by little." By such posturing, Mao wanted to show that he was morally superior to the Soviets, because the whole world would see that "I have not come to your Vladivostok; I have not come to your Khabarovsk, your Chita; but you have come to my Shenyang, Harbin, Changchun; therefore, you are unreasonable." In subsequent speeches, he continued to invite the Soviets to occupy northern China, perhaps seeing such rhetoric as a form of *wendou* ("verbal" struggle, frequently used against one's opponents in the Cultural Revolution).[26]

But what if the Soviet leaders took Mao up on this invitation? Mao took immediate comfort in the fact that the Soviets, like the Chinese, were making Zhenbao into a propaganda platform. If they really intended to wage war, Mao explained, they would be fighting, not demonstrating. Zhenbao would not lead to a big war, even if it showed the "ambitions" of socialism imperialism. The Soviets, Mao surmised, needed the conflict at Zhenbao Island for "internal reasons."[27] Their purpose was to "distract people's attention from the internal difficulties."[28] And yet, worried by prospects of the escalation, Mao himself ordered: "We should stop here! Do not fight any more!"[29] He added that China had to prepare for war by creating battalions in every county. "If we don't make the best of the opportunity to prepare, what will happen when we really fight a war?"[30] Mao was no longer confident about his predictions of future Soviet actions.

As the Chinese leaders grew more concerned about the Soviet threat, the United States began to show indications of a softer attitude toward China. Mao carefully studied Richard Nixon's 1967 *Foreign Affairs* article, "Asia after Viet Nam," in which the former vice president (and future presidential candidate) noted that "we simply cannot afford to leave China outside the family of nations." Nixon mentioned his readiness to enter into a dialogue with the PRC on several occasions during his 1968 election campaign. In November 1968, the United States offered to resume stalled ambassadorial talks in Warsaw, and the Chinese readily accepted. In his January 1969 inauguration address, Nixon announced that his administration's "lines of communication" would be open: "We seek an open world," he said, "a world in which no people, great or small, will live in angry isolation."[31] "Since [19]49 till today," Mao sarcastically commented, "they [the Americans] have savored the real taste of our angry isolation."[32] But he ordered Nixon's address published in *Renmin Ribao*, the official CCP newspaper, a careful signal that the president's feelers had not gone unnoticed.[33]

Changes were slow in coming. In a press conference on January 27, President Nixon said that US policy toward China would in fact remain the same unless Beijing changed its behavior. However, the defection of Liao Heshu, the Chinese chargé d'affaires in the Netherlands, on January 24 would spark a new round of recriminations. This development was a serious loss of face for the Chinese government, and it came only days after the Sino-American ambassadorial talks were scheduled to begin in Warsaw. On February 18, Beijing abruptly canceled the talks, just one day before the top Chinese leadership approved the attack at Zhenbao Island.[34] This seemingly irrational action—for clearly, an open channel of communication with the United States would benefit China at a time of a bloody conflict with the Soviet Union—only makes sense in the context of Mao's deep mistrust of US intentions. As Mao put it at a meeting on February 19, he found it "a little strange" that the Western media, which always reported on Soviet military moves in Europe, passed over in silence the Soviet buildup in the Far East.[35] "Strange," in this context, indicated Mao's suspicion that the United States was, in the ancient Chinese adage, sitting on the mountain to see two tigers fight, perhaps even tacitly encouraging Soviet war preparations.

With the flare-up at Zhenbao Island, China's isolation was compete. Its leaders lived in fear, their lines of communication with the outside world practically cut. Ironically, Soviet premier Alexei Kosygin tried to get through to Mao or to Zhou Enlai on March 21, but the telephone operator, cursing the Soviets, refused to connect the call.[36] Unbeknownst to the Soviets, the operator had acted without authorization. Zhou later fumed at this insubordination: "The two countries are at war; one cannot chop the messenger."[37] Yet instead of trying to get back in touch with Kosygin, on March 22 Zhou proposed to inform the Soviets via diplomatic channels that in view of the poor state of Sino-Soviet relations, direct conversations were "inappropriate."[38] The reason Zhou put forward for turning down Soviet overtures showed the extent of Beijing's apprehension: military reports suggested that the Soviets were maneuvering troops in the vicinity of Zhenbao Island with the likely intent (as

Zhou thought) of invading the island that very day. Kosygin, Zhou explained, was simply "posturing."[39] Mao agreed with this assessment but, in a bid to lessen tensions, called for immediate diplomatic negotiations with the Soviet Union.[40] On the same day, he gloomily summed up the state of affairs: "We are now isolated; no one understands us."[41]

During the Cultural Revolution, Chinese ambassadors, with the sole exception of Huang Hua in Egypt, were recalled for "re-education" at home. China's foreign policy apparatus practically broke down, and the Foreign Ministry itself was ridden with factional strife. One-time Foreign Minister Marshal Chen Yi had been purged in 1967, but now Mao longed for his advice. On February 19, 1969, he asked Chen to join marshals Nie Rongzhen, Ye Jianying, and Xu Xiangqian to debate the international situation in secret and come up with assessments of the likelihood that the Soviet Union and United States would invade China. The four marshals, shielded by Zhou Enlai from attacks by the radicals, worked through the spring, summer, and early autumn of 1969. On July 11, they submitted an extensive report to the Chinese leadership.

The most important finding of the July 11 report was that the Soviet Union and the United States were unlikely to wage a war against China, either jointly or separately. This conclusion was similar to Mao's assessment of the situation. The marshals restated some of the key arguments that Mao himself frequently had put forward in previous months: that the United States was more interested in Europe than in Asia; that its main adversary was the Soviet Union; that it had been burned by the "bitter" experiences of Korea and Vietnam and would not be morally or logistically prepared to fight another war across the Pacific. Nor were the Japanese in a position to help Washington in this respect. The Soviet leaders, the marshals thought, would not dare to order an invasion of China because they realized that the real threat emanated from the United States, not from China; because their industrial production was based in the western part of the country and they would be hard-pressed to fight in the east; and because the Soviet people would not support their leadership in waging an offensive war. Explaining the evident buildup of Soviet forces on the border with China, the report noted that the Soviets intended "to use military mobilization to consolidate their political control and to suppress resistance to them at home and in Eastern Europe."[42]

The marshals thus repeated some of the misconceptions that had blurred Mao's vision of the international situation. Two key misconceptions were that the Soviet Union did not perceive China as a credible threat and that its military buildup at the Sino-Soviet border was motivated by "internal" factors, much in the same way as some of Mao's external policies served as catalysts for internal mobilization. The Chinese leaders not only were unable to understand the level of concern with which China was perceived from the outside, but also projected a China-specific framework to the unfamiliar milieu of Soviet policymaking. Misinterpreting motivations for the Soviet military buildup in the Far East, the marshals found that the Soviets now posed a greater threat to China's security than that posed by the United States. Although this conclusion did not yet suggest readiness to mend fences with Washington, it showed that the Chinese policymakers were no longer putting US "imperialism" and Soviet "social imperialism" on the same plane. When, days after the marshals' report, Pakistan's Air Marshal Nur Khan visited China, he found that Zhou Enlai had little to say of the United States but instead "spent a great deal of time on [Chinese] fear and distrust of Soviets."[43]

Ten days after the four marshals presented their views to the central leadership, the *New York Times* reported that the Nixon administration would slightly relax its economic sanctions against China and would allow certain categories of US citizens to visit the PRC. Although the changes were economically unimportant, they were symbolically significant. As Senator Mike Mansfield put it, "Now the door is open if they [the Chinese] want to step in."[44] Mansfield also sent a personal message to Zhou Enlai through Cambodia's Prince Norodom Sihanouk, asking to be invited to China for a visit. Zhou turned down this request, but it made an impression on the Chinese leadership. And in late July, while on a tour of Asia, President Nixon announced that the United States would henceforth abstain from contributing troops to local conflicts, calling on US allies to protect themselves with "Asian hands."[45] Although Nixon's statement was criticized in Beijing as a means of setting Asians to fight Asians, the "Nixon doctrine" confirmed the trend toward de-escalation of US military presence in China's immediate neighborhood. These signals from Washington were noted by the four marshals as they continued to debate the international situation, and also by Mao, who began to ponder the possibilities of triangular diplomacy.

In her book *Anatomy of Mistrust*, Deborah Welch Larson has shown how mistrust in international politics is frequently rooted in cognitive failures and the lack of empathy. When policymakers attempt to explain another country's behavior, "they overestimate the contribution of internal sources and underestimate the impact of external forces. Leaders attribute the other side's hostile or aggressive behavior to its ideology or national character, and they overlook that the other side may be responding to their own actions."[46] Larson's observations are fully confirmed in Mao Zedong's assessment of Soviet behavior, for instance, in his insistence that Moscow's alleged aggressiveness was motivated by internal difficulties. Mao professed his lack of understanding of Soviet fear of China. His was an economically backward country with a minuscule nuclear arsenal: how could anyone fear it? Soviet fear, therefore, was disingenuous and quite possibly was a deliberate propaganda ploy aimed at deceiving public opinion and producing a pretext for a possible invasion of China. Given the long-standing mistrust in Sino-Soviet relations, it is easy to see how Mao would fail to appreciate the other side's point of view or see his own policies as threatening even when, as in March 1969, it was China that launched a preemptive attack on the Soviet Union.

But if such cognitive failures are understandable, it is less clear why the Chinese did so little to try to achieve some form of accommodation with the Soviets in order to avoid war. In 1962, the American social psychologist Charles Osgood formulated prescriptions for escaping the spiral of mistrust, calling it GRIT: "graduated and reciprocated initiatives in tension reduction."[47] The idea here was that in the absence of trust, one side or the other had to take a unilateral but not-too-costly initiative that would signal its benign intentions to the other. Each reciprocated initiative would increase mutual trust in the relationship and pave way to more generous initiatives by each side. Although it is unlikely that Soviet premier Alexei Kosygin had ever heard of Charles Osgood, his efforts of step-by-step engagement (e.g., reaching out to Zhou Enlai on the phone at the height of the Zhenbao crisis) were much in line with Osgood's approach. The Chinese showed no interest in reciprocating these feelers, even though Mao was clearly apprehensive about the possibility of a Soviet invasion and wanted to avert such a scenario. At the same time, the beginning of Sino-American engagement followed the GRIT-prescribed pattern perfectly. In other words, China was willing to reciprocate American initiatives and unwilling to reciprocate Soviet initiatives. One can explain this with reference to the fact that the Soviet Union presented a greater threat to China than the United States did. But threat is a subjective notion, and so it is also the case that the Chinese felt threatened because of the dismally low level of trust between them and the Soviets.

Soviet Policy toward China

China was a mystery for the Soviet leadership: when Sino-Soviet relations soured in the late 1950s, Moscow was perplexed. Mao Zedong claimed that his erstwhile allies had betrayed Marxism-Leninism, but neither Nikita Khrushchev nor, after his ouster, Leonid Brezhnev believed that ideological disagreements were the root cause of the deepening confrontation. China specialists at Soviet policy institutes, at pains to come up with a reasonable explanation as to how things could go so wrong in China, argued that Mao, under cover of pseudorevolutionary rhetoric, had joined forces with the military to create a military bureaucratic dictatorship, but those less academically endowed (such as General Secretary Brezhnev) could never quite come to grips with the twists and turns of Chinese politics, certainly not since the Cultural Revolution. "Unbelievable madness" was about as much as Brezhnev could say of the subject.[48]

In the immediate aftermath of the border clashes, the Soviet leaders appealed to Russian patriotic sentiments. Until then, Moscow had downplayed the Chinese "threat" in propaganda, but after the Zhenbao incident these self-imposed restrictions were lifted. On March 7 and 8, thousands of demonstrators marched by the Chinese embassy in Moscow under banners calling for the overthrow of the "Mao clique," hurling ink bottles and smashing glass windows. Soviet television showed border scuffles with the Chinese, and the newspapers were filled with articles promising a "resolute rebuff" to China should such "provocations" continue. The Soviets also made careful public hints of nuclear retaliation against China.[49] In the meantime, Soviet officials privately inquired about Washington's reaction to such a nuclear strike, claiming that it would not only deal effectively with China's military threat but also weaken Mao's domestic political base.[50] These inquiries proved counterproductive, as they encouraged the Nixon administration to develop a dialogue with China. In the short term, they fed worrisome speculations of impending war between China and the Soviet Union.

The appearance of greater Soviet assertiveness in relations with China masked bewilderment and uncertainty. Little is known of internal Soviet deliberations on the subject. In preparation for possible escalation, the Soviet military built up forces in the border region and in Mongolia, and issued secret orders to local party authorities to stockpile medical supplies and prepare civil militias who "could be armed and involved in the implementation of military tasks."[51] Surprised at Zhenbao, Soviet border guards were also more willing to use deadly force, as in the case of the robust Soviet response to a perceived Chinese border violation at Tielieketi/Zhalanashkol in what was then the Kazakh Soviet Socialist Republic. In a skirmish on August 13, twenty-one Chinese soldiers lost their lives.[52] But far from being a premeditated attack planned and directed from Moscow (as it is often depicted in the Chinese historiography) the Tielieketi incident was a local consequence of the Soviet decision to increase vigilance in the border area in the hope of deterring Chinese cross-border incursions.

Unable to understand the turn of events, the Soviet leaders harbored deep mistrust of the Chinese. Moscow's relations with the United States had suffered ups and downs, but the Soviets knew what to expect of their Cold War adversaries even in the time of crisis like the Cuban Missile Crisis in 1962 or the *Pueblo* crisis with North Korea in 1968. The seeming irrationality of the Chinese actions—as in 1958, when Mao ordered the shelling of the Guomindang-held islands without first consulting with the Soviet Union; as at the height of Cultural Revolution in 1967, when the Soviet embassy in Beijing came under siege; and, most recently, as at Zhenbao Island—eroded all basis for making informed predictions of what the Chinese may do. "Not honorable," "treacherous," and an "exceptionally sly and perfidious people" was how Leonid Brezhnev characterized the Chinese in a conversation with Richard Nixon in June 1973. For all his faults, Nixon was someone Brezhnev could relate to and respect, in contrast to "the feelings of distrust and disrespect" he felt for the Chinese leadership.[53] In these circumstances, the course of action that appeared most reasonable to the Soviet leaders was to build up their military force. As Brezhnev put it in June 1969, "the stronger the defense of our borders, the less danger there is of a really dangerous military confrontation at our eastern frontiers."[54] At the same time, the Soviet leader announced the Soviet proposal for a "collective security system" in Asia, which won few adherents but fed into Beijing's fears of hostile encirclement.

Even as the Soviet Union increased military and diplomatic pressure on China, Moscow offered to hold border talks in notes sent on March 29 and July 13, 1969. On July 26, the Soviets privately inquired whether the Chinese leaders would be open to a bilateral summit to resolve Sino-Soviet differences. But far from being interpreted in Beijing as gestures of good faith, these measures only deepened Chinese concerns about Soviet duplicity. The four marshals concluded that Moscow feared the prospect of warming relations between Beijing and Washington, and attempted to "play the China card" against the United States by softening its own position vis-à-vis the Chinese.[55] The concern, to be sure, was real. Since 1966, Moscow at least suspected that the real purpose of the anti-Soviet turn in China's foreign policy was to mend fences with the United States, an unfortunate misconception that seriously hindered Soviet efforts to understand the situation in China. Following Zhenbao, the Soviets redoubled their efforts to convince Washington that Beijing could not and should not be trusted. China was "everybody's problem," explained Soviet ambassador Anatoly Dobrynin in a conversation with Henry Kissinger, who then was Nixon's national security advisor. But Dobrynin, too, worried that the White House would "take advantage of the Soviet Union's difficulties." Despite Kissinger's reassurance that Nixon "was not playing for petty stakes," the Soviet leaders harbored grave suspicions.[56]

Nevertheless, the four marshals attributed more devious geopolitical thinking to the Soviets than there actually was. The duality of Soviet posture with respect to China—military pressure and hostile propaganda alongside appeals for negotiations—reflected the lack of consensus in the Kremlin on the most desirable course of action. Although no conclusive evidence has surfaced as yet, there are indications that Prime Minister Alexei Kosygin favored the path of negotiations even as the military hard-liners called for a tougher response.[57] After Khrushchev's ouster in 1964, Kosygin was at the forefront of the Soviet attempt to mend fences with China. In February 1965, he met with Mao Zedong in a futile bid to jump-start the failing alliance. In February 1967, when the Soviet embassy in Beijing came under siege, it was Kosygin who successfully urged Zhou Enlai to intervene on behalf of the Soviet diplomats.[58] And in March 1969, it was Kosygin who called Beijing to talk personally to Zhou and Mao about the ongoing crisis in Sino-Soviet relations. Despite being turned away by the Chinese leaders, Kosygin persisted in his search for a negotiated solution, not because he sought to play the China card against the Americans (as the four marshals incorrectly assumed) but because he believed that as two communist powers, China and the Soviet Union did not have problems that could not be overcome.

The Soviet approach to China in 1969 was in some ways a mirror image of the Chinese approach to the Soviet Union. Like the Chinese, the Soviets perceived the source of the conflict to be in the very nature of their opponent, not in external contingencies to which they, too, had contributed. The Soviets also failed to see themselves as a threat to their neighbor. Brezhnev's decision to build up military forces at the Sino-Soviet border as a way to increase Soviet security was a classic example of self-defeating behavior in a security dilemma. Soviet hints of nuclear retaliation reflected Moscow's deep mistrust of China; if Beijing retained any sense of trustworthiness, from the Soviet perspective, the Soviet leaders certainly would have found better ways to influence Chinese behavior than to threaten nuclear destruction. The latter move—born of the infamous misconception that one's opponent understands only force—actually undermined Kosygin's initiatives to reduce tensions. Seeing mixed signals, the Chinese perceived that the threatening signals represented Moscow's real intentions, while Soviet gestures of reconciliation were just deception and trickery.

Kosygin in Beijing, and the War Scare

In September 1969, Kosygin went to Hanoi for the funeral of Vietnamese leader Ho Chi Minh. Ho had struck an independent posture in the Sino-Soviet split and even had tried to mediate between Beijing and Moscow, though without success. But his death offered a rare and sober occasion for the Chinese and Soviet leaders to hold talks. Kosygin contacted the Chinese delegation through the Vietnamese with a proposal to meet in Beijing on his way back. After a delay of several days, Zhou Enlai agreed to a meeting. Kosygin, who had already left Vietnam for Moscow, zigzagged back to China. On September 11, he saw Zhou Enlai. Indicative of the frosty state of Sino-Soviet relations, their three-hour conversation took place in the Beijing airport.

Kosygin and Zhou tried to reassure each other than neither side wanted war. Zhou was especially emphatic: "We do not want war; we are carrying out a Cultural Revolution, and why would we want war? We have no forces abroad, and we don't want to have any there." Zhou accused the Soviet Union of building up a massive military force on the Soviet side of the border. For his part, he promised that China would "not take the initiative" in the border conflicts and would not use its nuclear weapons. But, Zhou added, if the Soviet Union bombed the PRC's atomic facilities, the Chinese would fight to the end. Kosygin agreed that "war is adventurism." "No one," he lied, "will believe that China is preparing for war." The Soviet Union, continued Kosygin, also had too many internal problems to be fighting wars. "I think … that in China they know perfectly well that the USSR is not preparing for war." Both premiers agreed that they should not allow the United States to profit from the situation and promised to find a peaceful solution to the border conflict.[59]

Yet while both Kosygin and Zhou showed interest in preventing the outbreak of a Sino-Soviet war, they also talked past each other. Kosygin clearly was more interested in arriving at a genuine rapprochement. He proposed to Zhou—whom he still called "comrade"—to incorporate Chinese economic requests into the Soviet Union's next Five-Year Plan, reappoint ambassadors to both countries, and resume foreign policy consultations. Zhou meekly promised to report these offers to the Chinese Politburo, but he was much more interested in avoiding further clashes by maintaining what he called the "status quo" at the Sino-Soviet border and withdrawing each side's military forces from all disputed areas. Zhou returned to this point again and again, but Kosygin was noncommittal, suspecting a trick: if the Soviets withdrew their forces, then the Chinese would simply send settlers in and later claim that the land was theirs all along. Zhou's claim that all border treaties between China and the Soviet Union had been "unequal" was also interpreted by the Soviets as a "trap." "Zhou Enlai," recalled one of the Soviet participants in the meeting, "spoke with a subtext and ambiguity."[60] Zhou's caution and fear were seen as conceit and trickery, these impressions only serving to reinforce Moscow's conviction that the Chinese could not be trusted.

For the Chinese, the talks between Zhou Enlai and Kosygin served two main aims. The first was to remove the immediate danger of a Soviet attack on China, which appeared quite likely after the clash at Tielieketi on August 13 and the subsequent escalation of Soviet rhetoric with its veiled nuclear threats. The second was to influence US thinking by raising the prospect of accommodation with the Soviet Union. By the time Kosygin made his appearance in Beijing, the Chinese had already learned that Richard Nixon was secretly extending feelers to China. During his visits to Pakistan and Romania that summer, Nixon passed messages to the Chinese leadership, promising that he would not try to "fence off" China and at the same time criticizing the Soviets for trying to do so through arrangements like Brezhnev's call for collective security in Asia.[61] Under these circumstances, Kosygin's visit made the Americans "nervous" and—in the assessment of the four marshals who met to consider the results of the talks—would make Nixon "exert himself to catch up."[62]

The marshals were thus beginning to move away from the even-handed July 11 report and to see benefit in closer engagement with the United States at Soviet expense. Marshal Ye Jianying cited the wisdom of strategist Zhuge Liang who, during the Three Kingdoms period in the third century CE, had argued in favor of the State of Shu uniting with the State of Wu in the east to oppose the State of Wei in the north, and Marshal Chen Yi compared China's predicament with the Soviet decision to sign a nonaggression pact with Adolf Hitler in 1939.[63] On September 17, the marshals submitted another report on the international situation to Zhou Enlai. Despite Kosygin's assurances, the new report struck a tone of alarm concerning Soviet intentions: "The Soviet revisionists indeed intend to wage a war of aggression against China."[64] They would not dare to launch a major war, however, because they were afraid of the American reaction. But Washington was "utterly unwilling" to see a Soviet victory in a war with China, as this would allow the Soviets to establish "a big empire" that would exceed America's in resources and manpower.[65] All indicators in the report thus pointed toward the importance of improving Sino-American relations, an idea so radical and dangerous that it was not explicitly articulated. But Chen verbally briefed Zhou about the "unconventional" thoughts that lurked between the lines of the September report: "Utilizing the Soviet-American contradictions in a strategic sense, we need to make an opening in Sino-American relations."[66]

If Zhou's talks with Kosygin thus served a useful strategic purpose in China's tentative try at triangular diplomacy, the Chinese leaders remained concerned about a possible Soviet attack. The marshals suspected that Kosygin's visit was a tactical ploy "to plug up internal holes, stabilize the situation in Eastern Europe, and to solidify and expand Soviet position in the Middle East and other parts of Asia."[67] In fact, what impressed the Chinese the most was not that Kosygin appeared accommodating but that, after his return to Moscow, he was not welcomed at the airport by other senior Soviet leaders. To Beijing's policymakers, this was a sure indication that Kosygin's talks in China had not met with the approval of his Politburo colleagues.[68] This conviction grew stronger after the September 16 publication of an article by Victor Louis, the Moscow-based correspondent for the *London Evening News*. Louis, who was thought to have connections to the KGB, spoke about a preemptive Soviet nuclear strike on Chinese nuclear facilities at Lop Nor: "the world would only learn about it afterwards." Louis also hinted that the Soviets might find an anti-Maoist group inside China who could be called upon to invite them in, like in the Czechoslovak case a year earlier.[69]

These insinuations touched a raw nerve with the Chinese leadership. For months, Mao, Zhou, and others had warned about the possibility of a repeat of the Czechoslovak scenario. Alexander Dubček's problem was that he "trusted the Soviets, which is why he failed."[70] Mao chose to rely on the People's Liberation Army; its positions were strengthened significantly after the Ninth Party Congress and continued to be strengthened in the summer of 1969 as the revolutionary chaos that Mao had unleashed in 1966 began to subside. But there was still unrest in many parts of China, including regions near the Soviet border. A "large group" of Xinjiang Uyghurs secretly informed the Soviet authorities in Kazakhstan that the "indigenous population is prepared to rise in the struggle of liberation against the Mao Zedong clique in order to attain self-determination up to secession from the PRC and the founding of an independent socialist state—the Republic of Eastern Turkestan." Soviet sources reported that the Uyghurs, considered politically unreliable, were being resettled inland from the border region.[71]

On July 23, following reports of chaotic factionalism in Shanxi province, the Central Committee put out a notice demanding an end to "armed struggle" and surrender of all weapons to the authorities.[72] On August 28, this notice was strengthened further with the Order for General Mobilization in Border Provinces and Regions, which prohibited "factionalism," mandated unity of the whole people and the whole army, and called for heightened vigilance in the face of possible "sudden attacks" by the enemy.[73] From June 20 to July 4, 1969, the Central Military Commission held a conference of three border regions (Northwest, North, and Northeast) to discuss war preparations. This conference, in the words of the Chinese historian Liu Zhinan, "marked the turn of the focal point of Chinese military strategic defense towards the Soviet Union."[74]

Although the Sino-Soviet border situation calmed down somewhat after Kosygin's visit, this de-escalation only raised suspicions among senior Chinese leaders that the Soviets were preparing a "sudden attack" against China.

Soviet diplomatic approaches were compared to Japan's negotiations with the United States in the run-up to the attack on Pearl Harbor: the Chinese leaders feared that Moscow would use talks as a "smoke screen" for a blitzkrieg.[75] In China, military preparations intensified in late September. Defense Minister Lin Biao suspected that the Soviets would strike on October 1, the twentieth anniversary of the PRC's founding, to catch the Chinese unprepared. That day came and went without incident, but paranoia did not abate. The Chinese leaders then feared that the Soviets would attack on October 20, to coincide with the beginning of the Sino-Soviet border talks in Beijing. In anticipation of a nuclear strike, senior leaders were evacuated from Beijing and dispersed across China. Only Zhou Enlai, as the prime minister, was left in the capital to run the government. When the war did not happen on October 20, the Central Military Commission issued instructions to expect war when the ice froze on rivers along the Sino-Soviet frontier, which would make it possible for the Soviet tanks to cross.[76] The war scare, with massive digging of tunnels and caves as a precaution against nuclear bombardment, continued well into 1970. "[We] should learn the ways of the mouse: the mouse digs tunnels, and so does the rabbit," Mao explained to North Korean leader Kim Il Sung in October 1970. (He learned, to his probable satisfaction, that the North Koreans too were digging tunnels).[77]

Conclusion

In 1969, Mao Zedong reached the very apex of his power. He was worshipped by millions. He had become a living god. But even gods make errors of judgment. One of the consequences of Mao's misjudgment of the international situation was the Sino-Soviet clash at Zhenbao Island. The ostensible purpose of the Chinese attack on March 2 was to teach the Soviets a "bitter lesson" and so dissuade Moscow from launching an invasion of China. The Chinese leadership viewed the ambush as a reaction against aggressive Soviet behavior but did not understand how threatening China itself appeared in the eyes of its neighbors, especially of the Soviet Union, which came under a barrage of hostile propaganda unlike anything hitherto experienced in Soviet foreign relations. Instead of dissuading Moscow, the Chinese attack reinforced Soviet feelings of mistrust and fear of China, and led, not unexpectedly, to a tough response at Zhenbao Island and along other sections of the Sino-Soviet border. This strong response, in turn, transformed Mao's anxiety about a possible war with the Soviet Union into a full-blown war scare.

A reconsideration of Chinese decision-making during 1969 reveals that the senior leadership in Beijing completely misinterpreted Soviet motivations in the border conflict with China. Trapped in wishful thinking born of revolutionary idealism, Mao looked for signs of deep crisis in the Soviet Union, which would explain its assertiveness in its border relations with China. He believed that the Soviet leaders were eager to distract their people's attention from internal difficulties, much as Mao had done when he used radical foreign policy moves to distract the attention of his own people from the chaos of the Cultural Revolution. In fact, Soviet assertiveness stemmed from uncertainty and fear in the face of the deep crisis of the Chinese revolution and in view of its own inherent weaknesses in Siberia and the Far East, which made the possibility of a Chinese invasion all the more worrying and led to a military buildup and to efforts to build an international front against a militant, unpredictable China.

Both Chinese and Soviet leaders recognized that their confrontation could not be taken in isolation from each country's relationship with the United States. But mutual misperceptions and mistrust that plagued Sino-Soviet relations made it difficult for either Beijing or Moscow to effectively engage in triangular diplomacy. The Chinese were ultimately unable to maintain equidistance between the two superpowers after the Soviets began to resort to nuclear threats, although they tried to do so in the summer of 1969. Instead of making the Americans "nervous" by improving relations with the Soviet Union, Mao had himself become so nervous that he hurriedly pursued rapprochement with his one-time archenemy: the United States. The Soviets, too, were eager to improve relations with China, but their good intentions were dismissed as posturing in Beijing, while their clumsy threats and military buildup at the border—meant as a warning to China—were interpreted as signs of bad faith, hostile intent, and perhaps imminent aggression.

The Soviets were deeply worried that the Nixon administration would take advantage of Moscow's difficulties to engage with Beijing, but they did not see the extent to which their own contradictory policies played into the Sino-American rapprochement. Soviet policymakers believed that Mao had unleashed the conflict at Zhenbao Island in order to improve his standing with Washington. In fact, such a strategic gambit was far from his mind when he pondered the international situation in late 1968. He had expected the breakout of a global war or a global revolution, "great chaos under the heaven."[78] Instead, what he got was great insecurity pregnant with the possibility of a Soviet attack on China, something that Mao, for all his bravado, was desperate to avert. In times of such uncertainty, Mao Zedong put his faith in the only premise that seemed sure to hold: that it was in the American interest to do everything possible to keep the Soviet threat to China in check. This premise became China's starting point on the road to Sino-American rapprochement.

37

Notes

1. Andrei Musalov, *Damanskii i Zhalanashkol, 1969* [Damanskii and Zhalanash-kol, 1969] (Moscow: Eksprint, 2005).

2. See, e.g., Yang Kuisong, "The Sino-Soviet Border Clash of 1969: From Zhen-bao Island to Sino-American Rapprochement," *Cold War History* 1, no. 1 (2000): 21–52.

3. See, e.g., Deborah Welch Larson, *Anatomy of Mistrust: U.S.-Soviet Relations during the Cold War* (Ithaca, NY: Cornell University Press, 1997); and Andrew H. Kydd, *Trust and Mistrust in International Relations* (Princeton, NJ: Princeton University Press, 2005).

4. Most famously, perhaps, in his speech at the Conference of Communist and Workers' Parties in Moscow on November 18, 1957. See N. G. Tomilina et al. (eds.), *Nasledniki Kominterna: Mezhdunarodnye Soveshchaniya Predstavitelei Kommunis-ticheskikh i Rabochikh Partii v Moskve (noyabr' 1957 g.)* [Heirs of the Comintern: The International Meeting of Communist and Workers' Parties in Moscow, November 1957] (Moscow: Rosspen, 2013), 372.

5. For an in-depth analysis of the Sino-Soviet polemics, see Alfred D. Low, *The Sino-Soviet Dispute: An Analysis of the Polemics* (Cranbury, NJ: Associated University Presses, 1976).

6. The Ministry of Foreign Affairs of the PRC and the Party Literature Research Center, eds., *Mao Zedong on Diplomacy* (Beijing: Foreign Languages Press, 2007), 251. For an in-depth discussion of this episode, see Shen Zhihua and Xia Yafeng, *Mao and the Sino-Soviet Partnership: A New History* (Lanham, MD: Lexington Books, 2015), 308–21.

7. Mikhail Suslov's report to the March (1965) Plenum, March 23, 1965, fond 2, opis 1, delo 776, list 17, Russian State Archive of Current History (RGANI).

8. Alexander Pantsov and Steven Levine, *Mao: The Real Story* (New York: Simon and Schuster, 2012), 538.

9. Romulus Budura, ed., *Relațiile româno-chineze, 1880–1974: documente* [Romanian-Chinese relations, 1880–1974: Documents] (Bucharest: Ministerul Afacerilor Externe, 2005), 901–2 (trans. Mircea Munteanu).

10. Speech by Zhou Enlai, September 2, 1968, in Song Yongyi (ed.), *Chinese Cultural Revolution Database, CD-ROM* (hereafter, *CCRD*) (Hong Kong: Chinese University of Hong Kong, 2002).

11. Budura, *Relațiile româno-chineze*, 904–5 (trans. Mircea Munteanu).

12. Mao Zedong, "About Two Possibilities for a World War," early 1969, *CCRD*.

13. Conversation between Mao Zedong and Beqir Balluku, October 5, 1968, Chinese Central Archive.

14. Conversation between Mao Zedong and Pham Van Dong, Beijing, November 17, 1968, in *77 Conversations between Chinese and Foreign Leaders on the Wars in Indochina, 1964–1977*, Cold War International History Project Working Paper No. 22, ed. Odd Arne Westad, Chen Jian, Stein Tønnesson, Nguyen Vu Tung, and James G. Hershberg (Washington, DC: Woodrow Wilson International Center for Scholars, 1998), 142, 137.

15. Zhou Junlun, ed., *Nie Rongzhen Nianpu* [The chronicle of Nie Rongzhen] (Beijing: Renmin Chubanshe), 2:1109.

16. Speech by Mao Zedong, April 5, 1969, *CCRD*.

17. Zhou, *Nie Rongzhen Nianpu*, 2:1109.

18. Conversation between Mao Zedong and Beqir Balluku, October 1, 1968, in Chen Jian and David Wilson, "All Under the Heaven Is Great Chaos: Beijing, the Sino-Soviet Border Clashes, and the Turn Toward Sino-American Rapprochement, 1968–69," *Cold War International History Project Bulletin* 11 (Winter 1998), 157.

19. Chen and Wilson, "All Under the Heaven Is Great Chaos."

20. G. V. Kireev, *Rossiia - Kitai: Neizvestnye stranitsy pogranichnykh peregovorov* [Russia – China: Unknown pages of border talks] (Moscow: Rosspen, 2006), 92.

21. Li Ke and Hao Shengzhang, *"Wenhua dageming" zhong de renmin jiefang jun* [The People's Liberation Army during the "Cultural Revolution"] (Beijing: Zhonggong Dangshi Ziliao Chubanshe, 1989), 318.

22. Cited in Kuisong, "The Sino-Soviet Border Clash of 1969," 27–28.

23. Nikita Khrushchev, *Vremia, Liudi, Vlast* [Time, people, power] (Moscow: Moskovskie Novosti, 1999), 2:413.

24. A. Elizavetin, "Peregovory Chzhou Enlaia i Kosygina v Pekinskom Aeroportu" [Negotiations between Zhou Enlai and Kosygin at the Peking Airport], *Problemy Dal'nego Vostoka* 5 (1992): 48.

25. Cited in Chen and Wilson, "All Under the Heaven Is Great Chaos," 162.

26. Comments by Mao Zedong, March 15, 1969, in Zhongong Zhongyang Wenxian Yanjiushi, ed., *Jianguo yilai Mao Zedong junshi wengao* [Mao Zedong's manuscripts since the formation of the People's Republic of China] (Beijing: Zhongyang Wenxian Chubanshe, 2010), 3:355–58.

27. Ibid.

28. Budura, *Relaţiile româno-chineze,* 904–5, 958.

29. Cited in Kuisong, "The Sino-Soviet Border Clash of 1969," 30.

30. Comments by Mao Zedong, March 15, 1969, in Zhongong Zhongyang Wenxian Yanjiushi, *Jianguo yilai Mao ZedongJunshi wengao,* 3:355–58.

31. "Richard Nixon: Inaugural Address," January 20, 1969, The American Presidency Project (ed. John Woolley and Gerhard Peters, University of California, Santa Barbara), http://www.presidency.ucsb.edu/ws/?pid=1941.

32. Liu Zhinan, "1969nian, zhongguo zhanlüe yu dui meisu guanxi de yanjiu he tiaozheng" [China's war preparations and balance toward Soviet-American relations in 1969], *Dangdai Zhongguo Shi Yanjiu* 3 (1999): 50.

33. Chen Jian, *Mao's China and the Cold War* (Chapel Hill: University of North Carolina Press, 2001), 245.

34. Li Danhui, "1969nian zhongsu bianjie chongtu: Yuanqi he jieguo" [The 1969 Sino-Soviet border incidents: Origins and outcome], *Dangdai Zhongshi Shi Yanjiu* 3 (1996): 47.

35. Wang Yongqin, ed., *Taipingyang shang kong de caihong* [Rainbow over the Pacific Ocean] (Beijing: Zhongyang Wenxian Chubanshe, 1998), 369–70.

36. Elizavetin, "Peregovory," 48.

37. Lorenz Lüthi, "Restoring Chaos to History: Sino-Soviet-American Relations, 1969," *China Quarterly* 210 (June 2012), 384.

38. Zhongong Zhongyang Wenxian Yanjiushi, *Jianguo yilai Mao Zedong wengao,* 13:21.

39. Ibid.

40. Ibid.

41. Wang Yongqin, *Taipingyang shang kong de caihong*, 374.

42. Report by Four Chinese Marshals—Chen Yi, Ye Jianying, Xu Xiangqian, and Nie Rongzhen—to the Central Committee, "A Preliminary Evaluation of the War Situation," July 11, 1969, in Chen and Wilson, "All Under the Heaven Is Great Chaos," 167.

43. State Department cable 130100 to US Embassy, Taipei, "Nur Khan's Meeting with Chou En-lai," August 5, 1969, National Archives, SN 67-69, in *The Sino-Soviet Border Conflict, 1969: U.S. Reactions and Diplomatic Maneuvers*, National Security Archive Electronic Briefing Book No. 49, ed. William Burr (Washington, DC: National Security Archive, June 12, 2001), http://nsarchive.gwu.edu/NSAEBB /NSAEBB49/sino.sov.8.pdf.

44. Peter Groses, "U.S. Acts to Relax Curbs on China Travel and Trade," *New York Times*, July 21, 1969, 1, 11.

45. "Nixon's Asian Doctrine," *New York Times*, August 3, 1969, E10.

46. Larson, *Anatomy of Mistrust*, 23.

47. On GRIT, see Charles E. Osgood, *An Alternative to War or Surrender* (Urbana: University of Illinois Press, 1962).

48. Leonid Brezhnev's speech at the December 1966 CC CPSU Plenum, December 12, 1966, fond 2, opis 3, delo 45, list 63, RGANI.

49. See, e.g., "Soviet No Paper Tiger, Moscow Radio Tells China," *New York Times*, March 21, 1969, 2; Raymond Garthoff, *Détente and Confrontation: American-Soviet Relations from Nixon to Reagan*, rev. ed. (Washington, DC: Brookings Institution Press, 1994), 237.

50. US State Department Memorandum of Conversation, "US Reaction to Soviet Destruction of CPR [Chinese People's Republic] Nuclear Capability; Significance of Latest Sino-Soviet Border Clash. . . ." August 18, 1969, in Burr, *The Sino-Soviet Border Conflict*, http://www.gwu.edu/~nsarchiv/NSAEBB/NSAEBB49/sino.sov.10.pdf.

51. Letter from the Directorate of Forces of the Eastern Border Region of the KGB to the Central Committee of Kyrgyz Soviet Socialist Republic, March 24, 1969, special dossier, Kyrgyz Party Archive.

52. Musalov, *Damanskii i Zhalanashkol, 1969.*

53. Conversation between Richard Nixon and Leonid Brezhnev (June 23, 1973), Brezhnev Visit June 18–25, 1973 Memcons, Nixon Presidential Materials Project, National Security Council Files, HAK Office Files, Country Files–Europe–USSR, Box 75, US National Archives and Records Administration.

54. Leonid Brezhnev's speech at Central Committee CPSU Party Plenum, June 26, 1969, fond 2, opis 3, delo 159, list 37, RGANI.

55. Xiong Xianghui, "Dakai zhongmei guanxi de qianzou" [The prelude to Sino-American rapproachement], *Zhonggong Dangshi Ziliao* 42 (1992), 77.

56. Conversation between Henry A. Kissinger and Anatolii Dobrynin, March 19, 1969, in *Foreign Relations of the United States, 1969–1976*, Vol. XII, *Soviet Union, January 1969–October 1970* (Washington, DC: US Government Printing Office, 2006), doc. 27, 96.

57. Lüthi, "Restoring Chaos to History."

58. Aleksei Kosygin's letter to Zhou Enlai, February 2, 1967, fond 100, opis 54, papka 228, delo 11, list 102, Foreign Policy Archive of the Russian Federation.

59. Elizavetin, "Peregovory."

60. Mikhail Kapitsa, *Na raznykh paralleliakh: Zapiski diplomata* [On different parallels: Diplomatic notes] (Moscow: Kniga i Biznes, 1996), 92.

61. Chris Tudda, *A Cold War Turning Point: Nixon and China, 1969–1972* (Baton Rouge: Louisiana State University Press, 2012), 26.

62. Xiong, "Dakai Zhongmei Guanxi de Qianzou," 83.

63. Ibid.

64. Chen and Wilson, "All Under the Heaven Is Great Chaos," 170.

65. Xiong, "Dakai Zhongmei Guanxi de Qianzou," 85.

66. Ibid., 87.

67. Ibid., 85.

68. Liu, "1969nian, zhongguo zhanlüe yu dui meisu guanxi de yanjiu he tiaozheng," 46.

69. Harrison E. Salisbury, "A War of Nerves," *New York Times*, September 18, 1969, 5.

70. Budura, *Relaţiile româno-chineze,* 901–2 (trans. Mircea Munteanu).

71. Speech by Dinmukhamed Kunaev, June 26, 1969, Moscow. fond 2, opis 3, delo 158, 24–27, RGANI.

72. Zhongong Zhongyang Wenxian Yanjiushi, *Jianguo yilai Mao Zedong wengao,* 13:54.

73. Chen and Wilson, "All Under the Heaven Is Great Chaos," 168–69.

74. Liu, "1969nian, zhongguo zhanlüe yu dui meisu guanxi de yanjiu he tiaozheng," 44.

75. Ibid., 47; see also Roderick MacFarquhar and Michael Schoenhals, *Mao's Last Revolution* (Cambridge, MA: Belknap Press, 2006), 314.

76. Liu, "1969nian, zhongguo zhanlüe yu dui meisu guanxi de yanjiu he tiaozheng," 49. Liu misdates the instructions as November 12; the instructions were issued on December 12, 1969.

77. Conversation between Mao Zedong and Kim Il Sung, October 10, 1970, B120-2-16, Shanghai Municipal Archive.

78. Chen and Wilson, "All Under the Heaven Is Great Chaos," 155–75.

41

2. "No Crowing": Reagan, Trust, and Human Rights

Sarah B. Snyder

Us president Ronald Reagan is well known for using the phrase "trust, but verify" in connection with Soviet-American arms control negotiations. It has not yet been sufficiently associated with his thinking on Soviet human rights practices, but he clearly sought to reduce mistrust with Soviet leaders to enable progress on human rights—one of a range of issues that Reagan sought to improve during his presidency. This chapter addresses Reagan's approach to negotiations with the Soviets over human rights issues, and the ways in which the development of a degree of trust facilitated Soviet progress in this sphere.[1] It focuses in particular on Reagan's interest in securing emigration visas for two Pentecostal families that had sought refuge in the US embassy in Moscow, his discussions with Soviet leader Mikhail Gorbachev about human rights at the 1985 Geneva and 1986 Reykjavik summits, and Soviet-American negotiations about improving Soviet human rights practices over the course of the Vienna Conference on Security and Cooperation in Europe (CSCE) Review Meeting (1986–89).[2] Taken together, these three cases show that Reagan's willingness to pursue "quiet diplomacy," a practice that was much maligned by observers in the Nixon years, may have been a key factor in establishing a greater degree of trust in Soviet-American relations and in facilitating Reagan's accomplishments in this area. This analysis also fits into growing efforts to introduce the history of emotions and the senses into international history.[3]

The relationship that Reagan forged with Gorbachev was surprising, given that before entering office Reagan had demonstrated a long record of anticommunism, dating to his efforts to root out suspected communist sympathizers in Hollywood during his leadership of the Screen Actors Guild in the early Cold War. He also expressed strong skepticism about the trustworthiness of Soviet leaders, particularly of their ability or willingness to uphold agreements. In his nationally syndicated radio broadcasts in the 1970s, Reagan had been broadly critical of negotiating with communist countries because, in his view: "violating agreements is standard operating procedure for communists."[4] Furthermore, during the 1976 presidential election, Reagan condemned President Gerald Ford's signature of the 1975 Helsinki Final Act. In Reagan's view, this agreement, which Soviet general secretary Leonid Brezhnev had also signed, offered the Soviets a considerable propaganda victory (an agreement to recognize the inviolability of frontiers) at little cost, given what he saw as the low likelihood that the Soviets would adhere to the act's more onerous tenets (a pledge to respect human rights and facilitate human contacts in Europe). In particularly strong language, Reagan alleged that the agreement had "put the American seal of approval on the Red Army's World War II conquests."[5] He used even more incendiary language in his first news conference as president in January 1981. In response to a question about the "intentions" of the Soviet Union, which in his memoirs Reagan characterized as asking if the United States could "trust" the Soviet Union, the president replied that "the only morality they recognize is what will further their cause, meaning they reserve unto themselves the right to commit any crime, to lie, to cheat, in order to attain that, and that is moral, not immoral, and we operate on a different set of standards, I think when you do business with them, even at a detente, you keep that in mind."[6] Reagan's concerns about the trustworthiness of communist leaders were heightened with the imposition of martial law in Poland in December 1981, which shocked and angered Reagan.[7]

Pentecostals in the Basement

Similarly unexpected was Reagan's attention to human rights as president.[8] Although Reagan did not rhetorically champion human rights in the way that his predecessor Jimmy Carter had done, he devoted considerable personal attention to a number of cases such as the Pentecostal families living in the US embassy in Moscow. In June 1978, the Vashchenko and Chmykhalov families forced their way into the US embassy in an effort to secure emigration from the Soviet Union. When permission to emigrate was not forthcoming, the two families began living in the embassy basement, fearing the consequences if they left the embassy. They did not leave for five years.[9]

Reagan raised his concern for the Pentecostal families during his first meeting with Foreign Service officer Jack Matlock, who was returning from the US embassy in Moscow. According to Matlock, Reagan's interest was driven by his concern for "identifiable human beings" and derived perhaps from his earlier work as a lifeguard in that he wanted to save people who needed help.[10]

In January 1982, Reagan pressed Brezhnev for exit visas for the Pentecostal families, citing the Helsinki Final Act in support of their right to leave the Soviet Union.[11] In February 1983, in his first one-on-one meeting with long-serving Soviet ambassador to the United States Anatoly Dobrynin, Reagan asked that the two families be allowed to emigrate as a signal of goodwill to the United States. Promising that the United States would not draw negative attention to any Soviet action, Reagan pledged that there would be no "crowing."[12] Foreign Service officer Tom Simons reported that in Reagan's meeting with Dobrynin, the president spent about "one-third of his time on human rights, with a special emphasis on the Pentecostalists."[13] According to Dobrynin's memoirs, Reagan's request that the Soviets release the Pentecostals as a symbol of improved US-Soviet relations confused him, given all of the other pressing issues in their relationship.[14]

Reagan viewed his commitment not to "crow" about positive steps taken by the Soviets as a means of building a relationship based on trust, which political scientist Deborah Welch Larson has argued is a "necessary (though not a sufficient) condition for states to cooperate."[15] Although there was not immediately a direct response, in Matlock's view, Reagan's personal emphasis facilitated the families' emigration several months later, after bilateral negotiations spearheaded by Max M. Kampelman, the US ambassador to the CSCE review meeting in Madrid.[16] The Soviet decision to allow the Pentecostals to emigrate was not unlike the confidence-building measures employed in the military sphere, in that Soviet action and Reagan's low-key response to their emigration suggested that Soviet-American negotiations could be productive after years of stagnation.

In his first term, Reagan's efforts at private diplomacy were largely unsuccessful.[17] Political instability in the Soviet Union, combined with repeated Soviet refusals to negotiate with the United States on human rights issues, prevented Reagan from successfully pursuing a highly personal role. Reagan attempted to exert influence in correspondence with Soviet leaders; however, Brezhnev and his successors Yuri Andropov and Konstantin Chernenko were each unwilling to engage substantively on human rights questions, regarding US interest as undue interference.[18] In his diary, Reagan recounts that in a draft letter he had assured Brezhnev that if the Soviet Union allowed Jewish refusenik Anatoly Shcharansky to emigrate to Israel, Brezhnev's action on this matter would be "strictly between us." Furthermore, Reagan wrote that if Brezhnev were to allow the Pentecostals to emigrate, "this is between the two of us and I will not reveal that I made any such request. I'm sure however you understand that such actions on your part would lessen my problems in future negotiations between our two countries."[19] Not surprisingly, Brezhnev reacted defensively in his response.[20] Reagan also expressed interest in the plight of other individual activists, such as physicist Andrei Sakharov and

Jewish refusenik Ida Nudel, in letters to the Soviet leader.[21] For Reagan, building trust was not an end in itself but rather was one means to secure the release of certain individuals from the Soviet system. In another tactic, Reagan wrote in his diary that he and Secretary of State George Shultz had agreed that in an upcoming meeting with Soviet foreign minister Andrei Gromyko, Shultz would "stay low key with regard to a summit[:] agree in principle but say we'd have to see some action. 1st – permission for Jews to emigrate, let the Pentecostals out of our embassy in Moscow. Seven of them have been trapped there for 4 years."[22] Yet Reagan's focus on these individual cases was never separate from the Cold War context.

The United States raised its human rights concerns in a number of other ways, including meetings between Gromyko and secretaries of state Alexander Haig or George Shultz, and Max Kampelman's meetings with the Soviets in Madrid.[23] According to Kampelman, Reagan personally pushed him to negotiate with the Soviets at Madrid to help Jewish refuseniks, saying, "Max, see what you can do to help these people," as he handed him a list of names.[24] Reagan also asked Kampelman to press for the emigration of the Pentecostals as part of a package agreement. Kampelman estimates that he spent 400 hours in bilateral negotiations with the Soviets at Madrid.[25]

As a result of these negotiations, in May 1983 Kampelman's Soviet counterpart outlined his country's position: it was willing to grant twenty-three exit visas for the Pentecostals, three Helsinki monitors would be released and allowed to emigrate, and there would be possible movement on Shcharansky and five other prominent cases.[26] According to one Soviet specialist, Andropov wanted to improve relations with the West and was therefore willing to make some "gestures" on human rights.[27] The Soviets, however, reneged on the agreement to release Shcharansky and several other Soviet dissidents, sharply angering Kampelman and suggesting that a good degree of mistrust remained between the two sides.[28] Ultimately, Kampelman did secure a pledge that if the Vashchenko and Chmykhalov families left the American embassy, they would be allowed to emigrate from the Soviet Union.[29] The significance that the White House attributed to the Pentecostals' plight can be seen in Shultz's handwritten letter to Reagan once the families had emigrated:

> Now that both Pentecostal families are out, you must feel relieved but also exhilarated. Giving freedom to a human being is a gift of great wonderment.
>
> Few people know how this all happened and I happen to be one of them. As someone with a ring side seat, let me express to you my admiration for the way you have handled this. You are a real pro and a deeply human person.[30]

45

As per its agreement with the Soviets, the United States did not publicize its role in aiding the Pentecostals. After the second Pentecostal family had emigrated, Reagan recorded in his diary, "Quiet diplomacy is working."[31]

Developing trust was complicated for Reagan and his ideological adversaries. As much as Reagan and Shultz were thrilled by the Pentecostals' release, they repeatedly were disappointed by other Soviet actions. For example, writing about a July 1983 meeting reviewing negotiations with the Soviets, Reagan commented, "The Soviets are being devious about their promise to let [Anatoly] Shcharansky go. We're going to hold them to it."[32]

Kampelman tried to encourage Soviet human rights progress by suggesting other potential areas for improvements in the US-Soviet relationship. He implied that "if they permit a plane load of monitors and activists to leave their prisons, many benefits to them would flow and we could be more flexible on specific human rights words in Madrid."[33] The concessions that Kampelman secured at Madrid were significant in that they demonstrated a Soviet willingness to negotiate on cases of humanitarian concern to the United States. Kampelman's progress, however, was a small gesture, given the vast scope of the problem. A broader commitment by the Soviet government was necessary. The circumstances for such a shift did not seem possible until after Gorbachev had been in office for several months and the two leaders began to develop a personal relationship.

Establishing a Personal Relationship in Geneva

In an important step for human rights improvements over time and the possibility of introducing a greater degree of trust in their relationship, at the November 1985 Geneva summit Reagan expressed a willingness to avoid anti-Soviet propaganda if the Soviets made some concessions on human rights.[34] Indeed, after the summit Reagan told his cabinet that he would no longer pressure the Soviet Union on human rights publicly.[35] Political scientist Andrew Kydd has defined "trust" as "a belief that the other side is trustworthy, that is, willing to reciprocate cooperation." In Kydd's view, "mistrust" is "a belief that that other side is untrustworthy, or prefers to exploit ones cooperation."[36] Reagan thus wanted to remove the impression that he hoped to exploit Soviet cooperation. As part of Reagan's new commitment not to "crow" when Gorbachev took positive steps on human rights, he declined to receive Soviet human rights activist Elena Bonner when she visited the United States for medical treatment.[37]

Over time, Gorbachev and a group of close advisers helped foster a culture of reform within the Soviet government. These reforms began with respect to military and security measures, including a progressive agreement signed at Stockholm in 1986 to allow on-site military inspections for the first time, and gradually evolved to include an array of human rights improvements. Given the secretive nature of the Soviet regime, especially on military matters, it had strongly opposed on-site inspections. Soviet negotiators claimed repeatedly that the United States and the West were using the Stockholm Conference on Confidence- and Security-Building Measures and Disarmament in Europe to gain "unilateral advantages" during the negotiations.[38] North Atlantic Treaty Organization (NATO) diplomats, however, were demanding that the confidence- and security-building measures be "verifiable," which was consistent with Reagan's long-held concerns about Soviet willingness to adhere to agreements. The Soviet concession on on-site inspections was psychologically costly, demonstrating a real commitment to concluding the talks successfully.[39]

Like his predecessors, Gorbachev initially was reluctant to address human rights with Reagan. In their first correspondence in early 1985, Reagan affirmed the United States' commitment to human rights. When Gorbachev replied, he indicated an interest in a summit meeting to ease Soviet-American tensions, but did not address Reagan's discussion of human rights.[40] In a subsequent letter, Reagan raised questions about Gorbachev's commitment to improving relations, citing continued Soviet human rights abuses in violation of CSCE agreements: "strict observance . . . of the Helsinki Final Act is an important element of our bilateral relationship."[41] Similarly, later that month, Reagan highlighted the gravity of human rights issues: "let me turn to an issue of great importance to me and to all Americans. As the Vice President informed you in Moscow, we believe strongly that strict observance of the Universal Declaration of Human Rights and of the Helsinki Final Act is an important element of our bilateral relationship."[42] Reagan's futile efforts with Gorbachev and previous Soviet general secretaries highlight the limits to personal correspondence. Reagan would raise human rights in their one-on-one meetings with greater success.

Gorbachev's overriding focus on invigorating the Soviet economy necessitated reducing Soviet military expenditures, which fed his strong interest in reaching arms control agreements with the United States. Arms control negotiations would succeed only with reciprocal (and often costly) concessions, which more likely would be achieved with greater trust. Gorbachev also saw that in addition to reducing military expenditures through arms control agreements, the moribund Soviet economy needed Western technology, trade, and financial support. In order to improve economic relations or garner international assistance, Gorbachev recognized that he would need to normalize relations with the West, which would be aided by the development of bilateral trust. A key element of enhanced trust would be a better Soviet human rights record.[43] Gorbachev may have felt more comfortable taking such steps, given Reagan's assurances that he would not use Soviet concessions for political purposes.

The 1985 Geneva summit offered Reagan and Gorbachev the opportunity to meet face to face, establish a personal relationship, lay a foundation upon which to build trust, and begin to forge agreements. There were also considerable risks. Nonetheless, according to Jack Matlock, Reagan, in his correspondence with Gorbachev, "stressed the need to build trust, reduce weapons to a common low level, and deal with regional issues and human rights." [44] At Geneva, the United States hoped to emphasize four main themes, one of which was human rights. To ensure that the Soviet-American relationship would not be dominated solely by arms control discussions, the Reagan administration developed a four-point agenda to be addressed in all bilateral talks. It included human rights concerns, regional issues, arms control, and bilateral issues.[45] On human rights, Reagan's briefing paper advised him to express American concerns at low Jewish emigration, human rights activist Andrei Sakharov's internal exile, political prisoners, and spouses divided by the Cold War, among other concerns. It also reported that the Soviets were attempting to "eliminate all forms of internal dissent" and that they had succeeded in dismantling the Moscow Helsinki Group by late 1982.[46] Reagan wrote notes to himself in advance of the meeting; of the four-and-a-half double-spaced pages that he drafted, one full page was devoted to his thoughts on human rights: "We are somewhat publicly on the record about human rights. Front page stories that we are banging away on them on their human rights abuses will get us some cheers from the bleachers, but it won't help those who are being abused."[47] Pressing the Soviets on human rights would certainly earn Reagan support from the many private citizens and politicians who wrote urging him to raise human rights issues with Gorbachev at Geneva, although Reagan wanted to affect change as well as score political points.[48] A number of commentators have suggested that Reagan's approach may have been influenced by Richard Nixon and Henry Kissinger's support for quiet diplomacy in the early 1970s. Political scientists Alexander Dallin and Gail W. Lapidus have argued that changes in the Reagan administration's objectives led to a shift from public to private diplomacy on the issue of human rights; the White House no longer sought publicity and propaganda, but rather achievements on this issue. Such a clear shift in objectives is not borne out by the evidence, however; Reagan's different tactics were more a reflection of the circumstances than a change in underlying US goals. For Reagan, vocal public diplomacy made more sense at a CSCE meeting, while quiet pursuit of Helsinki objectives was more effective at other times during his presidency.[49]

Nonetheless, it was clear Reagan wanted to institute a new approach with Gorbachev. Describing his objectives at Geneva, Reagan said, "Our purpose was to begin a fresh chapter in the relations between our two countries and to try to reduce the suspicions and mistrust between us." Gorbachev used the term mistrust as well, reporting that "one of the main results of my meeting with President Reagan is that, as leaders and as human beings, we were able to take the first step towards overcoming mistrust and to activate the factor of confidence."[50]

In their two days of meetings, among other issues, Reagan told Gorbachev about American concern for divided families, and he suggested that movement on human rights would facilitate other types of cooperation, such as trade.[51] In an important step for human rights progress and the future of their relationship, Reagan also expressed a willingness to avoid propaganda on the issue if the Soviets made some concessions on human rights. Gorbachev, in response, charged that anti-Soviet groups and even Reagan himself were using the issue of human rights for political reasons. Reagan assured Gorbachev he would not claim responsibility if the Soviets moved forward on some cases, and Gorbachev agreed to look at the cases.[52] The two did not make significant progress on human rights at Geneva, but discussing the issue seemed to have shifted the dynamic of their personal relationship.[53]

After Geneva, Reagan wrote to Gorbachev to outline his concerns about Soviet human rights, emphasizing that movement on human rights was central to improving the broader US-Soviet relationship. He noted with pleasure Soviet efforts to reunite divided spouses in the aftermath of the summit but also outlined a number of other areas he hoped that Gorbachev would address, including dual citizens and family reunification requests.[54] The issues, according to Reagan, included—

> the broad question of emigration, whether members of such groups as Jews, Armenians and others, or of some internationally known individuals. In both categories, we are talking about quite poignant cases. The young pianist I mentioned to you falls into the category of someone whose requests to emigrate have been refused. The political importance of resolving such well known cases as the Sakharovs, Scharansky [sic] and [Soviet physicist and human rights activist] Yuri Orlov cannot be overestimated. We are not interested in exploiting these cases. Their resolution will permit greater prominence for other issues in our relationship . . . the issues I have laid out in this letter are serious ones. Progress here would provide an enormous impetus to the resolution of other outstanding problems. Lack of progress will only hold us back.[55]

By ceasing to press human rights issues publicly, Reagan hoped to convince Gorbachev that respecting human rights was in the best interests of the Soviet Union, and he recognized that Gorbachev would be much more likely to implement changes if it did not appear that he was simply reacting to Western demands, particularly because Gorbachev had indicated that the Soviet Union would not change its policies under American pressure.[56] Reagan argues in his memoirs that his Geneva commitment to Gorbachev to use quiet diplomacy facilitated progress on human rights over time.[57]

Reagan succeeded in convincing Gorbachev of his interest in human rights, as Gorbachev later wrote that Americans had "an almost missionary passion for preaching about human rights and liberties" despite what he termed "a disregard for ensuring those same elementary rights in their own home."[58] In his memoirs, Gorbachev recounted his discussions with Reagan at Geneva, suggesting they had lasting resonance for him:

> Reagan began by saying that if the Soviet Union intended to improve its relations with the United States, it would do well to change its reputation with respect to individual freedom. He argued that the American public was very sensitive with respect to individual freedom. He argued that the American public was very sensitive about the issue and that therefore no American politician could ignore it.[59]

Facing American and other entreaties on the issue, Gorbachev said that he was willing to discuss human rights broadly with the West, but not individual cases.[60] His initial openness and overall less rigid demeanor compared with his predecessors offered American officials opportunities to influence Soviet policy in the long run. Larson has argued that more than simply a commitment to cooperation was required, but that "the identity of the individual leaders also mattered."[61] Reagan and Gorbachev may have been better suited to developing a working relationship than some of their predecessors.

For some observers, the 1985 Geneva summit marked a turning point in Gorbachev's views on human rights policy. Others have suggested that his actions at the time were calculated to maximize the public relations value of each human rights move.[62] Regardless, Gorbachev's small steps, such as resolving divided family cases, raised American hopes that the Soviets might make more significant changes.

Reducing Mistrust in Iceland

As in Geneva, the principal issue under discussion at the October 1986 summit in Reykjavik was arms control, which in Reagan's view required the development of trust between the two leaders.[63] In addition, Reagan intended to press Gorbachev on human rights issues, announcing he would link them to other areas of the US-Soviet relationship: "I will make it amply clear to Mr. Gorbachev that unless there is real Soviet movement on human rights, we will not have the kind of political atmosphere necessary to make lasting progress on other issues."[64] At Reykjavik, Gorbachev agreed to discuss what he called "humanitarian issues" but resented Reagan's efforts to press human rights before other, broader discussions occurred.[65] In their talks, Reagan told Gorbachev that he wished that the Soviets could go further on human rights to facilitate more cooperation, and he gave Gorbachev a list of 1,200 Soviet Jews who were waiting to emigrate.[66]

Reagan used the term trust when speaking to the American public about his summit meeting in Reykjavik:

> For all the progress we made on arms reductions, we must remember there were other issues on the table in Iceland, issues that are fundamental. As I mentioned, one such issue is human rights. As President Kennedy once said, "And is not peace, in the last analysis, basically a matter of human rights?" I made it plain that the United States would not seek to exploit improvement in these matters for purposes of propaganda. But I also made it plain, once again, that an improvement of the human condition within the Soviet Union is indispensable for an improvement in bilateral relations with the United States. For a government that will break faith with its own people cannot be trusted to keep faith with foreign powers. So, I told Mr. Gorbachev—again in Reykjavik, as I had in Geneva—we Americans place far less weight upon the words that are spoken at meetings such as these than upon the deeds that follow. When it comes to human rights and judging Soviet intentions, we're all from Missouri—you got to show us.[67]

Reagan's remarks show the clear correlation in his mind between improved human rights practices and the development of trust between him and Gorbachev. For Reagan, Soviet fulfillment of its pledges, whether in the Helsinki Final Act or elsewhere, would facilitate greater American trust of Soviet leaders. Such a connection is further demonstrated by Reagan's December 1987 remarks to human rights activists: "The real joy will come, and trust between East and West will flourish, not only when prisoners are released but when the instruments of repression are dismantled and repressive laws and practices are abolished."[68]

Some observers see Reykjavik as marking an important shift in Soviet attitudes toward human rights. In November 1986, after the summit, Gorbachev told the Politburo that the Soviet Union needed to improve its stance on human rights: "We need to work out a conception of human rights, both at home and abroad, and to put an end to the routine. It only produces dissidents."[69] Indeed, Matlock has argued that after Reykjavik, Gorbachev realized that he could achieve normalized relations with the United States only if he was willing to deal with "the full agenda of issues," which included human rights.[70] Yet other scholars such as political scientist Robert English have maintained that it was not Reykjavik, but rather the nuclear accident at Chernobyl in April 1986, that spurred Gorbachev to focus more on respect for human rights issues. Whether it was Chernobyl or Reykjavik that provided the tipping point, Gorbachev saw clear evidence that domestic problems and questions about Soviet trustworthiness prompted by noncompliance with the Helsinki Final Act and the secrecy surrounding the Chernobyl accident could negatively affect the Soviet image abroad. British prime minister Margaret Thatcher also warned Gorbachev that the Soviets would never develop international relations based on trust if they did not respect human rights and democracy.[71] This series of events had highlighted for Gorbachev what Western leaders had emphasized for some time, that the United States under Reagan, Britain under Thatcher, and other like-minded governments determined their relations with the Soviet Union based on its commitment to upholding international agreements such as the Helsinki Final Act—or, in another sense, if it could be trusted. Reagan's and Thatcher's messages seem to have penetrated Gorbachev's policymaking in late 1986, when his efforts to pursue domestic reforms to improve the Soviet image abroad accelerated during the Vienna CSCE Review Meeting, which opened in November 1986.

Demonstrating Progress in Vienna

Over the course of the Vienna meeting, Soviet and American negotiators developed a relationship of trust that enabled significant reforms in Soviet human rights practices. As a result of these negotiations, the Soviets ceased radio jamming, allowed increased emigration, released political prisoners, and altered their criminal code. Anatoly Adamishin and Richard Schifter, who negotiated on human rights for the Soviet and American sides respectively, wrote, "The Soviet-U.S. human rights dialogue of the late 1980s achieved significant results" because both Gorbachev and Reagan "wanted to remove the obstacle to good relations that disagreement on human rights issues presented."[72]

The Soviet Union undertook meaningful steps during the Vienna talks to improve its human rights record. Of particular significance to the United States was the emigration of Jewish refusenik Ida Nudel, whose case had first come to Reagan's attention in the 1970s. Shultz later said that he regarded the Soviet decision to grant Nudel an exit visa as one of his most significant accomplishments.[73] In a further sign of increased willingness to resolve human rights cases, the Soviet government responded for the first time to congressional entreaties by resolving 137 cases of the 442 that the Commission on Security and Cooperation in Europe, a US government monitoring body, had raised several months earlier. Democratic representative Steny Hoyer of Maryland called the Soviet response "a positive move forward because it is the first time the Soviets have ever responded directly to a list presented by the official U.S. commission monitoring the Helsinki Accords. Hopefully this is an indication that the Soviets are willing to take specific steps to fulfill their Helsinki humanitarian commitments." According to the commission, the 137 cases that the Soviets resolved involved more than 300 individuals who had long sought to emigrate from the Soviet Union.[74]

As CSCE diplomats negotiated in Vienna, George Shultz, Richard Schifter, and Arthur Hartman (the US ambassador in Moscow) pressed the Soviets in bilateral channels as well. Schifter describes considerable diplomacy outside of formal negotiations. In the first half of 1988, Soviet and American officials were meeting every six weeks to discuss human rights concerns.[75] According to Adamishin, by this point human rights had risen in significance as an issue in the Soviet view of its relations with the United States, such that at times it was regarded as being on a par with disarmament.[76]

Shultz's emphasis on the issue also slowly produced results, and he began to see genuine change in the Soviet position when Soviet foreign minister Eduard Shevardnadze told him in September 1987, "Give me your lists and we will be glad to look at them."[77] Clearly, the Soviets saw such steps as being in their interest, and trusted that American officials would not exploit such concessions for propaganda purposes. By October 1987, the Soviets had granted exit visas to 6,000 people, more than six times the number given in 1986, although 7,500 cases remained. After meeting with Shevardnadze in Moscow, Shultz believed that the Soviet system of reviewing applications was finally effective. Not only was Shevardnadze an improvement over his predecessor Andrei Gromyko in his willingness to listen to Shultz's concerns and occasionally act on cases that Shultz had mentioned, but by 1987, as Matlock has argued, "Shevardnadze actually began to try to change the system."[78] Nevertheless, the large number of exit visas outstanding indicated that many problems remained, raising questions about the depth of the Soviet commitment to change.

During the Vienna negotiations, Gorbachev and Reagan met several times. In one instance, when Reagan was en route to Moscow for a 1988 summit meeting with Gorbachev, he stopped in Finland, where he delivered a speech heralding the Helsinki Final Act as "a kind of way through the wilderness of mutual hostility to open fields of peace and to a common home of trust among all of our sovereign nations. . . . The Final Act set new standards of conduct for our nations and provided the mechanisms by which to apply those standards."[79] Reagan's rhetorical focus on trust suggests that he saw trust as an essential component of the improvement in Soviet-American relations. Yet he may have been slow to trust. In a June 1987 press conference, in response to a direct question, Reagan was not willing to say that he trusted Gorbachev.[80] Several months later, Reagan remained reluctant to describe Soviet-American relations as based on trust.[81] At the end of the year, Reagan acknowledged that there was "a certain chemistry between us," but would not characterize the relationship as one built on trust.[82] This pattern continued in a March 1988 interview.[83] It was not until December 1988, in his final news conference as president, that Reagan made a small but important concession. When asked if he trusted Gorbachev, Reagan said, "He hasn't shown me any reason yet that I shouldn't, but again, as I've said, that's why I kept referring to Dovorey no provorey—trust but verify."[84] By the end of 1988, Gorbachev also asserted that "fears and suspicion are gradually giving way to trust and feelings of mutual liking."[85] Reagan's final comments fit with a discernible shift in his rhetoric regarding trust and Gorbachev toward the end of his term, when he added a new line to his repetitive use of the "Russian proverb." In one speech, Reagan reportedly replaced "trust, but verify" with an American version— "Trust everybody, but cut the cards"—which suggests that even when trust exists, precautions should still be taken to ensure fair play.[86]

As Reagan and Gorbachev's meetings progressed, the Soviet Union made greater strides in the Vienna meeting and in improving its domestic human rights record. When the two leaders met again in New York in December 1988 and discussed human rights, among other issues, there was increasing evidence of Soviet progress. Reagan advocated the release of the remaining political prisoners and action on all long-time refusenik applications, objectives that the Soviets moved toward achieving.[87] In Shultz's view, the dialogue between Schifter and Adamishin "produced concrete results: an end to abuse of psychiatry [i.e., to confining political dissidents in psychiatric facilities], the release of political prisoners, the repeal of laws restricting freedom of expression, an end to the repression of religion, and a fundamental shift in the laws and regulations that governed emigration."[88] Of particular note, when Schifter was in Moscow in November 1988, he made significant progress on speeding up emigration. He secured a Soviet agreement to resolve the cases of 120 refuseniks before Reagan left office, based on a calculation of the number of working days remaining. Schifter was unprepared for such a concession, which indicated the degree to which the Soviets wished to demonstrate their dedication to reform.[89] As Larson has written, the "cost" of a concession indicates the depth of the conceder's commitment.[90]

Conclusion

Throughout his administration, Ronald Reagan showed he wanted concrete improvements in the Soviet human rights record. That the Soviets were willing to take such steps to, in a word, "verify" their promises of reform earned them esteem from the Reagan administration. Concurrently, Reagan's quiet responses to their prisoner releases and exit-visa decisions signaled to Gorbachev that the president was a suitable negotiating partner. Most important, the establishment of a relationship of trust, built in part on human rights negotiations, helped facilitate the end of the Cold War.

Notes

1. This chapter uses Deborah Welch Larson's conception of trust as a "belief that the other has benevolent intentions toward us." Deborah Welch Larson, "Trust" (keynote address at "Trust, but Verify: Confidence and Distrust from Détente to the End of the Cold War," Woodrow Wilson Center for International Scholars, Washington, DC, November 2011). In the relationship discussed here, that between Ronald Reagan and Mikhail Gorbachev in the late Cold War, diminishing mistrust was more easily accomplished than developing trust between the two adversaries. For discussion of a similar dynamic in their negotiations on arms control, see Nicholas J. Wheeler, Joshua Baker, and Laura Considine's chapter in this volume.

2. For a different approach to the same events, see Sarah B. Snyder, *Human Rights Activism and the End of the Cold War: A Transnational History of the Helsinki Network* (New York: Cambridge University Press, 2011).

3. See, e.g., Andrew J. Rotter, "Empires of the Senses: How Seeing, Hearing, Smelling, Tasting, and Touching Shaped Imperial Encounters," *Diplomatic History* 35, no. 1 (2011): 3–19; and Barbara J. Keys, *Reclaiming American Virtue: The Human Rights Revolution of the 1970s* (Cambridge, MA: Harvard University Pres, 2014).

4. "Indochina #2," April 1975, in *Reagan, in His Own Hand: The Writings of Ronald Reagan that Reveal His Revolutionary Vision for America*, ed. Kiron K. Skinner, Annelise Anderson, and Martin Anderson (New York, 2001), 49. See also Sarah B. Snyder, "Through the Looking Glass: The Helsinki Final Act and the 1976 Election for President," *Diplomacy and Statecraft* 21, no. 1 (2010), 91.

5. Leo P. Ribuffo, "Is Poland a Soviet Satellite?: Gerald Ford, the Sonnenfeldt Doctrine, and the Election of 1976," *Diplomatic History* 14, no. 3 (1990), 394.

6. Ronald Reagan, "The President's News Conference," January 29, 1981, The American Presidency Project (ed. John Woolley and Gerhard Peters, University of California, Santa Barbara), http://www.presidency.ucsb.edu/ws/?pid=44101. In 1980,

Reagan confided in a friend that he did not "really trust the Soviets"; James Graham Wilson, *The Triumph of Improvisation: Gorbachev's Adaptability, Reagan's Engagement, and the End of the Cold War* (Ithaca, NY: Cornell University Press, 2014), 17.

7. Gregory F. Domber, *Empowering Revolution: America, Poland and the End of the Cold War* (Chapel Hill: University of North Carolina Press, 2014), 25 and 46.

8. Reagan's support for human rights was episodic and clearly shaped by Cold War politics, in that he was largely inattentive to human rights abuses in South Africa, Central America, and countries allied with the United States.

9. Matlock regards Reagan's interest in Soviet human rights as genuine. Jack Matlock Jr., *Reagan and Gorbachev: How the Cold War Ended* (New York: Random House, 2004), 55–57. Further evidence of Reagan's concern can be found in his personal letters to author Suzanne Massie, *Manchester Union Leader* publisher Nackey Loeb, and businessman Armand Hammer, in which he discusses successful American efforts to secure the release of human rights activist Yuri Orlov and his wife and Soviet dissidents David and Cecilia Goldfarb. See Kiron K. Skinner, Annelise Anderson, and Martin Anderson, ed. *Reagan: A Life In Letters* (New York: Free Press, 2003), 382–83.

10. Jack Matlock, interview by author, April 3, 2006. Reagan's personal investment in these cases makes it unlikely he was only interested in the propaganda benefits of Eastern human rights abuses. Reagan did seem to sympathize with victims of communist repression, indicating that his strong anticommunism influenced his ideas on human rights.

11. Telegram, SecState to AmEmbassy Moscow, January 15, 1982, USSR: General Secretary Brezhnev, Box 38, National Security Council Records (hereafter, NSC Records) Head of State, Executive Secretariat, Ronald Reagan Library, Simi Valley, California (hereafter, Reagan Library). Brezhnev responded that the United States should not shelter the Pentecostals and instead force them to leave the embassy and seek exit visas through proper channels. Telegram, SecState to AmEmbassy Moscow, February 4, 1982, USSR: General Secretary Brezhnev, Box 37, NSC Records Head of State, Executive Secretariat, Reagan Library.

12. Matlock, *Reagan and Gorbachev*, 54. (For further discussion of Reagan's "rhetorical restraint," see Wheeler, Baker, and Considine's chapter in this volume.) In his account of the meeting, Dobrynin did not mention Reagan's promise; however, Dobrynin did not know that Soviet officials in Moscow were frustrated that Reagan treated the fate of the Pentecostals as if it was "the most important issue between us." Anatoly Dobrynin, *In Confidence: Moscow's Ambassador to America's Six Cold War Presidents* (New York: Crown, 1995), 517–21.

13. Interview with Tom Simons, Folder 8, Box 3, Don Oberdorfer Papers, Public Policy Papers, Department of Rare Books and Special Collections, Princeton University Library, Princeton, New Jersey. According to Haig, it was National Security Council staffers Richard Allen and Richard Pipes that spurred Reagan's interest in the Pentecostals living in the Moscow embassy. Alexander M. Haig, Jr. *Caveat: Realism, Reagan, and Foreign Policy* (New York: Scribner, 1984), 110.

14. Dobrynin, *In Confidence, 521.*

15. Deborah Welch Larson, *Anatomy of Mistrust: U.S.-Soviet Relations during the Cold War* (Ithaca, NY: Cornell University Press, 1997), 6.

16. Matlock's account offers important insight into the level, style, and areas of Reagan's personal involvement in United States foreign policy. Matlock, *Reagan and Gorbachev*, 57–58.

17. The Madrid CSCE Review Meeting offered a unique opportunity for bilateral negotiations on human rights, given that the Soviet noncompliance with the Helsinki Final Act was one of the dominant themes of the talks there.

18. According to Reagan's memoirs, Chernenko thought that the United States should not raise human rights issues with the Soviet Union because he regarded it as an internal matter. Ronald Reagan, *An American Life* (New York: Pocket Books, 1992), 601.

19. Douglas Brinkley, ed., *The Reagan Diaries* (New York: Harper, 2007), 13–15.

20. Brezhnev to Reagan, May 27, 1981, "USSR: General Secretary Brezhnev Cables," Box 38, NSC Records: Head of State File: Records, Executive Secretariat, Reagan Library.

21. Reagan had a long-standing interest in Nudel, at least since a 1976 radio broadcast in which he raised her inability to obtain an exit visa as a violation of the Helsinki Final Act.

22. Brinkley, *The Reagan Diaries*, 102.

23. Shultz replaced Haig in July 1982. Moore to Gradison, April 29, 1982, Folder 9, Box 1, HU, White House Office of Record Management (hereafter, WHORM) Subject Files, Reagan Library; and George P. Shultz, *Turmoil and Triumph: Diplomacy, Power, and the Victory of the American Ideal* (New York: Scribner, 1993), 122–23.

24. Kampelman also tried to gain Shcharansky's release. *Washington Post* columnist George Will argued for human rights gestures to be required in connection with a final agreement at Madrid and wrote explicitly that "no document should be signed with Anatoly Shcharansky in prison." Max M. Kampelman, "Rescue with a Presidential Push," *Washington Post*, June 11, 2004, A25; Matlock, *Reagan and Gorbachev*, 57–58; and George F. Will, "Helsinki Charade," *Washington Post*, August 21, 1983, Black Binder, Box 2442, Dante Fascell Papers, University of Miami, Coral Gables, Florida.

25. Max M. Kampelman, *Entering New Worlds: The Memoirs of a Private Man in Public Life* (New York: Harper Collins, 1991), 239; Kampelman to Kovalev, November 23, 1982, Box 13, Max M. Kampelman Papers, Minnesota Historical Society, St. Paul, Minnesota (hereafter, Kampelman Papers); Kampelman to Haig, September 10, 1981, Madrid Conference on Security and Cooperation in Europe August–September 1981, Box 15, ibid.; and William Korey, *Human Rights and the Helsinki Accord: Focus on U.S. Policy* (New York: Foreign Policy Association, 1983), 55.

26. Shcharansky was the subject of considerable discussion, with the Soviets suggesting that Shcharansky apply for a pardon. Kampelman pushed for Orlov and Sakharov also to be included in the deal. Kampelman suggested that he would accept a plane full of dissidents. Draft Telegram, Box 14, Kampelman Papers; Kampelman to Shultz, May 7, 1983, Madrid Conference on Security and Cooperation in Europe April–June 1983, Box 15, ibid.; Memorandum, Hill to McFarlane, October 19, 1983, Matlock CHRON October 1983 [0/11-10/24], Box 90888, Jack Matlock Files, Reagan Library; Telegram, EXTOTT to MDRID/CSCE, May 9, 1983, Volume 9121, 20-4-CSCE-Madrid, Volume 35, RG 25, National Archives, Ottawa, Ontario, Canada (hereafter, National Archives, Canada); and Delworth and Marchand to MacGuigan, September 5, 1982, Volume 9118, 20-4-CSCE-Madrid, Volume 21, RG 25, ibid.

27. Timothy J. Colton, *The Dilemma of Reform in the Soviet Union* (New York: Council on Foreign Relations, 1986), 183.

28. Telegram, WHDC to EXTOTT, July 6, 1983, Volume 9121, 20-4-CSCE-Madrid, Volume 36, RG 25, National Archives, Canada.

29. Kampelman eventually secured assurances for the two Pentecostal families and their extended relatives, between 60 and 80 people in all. See Kampelman, "Rescue With a Presidential Push"; and Kampelman, *Entering New Worlds*, 271.

30. Shultz to Reagan, July 18, 1983, Folder 12, Box 2, HU, WHORM, Reagan Library.

31. Brinkley, *Reagan Diaries*, 168.

32. Ibid., 166. Shcharansky was not released until February 1986 as part of an exchange for a Soviet spy.

33. Kampelman to Haig, September 10, 1981, Madrid Conference on Security and Cooperation in Europe August-September 1981, Box 15, Kampelman Papers; and Korey, *Human Rights and the Helsinki Accord*, 55.

34. Reagan, answering questions from Soviet journalists in the Oval Office, said, "I hope that in the summit maybe we can find ways that we can prove by deed—not just words, but by deeds—that there is no need for distrust between us. And then we can stop punishing our people by using our wherewithal to build these arsenals of weapons instead of doing more things for the comfort of the people." Ronald Reagan, "Remarks in an Interview With Representatives of Soviet News Organizations, Together With Written Responses to Questions," October 31, 1985, The American Presidency Project, http://www.presidency.ucsb.edu/ws/?pid=38015; and Ronald Reagan, "Interview With Foreign Broadcasters on the Upcoming Soviet–United States Summit Meeting in Geneva," November 12, 1985, The American Presidency Project, http://www.presidency.ucsb.edu/ws/?pid=38044.

35. Speaking about his summit meeting with Gorbachev, Reagan expressed hope that the two leaders had made a "fresh start." Ronald Reagan, "Written Responses to Questions Submitted by Foreign Publications," December 6, 1985, The American Presidency Project, http://www.presidency.ucsb.edu/ws/?pid=38153.

36. Andrew H. Kydd, *Trust and Mistrust in International Relations* (Princeton, NJ: Princeton University Press, 2005), 3.

37. Perhaps this was Reagan's own form of a confidence-building measure.

38. Statement, Oleg A. Grinevsky (USSR), October 12, 1984, CSCE/SC/Vol. 55, OSCE Archives, Prague.

39. Snyder, *Human Rights Activism and the End of the Cold War*, 497; and Ben Horne, "Conflict, Costly Concessions and Manipulative Mediation," http://econ.ucsd.edu/~bhorne/pdfs/paper1.pdf (accessed April 8, 2013), 7.

40. Gorbachev to Reagan, March 24, 1985, USSR GSG 8590272-8590419, Box 39, Executive Secretary NSC Head of State File, Reagan Library.

41. Reagan to Gorbachev, April 30, 1985, USSR GSG 85904/5-8590495, Box 39, Executive Secretary NSC Head of State File, Reagan Library.

42. "Reagan letter to Gorbachev," April 30, 1985, doc. 9, in *To the Geneva Summit: Perestroika and the Transformation of U.S.-Soviet Relations*, National Security Archive Electronic Briefing Book no. 172 (Washington, DC: National Security Archive, November 22, 2005), http://nsarchive.gwu.edu/NSAEBB/NSAEBB172/Doc9.pdf.

43. Daniel C. Thomas, "The Helsinki Accords and Political Change in Eastern Europe," in *The Power of Human Rights: International Norms and Domestic Change*, ed. Thomas Risse, Stephen C. Ropp, and Kathryn Sikkink (New York: Cambridge University Press, 1999), 229.

44. Matlock, *Reagan and Gorbachev*, 122.

45. In each of these areas, not just human rights, the United States tried to reduce mistrust with the Soviet Union. Shultz, *Turmoil and Triumph*, 266n.

46. "Human Rights in the Soviet Union," "Soviet Union (binder)," Box 91097, Tyrus W. Cobb Files, Reagan Library.

47. Matlock, *Reagan and Gorbachev*, 152.

48. For a representative example, see Hammen to Reagan, October 18, 1985, Folder 6, Box 2, FO 006-09, WHORM, Reagan Library; Adram to McFarlane, September 9, 1985, Folder 4, ibid; Broomfield to Oglesby, November 4, 1985, Folder 16, ibid; and Flis to Reagan, October 29, 1985, Folder 12, ibid; Specter et al. to Reagan, October 24, 1985, Folder 7, ibid; and D'Amato et al. to Reagan, November 5, 1985, Folder 1, Box 32, PR 007, ibid.

49. Lou Cannon, *President Reagan: The Role of a Lifetime*, rev. ed. (New York: Public Affairs, 2000), 676; and Alexander Dallin and Gail W. Lapidus, "Reagan and the Russians: American Policy Toward the Soviet Union," in *Eagle Resurgent?: The Reagan Era in American Foreign Policy*, ed. Kenneth A. Oye, Robert Lieber, and Donald Rothchild (Boston: Little, Brown, 1983), 223.

50. Ronald Reagan, "New Year's Messages of President Reagan and Soviet General Secretary Gorbachev," January 1, 1986, The American Presidency Project, http://www.presidency.ucsb.edu/ws/?pid=36367.

51. Cannon, *President Reagan*, 675; and Bernard Weinraub, "President Links Rights in Soviet to Summit Success," *New York Times*, October 8, 1986, Human Rights Issue, Box 1 Processed, Joint Baltic American National Committee Records, Immigration History Research Center, University of Minnesota, Minneapolis, Minnesota (hereafter, JBANC).

52. Matlock, *Reagan and Gorbachev*, 161; and Memorandum of Conversation, November 20, 1985, Geneva: Memcons (Reagan-Gorbachev Memcons Geneva Meeting 11/19–21/1985) 2 of 3, Box 92137, Jack Matlock Files, Reagan Library.

53. Matlock, interview, April 3, 2006.

54. Shultz to Reagan, December 4, 1985, USSR GSG 8591241-8591245, Box 40, Head of State File, Executive Secretary NSC, Reagan Library; and Reagan to Gorbachev, December 7, 1985, ibid.

55. Reagan, *An American Life*, 645.

56. Matlock, interview, April 3, 2006; and Memorandum, Shultz to Reagan, January 14, 1986, 90024, Box 40, USSR GSG 8690024-8690124, Head of State File, Executive Secretary, National Security Council, Reagan Library.

57. Reagan, *An American Life*, 686.

58. Mikhail Gorbachev, *Perestroika: New Thinking for Our Country and the World* (New York: Harper and Row, 1987), 215.

59. Mikhail Gorbachev, *Memoirs* (New York: Doubleday, 1996), 408.

60. Gorbachev, *Perestroika*, 205.

61. Larson, *Anatomy of Mistrust*, 239.

62. According to Senator Alfonse D'Amato (R-NY), the Soviet Union was making tactical concessions to disguise continued repression: "There is reason to believe that recent promising developments were nothing more than another cynical attempt by Soviet leaders to manipulate the Western media and, through them, Western political leaders and public opinion." Commission on Security and Cooperation in Europe Hearing, "Human Rights and the CSCE Process in the Soviet Union," February 27, 1986, 99th Congress, 2nd Session.

63. For further discussion, see Wilson, *The Triumph of Improvisation*, 112.

64. A host of other ethnic and human rights organizations, members of Congress, and private citizens wrote to Reagan asking him to raise different human rights concerns in his meeting with Gorbachev. Bernard Weinraub, "President Links Rights in Soviet to Summit Success," *New York Times*, October 8, 1986, Human Rights Issue, Box 1 Processed, JBANC; Overall Briefing Book, October 10–12, 1986, President Reagan's Trip to Reykjavik, Iceland, October 10–12, 1986: Overall Briefing Book, Box 92085, Fritz Ermath, Reagan Library; Letter and Attachments, Broomfield to Ball, October 7, 1986, 428917, Box 5, HU, WHORM, ibid.; and Hoyer et al. to Reagan, October 6, 1986, 451246, FO 006, WHORM, Reagan Library.

65. Matlock, *Reagan and Gorbachev*, 218.

66. Shultz proposed a working group to discuss human rights and regional issues. Matlock, *Reagan and Gorbachev*, 226; and Cannon, *President Reagan*, 687.

67. Ronald Reagan, "Address to the Nation on the Meetings With Soviet General Secretary Gorbachev in Iceland," October 13, 1986, The American Presidency Project, http://www.presidency.ucsb.edu/ws/?pid=36587.

68. Ronald Reagan, "Remarks at a White House Briefing for Human Rights Supporters," December 3, 1987, The American Presidency Project, http://www.presidency.ucsb.edu/ws/?pid=33765. See also Ronald Reagan, "Remarks to the World Affairs Council of Western Massachusetts in Springfield," April 21, 1988, The American Presidency Project, http://www.presidency.ucsb.edu/ws/?pid=35716.

69. Daniel C. Thomas, "Human Rights Ideas, the Demise of Communism, and the End of the Cold War," *Journal of Cold War Studies* 7, no. 2 (2005), 131; and Robert D. English, *Russia and the Idea of the West: Gorbachev, Intellectuals, and the End of the Cold War* (New York: Columbia University Press, 2000), 220.

70. Jack Matlock Jr., *Autopsy of an Empire: The American Ambassador's Account of the Collapse of the Soviet Union* (New York: Random House, 1995), 97.

71. Robert English, "The Sociology of New Thinking: Elites, Identity Change, and the End of the Cold War," *Journal of Cold War Studies* 7, no. 2 (2005), 66.

72. Anatoly Adamishin and Richard Schifter, "Introduction," in Anatoly Adamishin and Richard Schifter, *Human Rights, Perestroika, and the End of the Cold War* (Washington, DC: United States Institute of Peace Press, 2009), 3.

73. Shultz describes Nudel's phone call to him from Israel upon her arrival there as "a very emotional moment" for him. Rozanne Ridgway Interview, Folder 30, Box 2, Oberdorfer Papers; George Shultz Interview, Folder 2, Box 3, ibid.; and George Shultz Interview, December 18, 2002, Reagan Presidential Oral History Project, Miller Center, University of Virginia.

74. "Soviets Announce Resolution of Commission Cases," *CSCE Digest*, April 1987, CSCE Digest, Box 6, JBANC.

75. Schifter, "Putting the Vienna CSCE Meeting on Our Bilateral Agenda;" and Schifter, "A Goal-Oriented Human Rights Dialogue Begins," in Adamishin and Schifter, *Human Rights, Perestroika, and the End of the Cold War*, 144, 149.

76. Anatoly Adamishin, August 5, 1989 Interview Transcript, Folder 1, Box 1, The Hoover Institution and the Gorbachev Foundation (Moscow) Collection, Hoover Institution Archives, Stanford, California.

77. Shultz, *Turmoil and Triumph*, 986. According to Ridgway, Shultz's repeated entreaties convinced Soviet leaders that changing their human rights practices was

in the best interests of their reform efforts. Rozanne Ridgway Interview, Folder 30, Box 2, Oberdorfer Papers. Hill emphasizes Shultz's role in convincing Gorbachev and Shevardnadze that human rights violations were a "practical problem" for the Soviet Union. Charles Hill, written communication with the author, March 29, 2010.

78. Matlock, *Reagan and Gorbachev*, 265; and AP, "Soviets Sending Positive Signals on Human Rights, Shultz Says," October 22, 1987, Politics: Human Rights: General, 1987–1987, Box 19, New Code Subject Files, Soviet Red Archives, Records of Radio Free Europe/Radio Liberty Research Institute, Open Society Archives, Open Society Archives, Budapest, Hungary (hereafter, Open Society Archives).

79. See Stefan Lehne, *The Vienna Meeting of the Conference on Security and Cooperation in Europe, 1986–1989: A Turning Point in East-West Relations* (Boulder, CO: Westview Press 1991), 119–20.

80. Ronald Reagan, "The President's News Conference," June 11, 1987, The American Presidency Project, http://www.presidency.ucsb.edu/ws/?pid=34384.

81. Ronald Reagan, "Written Responses to Questions Submitted by the Swedish Newspaper Svenska Dagbladet," September 22, 1987, The American Presidency Project, http://www.presidency.ucsb.edu/ws/?pid=33461.

82. Ronald Reagan, "Remarks and a Question-and-Answer Session with News Editors and Broadcasters," December 11, 1987, The American Presidency Project, http://www.presidency.ucsb.edu/ws/?pid=33807.

83. Ronald Reagan, "Interview With Alastair Burnet of ITN Television of the United Kingdom," March 10, 1988, The American Presidency Project, http://www.presidency.ucsb.edu/ws/?pid=35534.

84. Ronald Reagan, "The President's News Conference," December 8, 1988, The American Presidency Project, http://www.presidency.ucsb.edu/ws/?pid=35251. Reagan's slow progress to this point, despite his admission in his memoirs that he was usually quick to trust, suggests that may have conceptualized "trust" as separate from the personal friendship he developed with the Soviet leader. For more on the distinction among friendship, sympathy, and trust, see Ute Frevert, "Emotions in History—TRUST and Confidence" (keynote address at "Trust, but Verify: Confidence and Distrust from Détente to the End of the Cold War," Woodrow Wilson Center for International Scholars, Washington, DC, November 2011).

85. Ronald Reagan, "New Year's Messages of President Reagan and President Mikhail Gorbachev of the Soviet Union," January 1, 1989, The American Presidency Project, http://www.presidency.ucsb.edu/ws/?pid=35313. Reagan wrote in his memoirs: "I tend to trust people until they give me reason not to." Reagan, *An American Life*, 184.

86. See, e.g., Ronald Reagan, "Remarks at a Campaign Fundraising Luncheon for Senator Pete Wilson in Irvine, California," August 23, 1988, The American Presidency Project, http://www.presidency.ucsb.edu/ws/?pid=36291.

87. "Text of Reagan's Rights Remarks," December 9, 1988, Human Rights deklaratsia, 1988–1990, Box 693, Old Code Subject Files, Soviet Red Archives, Records of Radio Free Europe/Radio Liberty Research Institute, Open Society Archives; Letter, Hornblow to Bauzys, January 13, 1989, Folder 9, Box 7, HU, WHORM Subject File, Reagan Library; and "Memorandum of Conversation: 'The President's Private Meeting with Gorbachev'," December 7, 1988, doc. 8, in *Reagan, Gorbachev, and Bush at Governor's Island*, National Security Archive Electronic Briefing Book no. 261

(Washington, DC: National Security Archive, December 8, 2008), http://nsarchive .gwu.edu/NSAEBB/NSAEBB261/us08.pdf.

88. Shultz, "Foreword," in Adamishin and Schifter, *Human Rights, Perestroika, and the End of the Cold War*, xiv.

89. Schifter had to scramble to get Soviet authorities a list of the 120 cases to be resolved. Richard Schifter, "Putting the Vienna CSCE Meeting on Our Bilateral Agenda," in Adamishin and Schifter, *Human Rights, Perestroika, and the End of the Cold War*, 169–72; and Richard Schifter, interview with author, May 5, 2008.

90. Larson, *Anatomy of Mistrust*, 28.

3. Trust between Adversaries and Allies: President George H. W. Bush, Trust, and the End of the Cold War

J. Simon Rofe

"**Y**ou can't develop or earn this mutual trust and respect unless you deliberately work at it." George H. W. Bush wrote these words in recounting a difference of opinion with Henry Kissinger regarding personal diplomacy and national interests when the latter was national security advisor to President Richard M. Nixon and embarking on the policy of détente.[1] As can be seen in his correspondence with Kissinger, Bush felt that trust was required to operate at the highest level of US and international politics.

This chapter argues that trust, and its double-edged capacity, was a hallmark of the George H. W. Bush administration's diplomacy and foreign policy making at the end of the Cold War. The reliance on trust was seen in three different capacities. First, with advisers such as Brent Scowcroft and James A. Baker III, Bush required trust to be able to contemplate unpalatable policy options and make decisions. Second, with allies like West German chancellor Helmut Kohl, British prime minister Margaret Thatcher, and French president François Mitterrand, trust was political capital that enabled Bush to garner

The author would like to thank the editorial team of Martin Klimke, Christian Ostermann, and Reinhild Kreis for their unstinting patience on this project, and to express gratitude for offering the opportunity to contribute to the colloquium in Washington, D.C., in November 2011, and subsequently to contribute to this volume. Equally, I would like to add my thanks to Shannon Granville and her colleagues at the Wilson Center. Elements of an earlier version of this analysis appeared in Michael Patrick Cullinane and Clare Frances Elliott, ed., *International Perspectives on Presidential Leadership: An International View of the White House* (New York: Routledge, 2014).

support for US policies on an international plain. Third, with Soviet premier Mikhail Gorbachev, reciprocal trust was vital to ensuring a peaceful end to the superpower conflict. These different capacities of trust illustrate how trust underpinned Bush's approach to personal diplomacy honed throughout his professional career. At the same time, the evidence demonstrates that the Bush administration was not always able to base its diplomacy on the president's personal outlook in the face of the fast-changing political topography of the end of Cold War. The tension between Bush's personal belief in the value of trust and the realities posed by the challenges of his administration meant that the former was not always in evidence.

Reflecting an intermestic approach, trust was also an important consideration on the domestic scene. Bush's capacity for trust would be challenged outright in the 1992 presidential election campaign. The Democratic opposition repeatedly pointed to his 1988 "read my lips" pledge in respect to raising new taxes on the American people,[2] a pledge that Bush had abrogated in 1990 in the face of an increased federal budget deficit. Yet even though the issue of trust ultimately would contribute to the end of his presidency, Bush's conception of trust was fundamental to his own diplomacy and thus was in part integral to the national security policy he pursued as president.

The chapter draws three conclusions. First, and most clearly, the Bush administration's understanding of and capacity to draw upon trust has been overlooked in literature of the period. Second, this oversight has been detrimental to understanding the era and the issues with which the Bush administration had to contend. Finally, the omission is all the more notable because the manner in which Bush sought to conduct diplomacy was based on his understanding of the Cold War in its final years. In revealing President Bush and his closest advisers' sophisticated and deliberate approach, underpinned by their conception of trust, the chapter makes use of the increasing volume of files available at the George Bush Presidential Library in College Station, Texas. It begins by providing an understanding of trust and its relation to distrust, mistrust, and risk, rooted in the work of Onora O'Neill. The chapter then looks at the foundations of Bush's understanding of the concept as it had developed by the time he became president, and turns to the application of trust during the Kuwait crisis of 1990–91. It then focuses upon the relations between Washington and Moscow in Bush's personal diplomacy and his individual relationships with Mikhail Gorbachev and Boris Yeltsin. Bush's relationship with his advisers is considered in the chapter's next section, before turning to contrasting expressions of trust in the domestic and foreign spheres. These instances illustrate in Bush the threefold application of trust with advisers, allies, and one-time adversaries.

Trust and the Roots of Bush's Personal Diplomacy

In delivering the BBC's Reith Lectures in 2002, under the title "A Question of Trust?," Baroness Onora O'Neill identified a "crisis of trust" in the modern world.[3] The crisis she identified was that faced by George H. W. Bush when confronted with a swiftly changing geopolitical landscape at the end of the Cold War, which centered on the fundamental question of what it takes to trust someone or something. For the Bush administration, this question meant applying trust in a number of scenarios, including judgments about Gorbachev's commitment to reform the Soviet Union, and Iraqi president Saddam Hussein's bona fides. A student of philosopher John Rawls, O'Neill argued that in seeking to build trust in an era when accountability and transparency are increasingly valued, society actually finds more and more reasons *not* to trust individuals and supposed evidence. Evidence of wrongdoing and mistakes, conscious or subconscious, undermine important aspects of "trustworthiness." "A more serious and practical approach to trust," O'Neill argued, "would concentrate on showing what we need in order to judge others' honesty, reliability, and competence so that we can place or refuse trust intelligently."[4] O'Neill's essential point was that trust is always a judgment; it can never be absolute: "Trust is needed precisely because all guarantees are incomplete."[5] Taking this point to its logical conclusion, the search for trust has the capacity to increase levels of mistrust: the more you know, the more evidence you have to mistrust others and to distrust the evidence you have.

The dilemma over trust and mistrust was one that the Bush administration faced, and it served to constrain a more active and assertive foreign policy. Instead, Bush's foreign policy was characterized throughout by caution as the administration learned more about the Soviet Union's predicament and the potential risks it still posed to US national security interests.[6] The certainties of the Cold War were replaced by questions, and there seemed to be no one to whom these questions could be directed, let alone anyone to provide definitive answers. Indeed, in relation to Bush and the end of the Cold War, the derivative question that arises is whether, in seeking to build a trusting relationship with Gorbachev, Bush ended up preventing greater levels of practical cooperation, given that he perhaps never could have gained the absolute guarantees from Moscow to have satiated the Cold War outlook of his inner circle. The question, in other words, is to what extent were Bush and his administration guilty of adopting a position that never could have been satisfied. The answer remains unclear, even though Bush and Gorbachev were able to achieve trust in their personal relations. What can be said with certainty from an examination of the files of the period is that the Bush administration failed to trust Moscow to the degree that would have seen further improvements of substance in relations between the two superpowers and former adversaries. One important consequence here is to highlight the difference between the personal levels of trust established between Bush and Gorbachev and the policies that their nations adopted. Of course, a chief executive is routinely presented with unrealized policy options. Nonetheless, given the extent to which the subsequent Clinton administration advanced US interests in relations with Russia—albeit perhaps recklessly in its faith in Boris Yeltsin—Bush's failure to push further at a crumbling Soviet state has given rise to critique of his presidency.

Such a critique is all the more misplaced, given that the Bush administration considered the establishment of trust a foundation for its diplomacy and foreign policy. As Bush expressed in his correspondence with Kissinger, he believed that trust had to be worked at in a pragmatic and dedicated manner, and so his approach supports O'Neill's notion that trust can never be absolute. For Bush and the key figures in his administration, trust manifested itself in considered policy deliberations and the careful application of policy decisions. They were ready to test, and retest, trust. The test they applied most readily was how far they could trust the correlation between "words" and "actions." This test applied on a number of levels, but it was expressed particularly in the president's diplomatic and personal relationships. Personal diplomacy meant being able to rely on people and the situation. In a 2011 interview, Secretary of State Baker explained how he and President Bush conceived of trust in this respect: "You're always better off if you can trust the guy across the table, but you'll never know that until you test him. If he agrees to some things, if he ever welshes on you or if he ever lies to you, then you've got a problem."[7] Baker's analysis closely aligns with the transient nature of trust that Deborah Welch Larson has identified when she states that "trust takes a long time to create, it can be destroyed in an instant."[8] The Bush administration understood the duality of trust, and adopted a cautious outlook in the face of the rapidly changing geopolitical landscape after the fall of the Iron Curtain in the second half of 1989. Brent Scowcroft, Bush's national security advisor, recalls having spent the first two years of the administration stressing the continuing threat posed by the Soviet Union by explicitly correcting Bush's speechwriting team: "For months, the President's speechwriters had included a phrase in speeches saying, 'The Cold War is over.' And routinely, I crossed it out and crossed it out and crossed it out."[9] Bush captured the reluctance to appear outwardly "victorious" in a conversation with Canadian prime minister Brian Mulroney in March 1991. Even in the afterglow of the apparently successful conclusion of the Gulf War, Bush remarked, "I think our best policy is steady as she goes."[10] Such sentiment can be applied to his entire presidency in this respect.

Although Bush was prepared to test trust in others, he also realized that trust had to be earned, and he endeavored to earn the trust of allies and adversaries alike with a consistent approach to policymaking and moderated presidential rhetoric. Therefore Bush's conception of trust aligns closely with the view put forward by Larson. "To build trust, a state should . . . maintain a consistent policy," Larson writes, "because people tend to believe that a state's actions in different areas, no matter how disparate the circumstances reveal its underlying motives."[11] Bush understood the importance of avoiding inconsistency in his administration's foreign affairs because of the destabilizing effect it could have on those with whom he had to negotiate. The Bush administration's reading of inconsistency in President Ronald Reagan's handling of Gorbachev and the latter's reforms contributed to its thorough reassessment of US policy toward the Soviet Union and the whole Eastern Bloc upon arriving in office. Even though Bush and many others in his administration had served in the Reagan administration, the distinction between the two administrations with regard to Gorbachev's commitment to reform is stark. The Bush administration adopted a notable "pause" in relations with Moscow upon assuming office in January 1989, and it was only after the Malta conference in December of that year that the tempo returned to US-Soviet relations. The differences between the two Republican administrations can be attributed to different understandings of trust and the importance subsequently placed upon trust in US foreign policy making.[12]

For Bush, being consistent in word and action was vital to establishing trust and being trustworthy oneself. The importance of consistency was an integral facet of the basis for negotiation: a central tenet of diplomacy. The Bush administration aimed to behave consistently with what it said it was going to do, even in the face of rapid change. Within this framework, the administration would adopt a pragmatic approach to crises as they arose and would seek to employ a diplomatic negotiated solution. With the Cold War backdrop to the vast majority of his professional life as part of the "Greatest Generation,"[13] Bush understood the value of negotiation, particularly as he understood that the alternative was worse; continuing to negotiate, as he saw it, was a means of preventing an escalation to military conflict. As esteemed scholar of diplomacy Geoff Berridge has noted, negotiation "can produce the advantages obtainable from the cooperative pursuit of common interests; and it is only this activity that can prevent violence from being employed to settle remaining arguments over conflicting ones."[14] However, the Bush administration's desire for a measured diplomatic response meant that Bush has since been critiqued for ponderous decision-making, most notably over his administration's seemingly hesitant response to the Tiananmen Square clampdown in May 1989. The historical record perhaps magnifies criticism of Bush's cautious approach, given that his presidency was bookended by the optimism of Ronald Reagan and the dynamic charm of Bill Clinton. Nonetheless, the key characteristic here of the Bush administration, and importantly one that worked in constraining escalating crises at the end of the Cold War, was that of caution.

Bush preferred to negotiate with individuals, often on a one-to-one or face-to-face basis.[15] It was in such an environment that he was most comfortable, and it was one that allowed him to most effectively further US diplomacy. Presidential scholar Jeffrey Engel has identified in Bush a "devotion to personal diplomacy."[16] The emphasis on the personal, however, is not meant to create a mutually exclusive distinction between the personal and political. As historian Frank Costigliola, writing about President Franklin Delano Roosevelt's predilection for personal diplomacy, has argued, "It remains impossible . . . to isolate what the precise impact of the "personal" would be on a hypothesized, wholly impersonal "political" interaction—not that such could ever occur among human beings."[17] That is to say, personal diplomacy is a political activity. Nonetheless, the practicalities of being president dictated that Bush would not always be able to undertake this type of personal diplomacy himself. In such circumstances, he had to rely on his advisers. With regard to foreign affairs, two individuals stand out: Secretary of State James A. Baker III and National Security Advisor Brent Scowcroft. These two men enjoyed the complete confidence and, more important, trust of the president due to their shared experiences of the Cold War and shared outlooks for the central place of the United States in the conduct of international affairs. Either directly or by proxy, trust was integral to the diplomatic approach that Bush sought in conducting US foreign relations.

Trust was to the fore of what is commonly held to be the high point of the Bush administration's foreign policy: the US-led United Nations response to Iraq's invasion of Kuwait in August 1990. The tale of US-Iraqi diplomacy during the summer of 1990 has been well told. Saddam Hussein's regime interpreted US ambassador April Glaspie's remarks as a "green light" from Baghdad's former sponsors in Washington to deal with Iraq's conflict with Kuwait in its own way. Saddam Hussein's misinterpretation bred mistrust more broadly in Washington, which conditioned the diplomacy preceding Operation Desert Shield that followed during late 1990 and early 1991. Bush did not tolerate Iraq's compromising of Kuwait's territorial integrity, and under the UN flag brought together a multinational coalition to liberate Kuwait. Prevalent in the administration's thinking was the drawing of a parallel between Saddam Hussein's actions in invading a small neighbor and

German chancellor Adolf Hitler's seizure of parts of Czechoslovakia in 1938 and the Munich agreement which followed.[18] Baker later recalled the administration's desire "to get rid of a Hitler."[19] After the Iraqi invasion on August 2, 1990, Washington's negotiations with Baghdad through Russian and Arab interlocutors centered on whether it could trust what Saddam Hussein professed as his peaceful intentions. In the final days before Operation Desert Shield gave way to the military action of Operation Desert Storm, Bush confessed to Gorbachev that "very candidly, to be honest with you, we have no trust anymore in anything the man [i.e., Saddam Hussein] says."[20] Given that Bush and his advisers saw the end of the Cold War as the ultimate closure of the Second World War, it is perhaps not surprising that they were so averse to appeasing, or even being perceived to appease. They did not want to be likened to British prime minister Neville Chamberlain, whose appeasement of Hitler following the seizure of Czechoslovakia labeled him as one of history's *"Guilty Men."*[21] As Onora O'Neill suggested in her discussion of trust, the application of trust is a judgment, and ultimately it is an imperfect one.

Bush, Trust, and the End of the Soviet Union

One of the most notable and celebrated personal relationships of the Bush administration was between President Bush and Mikhail Gorbachev, leader of the Soviet Union until its dissolution at the end of 1991. There was clear warmth in the relationship, as evidenced by the efforts that Bush made to confirm Gorbachev's personal safety after Gorbachev's position was challenged by a hard-line coup in August 1991.[22] Baker has identified the December 1989 Malta conference as a key moment in the two leaders' bond. According to Baker, the conference "was an important meeting, if for no other reason than to begin to establish a relationship between the two of them, . . . a relationship of cooperation and trust." The Bush administration came to know Gorbachev, which gave them a degree of confidence in their negotiations, despite previous skepticism of Gorbachev's commitment to reform in the Soviet Union and broader Eastern bloc. Baker also indicated the interrelationship of friendship, trust, and diplomacy in securing US national interests: "If you have the friendship—I call it a relationship of trust. If you have the trust, you can get a hell of a lot more done than if you don't. If you and I are trying to negotiate something and I know I can trust your word, we've got a better chance of getting there than we do if—and if you think the same about me." Baker concluded, "So it's not so much friendship as it is a relationship, knowing that you can trust your interlocutor."[23] According to Bartholomew Sparrow, the importance of these personal ties in US-Soviet relations was that they "eased difficult negotiations, allowed for frank discussions, and smoothed ruffled feathers (feathers that the press, domestic and foreign both, liked to ruffle)."[24]

The dynamics of Boris Yeltsin's challenge to Gorbachev's authority, and to the future of the Soviet Union, also illustrate the capacity for trust to shape Bush's relationship with Gorbachev, as well as the course of US-Soviet relations. (Yeltsin was then president of the Russian Soviet Federative Socialist Republic.) In the spring of 1991, Bush and his administration faced a dilemma over the stability and longevity of Gorbachev's leadership of the Soviet Union. Where once it saw a single leader—the head of the Central Committee of the Communist Party and president of the Soviet Union—Yeltsin's rise presented a quandary. Not only was Bush faced with the question of how far could he trust that Gorbachev would remain true to his pledge to reform in the Soviet Union, but how far could he trust that Gorbachev would remain the Soviet head of state? In March 1991, such a question was very much to the fore in Bush's mind. In conversation with Canada's Prime Minister Mulroney, Bush revealed the dilemma that Yeltsin posed as a challenger to Gorbachev and the dimension of trust that was at play. Mulroney began by asking Bush about his assessment of Gorbachev, and Bush was cognizant of his own domestic position: "I'm being criticised by both the Right and the Left for my support of Gorbachev. The thing about Yeltsin is that his values are good, but I don't know him." Bush succinctly summed up his predicament as he faced a fast-changing situation in the Soviet Union. National Security Advisor Scowcroft was more forthright. Scowcroft then opined, "Yeltsin may be a true demagogue; [he] does not appear to be a constructive force." Although the debate about Yeltsin's qualities continued to rage long after Bush left office, Scowcroft's remarks reflect a predisposition to question Yeltsin's trustworthiness. Following suit in a more reserved, almost confessional tone, Bush added, "I guess Yeltsin is not all bad, but we are not sure how to deal with him." He concluded, "We should stick with Gorbachev." Put colloquially, the implication of the conversation was "better the devil you know," and it revealed the difficulties that Bush had in placing trust in both individuals and the fast-changing situation.[25]

The importance of the internal political dynamics in the United States and the Soviet Union also presented Bush with difficulties in deploying trust in relations with Moscow. In early 1991, when the administration looked to Moscow, Bush was confronted with the unpalatable dilemma of choosing between Gorbachev and Yeltsin. Mulroney noted, "If you deal with Yeltsin, you will hurt Gorbachev."[26] Bush recognized the quandary, and lamented that his assessment of Gorbachev was being influenced by US domestic politics. "I have a congressional problem," he disclosed in conversation with French president François Mitterrand the day after meeting Mulroney. "They like to supervise." Although Bush knew that congressional supervision reflected the Founding Fathers' intentions for the executive branch of government, he recognized the potential to damage relations with Gorbachev: "Congress will invite Yeltsin over, and then I will have to see him." Mitterrand offered a succinct if structural retort—"Yeltsin is not in power and Gorbachev is"— and concluded that "it is not our responsibility to decide whether Gorbachev should remain in power or not." Bush agreed, stating that "we have to wait it out."[27] Gorbachev's domestic plight thus presented a further dimension to the quandary for Bush in placing trust between the individual and the state of the Soviet Union.

The international situation was complicated further by the domestic implications of Bush's policy in having to distinguish between a resurgent Russia and a Soviet Union that would cease to exist at the end of 1991. The economic dimension provides a critical insight into the dilemma the administration faced in maintaining trust with Gorbachev and the situation in Moscow. It was, in short, to whom would the United States lend dollars? The perception of many in Congress was that the Soviet Union, as the old enemy, did not warrant support, whereas a more democratic-leaning Russia with a readily identifiable and charismatic leader in Yeltsin was more palatable. When set against the economic recession that then was besetting the United States, Ed Hewitt, special assistant to the president for national security affairs, explained that "the provision of new credits for the Soviets will confront us again with the perception that the Administration is giving priority to foreign policy objectives over domestic concerns." Hewitt continued, "This must be given particular weight now in light of the current Congressional climate and the growing pressure for the President to introduce a domestic economic growth package."[28] Such an assessment was particularly apt, given the dramatic downturn in Bush's approval ratings from the high of 89 percent at the end of February 1991 in the aftermath of the Gulf War to just over 50 percent by the beginning of December that year.[29] This assessment again illustrates the difficult question of the relationship between Gorbachev as an individual and the state of US-Russian relations, while here paying particular attention to the domestic implications of both.

Even as Bush came to know Gorbachev as an individual, the administration also learned that Gorbachev's leadership was challenged by a dynamic Russian political milieu. In April 1991, the Central Intelligence Agency (CIA) Directorate of Intelligence presented a report to the National Security Council titled "The Gorbachev Succession."[30] The report began starkly: "The Gorbachev era is effectively over." The report saw Gorbachev as becoming

71

increasingly marginalized by both traditionalists and reformers, and questioned the likelihood that he would retain his position. The future, it proclaimed, was likely to be "messy," and presciently stated that "no matter what happens, the current political system in the Soviet Union is doomed." Importantly for Bush, the CIA report concluded by bringing together two levels of trust: "The Gorbachev succession is directly linked to the fate of the political system." What this statement served to do was to conflate Bush's judgment about the trustworthiness of his counterpart and the broader political situation. On a personal level, Bush trusted Gorbachev, but he did not have the evidence to support trusting Gorbachev's survival as premier of a nation that itself soon might not exist. Indeed, the more intelligence Bush received, the less likely the prospect of the Soviet Union's surviving seemed, thus confirming O'Neill's contention that the more information one has, the more grounds one has to distrust. Nonetheless, despite the CIA report's pessimistic outlook for the premier, Bush's personal trust in Gorbachev remained. He had confided to Mitterrand the previous month, "I hope Gorbachev survives, [he] has been good to work with so far."[31]

Trust, Personal Diplomacy, and the Role of the "Bush Triumvirate"

Bush and his administration's foreign affairs efforts especially were colored by a personal approach to diplomacy and the use of advisers, especially James A. Baker III and Brent Scowcroft—who, with the president, formed the "Bush triumvirate." Bush's personal approach is seen clearly in the manner in which one bilateral branch of the triumvirate operated with Secretary of State James Baker.

The diplomatic successes on behalf of the United States that the Bush-Baker relationship spawned can be attributed to the trust in their working relationship. Having worked for four presidents, Baker had some grounds for balanced comparison when he remembered in 2011, "This is a president, George Herbert Walker, who is unusually loyal to the people who work for him."[32] For Baker such loyalty, and the trust on which it was founded, meant that he was able to act without fear of being isolated in furthering US diplomatic interests and ultimately national security interests. "Most notably, and perhaps most important to his [Baker's] success," historian Michael Cairo has written, "Baker had the full support of President George H. W. Bush. Often called the *consigliere*—adviser or counselor—Baker was a loyal friend and instrumental in Bush's foreign policy success."[33] The highpoint of these successes was the efforts that the Bush administration undertook in 1990–91 to build and maintain a coalition in support of UN sanctions against Iraq's invasion of Kuwait. Indeed, the Bush administration's greatest diplomatic achievement—with

Baker as the key operator—was in keeping the coalition together once hostilities had commenced. Baker was integral to the process; journalist Bob Woodward estimated that Baker traveled over 100,000 miles to attend more than 200 meetings to discuss the invasion and the US response.[34] Baker's meetings allowed him to deliver President Bush's personal message to his interlocutors. The "personal message" as a feature of presidential diplomacy is not unique to Bush, but the value that Bush placed in personal relationship does distinguish his diplomacy at the end of the Cold War. Baker understood Bush's precautionary outlook, which meant that Bush regularly "deemed it better to do too little than too much."[35]

Among the most important of Baker's skills, recognized by Bush, was his ability to comprehend the "art of negotiation": "Baker had clear goals in the negotiations and understood whose cooperation he needed. He also knew how and when to bargain."[36] Mary Elise Sarotte has agreed with this assessment in her analysis of the disagreements over eastward expansion of the North Atlantic Treaty Organization (NATO).[37] Baker "understood the dynamic between negotiation and agreement," she argues; "that much could be said, contested, denied, or suggested in discussion, but that what resulted in writing at the end was what mattered." Subsequently, debates over any "promise" or "pledge" made by the Bush administration raged in popular politics and generated considerable bad feeling between Moscow and Washington, but this serves to overlook the trust Bush had in Baker.[38]

Baker was not alone in having a close and trusting relationship with the president. There was a real meeting of minds between Bush and National Security Advisor Brent Scowcroft as the other bilateral branch of the Bush triumvirate. "[O]utside the president," Bartholomew Sparrow argues, Scowcroft was "arguably the most influential person making US foreign policy and grand strategy between 1989 and 1993." The two were close; "they were pals—brothers almost—who went boating, fishing, golfing, and skiing together, among other joint activities."[39] The trust in their relationship—that of "pals"—was integral to their policymaking. The pair "shared political instincts, personal disposition, and years of foreign policy and governmental experience."[40] The antecedents of their relationship stretch back to shared experiences of the post–World War II world, when the quest for American preeminence and the global good appeared synonymous. "Committed to restoring the main tenets of post–World War II American foreign policy," David Schmitz argues, "the two men would be the last of the containment generation to guide American foreign policy, and they oversaw the final success of internationalism and the end of the Cold War."[41] Such a claim is testament to the pair's custodianship of US grand strategy.

The trust in Bush's relationship with Scowcroft was not only a function of outward-looking foreign policy, but was also manifest in the way that policy was made within Washington. "Bush and Scowcroft," Sparrow writes, "understood the importance of personal relationships among other US policymakers."[42] Notable among them was the relationship between Secretary Baker and the "more conservative (and pessimistic)" Secretary of Defense Dick Cheney.[43] Scowcroft's skill as Bush's proxy was to position himself between differing personalities without alienating either, meaning that "[n]ot only was Scowcroft trusted by the president, he was also uniformly trusted by his colleagues and staff."[44] The outcome was an operation which brought the best out of each individual as US government functionaries, while at the same time reflecting Bush's "steady hand" mantra. Indeed, Schmitz concludes of Bush and his personal approach that he "sought to re-establish trust in the structure of the government and faith in the individuals who made foreign policy."[45]

It couldn't get much worse: Could It? Trust at Home and Abroad

President George H. W. Bush was "a pragmatist, cautious to grandstanding responses to a rapidly changing geopolitical topography."[46] His administration's aversion to bold shifts in outlook and policy reveals an inherent conservatism: "They witnessed what could go wrong and preferred the devils they knew."[47]

In exploring trust, it is also important to recognize how mistrust operated in the Bush administration. Given the gravitas of the issues that Bush and his advisers faced from the demise of the Soviet Union, the reunification of Germany, and the Tiananmen Square protest, the administration feared throughout that anything other than a steady course could make the situation *worse*. In other words, the administration could not wholly trust their adversaries, and in part at least its members could not trust themselves to believe the extent of change that may have been possible during that period. The protagonists' Cold War experience of avoiding escalation left a legacy that made the Bush administration averse to actions that could destabilize, or be perceived to destabilize, the status quo. As historian Andrew Preston has noted, Bush "prioritised order over justice—he valued both, of course, but when the two conflicted, order usually prevailed."[48]

The difficulties in trusting are evident in returning to the dilemma that the Bush administration faced in 1991 as Gorbachev's authority in Moscow was challenged. In a conversation with Brian Mulroney, Bush revealed his fear that things could get worse, not better, in considering the dilemma of placing trust in an individual (in this case, Boris Yeltsin) and a fast-changing situation: "If we over play our relationship with him [Yeltsin], we could play into the hands of the worst elements within the Soviet Union." Bush continued, "In any case, there is a strong chance that if Gorbachev were replaced, it would be by someone from the Right, not by Yeltsin."[49] Here, Bush expressed his fear that hard-liners would be the beneficiaries of Gorbachev's demise, which illustrates how his mistrust of the political situation trumped his trust in the individual. Bush revealed to Mulroney that he had to tread carefully in discussing the future of the Soviet Union: "The Soviets need to have a place in the sun. It doesn't do us any good to stiff-arm them."[50]

The possibility of a Soviet renaissance was discussed within the Bush administration. In reviewing Bruce D. Porter's *National Interest* article, "The Coming Resurgence of Russia," Brent Scowcroft noted to his colleagues: "One can quibble with the detail, but I think the thrust of Bruce's argument is absolutely right—and should be reflected in our thinking, political dialogue, and even public commentary on the future of the Soviet Union."[51] Deborah Larson has agreed that fear of a deteriorating situation underpinned the Bush administration's thinking on Gorbachev's position: "A major concern of the Bush administration was that Gorbachev might be overthrown by hard-liners who would reverse his cooperative policies."[52] Indeed, this fear was foremost in the immediate aftermath of the August 1991 coup, which signaled the effective end of Gorbachev's leadership. In conversation with Polish president Lech Wałęsa, as events were still playing out in Moscow, Bush said that "[w]e have had a message from the self-appointed president (Gennady Yanayev) of the Soviet Union making some commitment to reform and democracy inside the Soviet Union, but we are not impressed."[53] Not impressed, nor indeed inclined to trust the words of someone who had turned against Gorbachev.

The fear of a worse outcome governed Bush and his administration in other areas beyond that of the leadership of the Soviet Union. In the field of nuclear arms, a subject that had dominated superpower rivalry during the Cold War, there was a dread of "loose nukes"—the possibility that Soviet nuclear weapons components might fall into unauthorized hands. This fear gave rise to the Cooperative Threat Reduction Program (P.L. 102-228), a bipartisan effort led by Democratic senator Sam Nunn of Georgia and Republican representative Richard Lugar of Indiana to "secure and dismantle" the former Soviet Union's weapons of mass destruction. The Bush administration supported the effort, signing off on the millions of dollars it took to get the program up and running. Nonetheless, while "the experience of the Cooperative Threat Reduction Programme (CTRP) showed that cooperation in even the most sensitive areas was possible," the administration's caution guided their approach.[54] Nonetheless, the program's success in decommissioning all weapons of mass destruction capabilities in Ukraine, Belarus, and Kazakhstan ranks as one of the most significant legacies of the period. The task of removing the weapons capabilities in these newly independent former Soviet states, and in a number of Russian facilities as well, would take a number of years to complete, but by 2012 over 7,500 nuclear warheads had been deactivated.

Further afield, Bush faced considerable domestic and international criticism in the aftermath of the Tiananmen Square crisis. Bush, while appalled by the actions of the Chinese communist leadership in brutally repressing the prodemocracy protest, maintained a measured dialogue with Beijing. Bush later argued that if he had "not kept the lines of communication open, it would have taken significantly longer for China-US relations to heal."[55] Jeffrey Engel neatly captures Bush's apprehension: the president was mindful that "that the wrong move at every turn could snatch defeat—and anarchy—out of the jaws of potential triumph and peace."[56] Such an approach may appear overly pessimistic, and Bush has regularly been labeled as a realist by international relations scholars on this basis, yet it is worth considering an alternative thesis: within the higher echelons of the Bush administration, there was a reflective awareness of the dangers of trusting in an uncertain future. This awareness manifested itself in a cautionary approach when opportunity presented itself and in recognition of the unknown. It was a later secretary of defense who has become synonymous with the concept of the "unknown unknown," but Donald Rumsfeld's words apply equally to the George H. W. Bush administration.[57] In the absence of complete knowledge, which would require him to make a trust judgment, Bush had concluded in his conversation with Brian Mulroney in March 1991 that "I think our best policy is steady as she goes." Such an attitude sums up his approach in the spring of 1991, when there would have been a great temptation to be triumphalist in the afterglow of the Gulf War, and to his administration as a whole.

Conclusions: Bush as a Cold War Peacemaker

Examining the presidency of George H. W. Bush and the concept of trust might, at first glance, lead to some fairly brief conclusions. An obvious narrative to trust in the domestic realm is to turn to his "read my lips" utterance and the unfavorable outcome of the 1992 presidential election; or in foreign affairs, to look to the administration's "pledge" not to condone any eastward expansion of NATO in Russian eyes and then condone the increase in NATO membership of states from the former Soviet sphere.[58] However, such an assessment oversimplifies matters and obfuscates a fuller analysis. Bush deployed a complex and multifaceted understanding of trust when faced with the demise of the Cold War order. On the one hand, he invested a good deal of time and effort personally and on behalf of his closest staff in establishing trust. On the other hand, he was unable to let go of the conditioning that the Cold War had provided to him and his colleagues, which meant that he had to perpetually test trust even when satisfying answers would not or could not be forthcoming. The tests that the Bush triumvirate applied to ally and foe alike were estimations of an individual's capacity to deliver on what they said they would in a consistent manner, or whether they "welshed," in Baker's words.[59] Given that the administration sought regular reassurance, they implicitly appreciated that time was a factor in delivering trust. It took time to evaluate the policies and rhetoric of others while establishing one's own course of action. In short, Bush's conception of trust rested on a brand of personal diplomacy and his concern for demonstrating consistency in his actions and the actions of the United States.

This chapter has outlined a number of instances when trust was a significant influence upon the Bush administration's foreign policy making, and it has used these examples to reveal another lens through which to view US foreign relations at the end of the Cold War. "Bush governed during tumultuous years indeed," as Jeffrey Engel has said with suitable understatement, describing the administration's period in office between 1989 and 1993 as a time when "the world itself seemed in flux."[60] President Bush recognized the gravity of his time. These are the "times that try men's souls," he told the nation in a televised address in October 1990, quoting Thomas Paine at the time of the American Revolution.[61] Yet Bush also recognized the seemingly endless assets of the United States that had allowed Charles Krauthammer to famously declare 1990 the "unipolar moment."[62] Bush's supreme confidence in American values and power, shared by the likes of Scowcroft and Baker, came from their reading of the "American Century." Bush was a creature of the mid-century height of American power as he came of age and first served his country, a member of the "Greatest Generation," and therefore it is unsurprising that his "world view" was shaped by "American leaders at the height of World War II and in the first years of the Cold War" who articulated an "American-led international order."[63] At the end of the Cold War, his administration had the opportunity to fulfill this opportunity, and in many regards the United States did achieve a position of preeminence during the 1990s.

Bush avoided dogma. His administration "favored flexible considerations of American needs and power above inviolable statements of principle" and "assess[ed] and pursue[ed] national interests on a case-by-case basis."[64] Retrospective reflections on Bush and his advisers' conduct have shown little regret for opportunities that might have been lost when set against the costs of getting it "wrong." Therefore, there should be little surprise that when Bush

77

and Scowcroft released their book *A World Transformed* in 1998, they pointed to their decision to cease the military campaign against Saddam Hussein after 100 hours as a cautionary tale. As they explained, "Had we gone the invasion route, the United States could conceivably still be an occupying power in a bitterly hostile land."[65] A prolonged occupation of that ancient land was a fate that would befall a later American administration.

Notes

1. George H. W. Bush, *All the Best* (New York: Scribner, 1999), 60–61.
2. "1988 George H. W. Bush Speech," C-SPAN video, 1:00:00, from the Republican National Convention in New Orleans, August 18, 1988, http://www.c-span.org/video/?3848-2/1988-george-hw-bush-speech.
3. Onora O'Neill, *A Question of Trust: The BBC Reith Lectures 2002* (Cambridge, UK: Cambridge University Press, 2002). A full audio archive of the lectures is maintained at http://www.bbc.co.uk/radio4/reith2002/.
4. Baroness O'Neill of Bengarve, "Perverting Trust" (Clare Hall Ashby Lecture, University of Cambridge, May 15, 2009), http://www.clarehall.cam.ac.uk/index.php?id=689.
5. Onora O'Neill, "Lecture 1 'Spreading Suspicion,'" in Onora O'Neill, *A Question of Trust: The BBC Reith Lectures 2002*, http://www.bbc.co.uk/radio4/reith2002/.
6. Jeffrey A. Engel, "'A Better World . . . but Don't Get Carried Away': The Foreign Policy of George H. W. Bush Twenty Years On," *Diplomatic History* 34, no. 1 (2010): 25–46.
7. James A. Baker III, interview with Russell Riley and James Sterling Young, March 17, 2011, George H. W. Bush Oral History Project, Miller Center, University of Virginia, http://millercenter.org/president/bush/oralhistory/james-baker-2011.
8. Deborah Welch Larson, *Anatomy of Mistrust: U.S.-Soviet Relations during the Cold War* (Ithaca, NY: Cornell University Press, 1997), 33.
9. General Brent Scowcroft, interview with Philip Zelikow, Ernest May, James H. McCall, and Fareed Zakaria, November 12–13, 1999, George H. W. Bush Oral History Project, Miller Center, University of Virginia, http://millercenter.org/president/bush/oralhistory/brent-scowcroft.
10. Memcon with Canadian Prime Minister Brian Mulroney, March 13, 1991, George H. W. Bush Presidential Papers, George H. W. Bush Presidential Library, Texas A&M University, College Station, Texas (hereafter, GHWB Library).
11. Larson, *Anatomy of Mistrust*, 5.
12. Sarah Snyder provides an account of the differences between the Bush administration and its predecessor in relation to the CSCE. See Sarah B. Snyder, "Beyond Containment? The First Bush Administration's Sceptical Approach to the CSCE," *Cold War History* 13, no. 4 (2013): 463–84.
13. The term "Greatest Generation," popularized by journalist Tom Brokaw, generally covers the generation of Americans who came of age during the Great Depression and were of an age to serve in World War II. See Tom Brokaw, *The Greatest Generation* (New York: Random House, 1998).
14. Geoff Berridge, *Diplomatic Theory from Machiavelli to Kissinger* (New York: Palgrave, 2001), 1.

15. Like others of high office, President Bush was rarely totally alone, so the idea of one-to-one conversations more accurately refers to meetings with limited participants where only Bush and two or three others were present. During the Bush administration, the most common participant would often be Chief of Staff John Sununu or, when discussing foreign affairs, Brent Scowcroft.

16. Engel, "A Better World," 28.

17. Frank Costigliola, *Roosevelt's Lost Alliance: How Personal Politics Helped Start the Cold War* (Princeton, NJ: Princeton University Press, 2011), 3.

18. "Hitler revisited. But remember when Hitler's war ended, there were the Nuremberg Trials." October 15, 1990, *Weekly Compilation of Presidential Documents* (Washington, DC: US Government Printing Office, 1991), 1594.

19. Baker, interview, March 17, 2011.

20. Telcon with Gorbachev, February 21, 1991, 91112-005, The Brent Scowcroft Collection, The Presidential Papers of George H.W. Bush, GHWB Library.

21. The "guilty men" thesis argued that the appeasement policy of British leadership under Prime Minister Neville Chamberlain was an act of cowardice in the face of Adolf Hitler's National Socialism in Germany. Cato [Michael Foot, Frank Owen, and Peter Howard], *Guilty Men* (London: V. Gollancz, 1940).

22. The personal dimension to US-Russian relations, and its policy implications, is discussed by Alex Marshall and J. Simon Rofe, "An Aborted Special Relationship?: US-Russian Relations in the Post–Cold War World, 1989–2007," in *America's 'Special Relationships': Foreign and Domestic Aspects of the Politics of Alliance*, ed. John Dumbrell and Axel Schafer (Oxford: Routledge, 2009), 132–51. Harold P. Smith Jr., President Clinton's assistant secretary of defense for nuclear, chemical and biological defense programs, stated of his role in the Cooperative Threat Reduction Programme that it "is amazing that it comes down to just a few individuals. I can't say more than that." Harold P. Smith Jr., in conversation with Harry Kriesler on University of California Television, January 26, 2006, quoted in Marshall and Rofe, "An Aborted Special Relationship?," 136.

23. Baker, interview, March 17, 2011.

24. Bartholomew H. Sparrow, "Realism's Practitioner: Brent Scowcroft and the Making of the New World Order, 1989–1993," *Diplomatic History* 34, no. 1 (2010): 153.

25. Memcon with Canadian Prime Minister Brian Mulroney, March 13, 1991.

26. Ibid.

27. Memcon with President of France, Francois Mitterrand, March 14, 1991 (Martinique), CF01728-009, National Security Files, The Presidential Papers of George H.W. Bush, GHWB Library.

28. 25 October 1991 memo for Ed Hewitt, Special Assistant to President for National Security Affairs and Senior Director Soviet Affairs, from David C. Mulford (Under Sec Inter Affairs), The Presidential Papers of George H.W. Bush, GHWB Library.

29. George H. W. Bush Approval Ratings, February 28–March 3, 1991, and December 5–8, 1991, available at Presidential Job Approval Center, Gallup (accessed January 24, 2016), http://www.gallup.com/poll/124922/presidential-job-approval-center.aspx.

30. Directorate of Intelligence, "The Gorbachev Succession," April 29, 1991, Central Intelligence Agency, Ed Hewitt Papers, National Security Council, GHWB Library

31. Memcon with President of France, Francois Mitterrand 14 March 1991 (Martinique).

32. Baker, interview, March 17, 2011.

33. Michael Cairo, "Consigliere: James Baker and the Persian Gulf War," in *Diplomats at War: The American Experience*, eds. J. Simon Rofe and Andrew Stewart (Dordrecht: Republic of Letters, 2012).

34. Bob Woodward, *The Commanders* (New York: Simon and Schuster, 1991), 333.

35. Engel, "A Better World," 39.

36. Cairo, "Consigliere."

37. Mary Elise Sarotte, "Not One Inch Eastward? Bush, Baker, Kohl, Genscher, Gorbachev, and the Origin of Russian Resentment toward NATO Enlargement in February 1990," *Diplomatic History* 34, no. 1 (2010), 127.

38. Mark Kramer, "The Myth of a No-NATO-Expansion Pledge to Russia," *The Washington Quarterly* 32, no. 2 (2009): 39–61. Kramer argues that evidence now available "undermines the notion that the United States or other Western countries ever pledged not to expand NATO beyond Germany," 41.

39. Sparrow, "Realism's Practitioner," 149.

40. Ibid., 148.

41. David Schmitz, *Brent Scowcroft: Internationalism and Post-Vietnam War American Foreign Policy* (Lanham, MD: Rowman and Littlefield, 2011), 88.

42. Sparrow, "Realism's Practitioner," 149.

43. Ibid., 147.

44. Ibid., 147.

45. Schmitz, *Brent Scowcroft*, 88.

46. J Simon Rofe, "H-Diplo Roundtable review: 'Special Forum: Reconsidering the Foreign Policy of the First Bush Administration, Twenty Years On,' *Diplomatic History* 34, no. 1 (2010)," H-Diplo, May 11, 2010, 9, http://h-diplo.org/roundtables /PDF/Roundtable-XI-25.pdf.

47. Sparrow, "Realism's Practitioner," 172.

48. Andrew Preston, "The Politics of Realism and Religion: Christian Responses to Bush's New World Order," *Diplomatic History* 34, no. 1 (2010), 102.

49. Memcon with Canadian Prime Minister Brian Mulroney, March 13, 1991.

50. Ibid.

51. Bruce D. Porter, "The Coming Resurgence of Russia," *The National Interest*, March 1, 1991, 14–23; and Brent Scowcroft April 1991, CFO 1613-004 Ed Burns and Nicholas Hewitt Files National Security Council, The Presidential Papers of George H.W. Bush, GHWB Library.

52. Larson, *Anatomy of Trust*, 29.

53. 19 August 1991 memo Telcon with Lech Walesa, CF01730-00 National Security Council, The Presidential Papers of George H.W. Bush, GHWB Library.

54. Marshall and Rofe, "An Aborted Special Relationship?," 132.

55. Randolph Kluver, "Rhetorical Trajectories of Tiananmen Square," *Diplomatic History* 34, no. 1 (2010), 71.

56. Engel, "A Better World," 27.

57. "Transcript: DoD News Briefing – Secretary Rumsfeld and General Myers," US Department of Defense, February 12, 2002, http://archive.defense.gov/transcripts /transcript.aspx?transcriptid=2636.

58. For a detailed account of the debate over interpretations of NATO expansion in Eastern Europe, see Sarotte, "Not One Inch Eastward?"

59. Baker, interview, March 17, 2011.

60. Engel, "A Better World," 26.

61. Thomas Paine, quoted by George H. W. Bush, October 2, 1990 televised address to the nation on the Budget. Box 143, White House Office of Records Management, The Presidential Papers of George H.W. Bush, GHWB Library.

62. Charles Krauthammer, "Unipolar Moment," *Foreign Affairs* 70, no. 1 (1990/1991): 23–33.

63. Engel, "A Better World," 28.

64. Engel, "A Better World," 25; and Sparrow, "Realism's Practitioner," 170.

65. George H. W. Bush and Brent Scowcroft, *A World Transformed* (New York: Alfred Knopf Inc., 1998), 489.

II. Risk, Commitment, and Verification: The Blocs at the Negotiating Table

4. Trust and Mistrust and the American Struggle for Verification of the Strategic Arms Limitation Talks, 1969–1979

Arvid Schors

The Strategic Arms Limitation Talks (SALT) between the United States and the Soviet Union were the first bilateral nuclear arms control negotiations during the Cold War. In a constant negotiation process from 1969 to 1979, SALT became "the flagship of détente"[1] and the linchpin of superpower relations in the 1970s. The negotiations spanned three presidencies and were conducted between not only permanent expert delegations but also top foreign policy officials. These channels went right up to direct contacts between the political leaders of both sides. In the haggling for hundreds upon hundreds of hours with the respective archenemy about the most prestigious—and most destructive—weapons that mankind had ever invented, the SALT process represented a new quality and shape of diplomatic cooperation, one without precedent at the time. In merely trying to seriously negotiate about their nuclear arsenals, the superpowers had to engage in a changed modus operandi of their relationship that can be characterized appropriately as "politics of dialogue" (*dialogische Politik*).[2] This novel means of dealing with the adversary placed a stronger emphasis on compromise, reconciliation, and reciprocal understanding, thus subliminally confounding the rigid black-and-white thinking that had been so prevalent in the previous decades of the Cold War. At the same time, though, the SALT process did not mark the end of the fundamental struggle between the archrivals. Rather, as Jussi Hanhimäki argues, a "central paradox"

A monograph by the author on the SALT negotiation process, titled *Doppelter Boden. Die SALT-Verhandlungen 1963–1979* [Uncertain ground: The SALT negotiations, 1963–1979], will be published by Wallstein Verlag in fall 2016.

emerged. On the one hand, "[d]étente was, for most of its practitioners, a conservative project that fit well with the previous decades' foreign policy"[3] and therefore was deeply rooted in and mostly consistent with the existent traditions and path dependencies of the Cold War. Following this reading, détente was "an attractive option not because it could end the Cold War but because it would allow them to fight it with a new toolkit in hand."[4] Yet on the other hand, and equally important, "some of its outcomes . . . were revolutionary" and "ultimately—often unintentionally—worked to undermine the validity of the Cold War itself."[5]

The issue of trust and mistrust was crucial not only in the minds of American politicians and experts but also for a public that was engaged with SALT. At the center of all reflections about this subject stood the question of how compliance could be secured. The overall value of every imaginable nuclear arms control agreement between the archenemies seemed to hinge crucially on the ability to reliably monitor if and to what extent the contractual partner was observing its provisions. This question of verification bundled together all the paradoxical elements of the SALT process. Moreover, in connection with the inherent need in the American democratic framework to consistently debate, scrutinize, and justify a foreign policy measure of such magnitude, the permanence and scope of the verification question offered for the general public a noteworthy translation of the often intricate and arcane SALT policies.

Paying special consideration to this public dimension, this chapter concentrates on the contemporary American discourse, examining the rhetoric of trust, confidence, and mistrust in connection with SALT verification and on the underlying ideas and interpretations associated with it.[6] It does not draw on a clear-cut definition of the elusive phenomenon of trust, nor does it operate under the assumption that trust as a definable phenomenon inevitably can be recognized at all. Rather, it intends to study the meaning that contemporaries attributed to this volatile notion, bringing into focus the multifariousness of trust and mistrust in the context of superpower relations. It aims to provide deeper insights into the various functions the notion of trust fulfilled as a political idea and ideal, rhetorical weapon, or public symbol during the Cold War.[7] Finally, it also highlights the importance of trust for an understanding of the history of détente in general and the SALT process in particular.

This chapter has a three-part approach. The first part underscores that the issue of trust and mistrust was of vital importance for the superpowers. Although the mode of nuclear arms control negotiations stood in marked contrast to the firmly established Cold War tradition of ostentatious mistrust, high-end verification technology now made it possible for the political actors to veil this significant deviation from the dichotomous Cold War worldview—thus bestowing Cold War legitimacy on the negotiation process. The second part deals with the evolution of the problem of trust and mistrust after practical questions of compliance emerged within the scope of treaty implementation. Precisely because SALT was publicly carried out in the name of Cold War mistrust, internally a rapprochement between the archrivals was facilitated and long-established Cold War dichotomies began to be called into question. In the final part, the intense public debate on SALT II and its ratification occupies center stage. The subtle but substantial shifts in the superpower relationship that came along with an evolved détente at the end of the 1970s partially blurred the boundaries of how to deal with the adversary, even in the minds of hawkish cold warriors. Although demands for absolute mistrust and respective testimonies now became even more radical and ubiquitous, on some level the SALT process was able to be uncoupled from these polemical but still influential slogans of the public debate.

Legitimizing SALT:
Reconnaissance Technology as a Substitute for Trust

The history of nuclear arms control negotiations during the Cold War was, if nothing else, a history of the US government openly flaunting that it could not and would not trust the Soviets under any circumstances. As early as the congressional hearings about the Nuclear Test Ban Treaty in 1963, for example, Secretary of State Dean Rusk felt obliged to campaign for its ratification with the reference that the "treaty is not standing upon the foundation of trust."[8] Arms control researcher Allan Krass points to one of the most important features of the US public debates about arms control negotiations and the verification of their results. He emphasizes that in demonstratively expressing their distrust of the Soviet Union, US government officials conducted a kind of "credibility ritual" to emphasize "that the speaker is not a sentimental disarmer or unwitting dupe of Soviet trickery."[9] This ostentatious and ritualized proclamation of mistrust in the public sphere points to the formation of strictures regarding what should and could be said in this regard—or, rather, should and could *not* be said. By submitting themselves to these strictures, the political actors were able to strengthen their basis of legitimacy, but paid the price of narrowing their own scope of legitimate action.

From a contemporary perspective, the question of trust and mistrust was inextricably linked with the issue of verification. This connection is palpable in a statement by Gerard Smith, director of the Arms Control and Disarmament Agency (ACDA), at a preparatory meeting of US government SALT experts in June 1969. Smith, the designated chief negotiator of the American

SALT delegation, stated that "[s]ince 1945–46 we have said that we wanted arms control but that we could not trust the other side. The principal obstacle has been inspection. To some extent this problem has been dissipated through development of national means of verification."[10] In this statement, Smith alluded to two facts. First, in former negotiations, the Soviets always had categorically rejected the possibility of on-site inspections on their home soil—a constant that would also shape the SALT process. Second, at the same time satellite reconnaissance devices on both sides were now technically mature enough to compensate for this constraint. A State Department working paper circulating inside the administration in May 1969 stated that "national means of verification will provide the foundation of an eventual agreement. It is only the development of such means which has made a realistic consideration of a limitation on strategic arms possible."[11] Underlying this prevalent notion among American government experts was the idea that high-end reconnaissance satellite technology could compensate for nonexisting—and even undesired—trust between the parties. Put differently, the surveillance capabilities made it legitimate and possible to pursue the innovative mode of intensive face-to-face negotiations while at the same time staying obedient to and maintaining established levels of mistrust.

An October 1972 *Houston Post* article popularized this argument in characteristic fashion and emphasized its power of attraction beyond circles of experts, commenting that "[i]n the past, negotiations over disarmament foundered on a single element—trust." According to the author, however, the SALT I talks had concluded successfully several months ago because the American satellite reconnaissance program "supplies an acceptable substitute for the missing ingredient of trust, and on that program rests all hope of reversing the arms race."[12] From this perspective, reconnaissance technology seemed to present a clear, mechanical, and (not least) depoliticized way out of the contradictions, insecurities, and incalculable risks of the Cold War and its nuclear arms race by detaching trust from any connections to subjectivity and emotionality. Although the prevalent undercurrent of mistrust identified above was itself profoundly subjective, it confined these emotional bearings *exclusively* to the one direction of all-encompassing mistrust. Satellites made it feasible to further uphold the one-sided reading that one would not trust the Soviets by any means, while actually moving in a more ambiguous direction.

Furthermore, this attempted superseding of trust with the aid of reconnaissance technology featured a striking similarity and continuity to patterns central to American Cold War thinking, patterns that were connected by their wrestling with the unsettling challenges of the nuclear age. In the end, they were about finding an intellectual backdoor to escape the existential implications of nuclear war against the background of the unpredictability of human behavior—whether it was expressed in the idea to make nuclear war unfeasible through the formation of deterrence theory, the alleged panacea of the Strategic Defense Initiative in the 1980s, or the reliance on nuclear superiority prevalent throughout the decades before SALT. This last-mentioned thought pattern of superiority was a feeling of almost proverbial invulnerability based on the quantitative and qualitative strength of US nuclear weapons systems vis-à-vis the Soviet Union. The loss of this clear dominance caused American experts and politicians tremendous discomfort in the 1970s, but at the same time it was one of the central reasons why the SALT process became feasible in the first place.[13] By means of advanced reconnaissance devices, this mind-set of superiority was partially transformed into the new reality of nuclear parity and was able to readjust to the changed circumstances of détente in a less martial and therefore more suitable way. As Central Intelligence Agency (CIA) deputy director Vernon Walters stated in 1975, drawing a comparison between the current balance of nuclear power and the Revolutionary War: "[W]e need it [intelligence] today because, in my opinion, the United States is in a tougher power situation than it has been since Valley Forge. Not since Valley Forge has any foreign country had the ability to destroy or seriously cripple the United States. That capability exists today."[14]

Accordingly, references to a feeling of technological strength and even intimations of superiority in the field of verification were not uncommon in government circles. As, for example, CIA director Richard Helms pointed out in a 1971 speech in reference to SALT satellite reconnaissance, "Certain details of the program must be kept from the Soviets if it is to remain fully effective. . . . They are aware of what we are doing, although not of the extent of our success."[15] And the following year, in accordance with the intelligence community's new task of monitoring Soviet compliance with the SALT I treaty, Helms underlined that the "country's intelligence knows so much about what the Russians have . . . that it is not like anything that has ever occurred in history before."[16]

Of course, these capabilities in which Helms took so much pride were also highly relevant in a practical sense, even if the attempt to fully escape the irretrievably political question of Soviet trustworthiness with the help of reconnaissance technology was finally a mirage intended specifically for public consumption. As the United States Intelligence Board Steering Group on SALT correctly emphasized as early as August 1972, "In SALT monitoring . . . , there is no possibility of achieving 100 percent assurance that collection and analysis programs, no matter how well conceived and executed, will provide timely warning of every feasible violation."[17] In reality, an assessment with clear-cut precision and in binary form was an unattainable goal, and even high-end verification technology ultimately could not change that. Furthermore, these emphases on surveillance capabilities are significant as an indicator of the prevalent hopes during détente. But above all, they opened an intellectual gateway that embedded the mode of the SALT negotiations in the existing beaten tracks and proven traditions of waging the Cold War that had been dominant during the preceding decades, thereby masking and diluting their peculiar novelty at the same time. The question of the relevance and meaning of trust and mistrust in regard to the Soviet Union was forcefully reraised by this mode of nuclear arms control negotiations that, at first glance, seemed to contradict or at least mitigate the established pattern of complete and unconditional mistrust toward the Soviet Union. Yet high-end verification now made it possible for the political actors to rhetorically bridge these deviations from the renowned traditions of conducting the Cold War. As a result, they temporarily were able to give the old and comforting assurance of comprehensive mistrust later on, while the relationship with the Soviet Union actually became more diverse.

The Utopia of Mistrust under Siege:
SALT Verification in the Field Test

For Henry Kissinger, President Richard Nixon's influential national security advisor, it was only possible to brief Congress about the concluded SALT I agreements in June 1972 against the background of verification technology, ultimately setting the tone for all following discussions about SALT. Kissinger successfully resorted to the communication strategy that "we advocate these agreements not on the basis of trust, but on the basis of the enlightened self-interests of both sides. This self-interest is reinforced by the carefully drafted verification provisions in the agreement."[18] In denouncing trust openly and underlining "self-interest" instead, Kissinger tried to make the groundbreaking nuclear arms control agreements semantically bulletproof for Senate ratification. Yet by forming this kind of defensive line, he removed from the picture the elements of SALT I that, in establishing an ongoing arms control relationship with the archenemy, inevitably clashed with traditional means of waging the Cold War.

This significant shift was particularly reflected in the Standing Consultative Commission (SCC), established within the framework of the 1972 Anti-Ballistic Missile Treaty as part of the SALT agreements to deal with questions of compliance regarding implementation.[19] From 1973, the SCC functioned as a permanent and private forum, "a joint U.S.-Soviet grievance board for monitoring SALT,"[20] as *Time* magazine later aptly called it.[21] In essence, the SCC symbolized the elements of SALT that ran contrary to the public atmosphere of ostensible mistrust; from that perspective, any uncertainty about compliance was self-contradictory, as there was only the salutary option of mistrust—or the option of trust, which inevitably would lead to disaster. At first, these contradictions went unnoticed, facilitated by the rhetorical fig leaf of mistrust and the fact that issues of verification would necessarily not be under close scrutiny for some time. Sidney Graybeal, the American SCC commissioner, could therefore report to Kissinger in June 1974 that in all "SCC sessions to date . . . neither side formally raised any questions concerning compliance with existing agreements or any related situations which may be considered ambiguous."[22]

Yet already in August 1974, the image of compliance changed, as a US ad hoc interagency working group considered several issues of SALT compliance and concluded that "while all of the suspicious Soviet activities are on the border of legality, that taken as a whole, they raise serious questions concerning Soviet attitudes toward compliance with the agreements."[23] From then on, press reports over alleged Soviet violations became a concomitant feature of the SALT process, along with public and secret appearances of officials putting these allegations into perspective and countering them.[24] The secret briefing that CIA director William Colby gave to the Senate Arms Control Subcommittee in February 1975, for instance, outlined several "types of ambiguous activity on the part of the Soviets" but acknowledged that "the Soviets probably do not view these activities as inconsistent with the treaty provisions."[25] Colby also pointed out that for the future, his agency "would not expect the SALT TWO era to be troublefree [sic] from a verification viewpoint. I have no doubt that we will continue to be confronted by ambiguities and suspicious activities."[26] In a March 1975 National Security Council meeting that dealt with the same questions, the attendant high-ranking government officials, including President Gerald Ford, agreed that several elements of uncertainty existed but no clear-cut violations were present. As Secretary of Defense James Schlesinger summarized: "[T]here are verification problems, but we can handle them. We are not in some Utopia."[27] Kissinger added that "these are all ambiguities that are the natural results of operating a large complicated strategic force."[28] In July 1975, Kissinger concluded a memorandum to Ford along similar lines: "[W]e believe that the Soviets are not in violation of any provisions of any of the SALT agreements. The ambiguities which have arisen relate principally to the issues of treaty language and the acknowledged inability to write treaty language that will unambiguously deal with all activities which could take place during the period of the agreement."[29]

Without doubt, these considerations were pragmatic overall. Yet it is especially striking how vigorously and consensually these mantra-like emphases on the inevitability of ambiguities now surfaced inside the administration—even from more hawkish officials. Schlesinger was right in highlighting that Cold War reality was not Utopia. He did, however, fail to make the connection to the contradiction that publicly the government had given assurances of some kind of utopia of mistrust where ambiguities were not to be expected—or rather, automatically represented Soviet violations of the agreements that would make the whole SALT process instantly futile. This is not to say that American government officials had developed trust in the Soviet Union in any way. Instead, the intricate combination of breaking new ground in actually negotiating and agreeing on concrete terms with the Soviets, and at the same time maintaining the public appearance of categorically not trusting them by touting the achievements of verification technology, was a hidden slippery slope that ran in opposite directions. In an idiosyncratic combination, these contradicting elements made the evolution of the SALT process possible and even facilitated the acceptance of an intellectual grey area as inevitable part of the superpower relationship, a perspective that was incompatible with a strictly dichotomous worldview of Cold War provenance. Yet at the same time and for the same reasons, that process became fragile and vulnerable to attacks that some kind of trust in the Soviet Union might almost inevitably be involved in its conduct, thus challenging its whole raison d'être.

No Easy Answers: Public Wrestling for and against SALT II

In February 1976, the Ford administration transmitted a paper to selected members of Congress that listed, in some detail, compliance issues raised by both sides in the SCC. The paper attempted to substantiate how uncertainties and misunderstandings could be dispelled, or at least calculably reduced, by the businesslike exchanges of the SCC. It concluded that "there have been no clear demonstrable Soviet violations of the SALT Agreements," although it mentioned a "debatable exception" that had indeed stopped after the United States raised the issue.[30] In 1978 and 1979, the Carter administration made several unclassified, updated, and modified versions of this report publicly accessible in order to dispel doubts about the verifiability of the SALT II treaty in the forefront of the ratification debate.[31] These updated versions came to similar overall conclusions.[32] As Secretary of State Cyrus Vance wrote to President Jimmy Carter in February 1978, on the occasion of the publication of one of these reports, "The Soviet 'cheating' argument will remain a major issue in the SALT ratification process, but this report will give us a sound, factual basis from which to deal with the charges," not least because "it does not 'white-wash' the Soviet record."[33] Vance's remarks emphasize that in this instance, the administration openly set its hopes on the persuasiveness of the matter-of-fact presentation of uncertainties—a notable attempt to mitigate the otherwise rhetorically dominant affirmations of mistrust. The reference to the persistence of the "Soviet 'cheating' argument," however, also highlights Vance's aware-ness of the limitations of this communicative strategy. These limitations were almost brutally substantiated during the debate on ratification.

The debate over SALT II ratification was dominated by fierce attacks on the agreement and on the administration's ability to verify compliance. These assaults all shared a barely concealed and uncompromising call for absolute verification, invulnerability, and mistrust toward the Soviet Union. Former high-ranking naval officers Elmo Zumwalt and Worth Bagley, for example, denounced the government's ability to verify the treaty in November 1978, arguing that "our photographs cannot invade Soviet research laboratories or the minds of Soviet decision-makers so its news will be late."[34] And the influ-ential conservative intellectual William F. Buckley wrote tellingly in Decem-ber 1978: "There are men in America who would trust the Russians even without invulnerable systems of verification. One hopes they are not running the government."[35] In their radical aversion to any uncertainties, the adminis-tration's critics ferociously attacked the phrase "adequate verification," which the administration had intended to underline that verification ultimately was inconceivable without elements of a judgment call. The critics not only dis-missed this qualifying limitation as "an Alice in Wonderland position,"[36] but also raised the rhetorical question if "any American [would] be satisfied by a wife or husband who was 'adequately faithful?'"[37] By applying the standard of marriage—an almost sacrosanct institution in American mainstream cultural thinking—to SALT, they obviously aimed at underpinning their argument in layman's terms. Yet this wording also implies that, regardless of their unequiv-ocal intentions, the paradoxical character of SALT subliminally blurred the boundaries of trust and verification even in the minds of these hawkish cold warriors. The standard of marriage, with its highly positive social connota-tions, was scarcely the appropriate benchmark in light of their critical read-ing that a "stable U.S.-Soviet truce based on mutual distrust is preferable to aberrations of friendship."[38] In fact, applying the metaphor of marriage to Soviet-American relations consequently would make the development of trust between the archrivals not just fully acceptable, but virtually essential.

Such inconsistencies in the position of the critics notwithstanding, their constant attacks and intransigent calls for across-the-board mistrust led the Carter administration to adopt a widespread strategy of openly discrediting, profaning, and tabooing every notion of trust toward the Soviet Union, exceeding previous efforts in that area. Matthew Nimetz, State Department counselor and the Carter administration's central SALT II campaign coordinator,[39] summarized the administration's public position in accordance with its internally circulated aim to "build confidence in the tough-minded realism of our negotiating strategy *and* stress to the public that SALT compliance does not depend on trust."[40] In a June 1978 *NBC Nightly News* story, Nimetz stated: "There's a healthy skepticism in the country. . . . I don't think the people should accept an important treaty like this just because, just on trust. . . . They don't trust the Soviets; they don't want an agreement that's built on trust; they want one that we can verify ourselves."[41] Accordingly, on June 18, 1979, in his address before a joint session of Congress on the signing of the SALT II Treaty at the recent Vienna summit meeting, President Carter himself emphasized that "[a]s I have said many times, SALT II is not based on trust"; instead, he stressed the United States' verification capabilities.[42]

To further support this strategy, the Carter administration finally decided, going back to a May 1978 initiative,[43] to disclose the fact that both superpowers were using satellite reconnaissance technology to monitor the agreements. This was "a notorious non-secret" that forced government spokespersons to refer to the abstract "euphemism National Technical Means"—a blanket term for satellite monitoring techniques and technologies—to deal with "public perceptions that the Soviets cannot be trusted" and allegations that "the US has an inadequate ability to verify compliance."[44] Against this background, the government hoped that "[d]eclassifying the 'fact of' photo-satellite reconnaissance could enable government spokesmen to make a more effective case for a SALT II agreement."[45]

In a practical sense, this disclosure, made in a speech by Carter on October 1, 1978,[46] was insignificant. Even government experts internally conceded that it was "already well-known to those who follow SALT." Rather, its aim was to "explain to the man in the street that our confidence in SALT compliance comes from our own capabilities, not our trust in the Soviets."[47] Yet the Carter administration understood this disclosure as an important step toward appealing to the broader public, almost desperately stressing its independent technological monitoring capabilities to dispel doubts that it did not mistrust the Soviets completely.

Even this modest announcement, however, happened "only after lengthy study and painstaking review"[48] and was accompanied by deep-seated discomfort inside the administration. CIA officials warned that "[d]eclassification of 'fact of' solely for SALT II without proof of capability, i.e. release of imagery, is an empty shell which will not convert any 'doubting Thomases.'"[49] At the same time, the CIA feared in turn that this disclosure could set a precedent and entail massive public pressure to publish imagery, thereby "enabling the USSR to take action to take better protective and concealment action against observation."[50] From this perspective, that step was inadequate on one level and went way too far on another. As this CIA assessment vividly underlines, a peculiar intermingling of divergent, paradoxical requirements took shape in the framework of the SALT process. These requirements inherently oscillated between both confrontational and cooperative elements and its public and internal dimension.

Consequently, in a paper on SALT II verification circulated inside the administration in April 1979, the ACDA's principal technical expert, James Timbie,[51] underlined once again the belief that "[l]ike most things in life, verification of arms control agreements is subject to some degree of uncertainty. No provision is either absolutely 'verifiable' or unverifiable.'"[52] Furthermore, he highlighted the multifaceted character of American SALT decisions in addressing "a tradeoff between flexibility for the US and verification considerations. . . . [I]t is to our advantage to be allowed to pursue certain options even though allowing the Soviets the same options complicates verification."[53] This abstract consideration had a concrete manifestation in the question of cruise missile limitation, "where the US position has been dominated by a desire to maximize US flexibility rather than to optimize verification. (The Soviet proposals were more verifiable and more restrictive.)"[54] Put differently, in some cases the US negotiators, to ensure prospective strategic advantages, had deliberately worked to craft treaty language that was more ambiguous and therefore less verifiable than would have been possible with their Soviet interlocutors. Yet in public, the administration could not promote and explain such finesses to underline its mistrust and toughness toward the Soviet Union. Not only would the Soviets have considered such open declarations of mistrust to be a blunt affront, but explaining the reasoning behind the negotiators' language choices could have called the Soviets' attention to critical elements of the treaty—for example, to the aforementioned passages about cruise missile limitations—that, from an American perspective, were best kept low-key.

Against the background of these diverging requirements and challenges, it was immensely difficult for the Carter administration to develop and maintain a consistent and appealing public strategy to support its SALT policy. As White House communications director Gerald Rafshoon wrote to Carter in May 1979, "By building trust in you as the chief negotiator and chief advocate of SALT II, we can build trust in the agreement itself. It won't be easy. The days are long gone when an Eisenhower could say, 'I've read the treaty and it's a good one.' The political and ideological dynamics of the SALT debate

95

are far too complex."[55] This highly polarized public "debate of the decade,"[56] as the administration aptly labeled it, finally ended on January 3, 1980, with President Carter's request to "delay consideration of the SALT II Treaty on the Senate floor."[57] Just over a week before, on December 25, 1979, the Soviet Union had invaded Afghanistan.

For both the SALT critics and the SALT defenders inside the Carter administration, trust and mistrust were central semantic reference points. But no matter which meanings they assigned to these terms for diametrically opposed purposes, both sides operated on the common ground of a deep-seated desire to return to a less complex, less ambiguous world—or at least one that seemed to be so. Trust and mistrust, with their underlying promise of emotional clarity and consistency, were rhetorical and intellectual devices for dealing with the paradoxical nature of détente—whether in discrediting or defending it—that subliminally confounded Cold War axioms.

Conclusion

These more or less blatant contradictions were essential to the SALT process, and marked its hybrid and at times even dysfunctional nature. Paradoxically, by standing with one foot firmly in the tradition of the Cold War even as the other simultaneously broke new ground and intellectually transcended its narrow framework, these frictions made SALT possible in the first place. Verification technology, which rhetorically marked trust as dispensable, was able to reconcile SALT with the well-established pattern of Cold War mistrust for a time. Yet it was exactly this reading that also made SALT highly vulnerable from the start, for relentless mistrust was the benchmark by which the agreement would be judged.

The prominence of the question of trust and mistrust for SALT verification, in its rigorous demand for dichotomy, reveals that this constant process actually blurred supposedly adamant intellectual boundaries of how to deal with one's enemy. The more uncompromising the rhetorical demands for and promises of verification, compliance, and all-embracing mistrust became, the more porous and diffuse these boundaries turned out to be. At first glance, it seems like a truism that gray areas and uncertainties regarding compliance could not automatically point to intended Soviet violations. Yet this realization entailed enormous potential impact: taken to its logical conclusion, it could shatter the subliminal dichotomic patterns of the Cold War. On the other end of the continuum, as the example of cruise missile limitation underlines, the Cold War conflict still continued, even though the communication challenges had grown more sophisticated. Despite the persistent rhetorical predominance of mistrust, by the end of the 1970s the intellectual Cold War landscape in the United States had become more diverse, so that even an action that conformed to its original pattern—maximizing every advantage that the United States could obtain in weapons technology—could be inappropriate for disclosure. It would, after all, run counter to the now equally established unwritten rules of superpower *cooperation*.

Contrary to interpretations that consider détente as a "well-intended political ambition that failed to materialize" and as "increasingly irrelevant to what was happening in the rapidly changing world of the late 1970s and early 1980s,"[58] the SALT experience left an influential legacy. Not only did it create a precedent as to how to temporarily bridge irreconcilable Cold War contradictions, but it also subliminally yet profoundly shifted the keystones upon which this epochal conflict was based.

Notes

1. Raymond L. Garthoff, *Détente and Confrontation: American-Soviet Relations from Nixon to Reagan* (Washington, DC: Brookings Institution Press, 1985), 127.

2. Eckart Conze, "Modernitätsskepsis und die Utopie der Sicherheit: NATO-Nachrüstung und Friedensbewegung in der Geschichte der Bundesrepublik" [Skepticism of modernity and the utopia of security: NATO nuclear expansion and the peace movement in the history of the Federal Republic], *Zeithistorische Forschungen/Studies in Contemporary History* 7 (2010): 228, http://www.zeithistorische-forschungen .de/16126041-Conze-2-2010.

3. Jussi M. Hanhimäki, "Conservative Goals, Revolutionary Outcomes: The Paradox of Détente," *Cold War History* 8, no. 4 (2008), 504.

4. Ibid., 510–11.

5. Ibid., 504.

6. Verification was not a problem that bothered only the Americans. Soviet ambassador Anatoly Dobrynin was convinced in retrospect "that our people in the military, too, in their own way, worried about verification." See Dobrynin's comments in "SALT II and the Growth of Mistrust: Transcript of the Proceedings of the Musgrove Conference of the Carter-Brezhnev Project at Musgrove Plantation, St. Simons Island, Georgia, May 7–9, 1994," ed. Svetlana Savranskaya and David A. Welch, National Security Archive (Washington, DC: George Washington University, February 5, 1995), 91, http://nsarchive.gwu.edu/carterbrezhnev/C-B%20-%20SALT%20II%20-%20 Musgrove%20master%20transcript.pdf. Yet overall, verification played a far more subordinate role for the Soviets because of two interrelated reasons. First, there were, of course, internal debates about questions of verification inside the Soviet government. But in the highly secretive dictatorship of the Soviet Union, with its closed society, there were no public discussions of these problems that can be placed on the same level with the landmark American public debates. There was no comparable pressure on the Soviet government to legitimate decisions and assessments in this field for a broader audience, as was the case in the American democracy. Second was the

fundamental asymmetry of information availability: The Soviets could receive reliable information about American weapons programs for verification purposes from open government publications, congressional hearings, or newspapers and magazines; the Americans, in turn, could rely only on their limited and costly intelligence capabilities to cut through the Soviet veil of secrecy. See Allan S. Krass, *Verification: How Much Is Enough?* (Lexington, MA: Taylor & Francis, 1985), 128–29. For the Soviet decision-making process in regard to nuclear arms control negotiations, see Aleksandr' G. Savel'yev and Nikolay N. Detinov, *The Big Five: Arms Control Decision-Making in the Soviet Union* (Westport, CT: Praeger, 1995), 1–54.

7. For another approach to the relationship of trust and verification from a social science perspective that, in spite of its different epistemological interest, methodology, and empirical base and focus, generally is consistent with the results and conclusions of this chapter, see Nicholas J. Wheeler, Joshua Baker, and Laura Considine's chapter in this volume.

8. *Nuclear Test Ban Treaty: Hearings before the Committee on Foreign Relations, United States Senate*, 88th Cong., 1st sess. Hearings (1963), August 12–15, 19–23, 26–27, 1963, 541, quoted in Paul Rubinson, "'Crucified on a Cross of Atoms': Scientists, Politics, and the Test Ban Treaty," *Diplomatic History* 35, no. 2 (2011), 313.

9. Krass, *Verification*, 160.

10. "Minutes of a Review Group Meeting," June 19, 1969, in *Foreign Relations of the United States, 1969–1976*, Vol. XXXII, *SALT I, 1969–1972* (Washington, DC: US Government Printing Office, 2010), doc. 20, 72.

11. "Strategic Missile Talks, Related Aspects of Satellite Reconnaissance Disclosure Policy, Discussion," undated, February 9, 2011, CIA-RDP72R00410R0001000 50031-9, CIA Records Search Tool (CREST), National Archives and Records Administration, College Park, Maryland (hereafter, NARA).

12. Donald R. Morris, "Spies in Sky Keep Two Big Powers in Balance," *Houston Post*, October 8, 1972.

13. For an intriguing historical analysis of nuclear parity in the 1970s, see Francis J. Gavin, "Wrestling with Parity: The Nuclear Revolution Revisited," in *The Shock of the Global: The 1970s in Perspective*, ed. Niall Ferguson et al. (Cambridge, MA: Harvard University Press, 2010), 189–204.

14. "Text of Address by Vernon Walters, Deputy Director, Central Intelligence Agency to American Security Council, July 23, 1975," February 9, 2011, CIA-RDP 80R01731R002000100007-6, CREST.

15. Richard Helms, "Strategic Arms Limitation and Intelligence, DCI's address to the National War College on 13 October 1971," *Studies in Intelligence* 17 (1973): 1–7, at 2, February 9, 2011, CIA-RDP78T03194A000400010002-9, CREST.

16. Richard Helms, "Director's State of the Agency Address, 30 June 1972," February 9, 2011, CIA-RDP84-00780R005500190006-8, CREST.

17. United States Intelligence Board Steering Group on Monitoring Strategic Arms Limitation, "SALT Monitoring Evaluation, 17 August 1972," February 9, 2011, CIA-RDP79B01709A000200020005-4, CREST.

18. Congressional Briefing by Dr. Henry A. Kissinger, June 15, 1972, Folder SALT—June 1972, Records of Under Secretary of State John N. Irwin, 1969–1973, Box 1, Record Group (RG) 59, NARA.

19. See Article XIII of the "Treaty on Anti-Ballistic Missile Systems, 26 May 1972," in *SALT Hand Book: Key Documents and Issues, 1972–1979*, ed. Roger P.

Labrie (Washington, DC: American Enterprise Institute for Public Policy Research, 1979),18–19.

20. "Trying to Soothe SALT's Critics," *Time*, March 13, 1978, 13.

21. For more details on the SCC, see Sidney N. Graybeal and Michael Krepon, "Making Better Use of the Standing Consultative Commission," *International Security* 10, no. 2 (1985): 183–99; see also "Standing Consultative Commission, May 26, 1976," February 9, 2011, CIA-RDP88-01315R000400400051-1, CREST.

22. Memorandum from Graybeal to Kissinger, June 20, 1974, Folder NSDM 252, National Security Council Institutional ("H") Files, Policy Papers (1969–1974), Box H-246, Richard Nixon Presidential Library and Museum, Yorba Linda, California.

23. Memorandum from Jan M. Lodal to Secretary Kissinger, August 2, 1974, Folder SALT (2), National Security Adviser, Presidential Subject File, (1973) 1974–1977, Box 18, Gerald R. Ford Library, Ann Arbor, Michigan (hereafter, Ford Library).

24. Exemplarily for such public allegations, one may refer to the influential article by former Secretary of Defense Melvin R. Laird, "Arms Control: The Russians Are Cheating!," *Reader's Digest* 111, no. 5 (December 1977): 97–101.

25. DCI Briefing for Senate Arms Control Subcommittee, February 11, 1975, Folder SALT (14), National Security Adviser, Presidential Subject File (1973) 1974–1977, Box 19, Ford Library.

26. Ibid.

27. Minutes: National Security Council Meeting, March 5, 1975, National Security Council Meeting Minutes, Gerald R. Ford Presidential Digital Library, http://www.fordlibrarymuseum.gov/library/document/0312/750305.pdf.

28. Ibid.

29. Memorandum from Henry A. Kissinger to the President, July 9, 1975, Folder SALT (18), National Security Adviser, Presidential Subject File, (1973) 1974–1977, Box 19, Ford Library.

30. See Attachment to Memo for Mr. Hal Sonnenfeldt from James P. Wade, Jr., February 2, 1976, Folder Def 18-1 SALT Congressionals, Office of the Counselor, Entry # A1 5339-B, Subject Files, Box 7, RG 59, NARA.

31. See Dan Caldwell, *The Dynamics of Domestic Politics and Arms Control: The SALT II Treaty Ratification Debate* (Columbia: University of South Carolina Press, 1991), 113. See, for this, "Going Public with Compliance"; see also the journalistic account of Strobe Talbott, *Endgame: The Inside Story of SALT II* (New York: Harper & Row, 1979), 142–45.

32. See, for example, the report Vance is subsequently referring to: Report on Compliance with SALT I, Attachment to a Letter from Counselor of the Department of State Matthew Nimetz to Paul Nitze, March 1, 1978, Folder 4, Box 160, Paul H. Nitze Papers, Manuscript Division, Library of Congress, Washington, DC (hereafter, PHNP).

33. Memorandum from Cyrus Vance for the President, February 28, 1978, Folder State Department Evening Reports, 2/78, Plains File, Subject File, Box 38, Jimmy Carter Library, Atlanta, Georgia (hereafter, Carter Library).

34. Elmo R. Zumwalt and Worth H. Bagley, "CIA Is Out in the Cold in Role as Carter Public Affairs Arm," *Navy Times*, November 13, 1978.

35. William F. Buckley Jr., "Skulduggery, the Satellite and SALT," *Washington Star*, December 3, 1978.

36. Verification, June 11, 1979, authorship unclear (possibly Nitze himself), Folder 4, Box 160, PHNP.

37. Talking Points for Admiral Zumwalt on Verification, authorship unclear, undated, Folder 4, Box 160, PHNP; see also Krass, *Verification*, 144–51.

38. Kenneth Adelman, "Can There Be a SALT III?," *Wall Street Journal*, August 28, 1978.

39. See Betty Glad, *An Outsider in the White House: Jimmy Carter, His Advisors, and the Making of American Foreign Policy* (Ithaca, NY: Cornell University Press, 2009), 108.

40. Matt Nimetz to SALT Coordinating Group, February 1, 1978, Folder S.A.L.T., Office of the Deputy Secretary, Records of Warren Christopher, 1977–1980 (RWC), Box 60, RG 59, NARA (emphasis in original).

41. Memorandum from Matt Nimetz to the Deputy Secretary, June 19, 1978, Attachment: NBC Nightly News, Sunday, June 11, Folder Memos from WC to P, E, T, M, C 1978, RWC, Box 19, RG 59, NARA.

42. See Jimmy Carter, "Address Delivered Before a Joint Session of the Congress on the Vienna Summit Meeting," June 18, 1979, The American Presidency Project (ed. John Woolley and Gerhard Peters, University of California, Santa Barbara), http://www.presidency.ucsb.edu/ws/?pid=32498.

43. See "Subject: Meeting of the SPRC on Declassification of the 'fact of' US Satellite Photoreconnaissance on 13 September 1978 at 1530 Hours," February 9, 2011, CIA-RDP81B00401R002000130002-7, CREST.

44. "Draft, Space Policy Alternatives Paper for Space Policy Review Committee, August 21, 1978, V. Satellite Reconnaissance Security Policy Alternatives," February 9, 2011, CIA-RDP83M00171R000500070008-8, CREST.

45. Ibid.

46. See "Memorandum from Zbigniew Brzezinski for the Secretary of State, the Secretary of Defense et al.; Subject: Public Acknowledgement of the 'Fact of' Photoreconnaissance Satellites, September 22, 1978," February 9, 2011, CIA-RDP87B 01034R000700040004-1, CREST. For the speech, see Jimmy Carter, "Remarks at the Congressional Space Medal of Honor Awards Ceremony," October 1, 1978, The American Presidency Project, http://www.presidency.ucsb.edu/ws/?pid=29897.

47. "Preparations for Declassifying 'Fact of'," undated, February 9, 2011, CIA-RDP81M00980R001300030060-9, CREST.

48. Memorandum from Acting Chief, Special Security Center on Presidential Policy Decision, Sept. 26, 1978, RAC Project Number NLC-21-54-7-3-9, Carter Library.

49. "Memorandum for Deputy to the DCI for Resource Management from John F. Blake, Deputy Director for Administration; Subject: Satellite Reconnaissance Security Policy Alternatives (C), 11 Sep 1978," February 9, 2011, CIA-RDP81-00142R000600070014-7, CREST.

50. Ibid.

51. See Talbott, *Endgame*, 144.

52. Top secret attachment "Verification of a SALT II Agreement" to a Memorandum from Roger Molander and Bob Rosenberg to Zbigniew Brzezinski and David Aaron, April 25, 1979, RAC Project Number NLC-17-16-1-7-8, Carter Library.

53. Ibid.

54. Ibid.

55. Memorandum from Jerry Rafshoon for the President, May 8, 1979, Folder SALT II Correspondence File, 4/24/79-9/27/79, Office of Congressional Liaison Beckel, Box 229, Carter Library.

56. "Selling the Treaty," *Congressional Quarterly, Weekly Report*, June 23, 1979, 1210.

57. Jimmy Carter, "Strategic Arms Limitation Treaty Letter to the Majority Leader of the Senate Requesting a Delay in Senate Consideration of the Treaty," January 3, 1980, The American Presidency Project, http://www.presidency.ucsb.edu/ws/index.php?pid=33072.

58. Olav Njølstad, "The Collapse of Superpower Détente, 1975–1980," in *The Cambridge History of the Cold War: Volume III: Endings*, ed., Melvyn P. Leffler and Odd Arne Westad (Cambridge, UK: Cambridge University Press, 2010), 155.

5. Trust and Transparency at the CSCE, 1969–1975

Michael Cotey Morgan

Trust and suspicion were central concerns of the Conference on Security and Cooperation in Europe (CSCE). These negotiations, which involved thirty-five North American and European countries and produced the 1975 Helsinki Final Act, addressed nearly every aspect of East-West relations, including the principles of international security, trade, and human rights. Ostensibly, the conference aimed to solve the outstanding problems of European security and cultivate mutual understanding in order to stabilize the Cold War. But before and during the negotiations, most members of the North Atlantic Treaty Organization (NATO) and Warsaw Pact suspected the motives of both their long-time adversaries and their own allies. The conference tried to build confidence between the blocs, but it often strained relations within them. Even as participants publicly affirmed the imperative of reducing East-West tensions, many of them privately doubted whether they could afford to trust their interlocutors on either side of the Iron Curtain.

Trust is rare in international relations. As Ute Frevert has observed, trust means expecting someone else to take one's own interests to heart, to act out of goodwill rather than selfish advantage.[1] Because states rarely have this luxury, they tend to mistrust each other, refusing to accept the vulnerability and uncertainty that trust entails.[2] States can nevertheless foster confidence by behaving predictably and following generally accepted rules. Aggression and competition erode confidence, but cooperation and conciliation can rebuild it, even despite incompatible goals.[3] The experience of the CSCE confirms this insight. Participants promoted East-West confidence by hammering out the basic principles of international conduct and a list of activities to advance mutual understanding. At the same time, however, many participants regarded confidence not as a goal in itself but as a weapon to wage the Cold War by other means. In the late 1960s, the Soviets touted the benefits of international confidence as they tried to persuade the skeptical Americans and Western Europeans to participate in a European security conference. The conference "would contribute to [the] improvement of [the] general political atmosphere in Europe and to [the] growth of trust," Anatoly Dobrynin, the Soviet ambassador to the United States, told Secretary of State William P. Rogers in 1969.[4] The Kremlin wanted to stabilize the international system, Dobrynin noted, but this would be impossible unless the superpowers trusted each other. President Richard Nixon and National Security Advisor Henry Kissinger agreed.[5] In none of these conversations, however, did anyone specify what "trust" meant. The leaders and diplomats involved in the CSCE agreed on the value of mutual confidence, but argued about how to build it. At the 1972–73 preparatory talks in Helsinki, and subsequently at the full conference in Geneva from 1973 to 1975, they struggled to find common ground. Negotiations that the Soviets hoped would take a few months dragged on for years, not least because participants disagreed about what the abstract principles on the agenda—including sovereignty, cooperation, and confidence—meant in practice.

These disputes illustrated a deeper conflict over the meaning of international security. In Moscow's view, security depended on upholding the power of the state and keeping Europe divided. The Eastern European revolts of the 1950s and 1960s demonstrated that the socialist governments had to maintain a tight grip on society and minimize their citizens' contact with the West. Peace demanded absolute respect for sovereignty and noninterference in states' domestic affairs. By contrast, Western governments insisted that security and confidence required more contacts between states and between individual citizens. Openness and transparency, not barriers and secrecy, would strengthen peace. The Soviets wanted to reinforce the Iron Curtain, but the Western allies hoped to puncture it. From 1972 to 1975, the fundamental incompatibility of these goals repeatedly brought the CSCE to a standstill. Yet Soviet leaders refused to let the negotiations collapse. Even though they distrusted Western motives, they made crucial concessions in order to reach a deal. As a consequence, the Helsinki Final Act—especially its provisions on humanitarian and military affairs—embodied NATO's approach to international security more than the Warsaw Pact's.

Clashing Visions of International Security

Soviet leader Leonid Brezhnev was the driving force behind the CSCE. If the Soviet Union hoped to maintain its power over the long term, he concluded,

103

it had to cement the political and military division of Europe while somehow reviving its economy. A successful conference would do both of these things, and more. By ratifying Europe's postwar frontiers, the CSCE would eliminate any doubts about the security of the Soviet empire. By broadening Eastern access to Western goods, capital, and technology, it would give the socialist economies a new lease on life and reinvigorate socialism in the eyes of Soviet citizens and foreign statesmen alike. Brezhnev understood that legitimacy and security were intertwined. The greater socialism's legitimacy, the less Moscow would have to rely on the threat of force to underwrite its suzerainty in Eastern Europe. And the stronger its ties to the West, the better it could deal with the growing menace of China.[6]

The Western powers agreed to participate in the CSCE only after several years of Soviet pressure. They suspected the Warsaw Pact's motives but decided that they could not reject the conference proposal outright, in large part because they worried about the popular legitimacy of their own governments and of NATO itself. By the late 1960s, Western Europeans' fears of a Soviet invasion had largely receded. The old logic of East-West confrontation no longer seemed to apply, and the Atlantic alliance increasingly looked like the relic of a bygone era. As a result, if the allies rebuffed even a facile Warsaw Pact overture to negotiate, voters might conclude that Western intransigence was unnecessarily prolonging the Cold War. Losing public legitimacy could endanger NATO's viability and, by extension, the very foundations of Western European security. Rejecting the conference proposal outright was therefore not an option.[7]

Western diplomats worked to make a virtue out of necessity. NATO agreed to participate in a security conference, but only if the Warsaw Pact satisfied three conditions. First, a modus vivendi had to be reached on the division of Germany and Berlin.[8] Second, the CSCE's security agenda had to include more than just the narrow declaration on the principles of international relations that the Soviet Union sought. In particular, the conference had to take concrete steps to reduce military tensions. Confidence-building measures (CBMs) would require governments to give advance notice of military exercises and movements and invite foreign officials to observe them. With luck, these steps would reduce mutual suspicions and fears of aggression. Finally, the conference had to expand human contacts between East and West. On this point, NATO championed the "freer movement of people, ideas, and information" in the hope of making the East-West divide less meaningful. Freer movement would make it easier for people to travel, emigrate, and read foreign books and newspapers.[9] The Western agenda emphasized openness and transparency at every turn.

These Eastern and Western approaches reflected divergent assumptions about international security. According to Western logic, peace required states to respect fundamental human rights. Because governments that did not respect their citizens were unlikely to respect their neighbors, human rights were not strictly a domestic matter but a valid diplomatic concern. The stability of the international system depended as much on states' inward character as their outward conduct. And because secrecy bred distrust, transparency would reduce the threat of conflict. "A genuine order of peace and cooperation in Europe will depend ultimately upon normalization of human contacts," the deputy American representative to NATO, George Vest, wrote in 1972. "More open relations and closer ties than now exist among people are the indispensable elements of progress toward mutual knowledge and understanding throughout the continent and toward the resolution of common problems."[10] As Eastern and Western governments and citizens came into closer and more regular contact, whether at a military or at a personal level, they would understand each other better. As their old suspicions faded away, they would be less likely to go to war.

It was no coincidence that these two principles—respect for human rights and transparency—threatened the foundations of Soviet power. Most Warsaw Pact leaders regarded military secrecy as necessary for the survival of communism, to say nothing of national and international security. The uprisings of the 1950s and 1960s—in East Germany, Poland, Hungary, and Czechoslovakia—demonstrated that domestic stability required curtailing citizens' civil rights and insulating them from Western culture and ideas. Freer movement and CBMs were hard to reconcile with preserving the communist status quo. For all these reasons, Western diplomats insisted on discussing these questions at the CSCE.[11]

The participants regarded trust as a powerful—and possibly dangerous—tool. They questioned their adversaries' motives and criticized their understanding of security. They feared that if they trusted too much, they would give away too much. Similar suspicions also taxed relations within each alliance and even within some governments. The Western Europeans questioned the Nixon administration's commitment to transatlantic solidarity. Some of the Eastern Europeans chafed under Moscow's demands for unconditional support in Geneva. Leaders on both sides sometimes wondered whether they could trust their own diplomats.

The CSCE therefore stretched far beyond the conference rooms and corridors in Helsinki and Geneva. It also encompassed negotiations within each alliance, secret back-channel talks between the superpowers, and deliberations among bureaucrats in the capitals of many participating states. The mutual trust—and mutual suspicion—of the many actors involved, from the

105

highest-profile statesman to the most obscure diplomat, affected every stage of the process. Even before they could lobby the West to participate in the conference, the Soviets had to get their own allies in line. The East Germans and Poles argued that the Soviets put too little emphasis on winning international recognition of Eastern Europe's postwar borders. By contrast, the Romanians, who did not share their Polish and East German counterparts' anxieties about the continent's frontiers, thought that the Soviets paid too much attention to the question.[12] The Warsaw Pact allies all agreed, however, that Western ideas on freer movement were weapons of ideological subversion. On the other side of the table, a number of Western diplomats contended that the Soviet Union's ostensibly peaceful goals for the CSCE concealed dangerous ambitions of a different sort. They suspected that the Soviets wanted to persuade Western voters that the new era of East-West understanding made NATO obsolete. Many Western European officials feared that, in pursuit of superpower comity, the Nixon administration would secretly collaborate with Moscow to undermine NATO's own objectives for the conference. In Washington, White House officials wanted to avoid confronting the Soviets over what they regarded as a meaningless diplomatic exercise and criticized the State Department for supporting Western European hard-liners. These currents of suspicion persisted throughout the CSCE, shaping the relationships of Cold War allies and adversaries alike.[13]

Puncturing the Iron Curtain

Formal negotiations to create the CSCE got underway in November 1972, when European and North American diplomats assembled at the Helsinki University of Technology to work out an agenda and rules of procedure for the conference. No one could foresee how long these multilateral preparatory talks (MPT) would last or whether they would succeed. The exercise tested the participants' willpower and their commitment to the CSCE. Trust played little role in the talks. Progress depended instead on a mixture of cajoling, horse-trading, bullying, and waiting. The lead Soviet negotiator, veteran diplomat Valerian Zorin, earned the nickname "the poisoned dwarf" from Western diplomats in recognition of his unfailingly aggressive tactics.[14]

Because the participants' ideas about security provided so little common ground, the MPT's success depended on Brezhnev's determination to make the CSCE work. His personal commitment to the conference was both an asset and a liability. Without it, the participants never would have convened in the first place. But it also prevented the Soviets from walking away in the face of steep Western demands. This dynamic gave the Western participants considerable leverage, and they knew it. At the same time, however, they too could ill afford to behave recklessly. Causing the CSCE to fail, even for good reason, risked undermining the public trust in NATO that they were so keen to rebuild. In this respect, the negotiations resembled a game of chicken. Each side wanted to demand as much as possible without provoking the other to leave the table. Moreover, in important respects, the negotiations were a zero-sum game. The CSCE could not declare that Europe's frontiers were both immutable, as the Soviets wanted, and open to peaceful change, as the West insisted. Sovereignty could not be both absolute and subject to the constraints of universal human rights. Security could not require both transparency and strict barriers between states.[15]

The negotiations over freer movement brought this conflict to a head. Mundane Western proposals to encourage the wider distribution of foreign newspapers and to reunite family members with their relatives abroad barely concealed lofty anti-communist ambitions.[16] In January 1972, Brezhnev warned his Eastern European counterparts that Western demands would turn what was supposed to be a peace conference into "another field of class struggle between the two social systems."[17] Bulgarian leader Todor Zhivkov denounced freer movement as "an open and shameless attempt to exploit the European conference for ideological subversion." The CSCE must not become "a pulpit for attacks against the socialist countries [and] . . . a means of broad ideological penetration into our countries," the Warsaw Pact's leaders agreed.[18] One cannot conclude that the Soviet bloc's leaders failed to anticipate the CSCE's potential impact on the stability of socialist rule. They identified the risks involved even before the negotiations began, but proceeded nonetheless. No international agreement could force them to adopt any domestic policy against their will, they reasoned. Sovereignty would protect them.

Besides, the Soviets were confident of blunting NATO's attack at the negotiating table. Two small problems complicated the task. Moscow's professed commitment to East-West cooperation meant that it could not refuse to discuss freer movement at all. Stonewalling might provoke the NATO allies to retaliate and obstruct the Soviet Union's desiderata on European frontiers. The Soviets therefore aimed to water down the West's proposals. They suggested replacing a straightforward endorsement of freedom of information with anemic language about cultural exchange programs, and insisted on subordinating any undertakings in this area to the prerogatives of state sovereignty. This tactic would preserve their rhetorical commitment to international cooperation and furnish an escape from any unpalatable provisions.[19]

The Western allies disagreed about how to respond. The Dutch refused to retreat from NATO's agreed goals. They reasoned that the Soviets eventually would grow tired of the stalemate and make concessions to get the agreement that Brezhnev so clearly wanted. The situation demanded patience. By contrast, the French called for flexibility. According to their analysis, by demonstrating their good faith now, the allies would reap the benefits from a more cooperative Soviet delegation over the long haul. This tactical dispute strained NATO's bonds of trust. Officials on either side of the argument insisted that they alone understood the West's best interests.[20] Eventually, the allies agreed to give way on a few minor points but maintain a united front. On the key issues, the Warsaw Pact would have to make the first move.[21]

Just as the Western hard-liners predicted, Moscow instructed its delegation in Helsinki to reach an agreement even at the price of substantial concessions. In June 1973, when the MPT finalized the agenda for the CSCE's so-called Basket III, which dealt with freer movement, the text closely matched the West's original demands. At the full conference, participants would discuss how to "facilitate freer movement and contacts" between people, "the freer and wider dissemination of information of all kinds," and the reunification of families that had been divided by the Iron Curtain. These measures would be implemented with "full respect" for the basic principles of international relations, including both sovereignty and human rights, which would be enumerated in Basket I.[22] The West got much of what it wanted, but a crucial question remained unanswered: Could the Soviets use this acknowledgment of sovereign prerogatives as a catchall defense against freer movement?[23]

The problem preoccupied senior leaders and junior diplomats alike once the CSCE itself opened in Geneva in September 1973. On one side, the West demanded "obligations of a normative character that will apply generally and in all circumstances" without exception, as a French official put it.[24] On the other, the Eastern Europeans rejected all sweeping commitments. Instead of a categorical endorsement of freer movement, they suggested holding film festivals and academic seminars.[25] They also tried to drive a wedge into NATO. Senior Soviet officials complained to their American counterparts that unreasonable Western demands threatened the success of the conference. The Soviet Union wanted better cultural relations, Brezhnev told Nixon, but it would never accept an agreement that infringed its sovereign rights. If the logjam in Geneva continued, superpower relations on the broadest scale might suffer.[26] On another occasion, Brezhnev asked Kissinger, "What kind of proposal is it if they want to arrogate to themselves the right to open theaters in the Soviet Union without any control by the Soviet administration?"[27] If Western European stubbornness torpedoed the CSCE, he warned, "there will be, instead of security, insecurity."[28] The Soviets expected that the Americans, duly chastised, would pressure their own allies to give ground.

The Nixon administration found itself on a diplomatic tightrope. Nixon and Kissinger wanted to keep détente on track, which required placating the Soviets. But they also wanted to maintain their allies' confidence, which required supporting the tough Western European position on freer movement. In the wake of the 1973 Year of Europe debacle, they could not risk a major transatlantic rupture, especially because the allies had long suspected—with good reason, as they discovered—that the White House was working secretly with Moscow to eviscerate the CSCE.[29] Even so, Kissinger regarded the allies' hopes for freer movement as absurdly ambitious and questioned the competence of the Western diplomats assigned to the negotiations. "I don't believe that a bunch of revolutionaries who manage to cling to power for fifty years are going to be euchred out of it by the sort of people we have got negotiating at the European Security Conference through an oversight," he told his staff.[30]

Kissinger worked both covertly and overtly to reconcile these competing priorities, exploiting the allies' trust in an attempt to undermine NATO's united front. Through the back channel, he told the Kremlin that state sovereignty should trump any commitments to freer movement.[31] But in order to camouflage this collaboration and preserve the façade of transatlantic solidarity, Kissinger and Soviet foreign minister Andrei Gromyko agreed that the neutral Finns would present the secret deal and pretend that it had originated in Helsinki.[32] Meanwhile, within NATO, Kissinger tried to rein in the allies' demands. He insisted that they spell out the minimum results that they would accept in Basket III. Without an explicit list of irreducible goals, he told French foreign minister Jean Sauvagnargues, there would be no end to NATO's demands in Geneva, and therefore no end to the negotiations.[33]

Washington's allies caught on to the subterfuge. They reacted with fury. When American diplomats in Geneva voiced their support for the Finnish preamble, the Western Europeans denounced it as the fruit of clandestine superpower collaboration.[34] They refused to draft a list of minimum Western objectives, regarding it as a capitulation to the Soviets. Doing as Kissinger asked would result "first in the abandonment of all requirements not included in the list; and secondly failure to achieve even our minimum requirements (as the Russians would certainly regard these as the starting rather than the ending point for subsequent negotiation)," a British diplomat argued.[35] Many of the allies wondered just whose interests the Americans were trying to advance. An underlying disagreement about what the conference could achieve provoked a long-running fight over how far to push the Soviets. An honest airing of differences within NATO seemed unlikely to settle the matter. Kissinger hoped to reconcile his irreconcilable goals and maintain his allies' trust while simultaneously avoiding a rupture with Moscow. Instead, his gambit backfired.

If the Soviets had expected Kissinger's intervention to weaken NATO's position and bring the CSCE to a painless conclusion, the results sorely disappointed them. Attempting to break the impasse on the preamble to Basket III, the neutrals proposed to soften the language on sovereignty.[36] Soviet and Eastern European diplomats in Geneva hesitated to accept a text that fell so far short of their initial goals, but Moscow insisted on settling the issue as soon as possible.[37] By the autumn of 1974, President Gerald Ford's new administration in Washington abandoned the campaign to codify NATO's minimum goals. The American position on Basket III hardened considerably, in part because of the growing domestic backlash against détente. Congress's December 1974 endorsement of the Jackson-Vanik Amendment, which denied most-favored-nation status to countries (like the Soviet Union) that restricted emigration, caused the administration particular concern. Eager to blunt the criticism of détente, Kissinger concluded that the United States should join its allies in standing up for human rights in Geneva.[38] As NATO's resolve stiffened, Soviet leaders concluded that they had to make concessions in Basket III if they wanted to avoid a stalemate. In Moscow, the KGB protested that the CSCE could endanger Soviet domestic stability, but Brezhnev maintained that the government could control its citizens no matter what happened at the negotiations. When NATO presented a take-it-or-leave-it Basket III proposal, therefore, the Warsaw Pact acquiesced.[39] As a consequence, the Final Act included many of the West's most ambitious demands, including commitments to family reunification, freer travel, and the wider distribution of foreign books and newspapers.

The Logic of Transparency

The CSCE's focus on international security meant that the talks had to pay at least some attention to military affairs. But what form should this discussion take and how bold an agreement should it produce? For strategic and domestic reasons, in 1968 NATO suggested working with the Soviets to cut the size of conventional forces in Europe. Because of the Warsaw Pact's long-standing and unchallenged conventional dominance, Western military security had long relied on nuclear superiority. But the Soviet Union's rapid nuclear buildup and the burden of the Vietnam War persuaded a number of Western officials to seek a diplomatic solution to the conventional imbalance in Europe. Mutual and balanced force reductions (MBFR), as NATO's proposal became known, offered domestic political benefits, too. The talks would show voters that Western leaders were serious about détente. MBFR would also blunt the growing danger that the US Congress would order unilateral troop withdrawals from Europe.[40]

In practice, however, MBFR was a dead end. The Warsaw Pact's conventional superiority made it difficult to envision a formula that would reduce troop numbers, maintain Western security, and stand a chance of winning Soviet support. Cutting Eastern and Western forces equally would just magnify the Warsaw Pact's advantage. Furthermore, the Soviets would never agree to reduce the Warsaw Pact's forces more than NATO's, even though this was the only way that MBFR might improve Western European security.[41] Despite this insurmountable conceptual roadblock, Western continued to push MBFR for purely domestic reasons.[42] But since it would be hard enough to reach a deal with only a few countries involved, it would be foolhardy to tackle MBFR at the CSCE, with dozens of delegations around the table. MBFR therefore had to run on a separate track.

Because some Western governments worried that their citizens would question the value of a security conference that had no military component, NATO devised the idea of confidence-building measures. The logic of CBMs had much in common with Western thinking about freer movement. CBMs aimed to reassure governments in East and West that they had nothing to fear from the routine business of defense. States would worry less about surprise attacks and have a harder time bullying their neighbors with shows of force. In the most optimistic interpretation, CBMs would build international peace on the basis of mutual confidence and cooperation rather than military deterrence and the threat of retaliation.[43] Alongside freer movement, they emphasized the connection between transparency and international stability. From this perspective, CBMs were the heir of President Dwight Eisenhower's Open Skies proposal.[44] Because secrecy was fundamental to the Soviet concept of security, robust CBMs would simultaneously reassure Western public opinion and complicate the Red Army's standard procedures. Their primary benefits were political and psychological, not military.[45]

This purpose was not lost on the Soviets, who attacked CBMs at the negotiations with their usual tactics. They tried to dilute the substance of the West's proposals and demanded that any undertakings on military security be contingent on respect for state sovereignty. During the preparatory talks in Helsinki, they indicated that they might consider discussing some elements of NATO's initial proposals, including the exchange of military observers at major maneuvers and advance notification of these maneuvers, so long as participation was strictly voluntary.[46] Advance notification of troop movements (as opposed to maneuvers), a point of central importance to the West, was out of the question. In addition, the Soviets wanted states to notify only their immediate neighbors, not every CSCE participant, and they insisted on exchanging military observers by invitation only, not as a matter of course. All told, one British diplomat noted, the Soviets were trying to make CBMs meaningless.[47] From the West's vantage point, this was no mere squabble over technicalities. NATO had to hold firm and put "Soviet good intentions to the test in a way understandable to public opinion." Even if progress on CBMs proved impossible, Western voters would recognize that the Soviet bloc was still untrustworthy. Despite improvements in East-West relations, the Red Army still posed a real threat and NATO remained the cornerstone of Western security.[48]

Much like Basket III, the discussion of CBMs ground to a halt in Geneva. The Soviets quietly appealed for American help to chip away at NATO's position. Western European proposals were "unacceptable" and "nothing short of ridiculous," Gromyko complained to Kissinger. "If anyone thinks that they can attempt to talk us into this position," he said, "they should know that it will fail."[49] Kissinger sympathized. "The trouble is that you have a bunch of bureaucrats in Geneva who are trying to impress each other with their toughness," he said. He hoped to end "this sterile debate" by working out a back-channel deal.[50] The White House pressured its allies to relax their demands, but despite Kissinger's promises of greater flexibility, the Western Europeans only stiffened their resolve. The West Germans, for example, declared that a robust agreement on CBMs was "essential" to the success of the whole conference. A number of allied diplomats even contemplated walking away from the CSCE if the Soviets refused to budge.[51]

Nevertheless, the Western Europeans gave way on two of the three central points of contention. The Soviets categorically refused to apply CBMs to regular troop movements, so the Western allies let the matter drop. And despite some grumblings that CBMs had to be mandatory to have any value at all, they agreed to make CBMs voluntary. This compromise was less significant than it appeared. Because no one on either side of the Iron Curtain wanted the CSCE to produce a treaty, none of its provisions would bind participants under international law, regardless of how strict the text on CBMs might be.[52]

On the third point, concerning the advance notification of maneuvers, the West made significant gains. The main parameters here were how many days' notice participants had to give; how many men had to be involved in a particular exercise for notification to be necessary; and to what proportion of Soviet territory these requirements applied. In early 1975, Soviet diplomats in Geneva privately admitted to their Western counterparts that it had been a mistake to allow CBMs on the conference agenda in the first place. And although military leaders in Moscow were blocking any concessions for the time being, the Soviets conceded that they would give ground eventually.[53] This is precisely what happened. After an extended period of haggling, the two sides reached agreement in July. The Washington-Moscow back channel had worked out a compromise deal, but the Western Europeans, predictably upset at Kissinger's secret diplomacy, refused to consider it. However, they agreed to a last-minute proposal from the neutrals that was only slightly tougher than what Kissinger had devised through the back channel. The participants would give twenty-one days' notice of any exercise involving more than 25,000 troops anywhere in Europe, including the band of territory 250 km from the Soviet Union's western frontier.[54]

The exact parameters mattered less than the underlying principles. The CBM deal represented a major Western victory not because of its military value but because of its political implications. The measures would lower "the huge barriers of secrecy within which the Russians, and above all the Soviet State, have always operated," the British delegation in Geneva concluded. Given the fanfare surrounding the CSCE's concluding summit in Helsinki in the summer of 1975 and the personal prestige that Brezhnev had invested in the negotiations, the Soviets would find it difficult to renege on their promises, even though compliance was voluntary.[55] Just a few years earlier, an agreement of this scope would have "seemed inconceivable," one Western diplomat noted.[56] The conference vindicated the Western Europeans' claim that security required openness and that transparency should trump secrecy.

Conclusion

Two visions of East-West relations collided at the CSCE. In the Soviet view (which the Nixon administration shared in part), the best way to encourage peace was to draw sharp lines between states and block fundamental changes to the international system. By establishing clear rules of international conduct and preventing states from interfering in each others' domestic affairs, the CSCE would build confidence and stability by making the Cold War predictable. In the Western European view, by contrast, peace required change, since the only way to escape the Cold War was to overcome the division of Europe. Transparency and openness were essential to achieve this goal. CBMs and the freer movement of people and information promised to lower the barriers on which Soviet power relied. From this perspective, the CSCE would serve as a Trojan horse to smuggle Western principles into the socialist bloc.

The CSCE did not reconcile these competing approaches. Instead, the Helsinki Final Act included elements of both. However, the Soviets' major concessions on a number of key points, including freer movement and CBMs, made the agreement a triumph for the Western European vision. The Soviets gave way not because NATO's arguments had persuaded them, or because they came to trust the Western allies, but because they wanted to get a deal.

In this respect, the negotiations demonstrated that states can conclude major agreements even in the absence of trust.

Tangled lines of trust and distrust made the CSCE complex, but also ultimately made it possible to reach agreement. The neutral states' reputation for trustworthiness helped them to break repeated logjams and convinced the Soviets to make compromises that they might not otherwise have contemplated. Henry Kissinger tried, unsuccessfully, to exploit the mutual confidence on which NATO relied to advance American interests at the expense of Western European ambitions. Leonid Brezhnev's confidence in the ability of his state to control Soviet society led him to endorse an agreement that, in numerous respects, threatened the power of his state. The Western allies devised proposals that used the logic of confidence to attack the suspicion and opacity at the heart of Soviet foreign and domestic policy. The various relationships at play in the negotiations—within each alliance, between the superpowers, and even within governments—required different kinds of confidence that were sometimes at odds with each other. Strengthening one might strain another. Gaining an adversary's confidence might require deceiving one's allies or even one's compatriots. Perhaps the CSCE's most significant lesson, therefore, is that confidence can be as important—and as dangerous—a weapon as any in the statesman's arsenal.

Notes

1. Ute Frevert, "Does Trust Have a History?" (Max Weber Lecture Series 2009-01, European University Institute, Florence, 2009), 5, http://cadmus.eui.eu/bitstream/handle/1814/11258/MWP_LS_2009_01.pdf.

2. See Deborah Welch Larson's conclusion to this volume.

3. See Larson's conclusion; and Ute Frevert, "Trust as Work," in *Work in a Modern Society: The German Historical Experience in Comparative Perspective*, ed. Jürgen Kocka (New York: Berghahn Books, 2010), 97.

4. Telegram from the Department of State to the Mission to the North Atlantic Treaty Organization, November 20, 1969, *Foreign Relations of the United States (FRUS), 1969–1976*, Vol. XXXIX, *European Security* (Washington, DC: US Government Printing Office, 2007), doc. 11.

5. See, for example, "Memorandum of Conversation (USSR)," February 14, 1969, in David C. Geyer and Douglas E. Selvage, eds., *Soviet-American Relations: The Détente Years, 1969–1972* (Washington, DC: US Government Printing Office, 2007), doc. 3; "Memorandum of Conversation (USSR)," February 17, 1969, ibid., doc. 6; "Note from the Soviet Leadership to President Nixon," undated [October 1969], ibid., doc. 32; and "Memorandum of Conversation (USSR)," December 20, 1969, ibid., doc. 41.

6. "Vermerk über ein Gespräch des Ministers für Auswärtige Angelegenheiten der DDR, Genossen Otto Winzer, mit dem stellvertretenden Außenminister der UdSSR, Genossen WS Semjonow," September 25, 1969, DY 30/3524, Stiftung Archiv der

Parteien und Massenorganisationen der DDR im Bundesarchiv, Berlin (hereafter, SAPMO); Memorandum from Winzer to Ulbricht, Stoph, Honecker, and Axen, "Einschätzung der sowjetischen Vorschläge über die Vorbereitung und den Inhalt einer europäischen Sicherheitskonferenz," September 29, 1969, DY 30/3524, ibid.; and "Speech by the Soviet Foreign Minister (Andrei A. Gromyko)," October 30, 1969, Parallel History Project (hereafter, PHP), http://www.php.isn.ethz.ch/collections /colltopic.cfm?lng=en&id=19860&navinfo=15699. See also Douglas Selvage, "The Warsaw Pact and the European Security Conference, 1964–69: Sovereignty, Hegemony, and the German Question," in *Origins of the European Security System The Helsinki Process Revisited, 1965–75*, ed. Andreas Wenger, Vojtech Mastny, and Christian Nuenlist (New York: Routledge, 2008); and Csaba Békés, "The Warsaw Pact, the German Question, and the Birth of the CSCE Process, 1961–1970," in *Helsinki 1975 and the Transformation of Europe*, ed. Oliver Bange and Gottfried Niedhart (New York: Berghahn, 2008).

    7. Pompidou-Rogers Memcon, December 8, 1969, Secrétariat général – Entretiens et Messages – Vol. 40, Archives du Ministère des Affaires Étrangères, Paris (hereafter, AMAE); Telegram from the American Embassy in London to the State Department, January 9, 1970, RG 59, Subject Numeric Files, 1970–73, Box 1703, National Archives and Records Administration, College Park, Maryland (hereafter, NARA); Minutes of a National Security Council Meeting, January 28, 1970, *FRUS, 1969–1976*, Vol. XXXIX, doc. 19; and Memorandum from Sous-Direction d'Europe Orientale to Pompidou, "Conférence sur la sécurité européenne," June 15, 1970, 5AG2/58, Archives Nationales, Paris (hereafter, AN). See also Drew Middleton, "Member Governments Remain Enthusiastic about NATO, but Popular Support Has Declined Sharply," *New York Times*, November 30, 1969, 14.

    8. See, for example, Telegram from External Affairs, Ottawa, to the Canadian Delegation to NATO, May 13, 1969, RG-25, Vol. 9054, File 20-4-CSCE, Vol. 1, Library and Archives Canada, Ottawa (hereafter, LAC); and Memorandum from Bahr to Brandt, "Aufzeichnung des Ministerialdirektors Bahr, z.Z. New York," September 21, 1969, in *Akten zur Auswärtigen Politik der Bundesrepublik Deutschland 1969* [Foreign policy documents of the Federal Republic of Germany, 1969] (Munich: R. Oldenbourg, 2000), doc. 296.

    9. Minutes of a National Security Council Meeting, January 28, 1970, *FRUS 1969–1976*, Vol. XXXIX, doc. 19, 44–48; telegram from London to the State Department, January 9, 1970, RG 59, Subject Numeric Files, 1970–73, Box 1703, NARA; and Pompidou-Rogers Memcon, December 8, 1969, Secrétariat général – Entretiens et Messages – Vol. 40, AMAE. See also Memorandum from Sous-Direction d'Europe Orientale to Pompidou, "Conférence sur la sécurité européenne," June 15, 1970, 5AG2/58, AN; and "Current West European Attitudes toward a European Security Conference," April 3, 1969, and Telegram from Oslo to the State Department, January 8, 1970, RG 59, Subject Numeric Files, 1970–73, Box 1703, NARA.

    10. Telegram from the US Delegation to NATO to the State Department, "POLADs Discussion of Freer Movement," March 1, 1972, RG 59, Central Foreign Policy Files, 1970–73, Box 2263, NARA. See also Letter from Sous-Direction d'Europe Orientale to Embassies in NATO and Warsaw Pact Capitals, "Conversations avec les Américains sur la Sécurité européenne," April 13, 1970, Affaires Étrangères – Fonds EU – Organismes Internationaux et Grandes Questions Internationales – Sécurité – 1966–70 – 2031,

AMAE; and Memorandum from the US Delegation to NATO, "Freer Movement of People, Ideas, and Information," April 8, 1971, Affaires Étrangères – Organismes Internationaux et Grandes Questions Internationales – Sécurité – 1971–1976 – 2921, AMAE.

11. See, e.g., US Delegation to NATO to the State Department, "NAC Meeting October 1—List of Issues for Possible Negotiation with the East," October 1, 1969, RG 59, Central Foreign Policy Files, 1967–1969, Box 2081, NARA; Memorandum From Helmut Sonnenfeldt of the National Security Council Staff to the President's Assistant for National Security Affairs (Kissinger), October 2, 1969, *FRUS 1969– 1976*, Vol. XXXIX, doc. 9, 8; "Declaration of the North Atlantic Council," December 5, 1969, *Selected Documents Relating to Problems of Security and Cooperation in Europe, 1954–77* (London: HMSO, 1977), 66; Memorandum from the French Delegation to NATO, "Conférence sur la sécurité européenne—Coopération culturelle, libre circulation des hommes, des idées et des informations," April 6, 1971, FCO 41/896, The National Archives, Kew, United Kingdom (hereafter, TNA); Memorandum from the US Delegation to NATO, "Freer Movement of People, Ideas, and Information," April 8, 1971, Affaires Étrangères – Organismes Internationaux et Grandes Questions Internationales – Sécurité – 1971–1976 – 2921, AMAE; and Memorandum from FE Maestrone to NATO's Political Committee, "Questions de Fond et Procédures pour d'Éventuelles Négociations Est-Ouest: Libre Circulation des Personnes des Idées et des Informations et Développement des Relations Culturelles," April 22, 1971, Affaires Étrangères – Organismes Internationaux et Grandes Questions Internationales – Sécurité – 1971–1976 – 2921, AMAE.

12. "Stenographic Transcript of the Meeting of the Executive of the Central Committee of the Romanian Communist Party," March 18, 1969, PHP, http://php.isn .ethz.ch/collections/colltopic.cfm?id=16493; GDR Politburo Memorandum, "Erwägungen zum Problem der europäischen Sicherheit," April 21, 1969, DY 30/3525, SAPMO; and "Foreign Ministry Memorandum to the HSWP Political Committee on Hungarian-Soviet Consultation re: European Security Conference," October 18, 1969, PHP, http://php.isn.ethz.ch/collections/colltopic.cfm?id=17007.

13. See, e.g., Memorandum From the President's Assistant for National Security Affairs (Kissinger) to President Nixon, April 4, 1969, *FRUS 1969–1976*, Vol. XXXIX, doc. 2; Memorandum from Rogers to Nixon, "Your Participation in the NATO Ministerial Meeting, April 10–11, 1969," April 7, 1969, RG 59, Executive Secretariat Conference Files, 1966–1972, Box 488, NARA; "Entretien entre le Président de la République et Monsieur Brosio," November 19, 1969, 5AG2/257, AN; Memorandum from Tickell to Wiggin, "Principles Governing Relations between States," June 15, 1972, FCO 28/1691, TNA; Telegram from French Embassy in Washington to the Quai d'Orsay, "Conversation du Ministre avec M. Rogers: CSCE et MBFR," September 22, 1972, Affaires Étrangères – Organismes Internationaux et Grandes Questions Internationales – Sécurité – 1971–1976 – 2924, AMAE; and "Conference on Security and Cooperation in Europe: Stage II Geneva: Steering Brief for the United Kingdom Delegation," n.d. [September 1973], FCO 28/2174, TNA.

14. Letter from Walden, UK Embassy in Helsinki, to Fall, FCO (Foreign and Commonwealth Office), "Despatch on the Conclusion of the CSCE," June 5, 1973, FCO 28/2166, TNA.

15. See, e.g., "Minutes of the Meeting in Crimea," July 31, 1972, PHP, http://www .php.isn.ethz.ch/collections/colltopic.cfm?lng=en&id=16044; Frigyes Puja, "Report on the 21–22 May 1973 Meeting of the Warsaw Treaty Countries' Deputy Foreign

Ministers," May 28, 1973, PHP, http://php.isn.ethz.ch/collections/colltopic.cfm?id= 17337; State Department Interagency Task Force, "Conference on Security and Cooperation in Europe: Interim Report to the Secretary of State," March 3, 1972, RG 59, Executive Secretariat, Briefing Books 1958–1976, Box 134, NARA; White House Memorandum, "Annotated Version of the General Declaration," n.d. [April 1973], FCO 41/1308, TNA; and Letter from Sykes, UK Embassy in Washington, to Brimelow, FCO, May 22, 1973, FCO 41/1303, TNA.

16. Memorandum from Walden to Tickell, "CSCE: Human Contacts," April 16, 1973, TNA, FCO 28/2172, TNA.

17. "Speech by the Head of the Soviet Delegation (Leonid Brezhnev)," January 25, 1972, PHP, http://www.php.isn.ethz.ch/collections/colltopic.cfm?lng=en&id=17104.

18. "Speech by the General Secretary of the Bulgarian Communist Party (Todor Zhivkov)," January 25, 1972, PHP, http://www.php.isn.ethz.ch/collections/colltopic .cfm?lng=en&id=18104&navinfo=14465. "Ideological subversion" was a common Eastern European phrase to describe the West's freer movement program. See also "About Some Current Questions Concerning the Multilateral Preparations for the European Security Conference," October 18, 1972, History and Public Policy Program Digital Archive, PA AA: MfAA C 372/78, http://digitalarchive.wilsoncenter.org /document/110100, as well as the other speeches given on January 25, 1972, at the meeting of the Warsaw Pact Political Consultative Committee: "Speech by the Head of the Soviet Delegation (Leonid Brezhnev)," "Speech by the General Secretary of the Romanian Communist Party (Nicolae Ceauşescu)," "Speech by the East German Head of State (Erich Honecker)," and "Speech by the Head of the Czechoslovak Delegation to the 1972 PCC Meeting," PHP, http://www.php.isn.ethz.ch/collections/colltopic .cfm?lng=en&id=17104.

19. "Pilna Notatka w sprawie radzieckiego projektu deklaracji programowej w związku z II-gim punktem porzadku dziennego EKBiW," November 17, 1972, in Wanda Jarzabek, *Polska wobec Konferencji Bezpieczenstwa i Wspólpracy w Europie* [Poland in the Conference on Security and Cooperation in Europe] (Warsaw: Instytut Studiow Politycznych Polskiej Akademii Nauk, 2008), doc. 9; "Speech by the Head of the Czechoslovak Delegation to the 1972 PCC Meeting," January 25, 1972, PHP; "Minutes of the Meeting in Crimea," July 31, 1972, PHP; and Hungarian Foreign Ministry Memorandum, "Report on Consultations of the Deputy Foreign Ministers," November 17, 1972, PHP. http://www.php.isn.ethz.ch/collections/colltopic.cfm?lng=en&id=173 29&navinfo=15700.

20. Telegram from Elliott, UK Embassy in Helsinki, to Wiggin, UK Delegation to NATO, May 12, 1973, FCO 41/1284, TNA; Telegram from Douglas-Home, FCO, to UK Embassy in Helsinki, "Meeting of Political Directors on 14 May: CSCE: Baskets I, II and III," May 16, 1973, ibid.; and Telegram from the French Embassy in the Hague to the Quai d'Orsay, "Attitude néerlandaise à l'égard de la CSCE," July 5, 1973, Affaires Étrangères – Organismes Internationaux et Grandes Questions Internationales – Sécurité – 1971–1976 – 2926, AMAE.

21. Telegram from Elliott, UK Embassy in Helsinki, to Douglas-Home, FCO, "CSCE/MPT," May 5, 1973, FCO 41/1291, TNA.

22. "Final Recommendations of the Helsinki Consultations," June 8, 1973, in *Selected Documents*, 149–51.

23. Letter from Elliott, UK Embassy in Helsinki, to Douglas-Home, FCO, "CSCE: The First Two Hundred Days," June 13, 1973, FCO 41/1293, TNA; and Memorandum

to the Secretary of State for External Affairs, "CSCE: Conclusion of Preparatory Talks," June 6, 1973, RG-25, Vol. 9054, File 20-4-CSCE, Vol. 35, LAC.

24. Memorandum from Sous-Direction CSCE, "Note concernant les objectifs et méthodes de travail de la CSCE (Commission III)," September 5, 1973, CSCE 1969–1975, Box 21, AMAE.

25. GDR Politbüro Memorandum, "Direktive für das Auftreten der Delegation der DDR während der zweiten Phase der Konferenz für Sicherheit und Zusammenarbeit in Europa," August 21, 1973, DY 30/J IV 2/2/1464, SAPMO; and "Vorschlag der Delegationen Bulgariens und Polens die Grundrichtungen der Entwicklung der Kulturellen Zusammenarbeit, der Kontakte und des Austauschs im Bereich der Information," n.d. [August 1973], DY 30/J IV 2/2/1464, SAPMO.

26. Letter from Brezhnev to Nixon, January 9, 1974, HAK Office Files, Box 69, Nixon Presidential Materials Project, College Park, Maryland (hereafter, NPMP).

27. Kissinger-Brezhnev Memcon, March 25, 1974, HAK Office Files, Box 76, NPMP.

28. Kissinger-Brezhnev Memcon, morning of March 26, 1974, HAK Office Files, Box 76, NPMP.

29. Telegram from the Mission in Geneva to the Department of State, June 24, 1974, *FRUS 1969–1976*, Vol. XXXIX, doc. 219. In 1973, the Nixon administration hoped to reinvigorate the Atlantic Alliance and rebuff Congressional criticism of NATO by proclaiming a "Year of Europe," but the initiative did more to alienate the Western European allies than reassure them. See Keith Hamilton, "Britain, France, and America's Year of Europe, 1973," *Diplomacy and Statecraft* 17, no. 4 (2006): 871–95.

30. Minutes of Secretary of State Kissinger's Staff Meeting, October 29, 1973, *FRUS 1969–1976*, Vol. XXXIX, doc. 177.

31. Nixon-Kissinger-Gromyko Memcon, February 4, 1974, HAK Office Files, Box 71, NPMP.

32. Action Memorandum from the Acting Assistant Secretary of State for European Affairs (Stabler) to Secretary of State Kissinger, "CSCE: The 'Laws and Customs' Issue in Basket 3," June 6, 1974, *FRUS 1969–1976*, Vol. XXXIX, doc. 208.

33. Memorandum of Conversation [Kissinger-Sauvagnargues], July 4, 1974, *FRUS 1969–1976*, Vol. XXXIX, doc. 232.

34. Telegram from the Mission in Geneva to the Department of State, June 24, 1974, *FRUS 1969–1976*, Vol. XXXIX, doc. 219; Telegram from the Mission in Geneva to the Department of State, June 21, 1974, ibid., doc. 216; Telegram from the Mission in Geneva to the Department of State, June 22, 1974, ibid., doc. 218; and Telegram from the Department of State to the Mission in Geneva, June 25, 1974, ibid., doc. 220.

35. Memorandum from Tickell to Private Secretary, "CSCE: Review of Objectives," July 5, 1974, FCO 41/1547, TNA.

36. Thomas Fischer, *Neutral Power in the CSCE: The N+N States and the Making of the Helsinki Accords 1975* (Baden-Baden: Nomos, 2009), 278–91.

37. Telegram from the Mission in Geneva to the Department of State, June 25, 1974, *FRUS 1969–1976*, Vol. XXXIX, doc. 221; and Memorandum from Winzer to the Politburo, "Zum gegenwärtigen Stand der Arbeit der Sicherheitskonferenz," July 30, 1974, DY 30/J IV 2/2J/5399, SAPMO.

38. Kissinger-Gromyko Memcon, February 16, 1975, RG 59, Records of the Office of the Counselor, 1955–1977, Box 8, NARA; and Ford-Kissinger Memcon, May 26, 1975, National Security Advisor Memoranda of Conversations, 1973–1977, Box 12, Gerald R. Ford Presidential Library, Ann Arbor, Michigan.

39. Letter from Alexander, UK Mission to Geneva, to Burns, FCO, "Basket III: Human Contacts," April 25, 1975, FCO 28/2671, TNA; Memorandum from Burns to Tickell, "CSCE: State of Play," April 29, 1975, FCO 41/1769, TNA; Letter from Alexander, UK Mission to Geneva, to Burns, FCO, "Basket III: Human Contacts and Information," May 16, 1975, FCO 28/2671, TNA; and Telegram from Hildyard, UK Mission in Geneva, to Callaghan, FCO, "CSCE: State of Play," June 7, 1975, FCO 41/1769, TNA. See also Marie-Pierre Rey, "The USSR and the Helsinki Process, 1969–75: Optimism, Doubt, or Defiance?" in Wenger, Mastny, and Nuenlist, *Origins of the European Security System*, 74–75.

40. "Opening Remarks by the Under-Secretary: Statement on East-West Relations," November 4, 1969, RG 59, Executive Secretariat, Briefing Books 1958–1976, Box 65; and Pompidou-Brandt Memcon, January 30, 1970; Schumann–Douglas-Home Memcon, July 15, 1970, Secrétariat général – Entretiens et Messages – Vol. 44, AMAE.

41. Memorandum from Kissinger to Nixon, "European Security Conference," October 19, 1970, HAK Office Files, Box 71, NPMP; Letter from Bridges, FCO, to Scott, UK Embassy in Moscow, "East-West Relations and MBFRs," July 23, 1971, FCO 41/833, TNA.

42. Minutes of a Senior Review Group Meeting, May 14, 1971, *FRUS 1969–1976*, Vol. XXXIX, doc. 48. See also Andreas Wenger, "Crisis and Opportunity: NATO's Transformation and the Multilateralization of Détente, 1966–1968," *Journal of Cold War Studies* 6, no. 1 (2004): 59; and Raymond Garthoff, *Détente and Confrontation: American-Soviet Relations from Nixon to Reagan* (Washington, DC: Brookings Institution Press, 1985), 114–15.

43. Johan Jørgen Holst and Karen Alette Melander, "European Security and Confidence-Building Measures," *Survival* 19, no. 4 (1977): 146–54; and Aurel Braun, "Confidence-Building Measures, Security, and Disarmament," in *Canada and the Conference on Security and Co-operation in Europe*, ed. Robert Spencer (Toronto: Centre for International Studies, 1984), 202–27.

44. On the rationale for Eisenhower's Open Skies proposal, see James J. Marquardt, "Transparency and Security Competition: Open Skies and America's Cold War Statecraft, 1948–1960," *Journal of Cold War Studies* 9, no. 1 (2007): 55–87; and David Tal, "From the Open Skies Proposal of 1955 to the Norstad Plan of 1960: A Plan Too Far," *Journal of Cold War Studies* 10, no. 4 (2008): 66–93.

45. See, e.g., Minute by Crispin Tickell, May 23, 1972, *Documents on British Policy Overseas* (hereafter, DBPO) Series III, Vol. 2: *The Conference on Security and Co-operation in Europe, 1972–1975* (London: The Stationery Office, 1997), doc. 9.

46. Anatoly Dobrynin Memorandum, "Talking Points with Dr. Kissinger (all-European conference)," n.d. [January 16, 1973], HAK Office Files, Box 70, NPMP; and Letter from Elliott, Geneva, to Douglas-Home, FCO, February 10, 1973, DBPO, Series III, Vol. 2, doc. 21.

47. Letter from Burns, FCO, to Adams, FCO, October 1, 1973, DBPO, doc. 48, footnote 12.

48. Memorandum from Tickell to Wiggin, Killick, and Private Secretary, December 20, 1973, FCO 41/1324, TNA.

49. Kissinger-Gromyko Memcon, February 4, 1974, HAK Office Files, Box 71, NPMP.

50. Ibid.

51. Telegram from the Department of State to Secretary of State Kissinger in Jerusalem, May 23, 1974, *FRUS 1969–1976*, Vol. XXXIX, doc. 205; and Telegram from

Elliott, Geneva, to FCO, "CSCE: General Situation: Political Directors Meeting in Bonn 27–28 May," May 22, 1974, FCO 28/2456, TNA.

52. Memorandum from Tickell to Private Secretary, "CSCE: Confidence-Building Measures," January 24, 1975, FCO 41/1755, TNA.

53. Ibid.

54. Fischer, *Neutral Power*, 298–307.

55. Letter from Hildyard, Geneva, to Callaghan, FCO, "CSCE: The Conclusion of Stage II," July 25, 1975, FCO 41/1769, TNA.

56. Telegram from Callaghan, FCO, to Certain Missions, "Conference on Security and Co-operation (CSCE)," July 28, 1975, FCO 66/793, TNA.

6. Trust or Verification? Accepting Vulnerability in the Making of the INF Treaty

Nicholas J. Wheeler, Joshua Baker, and Laura Considine[1]

In December 1987, US president Ronald Reagan and his Soviet counterpart General Secretary Mikhail Gorbachev met in Washington to sign a treaty abolishing an entire class of nuclear weapons. In the press conference before its signing, Reagan declared that the treaty reflected the wisdom in the old Russian proverb "*dovorey no provorey*—trust, but verify." With regard to the verification provisions of the treaty, Reagan claimed that "[t]his agreement contains the most stringent verification regime in history, including provisions for inspection teams actually residing in each other's territory and several other forms of onsite inspection."[2] The implication of Reagan's statement was that the signing and eventual implementation of the Intermediate-Range Nuclear Forces (INF) Treaty had become possible between two distrusting adversaries because it combined both trust and the promise of intrusive verification, and that without either of these elements there would have been no treaty. It also made clear that Reagan viewed trust and verification as distinct but complementary concepts. But these propositions raise the question left unanswered in Reagan's statement (and indeed in the Russian proverb) as to the causal relationship between trust and verification. Put differently, is trust a requisite for the agreement and implementation of verification regimes, or is verification merely a surrogate for the lack of trust?

The authors are grateful to Marcus Holmes, David Morris, and Dani Nedal for their comments on an earlier version of the chapter, and to the editors and the reviewers. They also thank Simon Copeland for his assistance in preparing the final bibliography.

To answer this question, the chapter sets up two competing approaches for conceiving the causal relationship between trust and verification, both of which challenge Reagan's notion that trust and verification are distinct but complementary ideas. The first approach conceives the relationship between trust and verification as an inverse one; the greater the level of verification that is sought, the lower the level of trust between two antagonistic states. In the case of the INF Treaty, this approach would hold that the intrusive verification mechanisms were themselves indicators of the lack of trust between the United States and the Soviet Union. Consequently, the argument goes, it is a misnomer to think in terms of "trust, but verify" because verification is itself a substitute for trust. In such a scenario, a verification regime would have to be established because the parties have no trust in each other. This logic has recently been at play in US-Iran interactions, where the Obama administration has sought to sell the 2015 Iran nuclear deal by stating that it is based on verification and not trust.[3] Obama administration officials have repeatedly demonstrated an example of the "surrogate" argument by stating that an intrusive, foolproof verification arrangement is needed because the US government cannot rely on trust in securing Iran's compliance with the terms of the deal.[4]

The second approach to understanding the relationship between trust and verification considers that states will agree to intrusive methods of verification only if they have expectations as to the other party's trustworthiness. Verification therefore is not a surrogate for trust, but in fact is highly reliant on the preexistence of trust, because implementing intrusive verification regimes (such as the INF Treaty) makes leaders vulnerable in multiple ways. As a result, this willingness to accept vulnerability is a key indicator that one party believes that the other potentially is trustworthy. Trust and verification are not, therefore, distinct but complementary concepts, as Reagan contended. Instead, they exist in a symbiotic relationship where each is dependent on the other if arms control agreements are to be successful. This chapter argues that it is this latter approach that best explains how the INF Treaty became possible, and it will show how Soviet perceptions, and crucially Gorbachev's, changed as to US (and crucially Reagan's) trustworthiness. It also shows how this approach to the INF Treaty reveals the limitations of the "trust, but verify" formulation, because Gorbachev's decision to enter into new and highly stringent verification arrangements was dependent on this expectation of Reagan's trustworthiness.

Trust and Verification during the Cold War

The dominant US approach to verification during the Cold War resembled the first of the two approaches outlined above. The US government assumed that verification was an essential component of arms control treaties because the Soviet Union could not be trusted to honor its agreements. The assumption was that when Moscow signed a treaty, its leaders did so in the firm knowledge that they would cheat on it, or for that matter, even if the current intentions of Soviet leaders were to comply, this could change in the future.[5] To prevent either of these outcomes, the US government demanded highly intrusive forms of verification.

The purpose of verification is to monitor a party's compliance with an agreement or treaty. Monitoring is crucial to verification because it is the process by which information is obtained to make assessments about whether others are complying or not. In the field of nuclear arms control and disarmament, non-compliance must be detected timely enough so that the other party or parties can either individually or collectively respond to militarily significant violations. What is deemed a militarily significant violation cannot be determined in the abstract, and it will depend upon the perceptions of decision-makers as to the risks and costs of any future breakout. Policymakers have to decide whether cheating has taken place, and if so, whether this cheating has exposed their state to a significantly increased risk of attack.

The issue of whether the Soviet Union had cheated on arms control agreements with the United States became highly politicized in the late 1970s and early 1980s. The Reagan administration charged Moscow in the early and mid-1980s with violating the 1972 Interim Agreement on Strategic Arms (SALT I) and the Anti-Ballistic Missile (ABM) Treaty, both of which they had signed in 1972. It was an article of faith among the "ideological fundamentalists"[6] driving US policy in the early 1980s that even if there was no direct evidence of Soviet cheating, it should be assumed that, given the Marxist-Leninist character of the Soviet state, Moscow's apparent compliance hid the real cheating that was taking place.[7] As such, even a pattern of Soviet compliance was interpreted by the first Reagan administration as Moscow's mimicking signals of trustworthiness to disguise its treaty violations. As Allan Krass wrote in 1985, "Under these assumptions it is, of course, impossible to imagine verification leading to a growth of trust. It will in fact lead only to demands for even more verification and even greater distrust."[8]

On the surface, the Soviet Union appears to have adopted a very different view to that of the United States on the question of the relationship between trust and verification. Rather than see verification as a surrogate for trust, Soviet negotiators have argued, in the words of Viktor Israelyan (when speaking to the Geneva-based Committee on Disarmament in 1981), that verification "should not be built upon the principle of total distrust by states of one another and should not take the form of global suspiciousness."[9] Instead, as Roland Timerbaev (then a senior official in the Soviet Foreign Ministry) contended in his 1983 book on verification, the Soviet view was that "[a] greements for restraining the arms race must be based on a certain degree of mutual trust among the parties to the agreements."[10] This chapter provides support for this view, arguing that the INF Treaty became possible because of the trust that was built between the two sides before the treaty was signed. The problem with US and Soviet thinking in the early 1980s was that both superpowers believed that the other had shown by its actions that it could not be trusted, and as a result, each believed the other would necessarily cheat on any arms control agreement. It was this deadlock in superpower relations that Gorbachev was to break, and he did so by developing a belief in the trustworthiness of his US counterpart that opened the door to new conciliatory actions, including the signing of the INF Treaty. Before turning to this story of changing perceptions of US and Soviet trustworthiness, it is necessary to provide the conceptual scaffolding to support this argument.

Trust, Trustworthiness, and Vulnerability

In emerging trusting relationships, the key litmus test of whether actors believe that another actor can be trusted, and the extent of that trust, is their willingness to accept new vulnerabilities and/or to live with existing ones. Aaron Hoffman similarly defined trust as "an attitude involving a willingness to place the fate of one's interests under the control of others in a particular context. This willingness is based on the belief, for which there is some uncertainty, that potential trustees will protect the interests placed in their control, even if they must sacrifice some of their own interests in doing so."[11] In this definition, Hoffman applied to international relations theory the standard cross-disciplinary definition of trust summed up by Denise Rousseau and her co-researchers in 1998: trust is "a psychological state comprising the intention to accept vulnerability based upon positive expectations of the intentions or behavior of another."[12] But Hoffman wanted to go beyond this psychological approach to trust and argue that what is important is whether actors act on this trust, not simply whether they intend to do so as in the abovementioned definition.[13] The key action that begins a trust-building process is the acceptance of vulnerability on the part of one or both parties.

This approach can be located within the cross-disciplinary literature in trust research that puts vulnerability at the heart of understanding and analyzing processes of trust-building. The paradox of vulnerability as a property of trust is that actors only take on the risks of making themselves vulnerable because they do not expect to be exploited. As the moral philosopher Annette Baier has expressed, "Trust *is acceptance* of vulnerability to harm that others could inflict, but which we judge that they will not in fact inflict."[14] Given the importance of vulnerability to this conceptualization of trust, it is necessary to make two important clarifications. The first is that an actor's acceptance of vulnerability—because they "judge" that the other will not harm them—does not mean that their judgment is necessarily correct. The existential reality might differ fundamentally from the actors' subjective perception. As the trust researcher Barbara Misztal has put it, "talking about vulnerability means taking into account subjective perception of a given situation, not only referring to objective or external risks."[15] In short, there is no objective measure of vulnerability against which to judge the behavior of the actors concerned.

This statement leads into the second point, which is that actors take on vulnerability in at least two different dimensions when they trust. The first relates to the concept of *trust as authenticity*, which refers to the idea that the trusting party (the trustor)—who takes on vulnerability—believes that the other party (the trustee) does not have malevolent intentions toward them or their state. The second is what we call *trust as capacity*, which can be defined as the belief on the part of the trustor that the trustee can deliver on their promises and commitments. Even if one actor believes in the authenticity of another, there could be uncertainty as to how far a trusted counterpart can deliver on their promises, given the tumultuous nature of domestic politics. Vulnerability, then, can be experienced in different ways and on different levels in an emerging trusting relationship.

This argument challenges the proposition of Vincent Keating and Jan Ruzicka, two prominent trust researchers in international relations, who have argued that trust and vulnerability are incompatible: "Actors in a trusting relationship will have little to no feeling of vulnerability precisely because trust functions to cognitively reduce or eliminate their perception of risk in the situation."[16] For them, the acceptance of vulnerability is not an indicator of trust because "the existence of a trusting relationship means that vulnerability is not knowingly experienced by the actor."[17] Admittedly, in established trusting relationships, such as that between the United Kingdom and the United States, actors may not always experience vulnerability consciously, yet Keating and Ruzicka's formulation fails to capture a situation where actors knowingly experience vulnerability but are not troubled in doing so because they trust the other party. Indeed, by writing vulnerability out of the story, Keating and Ruzicka neglect to see that, as Misztal puts it, "the act of trust needs to be seen as offering both a solution to the problem of our vulnerability, and as exposing us to more risks."[18] In highly embedded trusting relationships,[19] it is possible that habits and practices of trust can develop that do not rest on specific personal relationships of trust. However, in emerging trusting relationships such as between the US and Soviet leaderships in the mid-to-late 1980s, the development of trust can be so intrinsically tied to the interpersonal level that subjective feelings of vulnerability—both in terms of authenticity and capacity—may play a far greater role. Gorbachev, on the basis of increasingly positive expectations about Reagan's motives and intentions, took specific actions aimed at signaling the Soviet Union's trustworthiness that entailed accepting some degree of vulnerability.

Gorbachev's Changing Perceptions of Trustworthiness

When negotiations over reducing or eliminating the superpowers' INF forces began in 1982, there were few expectations of a breakthrough, given the deep enmity between the two sides. After the North Atlantic Treaty Organization (NATO) followed through on its 1979 decision to deploy US Cruise missiles to US bases in the United Kingdom and the Netherlands, and the US Pershing II missiles to US bases in the Federal Republic of Germany, the Soviet Union responded by walking out of all arms control negotiations. Although Moscow eventually returned to the negotiating table in March 1985, both sides continued to treat the negotiations as a continuation of their seemingly enduring competition. Yet just two years later, the frozen hostility of the Cold War was melting away in a manner that previously would have been unthinkable, and a key moment in this process was the signing of the INF Treaty in December 1987. A necessary (but not sufficient) condition of the INF Treaty was Gorbachev's changed perception of Reagan's trustworthiness, and crucial to this transformation was the personal trust that developed between Reagan and Gorbachev, as well as among their key advisors.

Reagan initially was hesitant about the possibility that Gorbachev would significantly change Soviet security and defense policy. As noted earlier, the first Reagan administration believed that the Soviet Union had persistently exploited previous arms control agreements. In an internal memorandum, Reagan stated that he anticipated no change in the underlying behavior of the new Soviet leader, who he saw as "totally dedicated to traditional Soviet goals."[20] Similarly, there was little optimism on the Soviet side about a thaw in relations. Pavel Palazchenko, the long-serving interpreter to Gorbachev and Soviet foreign minister Eduard Shevardnadze, depicted the atmosphere at the time as "quite pessimistic about the prospects of U.S.-Soviet relations, at least while Ronald Reagan was in office."[21] The prevailing mood was therefore not conducive to a departure from the "confrontational policies" of the past.[22]

However, the traditional practice of US-Soviet enemy imaging conflicted with Gorbachev's own conviction that the superpowers were caught in a spiral of fear and mistrust that was feeding an ever-escalating armaments competition. Gorbachev was strongly influenced by a group of key advisors within his inner circle that included Alexander Yakovlev, Anatoly Chernyaev, and Shevardnadze (who replaced Andrei Gromyko as foreign minister in 1985). These "new thinkers" pressed upon him the proposition that the only security in the nuclear age was mutual, what the 1983 Palme Commission had called "common security"—the notion that security should be achieved in common or not at all. Gorbachev officially expressed these ideas in February 1986 in a speech to the 27th Party Congress. In this speech, he outlined the necessity for a demilitarization of the US-Soviet relationship and the normalization of Soviet relations with the rest of the world, stating that "[e]qual security is the imperative of the times. Ensuring this security is becoming increasingly a political issue, one that can be resolved only by political means. It is high time to replace weapons by a more stable foundation for the relations among states."[23]

The new Soviet thinking on security showed an awareness of how both superpowers might be ensnared in what has been termed "security dilemma dynamics": hostility driven by mutual fear and not predatory ambition.[24] Gorbachev and his key advisors appreciated that even though the Soviet Union might profess defensive motives and intent, its enemies were not so easily reassured in the face of Soviet conventional capabilities that were configured for offensive operations against NATO forces. Gorbachev rejected the "ideological fundamentalism" that depicted the United States and its allies as inherently aggressive by virtue of their capitalist values and interests, and acknowledged that Soviet actions had created legitimate Western fears as to whether the Soviet Union had malign intent. Consequently, Gorbachev began developing new policies of common security that were designed to reassure the United States and NATO about the peaceful, defensive motives and intentions of the Soviet Union. An example of this shift in thinking can be seen in Gorbachev's discussions before the Reykjavik meeting, where he states that "nothing will come out of it if our proposals lead to a weakening of US security. The Americans will never agree to it. Thus, the principle is as follows: increased security for all on the way toward equal reduction of armaments levels."[25] Here, Gorbachev exercised what Booth and Wheeler have called "security dilemma sensibility," which is "an actor's intention and capacity to perceive the motives behind, and to show responsiveness towards, the potential complexity of the military intentions of others. In particular, it refers to the ability to understand the role that fear might play in their attitudes and behaviour, including, crucially, the role that one's own actions may play in provoking that fear."[26]

It was one thing to cognitively frame the US-Soviet conflict as an example of security dilemma dynamics, but it was quite another to make this empathetic awareness the basis of new Soviet trust-building initiatives, given the risk that the US government might exploit such policies. What appears to have been crucial in leading Gorbachev to act on this empathy and accept a new measure of vulnerability was the trust he placed in Reagan. The initial step on this journey was his first summit meeting with Reagan in Geneva in November 1985. Those involved in the summit meeting later stressed how important it had been in encouraging the two leaders to believe that they could work with each other.[27] Gorbachev himself recalled that "our dialogue was very constructive . . . and increasingly friendly the better we got to know each other."[28] The most important outcome of the summit was that each pledged that neither side would "seek military superiority."[29] This was a decisive rejection of the nuclear war-fighting policies that had characterized the first Reagan administration, and an acknowledgment of the reality that the only security in the nuclear age was common security.

The now declassified transcripts of the Geneva meeting reveal Reagan's and Gorbachev's awareness of the role that trust could play in improving US-Soviet relations. Both leaders spoke of the importance of increasing political dialogue at all levels and expanding opportunities for trade as a means of achieving increased trust.[30] Shortly after the Geneva summit, Anatoly Chernyaev, deputy head of the International Department of the Communist Party of the Soviet Union, observed in his diary that "something cardinal has occurred: the arms race is going on, nothing has changed in the military confrontation, but a turning point is noticeable in international relations."[31] Although it would be naive to think that one summit meeting could reverse decades of suspicion and animosity, the meeting went some way to convincing Gorbachev that he could work with Reagan. Moreover, it seems that Gorbachev increasingly appreciated that if trust were to be built between the leaders of the United States and the Soviet Union, this change would require more than declarations of good intentions. What was needed beyond such declarations were concrete actions that could begin to break down the "barrier of mistrust."[32]

Gorbachev's first attempt to let his actions speak louder than his words was his proposal on January 15, 1986, for global nuclear disarmament by the year 2000. However, he was disappointed by the US rejection of his disarmament vision and by what he saw as Reagan's continuing bellicose rhetoric.[33] Chernyaev describes a feeling at the time among Gorbachev and his closest advisors that the "hand [Gorbachev] extended was left suspended in mid-air."[34] The Chernobyl nuclear disaster three months later reinforced Gorbachev's developing belief that, in Soviet physicist Yevgeny Velikhov's words, "a great instinctive leap to break the old cycle"[35] of mistrust, suspicion, and secrecy in East-West negotiations was required. Gorbachev's first "leap" occurred the following month. In the face of strong opposition from "the General Staff, the Ministry of Defense, and the KGB,"[36] he instructed his chief negotiator, Ambassador Oleg Grinevsky, at the deadlocked Stockholm Conference on Confidence- and Security-Building Measures and Disarmament in Europe to accept unprecedented on-site inspections.[37] This concession was highly significant, not only because it made possible the signing of a new treaty that increased military transparency on both sides but also because it held out the promise that Moscow might be prepared to accept an equally demanding standard of verification in the nuclear arena.

Whether Gorbachev's willingness to accept on-site inspections in Stockholm would have still occurred in the absence of his first face-to-face encounter with Reagan in Geneva the previous November is a fascinating counterfactual. As noted above, Gorbachev was disappointed with the US response to his January 1986 disarmament proposal, and he was looking for more evidence that Reagan could be a partner in the task of ending the nuclear arms race. He was eager to meet Reagan again and proposed a meeting in Reykjavik.[38]

The two leaders came tantalizingly close to agreeing on the abolition of all nuclear weapons during their two days of negotiations in Iceland. But what stood in the way of the two leaders reaching such a momentous agreement was Reagan's insistence that nuclear disarmament proceed in tandem with the development and testing of the proposed US missile defense shield, the Strategic Defense Initiative (SDI). Reagan had announced his dream of protecting the US public from Soviet nuclear missiles in March 1983, and he remained fervently committed to the development of SDI at Reykjavik. Despite Reagan's and Gorbachev's failure to reach an agreement, the meeting was a crucial moment in the building of trust between the two leaders. Gorbachev reflected in 1992 to George Shultz that Reykjavik was the turning point in bringing about the end of the Cold War.[39] This opinion was confirmed by Chernyaev, who considered that "[a] spark of understanding was born between them, as if they had winked to each other about the future."[40] Such sentiments were shared by Reagan, who wrote in his memoirs that "[l]ooking back now, it's clear there was a chemistry between Gorbachev and me that produced something very close to a friendship."[41]

Gorbachev was disappointed with Reagan's subsequent response to his far-reaching arms reduction proposals at Reykjavik.[42] However, he made a crucial distinction after the summit between Reagan and his inner circle's motives and intentions, which he saw as peaceful and defensive, and the position of the hawks in Washington, who he considered had not given up the quest for nuclear superiority. For the hawks, Gorbachev reasoned, SDI could not be traded away because it was a critical component in their bid for a first-strike strategy. According to Anatoly Dobrynin, the veteran Soviet ambassador to the United States, Gorbachev told him after he returned from Reykjavik that "he could work with Reagan" and that he "saw in him a person capable of taking great decisions."[43] This view is supported by Chernyaev, who claimed that, after Reykjavik, Gorbachev began to think that in Reagan he had a partner with whom he could work to lead the world away from the abyss of nuclear destruction.[44] Rather than viewing Reagan as a representative of "US imperialism," Gorbachev, in Andrei Grachev's words, began to view him "as a trustworthy partner, who shared similar hopes and ideas."[45] After Reykjavik, Gorbachev began to put this conviction to the test, and in doing so showed his willingness to accept an increased level of vulnerability for both himself and the Soviet Union.

Gorbachev's Vulnerability in the Making of the INF Treaty

Gorbachev was anxious to turn the positive atmospherics that had developed between him and Reagan in Iceland into concrete agreements that would limit US-Soviet nuclear competition. To this end, he took some key decisions during 1987 that only became possible because he had come to believe that he could trust Reagan and his inner circle. As noted at the beginning of the chapter, it is in the nature of trust that actors only accept vulnerability when they have strong expectations that their trust will not be exploited. There is, however, always a degree of uncertainty in this regard. The unilateral trust-building steps taken by Gorbachev in 1987 indicate that he judged that his trust would not be exploited; yet he still made himself vulnerable in a number of interrelated ways.

The first major conciliatory move came in February 1987 when Gorbachev proposed delinking intermediate-range nuclear forces from SDI.[46] He confirmed this proposition at a meeting in April 1987 in Moscow with Shultz.[47] Gorbachev, writing in his memoirs in 1996, described this meeting as a "milestone."[48] He reflected that he had gained the impression, strengthened by Shultz's subsequent actions, that Shultz was a US policymaker who "genuinely wanted to sustain the dialogue" and who was prepared to work to transform "our agreement in principle into productive cooperation."[49] Interestingly, however, the accounts of this meeting at the time tell a different story. In his report to the Politburo, Gorbachev expressed his disappointment with Shultz for not reciprocating Soviet concessions and failing to bring anything new to the table. At the time, he explained this failing as Shultz being "too closely connected to the military-industrial complex."[50] From the memorandum of their conversation, it appears that Gorbachev felt let down that Shultz had not brought any concrete ideas to this meeting for further action following the Soviet Union's delinking proposal. Nevertheless, another major concession came in June 1987 when the Soviet Union finally agreed to on-site inspections of INF missile manufacturing and storage sites. And the third occurred the following month when Gorbachev proposed the global "double-zero" option that authorized the removal of all INF and short-range intermediate nuclear forces systems from both Europe and Asia.[51] These three concessions removed the obstacles to the signing of the INF Treaty, which Gorbachev claimed in his memoirs represented "the first well-prepared step on our way out of the Cold War."[52]

These moves that were so crucial in leading to the INF Treaty made Gorbachev increasingly vulnerable on several grounds. Even if Gorbachev had faith in the *authenticity* of Reagan and Shultz, and believed that they would not willingly and knowingly exploit his trusting moves, it was less clear to Gorbachev that they had the *capacity* to follow through with what they had agreed. Reagan was increasingly beleaguered in domestic battles at home; the Republicans had lost control of the US Senate in the November 1986 congressional elections, and the presidency increasingly was mired in the Iran-Contra scandal. Consequently, Gorbachev knew that there was a risk that Reagan, with less than two years left in office, might not be capable of delivering an agreement on strategic nuclear arms even if he wanted to do so.[53] This uncertainty in turn made Gorbachev politically vulnerable in the Soviet Union. If the INF Treaty negotiations had ultimately failed and Gorbachev had nothing to show for making these dramatic concessions, he would have been exposed to those hard-liners who continued to believe in the malign intent of the US government. Gorbachev was therefore becoming increasingly worried that Reagan was losing ground to the hard-liners in his own administration, and his uneasiness in this regard was made clear in the April 1987 meeting with Shultz, where he lamented the lack of US reciprocation of his delinking move by stating that "the position of the U.S. administration is one of very real extortion from its partner, it is a position of treating its partner disrespectfully."[54]

The proposition advanced in this chapter that Gorbachev's trust in Reagan played a pivotal role in making possible the INF Treaty runs up against the objection that Gorbachev had no choice but to cooperate, given the Soviet Union's desperate economic situation. Given the weaknesses of the Soviet economy, some scholars have argued that any Soviet leader at this time would have been compelled to make concessions in the way Gorbachev did.[55] Such a position, however, downplays the significance of Gorbachev's new thinking and his exercise of security dilemma sensibility in the transformation of US-Soviet relations. The material pressures exerted by a declining economy were important enabling conditions of Gorbachev's actions, and it is difficult to imagine that he could have secured domestic support for his new thinking had the Soviet Union not been so materially weak. But what is crucial to this argument is that material factors were insufficient by themselves to explain the trust-building actions that Gorbachev took in 1986 and 1987.[56]

The road of conciliation and cooperation was not the only one that the Soviet Union could have taken at this time, and Gorbachev's actions were not an inevitable response to the material pressures that the Soviet Union faced. Such a view finds support from Chernyaev, who asserted in a later interview that the influence of domestic economic pressures, though important, "does not definitively capture Gorbachev's motives," which also included his awareness of the potential devastation of nuclear war, his personal moral principles, and his belief that no one would attack the Soviet Union.[57] There were indeed others at that time—such as Victor Grishin and Grigory Romanov, the closest contenders with Gorbachev in 1985 for the Soviet leadership—who most likely would have adopted a more competitive approach to the US-Soviet relationship.[58] Robert English has maintained that the most likely outcome in the 1985 leadership competition in the Kremlin was a further continuation of East-West confrontation. The fact that a different course was chosen, English states, "was thanks to the singular influence of ideas and the singular leadership of Gorbachev."[59] Richard Ned Lebow and George Breslauer use counterfactual methods to likewise argue that if Grishin had been elected, it would be hard to imagine a similar process of deescalation.[60]

One striking aspect of the concessions that Gorbachev made in 1986 and 1987 is that there was no equivalent reciprocation on the part of the US government. Yet Gorbachev persisted in making progressively more significant concessions, especially after Reykjavik, despite knowing that some Politburo conservatives advocated confronting the United States.[61] Against these critics, Gorbachev insisted that to retreat from cooperation would strengthen the hands of the conservatives in the Reagan administration, which would escalate the arms competition, increase the risks of war, and place enormous strain on the Soviet economy. The Reagan administration did not positively reciprocate Gorbachev's moves, but it did not do anything to exploit them. Ken Booth and John Baylis have made an important distinction between "positive reciprocation" and "negative reciprocation." Positive reciprocation refers to actions taken in direct response to a conciliatory move that reward the initiating state with an equivalent concession. By contrast, in negative reciprocation the state that is rewarded with the initial concession does not seek to take advantage of the initiating state's move by taking steps that would make the initiating state less secure.[62]

Abraham Sofaer, then the legal advisor to George Shultz, reflected at a 2006 conference to mark the twentieth anniversary of Reykjavik that even though the Reagan administration did not engage in large-scale gestures, it did adopt three principles of action in response to Gorbachev's concessions. These were "regime acceptance" (the administration would not try to overthrow or undermine the legitimacy of the Soviet system), "limited linkage" (the US government would continue negotiations on arms control issues, despite differences in other areas such as human rights or espionage), and "rhetorical restraint" (promising not to publicly "crow" over any favorable Soviet actions).[63] US negative reciprocation of this kind was sufficient to reinforce Gorbachev's confidence that the Reagan administration would not exploit future conciliatory moves. Writing in 2007, Sofaer considered that "[t]he increased trust that Gorbachev and . . . Shevardnadze developed for Reagan and Shultz was based . . . on confidence that no effort would be made to challenge the legal legitimacy of the Soviet regime, that both sides would avoid linking their many differences, and that Soviet leaders would not be publicly embarrassed when they took actions favored by the United States."[64]

The claim that Gorbachev's trust in Reagan was pivotal to the making of the INF Treaty depends on the proposition that Gorbachev chose to accept a new level of vulnerability as a consequence of his developing belief in Reagan's trustworthiness. Gorbachev did accept a certain level of vulnerability in terms of *capacity*; the risk being that a politically weakened Reagan would not prove capable of delivering on his promises. However, there is also evidence that the Soviet Union's concessions also entailed a certain level of vulnerability in terms of *authenticity*. The argument has been made by a number of scholars that the Soviet Union's concessions were materially meaningless because their nuclear weapons capabilities gave them a "margin of safety" that allowed them to make these moves without decreasing their security.[65] What these arguments miss, however, is that what counts as an acceptable level of vulnerability is not fixed and should not be judged in the abstract.[66] It is, instead, the subject of political contestation and bureaucratic battles, and is decided upon subjectively by the actors themselves. An acceptable level of vulnerability for one actor may be very different for another. This difference is important to recognize: despite the "safety blanket" contention, some within the Soviet leadership, especially in the military, perceived Gorbachev's unilateral conciliatory moves as increasing the vulnerability of the Soviet state to potential US exploitation. As noted earlier, the move to agree to on-site inspections at the Stockholm conference, for instance, was strongly opposed by the defense establishment and the intelligence services.[67] According to ambassadors Lynn Hansen and Oleg Grinevsky, the US and Soviet representatives at the Stockholm conference, emotions had run high over this issue within the Soviet leadership; during the Politburo meetings on the topic, Marshal Sergey Akhromeyev, chief of the general staff and advisor to Gorbachev, repeatedly accused Grinevsky (who was in favor of agreeing to the inspections) as being guilty of "state treason."[68] Gorbachev's unilateral concessions were not made through a feeling of invulnerability, but rather through a belief he could trust in Reagan's *authenticity* not to exploit the Soviet Union's conciliatory moves.

Conclusion

Without Gorbachev's decision to apply the principle of on-site inspections to the issue of INF, there would have been no treaty in December 1987. Gorbachev's agreement constituted a trust-building action—one that entails an acceptance of vulnerability. Such an acceptance depended upon Gorbachev's belief that Reagan could be trusted not to exploit a conciliatory move of this kind. Gorbachev's confidence emerged from the interpersonal dynamics that had developed between him and Reagan between 1985 and 1987. Space has precluded a fuller discussion of how the face-to-face encounters between Reagan and Gorbachev and their officials built a climate of mutual trust.[69] But without Gorbachev's changed perception of Reagan's trustworthiness, Gorbachev would not have been willing to accept the vulnerabilities—both to himself and, to a lesser degree, the Soviet state—that came with the concessions that made the INF Treaty possible. This newfound trust in Reagan not only led to the signing of the treaty between the two leaders on the White House lawn in 1987, but it also facilitated a successful verification regime that endured beyond their leaderships.

The proposition that Gorbachev's acceptance of stringent INF verification measures was a trust-building action reveals the limitations of Reagan's framing of the INF Treaty in terms of "trust, but verify." In the case of INF, verification did not simply operate as complementary to trust; the Soviet agreement to accept on-site inspections was dependent on prior changes in Gorbachev's perceptions of Reagan's trustworthiness. The problem with Reagan's use of "trust, but verify" was that it appeared to present these two concepts as dichotomous. Such an understanding fails to recognize that, in some contexts, decisions to accept more intrusive forms of verification might themselves be acts that depend on a prior level of trust and contribute, in turn, to increasing that trust.[70] At the same time, the developing trust between Reagan and Gorbachev was not sufficient to obviate the US or Soviet requirements for highly intrusive verification provisions. Even if Reagan and Gorbachev trusted in each other's *authenticity* on the INF issue, they could not have carried, in the absence of these provisions, those within their governments who remained deeply suspicious of the other leader's intentions.

Notes

1. The chapter was originally presented by Wheeler and Considine at the "'Trust but Verify': Confidence and Distrust from Détente to the End of the Cold War" conference, organized by the German Historical Institute and held at the Woodrow Wilson International Center for Scholars, Washington, D.C., November 7–9, 2011. The chapter has been updated to take into account later work by Wheeler, especially his forthcoming book *Trusting Enemies* (Oxford University Press, 2017), and the chapter has been finalized with the addition of Joshua Baker.

2. Ronald Reagan, "Remarks on Signing the Intermediate-Range Nuclear Forces Treaty at the White House," December 8, 1987, Ronald Reagan Presidential Library and Museum, University of Texas, Austin, http://www.reagan.utexas.edu/archives/speeches/1987/120887c.htm.

3. For example, as US secretary of state John Kerry said, "There is a not a single sentence, not a single paragraph in this whole agreement that depends on promises or trust, not one. The arrangement that we worked out with Tehran is based exclusively on verification and proof." John Kerry, "Remarks on Nuclear Agreement with Iran," US Department of State, September 2, 2015, http://www.state.gov/secretary/remarks/2015/09/246574.htm.

4. Barack Obama, "Statement by the President on Iran," White House Press Office, July 14, 2015, https://www.whitehouse.gov/the-press-office/2015/07/14/statement-president-iran.

5. Allan S. Krass, *Verification: How Much is Enough?* (Stockholm: Stockholm International Peace Research Institute, 1985), 161.

6. The concept of ideological fundamentalism is defined by Ken Booth and Nicholas Wheeler as a mindset of decision-makers that "assigns enemy status because of what the other is—its political identity—rather than how it actually behaves." Ken Booth and Nicholas J. Wheeler, *The Security Dilemma: Fear, Cooperation, and Trust in World Politics* (Basingstoke, UK: Palgrave Macmillan, 2008), 64–65.

7. Allan S. Krass, "Focus on: Verification and Trust in Arms Control," *Journal of Peace Research* 22, no. 4 (1985), 286.

8. Ibid., 286.

9. Quoted in Krass, *Verification*, 161.

10. Quoted in Warren Heckrotte, "A Soviet View of Verification," *Bulletin of the Atomic Scientists* 43, no. 2 (1987): 12–15. Timerbaev's original account is *Verification of Arms Control and of Disarmament* (Moscow: International Relations Publishers, 1983).

11. Aaron M. Hoffman, *Building Trust: Overcoming Suspicion in International Conflict* (New York: State University of New York Press, 2006), 17.

12. Denise M. Rousseau, Sim B. Sitkin, Ronald S. Burt, and Colin Camerer, "Not So Different After All: A Cross-Discipline View of Trust," *Academy of Management Review* 23, no. 3 (1998), 395.

13. Hoffman, *Building Trust*, 17.

14. Annette Baier, *Moral Prejudices: Essays on Ethics* (Cambridge, MA: Harvard University Press, 1995), 152 (emphasis added).

15. Barbara A. Misztal, "Trust: Acceptance of, Precaution Against and Cause of Vulnerability," *Comparative Sociology* 10, no. 3 (2011), 364.

16. Vincent Charles Keating and Jan Ruzicka, "Trusting Relationships in International Politics: No Need to Hedge," *Review of International Studies* 40, no. 4 (2014), 7.

17. Ibid.

18. Misztal, "Trust," 364–65.

19. Booth and Wheeler, *The Security Dilemma*, 197–200.

20. Quoted in Jack F. Matlock Jr., *Reagan and Gorbachev: How the Cold War Ended* (London: Random House, 2004), 150. In his memorandum to President Reagan prior to the Geneva summit, Secretary of State George Shultz also warned that the "new Soviet leadership is skilled and determined to protect the legacy they inherited from Brezhnev, Andropov and Chernenko" (Memorandum for the President, November 7, 1985). In addition, a November 1985 National Intelligence Estimate on Soviet domestic stresses predicted Gorbachev's measures to be "activist, but essentially conservative"; Director of Central Intelligence, "Domestic Stresses on the Soviet System," National Intelligence Estimate NIE 11-18-85, Central Intelligence Agency (CIA), November 1985, 4, http://www.foia.cia.gov/sites/default/files/document _conversions/89801/DOC_0000681980.pdf.

21. Pavel Palazchenko, *My Years with Gorbachev and Shevardnadze: The Memoir of a Soviet Interpreter* (University Park: Pennsylvania State University Press, 1997), 38. Martin Walker also describes the contemporary Soviet view of the Reagan administration as being "concerned, threatening and relentless"; see Martin Walker, *The Cold War: A History* (New York: Henry and Hook, 1993), 38.

22. Matlock, *Reagan and Gorbachev*, 154. For example, a CIA evaluation of Gorbachev's agenda for the 1985 Geneva summit was pessimistic, stating that the Soviet leader "probably approaches the November meeting with little expectation of any major substantive breakthrough on arms control or regional issues." "CIA Assessment: Gorbachev's Personal Agenda for the November Meeting," n.d., doc. 14, in *To the Geneva Summit: Perestroika and the Transformation of U.S.-Soviet Relations*, National Security Archive Electronic Briefing Book no. 172 (Washington, DC: National Security Archive, November 22, 2005), http://nsarchive.gwu.edu/NSAEBB /NSAEBB172/Doc14.pdf. See also Anatoly Dobrynin, *In Confidence: Moscow's Ambassador to America's Six Cold War Presidents (1962–1986)* (New York: Random House, 1995), 482–83; and Vladislav Zubok, "Gorbachev and the End of the Cold War: Different Perspectives on the Historical Personality," in *Cold War Endgame: Oral History, Analysis, Debates*, ed. William C. Wohlforth (University Park: Pennsylvania State University Press, 2003), 209.

23. Mikhail Gorbachev, *Political Report of the CPSU Central Committee to the 27th Congress of the Communist Party of the Soviet Union* (Moscow: Novosti Press Agency Publishing House, 1986). This vision had previously been articulated in a speech to the Central Committee in 1985 which remains unpublished; see Raymond L. Garthoff, *The Great Transition: American-Soviet Relations and the End of the Cold War* (Washington, DC: Brookings Institution Press, 1994), 257.

24. For a discussion of security dilemma dynamics, see Booth and Wheeler, *The Security Dilemma*; and Nicholas J. Wheeler, "'To Put Oneself into the other Fellow's

Place': John Herz, the Security Dilemma and the Nuclear Age," *International Relations* 22, no. 4 (2008): 493–509.

25. "Anatoly Chernayev's Notes: Gorbachev's Instructions to the Reykjavik Preparation Group," October 4, 1986, doc. 5, 4, in *The Reykjavik File: Previously Secret U.S. and Soviet Documents on the 1986 Reagan-Gorbachev Summit*, National Security Archive Electronic Briefing Book no. 203 (Washington, DC: National Security Archive, October 13, 2006), http://nsarchive.gwu.edu/NSAEBB/NSAEBB203/Document05.pdf.

26. Booth and Wheeler, *The Security Dilemma*, 7.

27. George P. Shultz, *Turmoil and Triumph: My Years as Secretary of State* (New York: Scribner, 1993), 606–7; and Matlock, *Reagan and Gorbachev*, 169 and 173.

28. Mikhail Gorbachev, *Memoirs* (London: Doubleday, 1996), 405.

29. "Union of Soviet Socialist Republics–United States: Documents from the Geneva Summit," *International Legal Materials* 25, no. 1 (1986), 102.

30. See "Memorandum of Conversation: Reagan-Gorbachev Meetings in Geneva, November 1985 – Second Private Meeting," November 19, 1985, doc. 19, in *To the Geneva Summit*, http://nsarchive.gwu.edu/NSAEBB/NSAEBB172/Doc19.pdf.

31. "Excerpt from Anatoly Chernyaev's Diary, November 24, 1985," November 24, 1985, doc. 26, in *To the Geneva Summit*, http://nsarchive.gwu.edu/NSAEBB/NSAEBB172/Doc26.pdf.

32. Andrei Grachev, *Gorbachev's Gamble: Soviet Foreign Policy and the End of the Cold War* (Cambridge, UK: Polity, 2008), 65.

33. Gorbachev, *Memoirs*, 412. Gorbachev was also discouraged by combative statements from the Reagan administration on Afghanistan and what he described as an "unrestrained anti-Soviet campaign" of propaganda undertaken by the United States after the Chernobyl disaster; Garthoff, *The Great Transition*, 277.

34. Anatoly C. Chernyaev, *My Six Years with Gorbachev* (University Park: Pennsylvania State University Press, 2000), 56.

35. Velikhov was a member of the Soviet delegation to the nuclear and space talks in Geneva. Quoted in Robert English, *Russia and the Idea of the West* (New York: Columbia University Press, 2000), 217.

36. Lynn Hansen and Oleg Grinevsky, "Negotiating CSCE," in *Confidence Building and Verification: Prospects in the Middle East*, ed. Shai Feldman (Tel Aviv: Jaffee Center, 1994), 59.

37. Ibid., 59.

38. "Mikhail Gorbachev letter to Ronald Reagan," September 15, 1986, doc. 1, in *The Reykjavik File*, http://nsarchive.gwu.edu/NSAEBB/NSAEBB203/Document01.pdf.

39. Richard Rhodes, *Arsenals of Folly: The Making of the Nuclear Arms Race* (London: Simon & Schuster, 2008), 271.

40. Quoted in David Reynolds, *Summits: Six Meetings that Shaped the Twentieth Century* (New York: Allen, 2007), 363.

41. Quoted in Reynolds, *Summits*, 366.

42. See, e.g., Anatoly Chernyaev's notes from a conference with Politburo members, "Gorbachev Conference with Politburo Members and Secretaries of the Central Committee," December 1, 1986, doc. 28, in *The Reykjavik File*, http://nsarchive.gwu.edu/NSAEBB/NSAEBB203/Document28.pdf.

43. Quoted in William Jackson, "Soviet Reassessment of Ronald Reagan, 1985–1988," *Political Science Quarterly* 113, no. 4 (1998), 633. See also Mikhail S.

Gorbachev, *Perestroika: New Thinking for Our Country and the World* (London: Collins, 1987), 240.

44. Chernyaev, *My Six Years with Gorbachev*, 85.

45. Grachev, *Gorbachev's Gamble*, 95.

46. "Politburo, February 26, 1987: On Soviet-American Relations and Negotiations on Nuclear and Space Armaments," February 26, 1987, in *The INF Treaty and the Washington Summit: Twenty Years Later*, National Security Archive Electronic Briefing Book no. 238 (Washington, DC: National Security Archive, December 10, 2007), http://nsarchive.gwu.edu/NSAEBB/NSAEBB238/russian/Final1987-02-26%20 Politburo.pdf.

47. "Memorandum of Conversation between M. S. Gorbachev and U.S. Secretary of State George Shultz," April 14, 1987, in *The INF Treaty and the Washington Summit*, http://nsarchive.gwu.edu/NSAEBB/NSAEBB238/russian/Final1987-04-14%20 Gorbachev-Shultz.pdf.

48. Gorbachev, *Memoirs*, 440.

49. Ibid.

50. "Politburo, April 16, 1987: About the Conversation with Shultz," in *The INF Treaty and the Washington Summit*, http://nsarchive.gwu.edu/NSAEBB/NSAEBB238 /russian/Final1987-04-16%20Politburo.pdf.

51. For a discussion of Soviet INF concessions, see also Daniel Druckman, Jo L. Husbands, and Karin Johnston, "Turning Points in the INF Negotiations," *Negotiation Journal* 7, no. 1 (1991): 55–67.

52. Gorbachev, *Memoirs*, 443.

53. David E. Hoffman, *The Dead Hand: Reagan, Gorbachev and the Untold Story of the Cold War Arms Race* (London: Icon Books, 2011), 275; and James Graham Wilson, *The Triumph of Improvisation: Gorbachev's Adaptability, Reagan's Engagement, and the End of the Cold War* (Ithaca, NY: Cornell University Press, 2014), 123–24.

54. "Memorandum of Conversation between M. S. Gorbachev and U.S. Secretary of State George Shultz," 7.

55. See William C. Wohlforth, "Realism and the End of the Cold War," *International Security* 19, no. 3 (1994); Stephen G. Brooks and William C. Wohlforth, "Power, Globalization and the End of the Cold War: Reevaluating a Landmark Case for Ideas," *International Security* 25, no. 3 (2000): 5–53; and Stephen G. Brooks and William C. Wohlforth, "Economic Constraints and the End of the Cold War," in Wohlforth, *Cold War Endgame*, 273–310.

56. Nicholas J. Wheeler, "Investigating Diplomatic Transformations," *International Affairs* 89, no. 2 (2013), 492–95; and Wheeler, *Trusting Enemies*.

57. Chernyaev, oral history transcript, published in Wohlforth, *Cold War Endgame*, 20.

58. George W. Breslauer, and Richard Ned Lebow, "Leadership and the End of the Cold War: A Counterfactual Thought Experiment," in *Ending the Cold War: Interpretations, Causation and the Study of International Relations*, ed. Richard K. Hermann and Richard Ned Lebow (New York: Palgrave Macmillan, 2004), 161–88; and Zubok, "Gorbachev and the End of the Cold War," in Wohlforth, *Cold War Endgame*, 208.

59. English, *Russia and the Idea of the West*, 272.

60. Breslauer and Lebow, "Leadership and the End of the Cold War."

61. English, *Russia and the Idea of the West*, 263.

62. Ken Booth and John Baylis, *Britain, NATO and Nuclear Weapons: Alternative Defence versus Alliance Reform* (Basingstoke: Macmillan, 1989), 205. See also Alan Collins, *The Security Dilemma and the End of the Cold War* (Edinburgh: Edinburgh University Press, 1997), 193.

63. Abraham D. Sofaer, "A Legacy of Reykjavik: Negotiating with Enemies," in *Implications of the Reykjavik Summit on Its Twentieth Anniversary*, ed. Sidney D. Drell and George Shultz (Stanford, CA: Hoover Institution Press, 2007), 132. The Reagan administration's principle of not crowing over Soviet concessions was also practiced in the human rights arena, as explored by Sarah Snyder in her chapter in this volume.

64. Sofaer, "A Legacy of Reykjavik," 133.

65. Evan Braden Montgomery, "Breaking Out of the Security Dilemma: Realism, Reassurance and the Problem of Uncertainty," *International Security* 31, no. 2 (2006), 181, 183; Andrew Kydd, "Trust, Reassurance, and Cooperation," *International Organisation* 54, no. 2 (2002), 343; Andrew H. Kydd, *Trust and Mistrust in International Relations* (Princeton, NJ: Princeton University Press, 2006), 222; and Charles L. Glaser, *Rational Theory of International Politics: The Logic of Competition and Cooperation* (Princeton, NJ: Princeton University Press), 208.

66. Misztal, "Trust," 364.

67. Hansen and Grinevsky, "Negotiating CSCE," 59.

68. Ibid., 61.

69. See Wheeler, "Investigating Diplomatic Transformations"; Wheeler, *Trusting Enemies*; and Marcus Holmes, *Face Diplomacy* (manuscript on file with the author).

70. For this argument applied to the 2015 Iran nuclear deal, see Joshua Baker and Nicholas J. Wheeler, "Iran Nuclear Deal Is Built on Trust As Well As Verification," *Birmingham Brief*, University of Birmingham, July 16, 2015, http://www.birmingham.ac.uk/news/thebirminghambrief/items/2015/07/iran-nuclear-deal-16-07-15.aspx.

III. Between Consolidation and Corrosion: Trust inside the Ideological Blocs of East and West

7. Whom Did the East Germans Trust? Popular Opinion on Threats of War, Confrontation, and Détente in the German Democratic Republic, 1968–1989

Jens Gieseke

"Repeatedly, one can identify statements which show a certain 'trust' in the Brandt administration. To some extent illusions exist that this government could achieve certain 'progress' in intra-German policy and in rapprochement between the two German states.... The Brandt government is said to be dealing with 'real' issues and humanitarian concerns. They represent the interests of working people."[1]

Trust in the Cold War: An Intermestic Approach to Popular Opinion in State Socialist Societies

This chapter focuses on the history of the Cold War as a competition between political systems and grand ideologies. In this competition, the respective societies functioned as battlegrounds and resonant bodies. It deals with trust relationships between populations and governments or supranational actors involved in international politics and military policy, which in one way or another claimed to represent their interests and to act on their behalf. The starting point for the characterization of trust relations within communist regimes is often the assumption, following Hannah Arendt, that because of the atomization and powerlessness of the subjects under totalitarian rule there existed neither a need for rulers nor a space for agency for the population able to constitute trust relations in these societies.[2] This paper starts from the opposite assumption regarding the society of communist East Germany and for all post-Stalinist societies of Eastern Europe in general.

It goes without saying that in those societies, trust regimes were not based on democratic control mechanisms and conditional, limited, and revocable trust. Such participatory trust relationships were not institutionalized, neither for the regime itself nor in respect to other external actors.[3] Nevertheless, several types of different trust relationships can be found in these societies for two reasons. First, contrary to the atomization thesis, in these societies a communicative space did indeed exist in which attitudes and value orientations were formed in a discursive process. This process took place under dictatorial conditions (e.g., no independent press, impact of government propaganda, prohibition of organized groupings) and thus was not an ideally conceived "free discourse," but it did take place—certainly in the private sphere, but also in "small" public spheres of encounters on the street, in the shopping queue, or at the workplace, and sometimes even to a certain degree in public events (such as readings by critical authors).[4] Opinion-building in these "small publics" was fueled by a mixture of regime propaganda; alternative perspectives voiced by external sources like the Western electronic media or internal opposition (such as the church and dissidents); the horizon of experiences in the personal environment, like impressions about the supply situation or productivity in the workplace; and the informally passed-on stock of traditional attitudes and mentalities from generational experience, historical consciousness, and national or regional stereotypes. Value orientations formed on this basis included a variety of emotional bonds or reservations toward political actors, which can be conceptualized as trust (or mistrust) relationships.

In terms of form and inner structure, three types of trust relationships can be identified in the state socialist society:

1. *The official trust regime of the communist state.*[5] Communist regimes justify their rule from a politico-religious legitimacy. They claim the insight of a higher, unquestionable authority, and require belief in the power and insight of the communist party in the laws emanating from it.[6] What was actually demanded of the people was not participation but allegiance, based on a Right-Hegelian concept of statehood in which society had to serve the state and not vice versa. Bertolt Brecht called to mind this concept in precise fashion with his famous sarcastic note after the June 1953 people's uprising, in which, following the East German regime's statement that the people had lost the government's trust, he suggested that the East German communists should vote to elect a new people.[7]

In this respect, the trust relationship sought between party regime and population was similar to a premodern "trust in God."[8] Although these dictatorial regimes were based first and foremost on force, this trust regime was crucial for their self-legitimation. Therefore, "trust" was always important in the rhetoric of party propaganda and forced "official" statements of ordinary people, which were full of emotionalized anthropomorphisms such as "friendship." This trust relationship fitted into the concept of an authoritarian yet nurturing paternalism, not only in respect to the assurance of material welfare and social security but also in the sense of a fabric of "warm" quasifamilial emotional bonds. Besides the Marxist-Leninist "historical" legitimation, this concept gained more and more importance with the loss of utopian perspectives during the seventies, as part of demarcation against the "cold" modernity of the capitalist Western model.[9]

At the same time, the rhetoric of "religious" faith and family-style emotionalization in official culture can be read as expressions of the precarious state of real trust within the population—following Pjotr Sztompka's rule of thumb that "the more trust is talked about, the less it is actually available."[10] The communist regimes built broad surveillance structures to compensate for the lack of confidence in their compliance. They acted as "incarnations of mistrust."[11] Nevertheless it is appropriate to keep the official trust regime in sight for two reasons. For one, while calls for "trust by faith" were apparently pretty ineffective for the majority, they were at the same time pivotal with respect to the active loyalty of the ideological and power-securing elites of party rule; namely for those 15, 20, or 30 percent of the population that guaranteed the existence of the regime. As a glance at the late eighties shows, the loss of faith within the ranks of this elite was one of the determining factors for the collapse of, or where relevant incremental transformations in, the regimes.

2. *Conditional vertical trust.* These trust relations were thematically focused, divided between and directed to a variety of institutions. They could include trust in certain features of the West, such as market economy, representative democracy, or the welfare state, or of the East, such as social justice, job security, or the absence of Nazism. Other forms of trust were more specific and limited to singular issues, like certain types of politicians. Within the framework of limited but relatively diverse information resources, these trust relationships were structurally open and based on individual preferences. In this, they were conditional and revocable in case of disappointments or new points of view. However, these were not "full"

145

conditional trust relationships as in modern democratic statehood, as emerging mistrust remained without chances for sanction or participation, but were limited to a virtual "goodwill" relationship.

3. *Horizontal trust.* Contrary to the Orwellian visions of total mistrust, horizontal trust based on reciprocity played a major role, at least at the level of face-to-face relationships within the family and personal environment (e.g., work colleagues, neighbors, friends). In some respects this type of trust was even strengthened by state pressure, the flaws of the planned economy, and surveillance. Some practices of state socialist society could not be imagined without such types of trust, from the shadow economy as a lubricant of economic life to many forms of informal arrangements "just between us," even up to high-ranking state and party functionaries. This kind of horizontal trust was also present beyond personal acquaintance to a certain degree, as for example in some socio-moral milieus such as the educated middle class or circles of bohemian artists.[12] The formation of such horizontal trust relationships on a larger scale was a crucial process for the establishment of civil society before the revolution.

In the East German case, to a relatively pronounced extent, matters of "big politics" (and thus of international politics during the Cold War) were subject to subcutaneous discourses and opinion-building processes, owing to the strong presence of Western electronic media. Despite all the sanctions against people watching Western television programs, a relatively symmetrical plurality of information resources and offers of value orientation from a variety of potential sources and addressees of trust was the basic feature of this field. As the sources used in this analysis show, residents were able to form their own opinions, perspectives, and interpretations about the policies and ideologies, for example, of the various international actors. Moreover, it was part of the political culture of the Cold War that the international players claimed more or less explicitly to act as figures of trust for and representatives of the East German or Eastern European populations. This claim included at least the offer of establishing virtual "intermestic"[13] relations of trust and distrust to actors beyond the domestic regime—and one question to be addressed in this chapter is how East Germans responded to that offer.

The Cold War as a Subject of East German Popular Opinion

The present analysis is part of a reconstruction of East German "popular opinion." This project is based primarily on intelligence reports and opinion polls, both from East and West Germany. In the following, two of these series will be examined. The first set is a series of reports on the "reaction of the population," produced by the East German Ministry for State Security (MfS, or Stasi). The second set is the results of a survey program of the Federal Republic of Germany's (FRG) opinion research institute Infratest in Munich, which from 1968 to 1989 conducted annual proxy interviews with West German visitors to the German Democratic Republic (GDR) about the "attitudes and behavior" of their East German hosts, relatives, and friends. The Infratest reports were funded by (and delivered exclusively to) the West German federal government.[14]

The two series provide not only competing images of trust regimes, but are part of these regimes themselves. The MfS reports can be read as a direct expression of distrust by the Sociality Unity Party (Sozialistische Einheitspartei Deutschlands, SED) leadership in its paternalistic relationship with the population. The West German Federal Ministry for Intra-German Relations, by contrast, drew from the survey program information on the expectations, needs, and political attitudes of East Germans. In effect, it was designed to substitute for the absence of open society feedback via media and elections, and among other results to measure the results of West German policy toward the East. Both series provide us with filtered, distorted, and biased images of the East German population, but they also show remarkable similarities and mutual complements, resulting in a dense and detailed overall picture.

Problems of international politics were mentioned in both source series only occasionally. The main focus was rather on the internal situation in the GDR against the backdrop of competition between systems. This approach reflected not only the respective interests of the two institutions, but also the priorities of the East Germans themselves. Especially concerning the "silent majority," it can be stated that their value orientations were not very ideological (neither in the Western nor Eastern sense) but were shaped above all by a pragmatic attitude in respect to their material and spiritual life chances. This pragmatism resulted in a preference for many aspects of the Western model, but also contained a certain openness to the offers of the socialist system.[15] This pattern is of crucial importance for perceptions and judgments of the East German population in the Cold War as a trial of military strength, as a battle of grand ideologies, and as a competition about the most attractive standards of living.

A Time of Great Expectations:
New Ostpolitik as a Trust Relationship, 1969–75

By the end of the 1960s, a phase of reorientation lay behind the East German population.[16] In a painful process, East Germans had had to adjust themselves to a new status quo after the building of the Berlin Wall. The closure of the border was followed by a relaxation of internal pressure, offers for integration, and a temporary liberalization. From the perspective of the East German population, this reorientation meant above all finding a mental accommodation with the immutable circumstances. In this period, the last expectations for liberation by the West and a revision of the postwar order in Europe disappeared from the mindset of broad layers of the population.[17] Thus, according to the first Infratest survey from 1968, the hope for military liberation was articulated at this time by only 2.5 percent of East Germans. At the same time, however, 91 percent stated that they did not feel threatened by the Federal Republic, and thereby marked clearly their distance from the anti-Western propaganda of the East German leadership.[18]

Nevertheless, hopes for a reopening of the border, fundamental liberalization, and reunification remained present. The division of the nation was still fresh and recognized as "abnormal" in the minds of contemporaries. But over the decade after the building of the Wall, emphasis had shifted: an attitude of confrontation held no prospects, and sympathies grew for political options of cooperation and détente between the blocs. This shift was accompanied by an obviously deep-rooted pacifism, based in the traumas of the Second World War and revived by horrific visions of a nuclear war. At least in this respect, the status quo was seen as a value per se, including some acceptance for the limits of action on the Western side. The Soviet Union, which in the domestic context was perceived first and foremost as an occupying power, had been increasingly recognized as an international actor with at least a certain degree of reliability. Here, then, its confessions of "peaceful coexistence" found some positive responses even beyond party circles.

And what of the basic constellation in terms of trust relationships at the beginning of détente in the early seventies? As the intense positive reactions to the first efforts of rapprochement between the SED and the West German Social Democratic Party (Sozialdemokratische Partei Deutschlands, SPD) during the sixties show, the prospects of détente were accompanied by far-reaching expectations, in particular at the German-German level. Détente was consistently aimed at maintaining peace, oriented toward cooperation and compromise, and at the same time remained pragmatic and open for the most urgent value preferences and political priorities of the East German population.

The East German government noticed this intense bond of trust immediately as West German chancellor Willy Brandt in 1970 sparked a spontaneous manifestation of sympathy from the East German people during his first visit to Erfurt, East Germany. The trust relationship that became palpable in the famous brief glance out of the hotel window—responding to the public's

Table 7.1. Infratest 1972 on the Eastern Treaties

Arguments for and against the "Eastern treaties" (in percent, reasons: multiple answers possible)

For treaties	81	Against treaties	9
Reasons		*Reasons*	
General relaxation	77	Federal government makes too many concessions	69
Relaxation between FRG and GDR	68	Too few/no advantages for East German population	67
Better intra-German travel regulations	67	Advantages for GDR government only	46
Travel opportunities for citizens of the GDR to the West	64	Renunciation of German interests/ reunion	29
Facilitation of intra-German negotiations	52	Disadvantages for East German population	20
Alleviations for East and West German populations	59	Others	9
Improvement of trade	42		
Recognition of the GDR	32		

Source: Infratest GDR program 1972, questions 58A (N = 455) and 58 B (N = 67).

demand for him to make an appearance—and also his levelheaded look at his chances of meeting the public's expectations, set the basic tone for the next five years of negotiations and their modest results.

First, it should be noted that the East German leadership was praised at every step for having a constructive attitude in the negotiations. However, it was generally subject to a structural mistrust. In contrast, the West German government still enjoyed a high reputation in terms of strong emotional bonds and expectations one decade after 1961. From all sources, it becomes clear how intense the attention focused on Bonn really was. The Stasi reported broadly on the fruitfulness of the new Ostpolitik and the public appreciation for the constructive approach of this policy.[19] Above all, the style and content of détente corresponded with the expectations of the East German majority and brought about an intense trust relationship. This basic pattern of results was repeated across a variety of Infratest surveys and Stasi reports between 1969 and 1974.

Infratest data from 1972 (table 7.1) show a large majority (81%) of West Germans classifying the West German treaties with the Soviet Union and Poland as "rather positive." General relaxation and the positive effects on relations between the two German states were the most important arguments for this support, followed by the expectation of better travel regulations in the future, especially for East Germans' trips to West Germany. Among the minority who opposed the contracts, the dominant accusations were that the West German government had made too many concessions and that the East German population would receive few to no benefits from the treaties.

In this context, the Stasi explicitly referred to the concept of "trust," and used it in more than just the sense of confidence between two horizontally negotiating partners in their mutual reliability. Rather, it noticed with disappointment the strong vertical trust relationship that linked broader layers of East German population with the Brandt administration.

According to the MfS, the West German social-democratic-liberal coalition was seen as a "workers' government" and enjoyed "enhanced appreciation." Such positions were to be found in "all layers of the population." Statements like these culminated in a report to East German leader Erich Honecker and SED propaganda chief Werner Lamberz about East German reactions to the West German elections of November 19, 1972:

> The parliamentary elections in the FRG were followed with great interest. It was emphasized by broad sections of the population that the outcome of the elections would have a major influence on future political developments in Europe and on the relationship between the two German states.[20]

This passage was followed by a sentence that speaks volumes in its ambiguity: "The population of the GDR predominantly welcomes the victory of the Social Democratic [SPD] and Liberal Party [Freie Demokratische Partei, FDP] coalition." Such a statement was in accordance with the official SED position. But the connotations within the population went much further and came along with "various illusions and expectations": "At the top of such attitudes, views can be found that the SPD with Brandt at the top has a mobilizing effect upon the entire development in Europe." There were signs for a "process of democratization" in Eastern Europe, "while the GDR was lagging behind with its policy." With these "politically unclear" (in Stasi terms) positions, further requests were associated with the East German regime: "Is the FRG on the road to socialism under the leadership of the SPD as a workers' party?" And also: "Couldn't it make sense to take the Bundestag election in the FRG with its 'democratic approach' as a 'role-model' for the GDR?" Here, the whole spectrum of domestic and intra-German political desires was on the table.

The MfS also highlighted the general positive attitude in the East German population toward all political actors that showed a "willingness to understanding and compromise" and a policy of "moderate tone." From this angle, even the Soviet Union was appreciated for abandoning its "strategic long-term goal" of a change in the status quo with the new policy and accepting the balance of power. In contrast, the East German leadership was blamed for pursuing a "too 'dogmatic' policy" and a "rigid attitude," and would be forced by the West German–Soviet treaty to adopt a compromise-oriented policy.[21] According to Infratest 1970, about two-thirds (68%) of the East German population held the view that the GDR would not be willing to make concessions.[22] Two years later, 36 percent still assumed that the GDR was open to negotiations only as a result of Soviet pressure, whereas 32 percent recognized a "general will to negotiate." Eighteen percent saw a pronounced flexible negotiating stance, while 11 percent perceived a rigid posture with no willingness to make concessions.[23]

The contrary trust relations became even more visible in the attribution of the respective aims to both governments. According to Infratest interviews in 1973 and 1974 (table 7.2), East Germans saw their own government as particularly interested in enhancing its international relationships and increasing its political influence (68 percent and 71 percent of statements, respectively),

Table 7.2. Infratest 1973/74 on East and West German Government Aims and Intentions

What does person X think about the aims and intentions of the Federal Government and the East German government with respect to talks on treaties and a policy of normalization and relaxation? (In percent, multiple answers possible from a list, selected statements)

	GDR		FRG	
	1973	1974	1973	1974
Seeks to promote itself internationally/expand its political influence	68	71	5	29
Would have economic benefits	59	66	9	17
Wants regularized relations, but is otherwise interested in dissociation	56	68	11	10
Wants to win ideological influence on the citizens of the other state	37	47	9	17
Is interested in both German states accepting and respecting each other	41	–	45	–
Is acting under pressure from its allies	28	37	6	7
Has honest intentions of peace and relaxation/Wants to do something for peace	21	27	62	59
Is interested in improvements for the people of the two German states	17	15	75	83
Is interested in real convergence	12	–	60	–

Source: Infratest GDR program 1973, questions 41 and 42 (N = 818); and Infratest GDR program 1974, questions 20 and 21 (N = 581).

but as interested in dissociation in all other respects (1973: 56%; 1974: 68%). For the West German government, however, the highest approval ratings of 75 percent in 1973 and 83 percent in 1974 were ascribed to the aim of achieving improvements for the people of both German states. Furthermore, West Germany was perceived as primarily interested in peace and relaxation between the geopolitical blocs (1973: 62%; 1974: 59%).

As the Stasi reports show in more detail, East Germans were focused mainly on the practical results of negotiations, particularly travel opportunities and the general hope that the border would be more pervious from East to West. In the wake of the signing of the German-German traffic treaty in 1972, the Stasi noted a wave of some 2,000 requests from East German citizens who inquired about new regulations for trips to West Germany.[24] With clear majorities, the East Germans also expressed their hope for a "lifting of the security measures at the border" and "further rapprochement between the two states, towards the reunification of Germany" as final results of the talks.[25] Again and again, expectations were voiced that the German-German rapprochement would lead to a "wave of liberalization"[26] in all areas of East German society. All of these findings resulted in ongoing and intense trust for the West German government, except for one issue: in 1971, a majority of East Germans (55%) voted in favor of the West German government's full recognition of East Germany in return for concessions, which remained unacceptable for the West.

Two groups within the East German population differed remarkably from this general pattern of a pragmatic orientation on results, a basic trust in the intentions of the West German government and mistrust of the East German leadership. A minority, mostly of older people, positioned themselves as even more hostile to the East German regime and rejected any kind of concession by the West German negotiators. On the opposite pole, a consistent and slightly growing group of "trust by faith" supporters of communist rule identified strongly with the Eastern side. Their trust was directed at the East German actors only, while the West German government was accepted as acting cooperatively but also seen as an adversary. For example, 71 percent of SED members (amounting to approximately 15 percent of the adult population) favored an unconditional recognition of the East German state by the West, while only 25 percent of them wished for "concessions" in return.[27]

The asymmetry of trust relations became apparent on the level of individual political actors and their personalities. The change in leadership from Walter Ulbricht to Erich Honecker in 1971 did not fulfill any existing expectations of noteworthy change. According to Infratest, 55 percent of East Germans expressed the opinion that their government's policies would remain unaffected; 48 percent scored the political skills of both functionaries as rather similar, and 39 percent saw a similar degree of sympathy (or antipathy) for Honecker within the population as for his predecessor. The majority of those who saw differences expected a worsening of the situation: 31 percent considered Honecker to be "a hindrance" to German-German rapprochement, and only 14 percent saw him as "rather beneficial." Forty-three percent thought that he was classified in the GDR as "less sympathetic" than his predecessor, with only 15 percent seeing him as more sympathetic.[28] The personalization of different political lines, as found even in the communist systems at least on the level of top functionaries, apparently played a minor role in this case—both were considered "character masks" of their official role. Honecker gained somewhat better results in the following two years due to his welfare state policies, such as salary increases and commitment to a housing program. Yet these benefits changed little in the general situation.[29]

In contrast, the Stasi explicitly pointed out the charismatic appeal of Willy Brandt: East German citizens were full of gratitude toward him because he "had done so much for them" by initiating the negotiation process on "humanitarian relief"; he was said to be the "German Peace Chancellor" and to have exceptional skills as a statesman with his "true-to-life and worker-friendly policy."[30] The personal admiration that Brandt enjoyed among the East German population as a "statesman" and a Social Democrat was striking and presumably rankled Erich Honecker. It personalized Honecker's major problems with the West: the appeal of the Federal Republic, the success of the SPD's "workers' party," the model of democratic elections, and even the hoped-for immediate use of the new Ostpolitik for East German citizens in terms of travel regulations and personal contacts across the border.

As intense as expectations were toward the West German government in representing East Germans' interests in the German-German negotiations, the results after five years of Ostpolitik were equally ambiguous. Hardly any of the principal wishes had been met. There was a significant improvement in atmosphere, more favorable regulations for personal contacts across the border, and a steep rise in the number of trips by West Germans to the East. But none of the three main points—opening of the border and improvements in East-West travel regulations, liberalization of the political system toward free elections, and reunification—was significantly closer to realization. Nonetheless, these circumstances did not change anything in the general allocation of trust relationships. The interests of the East German population were seen as represented in principle by the FRG, while poor results were seen as caused by the GDR. Yet this constellation of trust relationships with its strong focus on the West German government came to a kind of completion with Brandt's resignation in 1974, after the unmasking of an East German spy in the Chancellor's Office. The sympathetic reactions of East Germans affirmed their strong emotional bonds toward Brandt. However, his successor, Helmut Schmidt, did not manage to forge emotional bonds with the same intensity.[31] Moreover, negotiations had come to a standstill. East Germans were not totally surprised by this development and showed a levelheaded attitude.

The matter-of-fact attitude of East Germans toward German-German relations was confirmed by Infratest in 1975 (table 7.3): 38 percent saw "disappointingly little" progress, 42 percent also saw little progress but stated that "more was probably not to be expected," while only 13 percent saw "significant, satisfying progress." Consequently, 70 percent believed that "in the foreseeable future little or no changes" would be realized. Only a minority (30%) still maintained the opinion that improvements would be implemented, particularly in terms of travel opportunities to West Germany and more informal and unforced encounters between East and West Germans. This attitude was revealing; on the one hand, it showed an entirely realistic assessment of the concrete results of the negotiations, but on the other hand, the process of political and cultural opening—considered, in hindsight, as the true engine of internal dissolution of state socialism as an ideological bloc—was seen as totally irrelevant. Only 17 percent of East Germans expected more informal contacts, 12 percent better access to Western consumer goods, and 6 percent to Western cultural goods.[32] In the short-term view, the "aggression in felt slippers" (to use Egon Bahr's expression) was so quiet that the GDR was perceived as much more successful in terms of the outcomes of Brandt's Ostpolitik. In respect to trust relations, this change was pivotal: the key figure of trust, Willy Brandt, departed the stage, and progress on the basic issues hit a logjam. This did not challenge trust relations in general, but it did de-emotionalize them. Moreover, the East Germans' virtual relationship with the West German government lost importance due to the latter's diminishing significance as an actor in the field of Cold War and détente.

Table 7.3. Infratest 1975 on the Inter-German Relationship

How has, according to X, the FRG-GDR relationship developed in recent years?

	Percentage
Absolutely no progress	8
Progress, but disappointingly little	38
Little progress, but more was probably not to be expected	42
Significant, satisfying progress	13

Source: Infratest GDR program 1975, question 46 (N = 1004).

Distance and Mistrust toward the Superpowers: The CSCE and the Second Cold War, 1975–85

After the German-German dialogue cooled, attention for Cold War issues shifted back to the international arena. However, general interest was significantly lower than in the preceding period. For example, West German Infratest respondents frequently were not able to comment on the CSCE process because they had not talked about it with their East German partners. Sympathy with cooperation and détente was still widespread, but East Germans had developed a more distanced attitude toward the actors at the international level. This loss of emotional bonds toward external actors pertained for the CSCE process and continued in the new confrontation of the so-called Second Cold War of the late 1970s and early 1980s.[33]

The Western willingness to cooperate in the CSCE in the second half of the 1970s was seen more as an expression of weakness, while the Soviet Union's performance was perceived as a significant increase in power and force, both in terms of results of negotiations as well as in the arms race (table 7.4).[34] Therefore, the Helsinki Final Act, signed in 1975, was first and foremost seen as a success for the Eastern bloc and particularly for the GDR (40%). In second place stood the impression of a useless "show by politicians," followed closely

Table 7.4. Infratest 1975 on the CSCE

What does X think about the results of the CSCE in Helsinki? (Multiple answers possible, select statements)

	Percentage
The conference was a thorough success for the GDR. Its sovereignty and full equality alongside the FRG was demonstrated to the world and endorsed by all participating states.	40
The conference was basically just a big show by politicians. Probably nothing will change, and the existing conflicts in the world could not be solved.	37
The conference is a great success for the Soviet Union. The Soviet sphere of influence in Europe has now finally been recognized by the Western states.	36
The conference is a milestone on the path of international détente. Peace is more secure now.	30
The result of this conference is equally advantageous for all countries in East and West. There are no winners or losers.	27
The results of the conference will in the end bring more civil liberties and rights to the people of the GDR.	12
The conference did not take place as originally intended by the Soviet Union. The Western and neutral countries have prevailed with their ideas of détente for the benefit of mankind.	7

Source: Infratest GDR program 1975, questions 54 and 55 (N = 128).

Table 7.5. Infratest 1978, 1980, and 1982 on Superpower Armed Conflict

Does X believe that an armed conflict between the two military blocs is possible in the foreseeable future?

	1978	1980	1982
Yes	8	20	31
No	90	78	67
Not specified	2	2	1

Source: Infratest GDR program, 1978, question 60 (N = 426); 1980, question 63 (N = 573); and 1982, question 63 (N = 571).

by the perception that the West (by their signatures in Helsinki) had accepted the Soviet Union's hegemonic sphere. Retrospective assessments were of marginal importance at that time: only 12 percent expressed the view that the results of the conference would generate "more civil liberties and rights for the people of the GDR"; and 7 percent stated that the Western powers, contrary to the original Soviet intentions, prevailed with "their ideas of détente for the benefit of mankind." Finally, 12 percent expressed the view that the results of the conference would generate "more civil liberties and rights for the people of the GDR."

As for the Central European and global military and political situation, the following years were marked by the fierce debates about the North Atlantic Treaty Organization's (NATO) double-track decision to deploy medium- and intermediate-range nuclear weapons in Western Europe and the resulting "second Cold War." In this scenario, three tendencies ascended in East German attitudes, all three of which resulted in growing distance and general mistrust. First was a general increase in the fear of war; second was a certain alienation from the policy of the West, particularly the United States; and third was a self-perception of being the helpless object of the superpowers, with adverse consequences even in peacetime.

"Does X believe that an armed conflict between the two military blocs is possible in the foreseeable future?," Infratest asked in 1978, 1980, and 1982 (table 7.5). At all times, at least a two-thirds majority judged war to be unlikely. Obviously, a fundamental confidence in the stability of the status quo, the desire for peaceful coexistence, and mutual nuclear deterrence were still taken for granted. Nevertheless, in that six-year time frame, the portion of those who considered war to be possible rose from 8 to 31 percent.

The most important risk in that respect was not seen in a strategically planned attack by any party, but rather as escalation by accident. Predominant was the perception of a fatal dynamic, regardless of whom the East Germans viewed as the driving force. These fears were reflected in a distanced attitude

Table 7.6. Infratest 1981 on the NATO Double-Track Decision

Does X rate the NATO double-track decision basically positive or negative? Is it in the opinion of X rather a unilateral rearmament or a NATO response to increased defense of the East?

Opinion on Decision		Reason for Decision	
Positive	33	Unilateral rearmament	40
Negative	64	Reaction	60
Not specified	3	Not specified	0

Source: Infratest GDR program 1981, questions 34 and 35 (N = 257/267).

toward the NATO double-track decision and generally toward Western expansion of nuclear armament (table 7.6). In 1981, 64 percent rated the double-track decision negatively, although almost as many (60%) shared the opinion that it was not a step toward unilateral armament but a response to the Warsaw Pact's deployment of mid-range nuclear missiles in Central Europe.

Three years later, the East Germans responded to the failure of the 1985 Geneva talks between US president Ronald Reagan and Soviet leader Mikhail Gorbachev with a more-than-equidistant position: a slight majority (51%) blamed both sides equally for the failure of the talks, 29 percent held the United States responsible, and only 16 percent made the Soviet Union liable for it.[35]

The Stasi's surveys broadly reflected these perceptions of the Second Cold War, given that as an organization it was interested in the effectiveness of the East German government's own peace propaganda. Particularly in this period, the SED recognized peace policy as a field for building up trust relations with those parts of the population that had maintained distance toward party rule by addressing the widespread pacifist mood—establishing a classical field for "conditional trust." Moreover, the East German government saw a chance to win a hegemonic position in West German public opinion, presenting East Germany as a reliable partner in contrast to the "untrustworthy," aggressive United States. However, the success of this strategy was limited.

The MfS located the growing fear of war, especially among elderly people who were influenced by the personal memories of the Second World War and remembered the prewar situation of 1938–39.[36] Moreover, mainly women and girls expressed their concern about "fear of an uncertain future" and decided against bringing "children into the world."[37] Apart from these concerns, fatalism about the "mutual distrust"[38] mushroomed among the population and turned into a deepened feeling of subjection and helplessness, particularly after the deployment of Pershing II missiles in Western Europe in 1983. The superpowers would not let themselves be influenced and "acted at their own discretion." "'Germany' [will] again be in the spotlight of war preparations," with the result that "the population of the GDR will be threatened by the stationing of missile complexes exactly as the population of the FRG now." In these views, danger had increased "that by 'chance' and minor incidents at the political level someone could 'press the button'."[39]

However, the confrontational course of the new US administration under Ronald Reagan did not find favor with the broad majority of East Germans. As early as 1981, the Stasi was pleased to report critical statements about Reagan's "scandalous statements," his "collision course" toward confrontation with the Soviet Union, and the increase in the US military budget. All of these developments were rejected by many parts of the East German population.[40] In a triumphant tone, the Stasi reported about the public's negative attitude: "To a larger degree GDR citizens show an anti-Reagan stance." The Stasi explicitly noticed that this distance from US policy exceeded the usual "progressive circles."[41]

However, the repercussions were sharper after the stationing of Pershing II missiles, when the Soviet Union followed suit with further missile deployments of its own. This response would, according to the reports of the Stasi, trigger serious military and economic consequences and not least weaken the Western peace movement: "Why do we deploy so quickly? Everywhere in the GDR, there are protests against the deployment in the West and Western Europe, and now we are practicing the same. How does that match?" The Warsaw Pact was said to be "at war course" now. This outlook was followed by a summary that knocked out the effort to gain ground in the peace movement: "All previous appeals for peace by the socialist countries [were] to be regarded merely as agitation . . . , as they now practiced the same as the NATO states."[42] Germans in the East and West "have to pay again for the great powers. . . . The ordinary citizen has to look on helplessly and pay the bill."[43] Overall, mistrust and the impression of an insurmountable distance toward both superpowers had reached a peak. The arms race between the superpowers was perceived as an uncontrollable fate, one that increased the risk of a nuclear inferno and did not bode well for the issues that the East German population perceived as most urgent, such as improved economic performance, not to mention the blocking effects for all questions of liberalization (in terms of domestic issues and freedom of movement).

During this confrontation, the role of the West German government as a proxy figure of trust with respect to those issues lost some importance. Yet in general it remained intact, as Infratest and Stasi agreed upon, though they drew reverse connotations from this finding. For example, in 1984 the MfS complained about "tendencies of underestimating the dangerousness and aggressiveness of FRG imperialism," particularly among young East Germans.[44] Even the "inventor" of the double-track decision, Chancellor Helmut

Schmidt, was seen as "variable" and also as sympathetic to the Soviet position; parts of the East German population "overestimate[d] Schmidt's role in the détente process and in particular attributed to his person all kinds of progress in the relationship between the two German states."[45] This tendency was also supported by Stasi reports in connection with Schmidt's visit to the GDR in 1981.[46] According to Infratest, in 1979 the East German population feared increased confrontation and a consequent deterioration of relations in the event of a change of government in West Germany, but in 1983 they seemed to notice that, reassuringly, the new West German administration under Helmut Kohl sought no fundamental change in German-German relations.[47]

Erich Honecker tried to benefit from this mood by ostentatiously maintaining close contacts with Bonn and continuing his preparations for a visit to the Federal Republic (which, due to Moscow's veto, he realized only in 1987). As the Stasi reported, an unspecified number of voices supported the GDR's "farsighted" policy of not burning its bridges with the FRG.[48] In 1984, Infratest estimated that 36 percent of those questioned perceived that the two German states were expending the same amount of effort on trying to keep inner-German relations separate from East-West tensions, while 29 percent saw only the FRG and 17 percent saw only the GDR as taking the lead in this role.[49]

As these data indicate, Honecker achieved only a limited growth in confidence with this maneuver. He benefited from the fact that the East Germans evaluated every gesture of cooperativeness positively, regardless of the side from which it came. Nonetheless, the lack of legitimacy of the East German regime was always present. According to the MfS, Erich Honecker's signals were classified as hypocritical. Principally in church circles and by those who followed the Western media, the following argument was made: "The GDR government made a lot of noise against the stationing of US medium-range missiles in the FRG, but in the GDR the population had not even been asked whether they agreed with the announced countermeasures [i.e., the stationing of Soviet weapons in East Germany]."[50] Other voices from the East German population in 1984 expressed their distance from the East German peace propaganda; they saw "the threat posed by the FRG with the stationing of missiles as exaggerated. The party and state leadership of the GDR is too extreme in these matters, as the FRG citizens also don't want war."[51]

A Harbinger of Self-Confidence?
Dialectics of the International Peace Movement

In some respects, vertical trust relationships and emotional bonds toward other international actors reached bottom on both sides in the early and mid-eighties.

In security and disarmament policy, the situation was deadlocked. There was no prospect that the clear preferences of East Germans—on the one hand for cooperation and détente, on the other for a gradual or fundamental change to the East German communist system and the divided status of Germany—would have a chance of success. The nuclear standoff with its relentless series of propaganda initiatives and negotiations led to some stability, but promised no chance to satisfy any further desires. In the perception of East Germans, the increase in US military spending forced the Soviet bloc to its knees. Yet no resolution of this situation to their advantage was in view.

The international debate on the arms race in the early eighties, however, took a dialectical twist in respect to trust relations. It led at least to a reconstitution of horizontal trust that went beyond the small-scale personal environment and established a base for action in society as a whole. In that respect, the role of alternative peace groups as nuclei of East German civil society usually is mentioned. In the long run, the deciding point was that these peace activities were not limited to small circles of organized dissidents, but to a certain extent paved the way for broader mobilization. Although the SED vigorously criminalized the independent peace movement, through its own official peace propaganda it paradoxically created a discursive space for the formation of mutual horizontal trust as a basis for collective action and the rise of the revolutionary mass movement of 1989.

In 1983, the Stasi noticed these incipient stages of repoliticization within the population and attributed them to the success of the SED's peace propaganda efforts. In late 1983, at the peak of the West German protests against the planned deployment of NATO missiles, the MfS reported: "Larger portions of the population of the GDR in recent times monitored with more interest the international development and the exacerbating situation provoked by the United States. Apparently mass actions of the population of the FRG and other Western European countries have left impressions and promoted insights among both critical and loyal parts of the population."[52] This basic sentiment survived the tailing off of the peace movement, as was noted in 1985 in respect to reactions to a meeting of US and Soviet foreign ministers: "What is remarkable is . . . the extent of such statements and discussions articulated by people who previously appeared to remain politically apathetic."[53] However, the Stasi also noted a small but remarkable wave of protests in early 1984, after the deployment of Pershing II missiles in West Germany and the Eastern countermeasures. In the three months after the deployments, more than 400 "pseudo-pacifist" and "neutralist" petitions criticizing the reactions of the Warsaw Pact were counted, including over one hundred collections of signatures with about 4,000 participants.[54]

Table 7.7. Infratest 1982 on the International Peace Movement

What does X think about the international peace movement?

	Percentage
Can make global peace more secure	60
Helps to ensure that the arms race will be stopped in East and West	48
Has forced the West to finally pick up arms reduction talks with the East	34
Does not make global peace more secure	20
In the FRG, is controlled primarily by the East	12
In the FRG, serves the interests of the East and harms the West	10
Undermines readiness for defense against attacks from the East within the population of the FRG	6

Source: Infratest GDR program 1982, question 37 (N = 298).

Infratest took note of the vague but widespread basic sympathy for the peace movement as a whole as early as 1982 (table 7.7). According to its polls, 60 percent of East Germans approved of the statement that the international peace movement could make "world peace more secure," while 48 percent saw the peace movement as a means to stop the arms race in East and West. The Western critical argument that the peace movement acted as a Soviet fifth column and risked undermining Western defense readiness, in contrast, found only low support (6%). When asked for more specific assessments of interest in the peace movement, the 1982 Infratest respondents estimated that some 59 percent of their East German interlocutors were sympathizers and another 17 percent were active supporters of the independent peace movement in East Germany.[55]

In the context of Cold War history in this period, it is worth mentioning the independent peace movement as a harbinger of this horizontal, revolutionary self-confidence (the influence of the Solidarność movement in Poland, which is beyond the scope of this discussion, notwithstanding). Although there was no mass base for public action, a fundamental sympathy for forms of civil resistance was apparently growing from the edges of East German society, such as the Protestant and alternative milieus. In the following years, these new forms of collective agency based on mutual trust—in the face of a purposefully designed surveillance environment—functioned as an important initial step for the prodemocracy movement. These efforts transcended the limits of small dissident circles and paved the way for a horizontal protodiscourse on political issues, based on mutual trust within the population. Even with the widespread and pervasive awareness of the pointlessness of political action, the harsh threats of repression, and limits of international support, for East Germans the issues of war and peace, mutual threats and armament, militarization, and civility offered some approaches to the discourse of official peace policy. In this form, the independent peace movement proved to be an ideal field in which new forms of trust relations could develop as a basis for future strategies.

Conditional Trust in an Inescapable World Order: Some Conclusions on East German Trust Relations in the Cold War

This analysis has confirmed and illustrated the presupposition that in societies under totalitarian and authoritarian regimes, a variety of protoconditional trust relations can be found, based on the existence of a space of popular opinion, negotiated by informal communication and fueled by various resources under the conditions of modern mass communication and media. During the Cold War, communist regimes countered this plurality of trust relations with the claim of a single "trust by faith" relation, yet this claim reached only a minority. Thus, the regimes were forced to position themselves in competition with alternative trust-providers, as far as they sought to base their rule on a broader base of legitimacy beyond pure coercion.

In the Cold War as a military and ideological conflict of system competition, the East German population positioned itself with a set of relatively independent value preferences. From the 1960s to the 1980s, these values were relatively nonideological, pragmatic, and focused on the material and spiritual quality of life. At the same time, attitudes about international policy were decidedly hospitable to cooperation and were based on an antiwar attitude. As far as political programs corresponded to these ideas, they enjoyed support within the East German population and created a basis for a protoconditional trust relationship, without an option to impose sanctions.

Trust bonds could be directed toward social systems and states in general, but also could include individual politicians and could be highly differentiated for certain issues. The general amount of trust in the East German leadership and the Soviet Union was low, but that low overall level of trust did not exclude trust in specific areas: the desire for peace, social security, or a "down-to-earth" attitude were certainly rewarded, while the rigid position in the arms race or in the shaping of the German-German situation were seen with suspicion and distance. Conversely, there was a general preference in favor of the West, paired with mistrust toward ideological and political aggression inasfar as the conduct of Western politicians confirmed Eastern anti-imperialist propaganda. Based on these values, the trust relationship with the West German government was characterized by an exuberant intensity in the Brandt era of the early 1970s, followed later by a rather disillusioned basic sympathy during the Schmidt and Kohl administrations of late 1970s and early 1980s. Finally, trust in the Kohl administration shot up at the moment of the communist system's disintegration. Other Western actors did not play such an important role, although prominent political personalities (such as John F. Kennedy or Ronald Reagan) were able to provoke strong expressions of trust or mistrust, respectively.

For most of the Cold War, a feeling of a general distance and powerlessness toward the "big powers," derived from the conditionality of vertical relationships of trust with respect to the international Cold War players, had become widespread in East Germany. It corresponded with a self-positioning of personal attitudes into "submissiveness," as objects of rule. This attitude was ambivalent. It guaranteed stability and personal security within a framework of political coercion, but the alternative model of social self-organization based on horizontal trust also challenged it. For East Germans, this ambivalence tilted only at a very late stage into a revolutionary consciousness.

Notes

1. MfS, Information 863/70 über die Reaktion der Bevölkerung der DDR auf den Abschluss des Vertrages UdSSR – BRD und die Reise von Brandt nach Moskau; n.d., Federal Commissioner for the Stasi Records, Central Archives Berlin (BStU, ZA), Central Analysis and Information Group (ZAIG) 1844, Bl. 13.

2. See Hannah Arendt, *The Origins of Totalitarianism* (New York: Harcourt, Brace, 1951).

3. See Piotr Sztompka, "Trust, Distrust and Two Paradoxes of Democracy," *European Journal of Social Theory* 1, no. 1 (1998): 19–32.

4. Jürgen Gerhards and Friedhelm Neidhardt, "Strukturen und Funktionen moderner Öffentlichkeit: Fragestellungen und Ansätze" [Structures and functions of modern community: Issues and approaches], in *Öffentlichkeit, Kultur, Massenkommunikation* [Community, culture, mass communication], ed. Stefan Müller-Doohm and Klaus Neumann-Braun (Oldenburg: BIS, 1999), 34–35.

5. For the following see Ute Frevert, "Vertrauen – eine historische Spurensuche" [Trust: A historical search for clues], in *Vertrauen: Historische Annäherungen* [Trust: Historical approaches], ed. Ute Frevert (Göttingen: Vandenhoeck & Ruprecht, 2003), 7–66; and Jan C. Behrends, "Soll und Haben: Freundschaftsdiskurs und Vertrauensressourcen in der staatssozialistischen Diktatur" [Debit and credit: Friendship discourse and trust resources in the state socialist dictatorship] in ibid., 338–66.

6. See Emilio Gentile, *Politics as Religion* (Princeton, NJ: Princeton University Press, 2006), xv.

7. Bertolt Brecht, *Die Lösung* [The solution], quoted in Arnulf Baring, *Der 17. Juni 1953* [June 17, 1953], 2nd ed. (Stuttgart: Deutsche Verlags-Anstalt, 1983), 196 ff.

8. Frevert, "Vertrauen," 16–17.

9. See Sigrid Meuschel, *Legitimation und Parteiherrschaft in der DDR* [Legitimacy and party rule in the GDR] (Frankfurt/Main: Suhrkamp, 1992).

10. Sztompka, "Trust and Distrust."

11. Frevert, "Vertrauen," 31.

12. Christoph Kleßmann, "Relikte des Bildungsbürgertums in der DDR" [Relics of the educated middle class in the GDR], in *Sozialgeschichte der DDR* [Social history of the GDR], ed. Hartmut Kaelble, Jürgen Kocka and Hartmut Zwahr (Stuttgart: Klett-Cotta, 1994), 254–70; and Georg Wagner-Kyora, *Vom „nationalen" zum „sozialistischen" Selbst: Zur Erfahrungsgeschichte deutscher Chemiker und Ingenieure im 20. Jahrhundert* [From "national" to "socialist" self: Experiencing the history of German chemists and engineers in the twentieth century] (Stuttgart: Steiner, 2009).

13. See Bayless Manning, "The Congress, the Executive, and Intermestic Affairs: Three Proposals," *Foreign Affairs* 55, no. 2 (1977): 306–24.

14. The "information on reactions of the population," issued by the MfS from 1958 to 1989, contained several hundred single-issue reports of about two to ten pages each. The Infratest GDR program was based on representative surveys of West German visitors of East Germany, summarized in annual reports of several hundred pages. The program ran from 1968 to 1989. For methodological questions, see Jens Gieseke, "Bevölkerungsstimmungen in der geschlossenen Gesellschaft: MfS-Berichte an die DDR-Führung in den 60er und 70er Jahren" [Population moods in the closed society: Stasi reports to the GDR leadership in the 1960s and 1970s], *Zeithistorische Forschungen* 5, no. 2 (2008): 236–57.

15. See Jens Gieseke, "Auf der Suche nach der schweigenden Mehrheit Ost. Die geheimen Infratest-Stellvertreterbefragungen und die DDR-Gesellschaft 1968 bis 1989" [Looking for the silent majority east: The secret Infratest proxy surveys and East German society from 1968 to 1989], *Zeithistorische Forschungen* 12, no. 1 (2015): 66–97.

16. The following summary is based on an analysis of the MfS reports of the years 1958 to 1968 on international and German-German issues, and of a number of early Infratest studies, based on proxy and refugee reports. Findings will be presented in more detail in a monograph in progress. See Daniela Münkel, *Die DDR im Blick der Stasi 1961* [The GDR in the view of the Stasi, 1961] (Göttingen: Vandenhoeck & Ruprecht, 2011); and Daniela Münkel, "Unruhe im eingeschlossenen Land: Ein interner Stasi-Bericht zur Lage in der DDR nach dem Mauerbau" [Unrest in the closed country: An internal Stasi report on the situation in East Germany after the fall of the Wall], *Vierteljahrshefte für Zeitgeschichte* 59, no. 4 (2011): 579–608.

17. See Bernd Stöver, *Die Befreiung vom Kommunismus* [The liberation from communism] (Köln: Böhlau, 2002); for Poland, see Dariusz Jarosz, "Kriegsgerüchte in Polen, 1946–1956" [Rumors of war in Poland, 1946–1956], in *Angst im Kalten Krieg* [Angst in the Cold War], ed. Bernd Greiner, Christian Th. Müller, and Dierk Walter (Hamburg: Hamburger Ed., 2009), 310–21.

18. Infratest GDR program 1968, question 32 (N = 347).

19. MfS, Information 863/70, BStU, ZA, ZAIG 1844, Bl. 10.

20. MfS, Information 1100/72 über die Reaktion der Bevölkerung der DDR zur Politik der Brandt/Scheel-Regierung im Zusammenhang mit dem Ergebnis der Bundestagswahl vom 19.11.1972, 5.12.1972, BStU, ZA, ZAIG 2095, here Bl. 2; the following quotations Bl. 3–5 and 13.

21. MfS, Information 863/70, BStU, ZA, ZAIG 1844, Bl. 1–17.

22. Infratest GDR program 1970, question 60 (N = 442).

23. Infratest GDR program 1972, question 63 (N = 226).

24. MfS, Information 609/72 über verstärkte Anfragen von Bürgern der DDR, besonders an staatliche Organe, über Reisemöglichkeiten in die BRD und nach Westberlin, 28.6.1972, BStU, ZA, ZAIG 2049, Bl. 1.

25. MfS, Information 294a/70 über die Reaktion der Bevölkerung der DDR zum bevorstehenden Treffen Stoph – Brandt in Erfurt, 17.3.1970, Bl. 7–8.

26. MfS, Information 863/70, BStU, ZA, ZAIG 1844, Bl. 12.

27. Infratest GDR program 1971, question 60 (N = 44).

28. Infratest GDR program 1971, questions 65 (N = 158) and 68 (N = 147).

29. Infratest GDR program 1972, question 67A (N = 212).

30. MfS, Information 1100/72, BStU, ZA, ZAIG 2095, Bl. 13.

31. MfS, Erste Hinweise zur Reaktion der Bevölkerung der DDR zum Rücktritt Brandts vom Amt des Bundeskanzlers (Stand: 13.5.1974), 13.5.1974, BStU, ZA, ZAIG 4088.

32. Infratest GDR program 1975, questions 47 (N = 956) and 48 (N = 287).

33. Fred Halliday, *The Making of the Second Cold War* (London: Verso, 1986).

34. For general perceptions, see question 49 from the Infratest GDR program 1975: "Who benefited from détente and cooperation?" (Both sides 59%, Soviet Union 32%, the West in the long run 8% [N = 649]).

35. Infratest GDR program 1984, question 28 (N = 192).

36. MfS, Hinweise über Reaktionen der Bevölkerung der DDR auf die jüngsten Abrüstungsvorschläge der UdSSR und der Staaten des Warschauer Vertrages, 10.1.1983, BStU, ZA, ZAIG 4168, Bl. 2–5; and MfS, Erste Hinweise zur Reaktion der Bevölkerung der DDR zu den von der UdSSR, der DDR und der CSSR beschlossenen ersten Gegenmaßnahmen auf die Stationierung neuer USA-Raketen in Westeuropa, 26.10.1983, BStU, ZA, ZAIG 4172, Bl. 60–65.

37. MfS, Hinweise zur Reaktion der Bevölkerung der DDR zu den von der UdSSR, der DDR und der CSSR beschlossenen ersten Gegenmaßnahmen auf die Stationierung neuer USA-Raketen in Westeuropa (2. Bericht) 28.10.1983, BStU, ZA, ZAIG 4172, Bl. 51–58, here Bl. 53.

38. MfS, Weitere Hinweise zur Reaktion der Bevölkerung der DDR zum XXVI. Parteitag der KPdSU; 9.3.1981, BStU, ZA, ZAIG 4155, Bl. 11–16, here Bl. 12.

39. MfS, 26.10.1983, BStU, ZA, ZAIG 4172, Bl. 60–65, quotes Bl. 61.

40. MfS, Erste Hinweise über die Reaktion der Bevölkerung der DDR zum XXVI. Parteitag der KPdSU, 2.3.81, BStU, ZA, ZAIG 4155, Bl. 18–23, here Bl. 21; and MfS, Hinweise zur Reaktion der Bevölkerung der DDR (X. Parteitag) 10.4.1981, BStU, ZA, ZAIG 4158, Bl. 43–48, here Bl. 44.

41. MfS, 10.1.1983, BStU, ZA, ZAIG 4168, Bl. 4.

42. MfS, 26.10.1983, BStU, ZA, ZAIG 4172, Bl. 62.

43. MfS, Hinweise zur Reaktion der Bevölkerung der DDR zu den von der UdSSR, der DDR und der CSSR beschlossenen ersten Gegenmaßnahmen auf die Stationierung neuer USA-Raketen in Westeuropa, 14.11.1983, BStU, ZA, ZAIG 4172, Bl. 44–49, here Bl. 46.

44. MfS, Weitere Hinweise zur Reaktion der Bevölkerung der DDR auf die Gegenmaßnahmen der Staaten des Warschauer Vertrages und in diesem Zusammenhang getroffene Aussagen auf der 7. Tagung des ZK der SED sowie auf damit im Zusammenhang stehende Eingaben, Petitionen u.ä. Schreiben, 10.1.1984, BStU, ZA, ZAIG 4172, Bl. 9–19, here Bl. 10.

45. MfS, Erste Hinweise zur Reaktionen der Bevölkerung der DDR im Zusammenhang mit dem bevorstehenden Arbeitstreffen zwischen dem Generalsekretär des ZK der SED und Vorsitzenden des Staatsrates der DDR, Genossen Erich Honecker, und dem Bundeskanzler der BRD, Schmidt, 20.8.1980; BStU, ZA, ZAIG 4150, Bl. 2–8, here Bl. 5.

46. MfS, 20.8.1980, BStU, ZA, ZAIG 4150, Bl. 2; Bericht zur Reaktion der Bevölkerung der DDR im Zusammenhang mit dem bevorstehenden Treffen zwischen dem Generalsekretär des ZK der SED und Vorsitzenden des Staatsrates der DDR, Genossen Erich Honecker, und dem Bundeskanzler der BRD, Helmut Schmidt, 22.8.1980, BStU, ZA, ZAIG 4150, Bl. 9–16; Erste Hinweise zur Reaktion der Bevölkerung der DDR zum Treffen Honecker-Schmidt 5.12.1981, BStU, ZA, ZAIG 4164, Bl. 2–3.

47. Infratest GDR program 1979, question 66 (N = 454); and Infratest GDR program 1983, questions 28 (N = 717) and 29 (N = 806).

48. MfS, Erste Hinweise zur Reaktion der Bevölkerung der DDR auf den Stationierungsbeschluss des BRD-Bundestages, auf die Gegenmaßnahmen der Staaten des Warschauer Vertrages und in diesem Zusammenhang getroffene Aussagen auf der 7. Tagung des ZK der SED, 6.12.1983, BStU, ZA, ZAIG 4172, Bl. 33–42, here Bl. 34.

49. Infratest GDR program 1984, question 29 (N = 234).

50. MfS, 6.12.1983, BStU, ZA, ZAIG 4172, Bl. 38.

51. MfS, Erste Hinweise über Reaktionen der Bevölkerung der DDR auf das Interview des Genossen Honecker "Zu einigen aktuellen Fragen der Innen- und Außenpolitik der DDR," 28.8.1984, BStU, ZA, ZAIG 4179, Bl. 2–5, here Bl. 4.

52. MfS, 26.10.1983, BStU, ZA, ZAIG 4172, Bl. 60–65.

53. MfS, 10.1.1983, BStU, ZA, ZAIG 4168, Bl. 2–5; MfS, Erste Hinweise über Reaktionen der Bevölkerung der DDR auf das Treffen der Außenminister der UdSSR und der USA in Genf, 14.1.1985, BStU, ZA, ZAIG 4187, Bl. 2–5, here Bl. 2.

54. MfS, 10.1.1984, BStU, ZA, ZAIG 4172, Bl. 14.

55. Infratest GDR program 1982, question 43 (N = 243).

8. Not Quite "Brothers in Arms": East Germany and People's Poland between Mutual Dependency and Mutual Distrust, 1975–1990

Jens Boysen

Conceptual Considerations:
Trust as a Factor in Intrabloc Relations in the Warsaw Pact

During the thirty-six years of its existence from 1955 to 1991,[1] the Warsaw Treaty Organization, also known as the Warsaw Pact, was the most important framework for political coordination among its member states, the so-called people's democracies. Official statements and propaganda slogans, directed in significant part toward the West, always stressed the unshakable unity and unanimity of this "socialist community of peoples,"[2] based on the allegedly complete identity of its political interests and principles.

In view of this staunch claim of supranational cohesion, it seems appropriate to inquire whether trust was a central basis and pivotal resource for such unity. The issue will be addressed in terms of the extent to which one can identify common interests of the Warsaw Pact member states based on common identities and characteristics that would lead to common policies. These are elements that, if they can be identified, may be taken as evidence of a tendency toward some degree of supranational integration.[3] The issue has so far been little discussed with regard to the Warsaw Pact members after the end of their alleged uniformity as the "Eastern bloc," but it deserves more attention in the light of the pact's long-term existence and the small likelihood that, after the initial phase of direct regime enforcement that ended in 1956, this huge and heterogeneous space was held together only through Soviet coercion. Most obviously, the non-Soviet communist elites played an active, receptive, or even creative part in the Sovietization of Eastern Europe[4] and the functioning of the Warsaw Pact.

In this context, the issue of trust seems particularly important in the light of the process of détente that triggered a change of political climate for the Warsaw Pact and the North Atlantic Treaty Organization (NATO) in the 1970s. Détente, as we now know, served in the long run to undermine the Warsaw Pact, not least by allowing national rivalries among its member states to reveal themselves. This chapter will examine in particular the role of trust during the Cold War, and to that end it focuses primarily on the intrabloc relationship between the German Democratic Republic (GDR) and the Polish People's Republic after the signing of the Helsinki Final Act in 1975. The strain that arose in the region related to issues surrounding the interpretation of socialism and the presocialist past.

Historical materialism provided the ideological backdrop for the construction of the "socialist community" of the Warsaw Pact. The doctrine foresaw a "historically necessary" transition from capitalism to socialism that would offer the members of the socialist camp the opportunity to build a new order unburdened by the past of unjust societal relations. In security terms, this notion translated into the concept of a "brotherhood in arms" uniting the treaty states of the pact. This concept meant much more than a mere military coalition of the type that had existed in earlier epochs. It called for a civil-military community that would defend the "common achievements of socialism" in the spirit of "proletarian internationalism," based on a "class-conscious interpretation of international politics." In external affairs, the supposed harmony of fundamental goals would translate into "foreign policy coordination," which would operate "to combine, in an organic manner, the interests of the community with those of the individual brother countries." This coordination, to be carried out by the ruling parties, would "realize in a Leninist way the objective dialectical unity of national and international aspects within the foreign policies of the sovereign socialist states." The end result would be "the unitary behavior of the Warsaw Pact countries in the international arena," which would in turn help the pact "to keep the initiative in global affairs."[5]

At a more mundane level, both friend and foe acknowledged throughout the Cold War that the primary (though not the only) factor determining and steering the collective policies of the Warsaw Pact was the military, political, and economic domination of the Soviet Union over Central and Eastern Europe, established during the final stages of the Second World War and its aftermath.[6] Soviet preeminence made the region appear to be the external empire of Moscow rather than a genuine alliance of relative equals like NATO. From this perspective, historical materialism mainly represented an ideological superstructure that served to camouflage a political reality based on military power. As time went by, however, the states ruled by communist parties corresponded more to the "realist" ideal of internally unified international actors than did the liberal and pluralist countries of the West.[7] In theory, had the Warsaw Pact members indeed been guided by the same perception of international relations, they might have fairly accurately followed the path prescribed by Marxist-Leninist ideology.

But scholars have long since determined that the familiar notion of the Eastern "bloc" found its limits in the recognizable differences among the national interests of the member states, or, stated differently, among the varying ways in which they understood the raison d'être of the alliance. These differences were traceable to different legacies of historical development, social and economic structure, political culture, and general mentality. During the early phases of the Soviet "external empire," specifically between 1945 and the late 1960s, these disparities created a situation of mutual distrust and distancing rather than one of cooperation.[8] Yet even among themselves, the representatives of the ruling communist parties would often voice dissenting opinions and attempt to influence the alliance's policies to promote their national interests, especially after the member countries achieved greater military and political integration in the mid-1960s. Thus the "bloc" did not manage to or even intend to eliminate national diversity.[9] Even formally, beneath the superior multilateral level established in 1955, the bilateral treaties on mutual assistance that the Soviet Union had first concluded with its allies remained in effect, and the other member states later entered into such treaties among themselves.[10]

The Warsaw Pact came into being in 1955, officially as a reaction to West Germany's accession to NATO in that year. The pact could be interpreted as a step toward greater integration, but at the same time it effectively served as a compensatory arrangement, offsetting the fact that after Joseph Stalin's death the Soviet Union neither could nor would control the allied armies through direct supervision and intervention. When the Gomułka regime in Poland sought changes after October 1956 in both the bilateral Polish-Soviet regulations of military cooperation and the multilateral, pact-based ones, a memorandum drafted by the Polish army command in November of that year noted that the existing regulations were "at variance with the policies of independence and sovereignty as proclaimed by the Party leadership and the government." This statement referred in particular to the "supranational" status of the (Soviet) Supreme Commander of the United Armed Forces and the subordination of non-Soviet units to him.[11] Although the memorandum expressed no distrust as to Soviet intentions, Polish cooperation in the alliance was conditional on the de jure, if not de facto, inviolability of its national sovereignty.

Likewise, because the Soviet Union's global activities consumed much of its resources in the 1950s and 1960s, it sought to redistribute the financial, organizational, and military burden of defending its European "external empire" in a way that demanded a significantly greater contribution from its non-Soviet allies. Though this development could be considered an expression of the Soviets' trust in the allies' capabilities and loyalty to the common cause, the allies were already burdened with large costs associated with the presence and supply of the Soviet troops stationed in their countries. Moreover, the Soviet requests were not accompanied by any substantial offers of increased sharing in leadership functions or high-ranking staff positions or the like.[12] As an illustration, in January 1966 the Polish army command, which exerted a good bit of influence on the military policy of the Polish United Workers' Party (Polska Zjednoczona Partia Robotnicza, PZPR),[13] proposed that "[t]he general staff of the United Armed Forces [should] be composed of the representatives of all armies in proportion to the number of forces assigned to them. It is assumed that the Soviet participation in the staff will be percentage-wise smaller than their actual contribution to the Pact."[14] This proposal, however, did not produce any tangible results. As for the East German National People's Army (Nationale Volksarmee, NVA), it would remain silent on all such issues, because its political framing and control through the Ministry for State Security (Staatssicherheit, or Stasi) ensured its complete internal and external loyalty to the party line (Linientreue), and the National Defense Council (Nationaler Verteidigungsrat), a de facto extension of the Socialist Unity Party's (Sozialistische Einheitspartei Deutschlands, SED) Politburo, adopted the guidelines of the GDR's military policy.[15] Both the Polish and East German armies are further discussed below.

Despite such potential tensions between the member states and the hegemon, as well as tensions among non-Soviet members, the Warsaw Pact exercised a considerable influence upon the national policies of its members and represented a considerable collective force that held NATO strategically in check over several decades. The question thus arises as to the foundations on which, apart from sheer Soviet coercion, as mentioned above, the "socialist community" was actually built, and its capacity for any real supranational integration.

As a related matter, it is necessary to examine the even further-reaching notion of any transnational character in the multilateral relations among the Warsaw Pact member states and their societies. So far as "socialist" countries are concerned, scholars have to date applied the concept of transnationality mostly to political opposition movements. For regime elites, a similar scholarly process is still in the making.[16]

For purposes of this discussion, the existence or building of trust is a crucial, if "soft," resource for the shaping of political relations, whether domestic or international, and the development of trust involves both structural/institutional and (inter)personal dimensions. In keeping with its dynamic character, trust is said to have a history.[17] This means that relations built on trust change over time and have to be understood for any given historical situation. Given the ideological claim of a predetermined identity of interests among the "socialist brother countries," the Warsaw Pact members could not acknowledge the need to provide any formal mechanisms for actual negotiations or to create a confidence-building framework. As Piotr Sztompka has noted, the assumed unanimity of pact members probably resulted in much less "institutionalization of distrust" within the "socialist camp" than occurred when détente between the Eastern and Western blocs came about.[18]

Owing to the pact's specific ideological and political background, the term "trust" rarely was used explicitly, at least in public, by representatives of the socialist regimes to describe their mutual relationships. Instead, terms such as "friendship" and "brotherhood" prevailed. These terms implied a preset state of affairs, fixed and stable, that served as the basis for a common policy toward the outside world. A different, though related, issue is how domestic trust could be built in the societies of "real socialism" despite the paralyzing "harmony" among the classes; a relatively severe control policy on the part of the authorities; and the absence, or at least scarcity, of autonomous societal associations.[19]

Each Warsaw Pact member country was subject to very specific conditions as a result of its historical path and the existing Cold War environment. Basically, the principal foundation of the "socialist community" was interparty relations, to which interstate relations were subordinate. It therefore seems reasonable to look principally at interparty relations to discern the motives and interests that shaped neighborly relations, while keeping in mind that this examination will not produce a comprehensive picture. The guiding question may be stated as follows: How did the East German and Polish leaderships perceive each other's political priorities, and how did these perceptions and the assessments based on them affect their readiness for cooperation as "brother countries" during the 1970s and 1980s?

In addressing these questions, one must consider the "external" political forces brought to bear by the Soviet Union and the Federal Republic of Germany (FRG). The former, as the hegemon of East Germany and Poland, provided them with military protection but also exploited their respective views and interests—which from a bilateral perspective often appeared incompatible—in a divide-and-rule fashion so as to consolidate its control over the western fringe of its external empire. As a related matter, one thing that may cast doubt on the very idea of trust within the Soviet sphere of influence is the widely held view that the Russian imperial legacy, the country's specific historical experience of both self- and foreign-inflicted catastrophes since 1917, the resulting sociopsychological distortions, and the utterly different heritage of the European allies caused the Soviet leadership to regard those allies and their "unruly" populations with an "oversensitive mistrust."[20] The following discussion will attempt to shed some light on this issue also.

The FRG grew over time into the most important interbloc contact for the GDR and Poland. Initially, both these countries vilified the Bonn Republic as the main threat to the postwar order, because it questioned their borders and, in the case of the GDR, its very existence. It was also thought to harbor "revanchist" schemes that sought to restore the prewar borders of the German state. But beginning in the 1970s, the GDR and Poland sought the FRG's economic and technological cooperation to enhance their own standards of living.

In this context, and from the perspective of developments over the course of forty years, the threat perceptions of East Germany and Poland with respect to each other may appear contradictory. It may be that the Warsaw Pact gave each country sufficient support to pursue such "dangerous" contacts, or that certain beneficial factors outweighed the mistrust built into the bipolar conflict. The security dilemma described by Ken Booth and Nicholas Wheeler as the "dilemma of interpretation" may be relevant here to the intentions of the East German and Polish comrades, whose policies often appeared unclear in the light of the purported common cause. Each state had to rely on the other's continuing to play its part in maintaining the common politico-military framework. When, after 1975, East Germany and Poland developed divergent views of how best to behave as members of the socialist camp, this development made their perception of each other into an issue similar to, and perhaps more complex than, reconnaissance of the "class enemy" on the other side of the Iron Curtain. Given their mutual dependence as those parts of the Soviet strategic glacis that were under the most stress from war preparations and most exposed to potential destruction, one can also apply the integrity/reliability pair.[21] In any case, the kind of trust needed between the "brothers in arms" had less to do with strategic action in the interbloc dimension—the domain, generally, of the Soviet Union—than with maintenance of the status quo within the Warsaw Pact. Here, neighborly relations were of crucial importance.

Difficult Neighbors: Historical Legacies as an Impediment to "Brotherly" Relations between East Germany and Poland after 1945

After the Second World War, conditions were extremely unfavorable to the creation of good relations between East Germany and Poland. Stalin initially kept Germany's fate open, hoping for an all-German settlement that would satisfy his less-than-wholly-obvious security needs. As late as 1952, in the face of increased efforts by the Western allies to integrate West Germany politically and militarily, he made a proposal for a reunited, neutralized Germany. The seriousness of this offer is disputed even today.[22] But already, when any all-German option visibly faltered after 1947, Stalin had begun to turn the Soviet-occupied zone into an effectively separate communist state, in parallel with the Western allies' efforts in their respective zones. This development entailed the limited empowerment of the German communists and a plan for the GDR, founded in 1949, to advance from being a pariah nonstate to becoming a formally equal member of the Soviet external empire. The final major step toward this goal would be the inclusion of the GDR in the Warsaw Pact and the creation of the NVA in 1955–56. In the West, the Federal Republic set out on an analogous path of development. In 1955 it created the Federal Defense Forces (Bundeswehr) and simultaneously became a member of NATO. Admittedly, the leaders of both German states, Konrad Adenauer and Walter Ulbricht, gave priority to normative and physical anchorage in their respective camps and effectively treated national unity as a desirable but secondary issue.

In the GDR, apart from Soviet coercion, an important means to secure popular acceptance of this development (which included the partition of Germany) was a class-based narrative in which the GDR figured as the state of the "good," antifascist forces within the German people who, regardless of the apparent significance of such events as occupation, massacres of the civilian population by Soviet soldiers, territorial losses, partition, and universal denunciation, had been "liberated" by the Soviet Army and found themselves among the "victors of history" alongside the Soviet Union. Beneath the surface, however, were lasting disadvantages and uncertainties that also helped the Soviet Union keep its grip on "its" part of Germany:

- Throughout its existence, the GDR confronted the political, ideological, economic, and cultural challenge posed by the FRG, and thus depended significantly on Soviet political and material support.
- The GDR's position as the westernmost outpost of the Warsaw Pact made it very valuable to the Soviet Union but at the same time reduced its strategic leeway to practically zero.
- The Soviet Union never ceded its rights under the Four Powers' responsibility for "Germany as a whole," which not only allowed it to override East German sovereignty but also left it the possibility to "trade" the GDR for another, preferable, security arrangement.

For their part, the Polish communist forces, meaning the Polish Committee of National Liberation (Polski Komitet Wyzwolenia Narodowego; also called the Lublin Committee after its place of foundation) and its Polish People's

173

Army, had been busy between 1944 and 1947 supporting the Soviet Army during the final stages of the war against Germany; taking possession of the formerly German eastern territories and expelling the remaining Germans; and eliminating the remnants of the Home Army, the mostly right-wing forces subordinate to the London-based government in exile.[23] The official status of Poland as a member of the anti-Hitler coalition and a "victorious power" differed greatly from that of occupied Germany. But Stalin made an offer to the communist Polish regime similar to the one made to the East Germans. It contemplated a formal alliance based on nominal equality and, most important, a securing of Poland's new western border against West German claims. The price was the reconstruction of Polish society essentially according to the Soviet model. The main problem for the Polish communists was their lack of societal and political legitimacy. In a response that was a portent for the nature of their regime, they managed to win over the majority of the population essentially by emphasizing the need for Soviet protection from Germany. In so doing, they endorsed two major principles that came to shape Polish politics until the 1980s: first, an anti-German stance and a radical nationalism in general[24] and second, the primacy of foreign policy.

Thus, Polish readiness in the late 1940s to accept the East Germans as allies within the Soviet-led camp, more or less explicitly labeled "Slavic" after 1941, was extremely limited.[25] It did not help that communists ruled both countries, a fact that revealed the superficiality of the often-propagated "myth of proletarian internationalism."[26] Not only were the economic, societal, and political preconditions for building "socialism" widely different in East Germany and Poland, but events during and after the war had created a mutual feeling of incompatibility that hampered cooperation. Not least among these events was the loss to Poland of vast German territories east of the Oder and Neisse rivers. This was a situation that even the German communists could not imagine as permanent, but the lasting possession of these territories was central to the Polish communists' remaining in power.

The Cold War and an Imposed "Friendship": East Germany and Poland as Allies

An official German-Polish rapprochement started only after 1947, when the Soviet Union decided to turn its Eastern European zone of domination into a permanent structure and forced its client regimes to present themselves as a tight-knit community. In this way, the "myth of Stalinist brotherhood" came into being.[27] In the treaty named for the border town of Görlitz/Zgorzelec and signed on July 6, 1950, the GDR accepted the new border with Poland along the Oder and Neisse rivers, thus ceding Germany's eastern provinces to Poland and the Soviet Union.[28] Officially, the GDR acted in the spirit of the "historically new" neighborhood, but the treaty was indeed signed under Soviet pressure. Acceptance of the Oder-Neisse border was not only a Soviet-imposed prerequisite for any East German–Polish cooperation but also a measure deemed necessary to obtain Soviet support. At the time, the German communists were challenging West Germany's leaders for ideological and political leadership of the nation, and it was thought that Soviet support had to be obtained at any cost.

However, the acceptance of the territorial losses and the need to integrate several million refugees put a strain on the political legitimacy of the East German communist regime and its neighborly relations with Poland.[29] Despite the "invented"[30] and "imposed friendship"[31] under which both sides started lauding each other's "socialist achievements," neither the people nor the leaders of the GDR could easily overlook the price they had paid for this new status. Similarly, the Polish leadership, while spinning an official narrative of the GDR as the heir and guarantor of German antifascism, did not trust a change of mind by the German communists that they knew to be enforced by Moscow. In addition, the Polish leadership adhered to a nationalistic view of politics and harbored resentments against the Germans in general.[32] The new Oder-Neisse "peace border" was heavily guarded, and before 1971 it hardly could be crossed by ordinary citizens. Official meetings and other "public show[s] of affection [merely] masked the fundamental lack of trust between the Polish and East German communists that had developed after the war."[33] In the circumstances, no environment of trust could develop. What continued to work, however, and to guarantee a minimum of cooperation was the loyalty displayed by both regimes toward Moscow, their common external point of reference.[34] A later joint publication from the 1970s by the ruling parties of the GDR and People's Poland, the content of which was mostly provided by the Poles, acknowledged that a unilateral change of attitude by the Germans after 1945 had been a necessary precondition for the creation of trust between the two neighbors.[35] This change had been facilitated, from the East German perspective, by the SED's class-based view of history, and later, in the 1970s, by the adoption of the concept of a "socialist nation" and the policy of opening that promised to lead to an integrated socialist community.[36]

The simultaneous process of Sovietization, especially after 1948, had produced a certain similarity in the internal development of both countries. But after 1956 their paths began to diverge for good. The PZPR aimed to roll back Sovietization. It drew heavily on an idea of "national agreement" and thus tolerated pockets and even whole subcultures of cultural liberalism and pluralism—such as the intellectual Klub Krzywego Koła (Crooked Circle Club) in the late 1950s or the Catholic independent milieu around the Tygodnik Powszechny (The General Weekly) magazine founded in Kraków in 1945—so long as these groups did not openly question its leadership. In contrast, the SED tightened its control over both party and population after the erection of the Berlin Wall in 1961. The SED referred ostentatiously to Marxism-Leninism and built up an authoritarian police state. Ideological orthodoxy became its ersatz nationalism, which it held up against the less "devout" brethren in the socialist camp, typically the Poles. Consequently, tensions with Poland were fueled both by fundamental contradictions of national interests and by different ideological points of view. Until 1970, the situation was aggravated by the personal enmity between East Germany's leader Walter Ulbricht and Poland's Władysław Gomułka. What resulted has been called a "Cold War in the Soviet bloc." Even today, renowned scholars cite the East German–Polish relationship as prototypical for the "'false sense of . . . friendship" within the Warsaw Pact.[37] The hoped-for medium of the "collective identity"[38]—the "socialist community"—took shape only superficially, by covering over rather than eliminating those forces (such as nationalism) that seemed to run counter to "socialist trust-building." Ironically, though nationalism was in theory a "bourgeois relict," the Soviet Union exploited it to build a flexible but stable external empire. Contrary to the hopes of the SED, another factor inhibited the further fusion of national interests in the 1960s. The erection of the Berlin Wall in 1961 significantly reduced the danger of "West German imperialism"[39] in the view of the Poles and the Czechs as well. This fact did not prevent either the Polish or the Czech leadership from using that term whenever suitable. But all the while, for better or worse, they continued to treat the East Germans first and foremost as Germans.

Well after the foundation of the Warsaw Pact and the numerous crises between 1956 and 1968, the Soviet Union decided to advance the multilateral military integration of its allies as the main pillar of its strategic security system. This step was expected to buttress its continued strategic hegemony by allowing for some degree of national "coloring" on the part of its allies.[40] To some extent, the invasion of Czechoslovakia in August 1968, in which Poland and East Germany participated (though the latter did not directly deploy troops), brought about a more united phase in the history of the pact. One might even speak of a common crime that bonded the allies (albeit less so for Romania, whose armies did not take part in this action). That more united phase required a more substantial structural and procedural integration at the political level; moreover, it enhanced the role and responsibility of the non-Soviet member states. Consequently, both East Germany and Poland sought to influence the alliance's collective performance in accordance with their own priorities.

Here, significant differences of strategic interest began to make themselves felt between East Berlin and Warsaw. One of the first issues discussed within the freshly founded Warsaw Pact had been Polish foreign minister Adam Rapacki's 1957–58 plan to create a nuclear-free zone in Central Europe. The GDR leadership criticized the plan, which it viewed as principally an attempt to reduce Soviet influence in that region. A short time later, in 1958, Poland displayed serious doubts about Ulbricht's and Soviet leader Nikita Khrushchev's handling of the second Berlin crisis.[41] In 1964, a similar disagreement developed over Gomułka's renewed version of the Rapacki Plan, which envisaged a freeze of the US and Soviet nuclear armaments on the soil of the two German states. The East Germans wanted to see the nuclear weapons removed entirely.[42] Tensions continued when, in 1969, the pact members began to discuss their negotiating position for the planned European Security Conference. Initially, East Germany and Poland agreed to make West German recognition of the inter-German border and the Oder-Neisse line a precondition for talks. Despite this plan, the Poles—in a move that was typical of their rather egocentric comportment—presented without previous coordination a draft that the East Germans considered dangerous. They viewed it as suggesting asymmetrical arms reductions by the Eastern bloc, a measure that they believed would allow the West to drive a wedge between the Warsaw Pact members.[43]

However, it was also during that period, especially between 1967 and 1969, that the two neighbors, worried about what they perceived as Soviet recklessness toward the centrality of the European theater for the Cold War and afraid of being "sold" by Moscow, briefly cooperated to fend off West German "pre-détente" lures. Each viewed the other as a guarantor of the inter-German border as well as the German-Polish one.[44] Here one might see, albeit in limited fashion, an example of the integrity/reliability pair as found in Booth and Wheeler's analysis. But this phase of relative solidarity ended when, between 1969 and 1972, West Germany concluded cooperation treaties with the Soviet Union, Poland, and East Germany, and successfully used the divergent national interests of those countries to secure significant influence for itself.

Subsequently, during the "good" decade of the 1970s, East German and Polish foreign policy interests came more and more into a state of rivalry. Nonetheless, precisely at that time, their bilateral relations were officially characterized as a "brotherly association" (Bruderbund) and the neighbors claimed to have achieved a state of mutual "trust, respect, and friendship."[45] Because their domestic policies continued to diverge, these claims could not be explained in rational terms, and incidents of disagreement were interpreted in opposite ways: Whereas the GDR's orthodox Marxist leaders pointed to their Polish comrades' "ideological deviations," the Poles came to judge their western neighbors mainly with reference to their own primordial source of legitimacy, a precommunist amalgam of national interest and geopolitical thinking.[46] This conceptual gap could never be closed. Nonetheless, a large degree of pragmatic cooperation and community of interest persisted into the late 1980s.

In these developments, one can discern a tacit struggle between the GDR and People's Poland involving two notions of statehood: in Poland, a traditional, habitual "realist" one that insisted upon viewing the nation-state as the primary form of political life, and in East Germany, a more "postmodern" Marxist one maintained by the SED that reduced nation-states to temporary structures of historical progress and suggested their possible fusion into a transnational, ideally global, communist community. The conceptual tension made itself felt particularly in the context of the pact's common defense policy.

"Brotherhood in Arms" as a "New Type of Military Cooperation among Socialist Countries"

As noted previously, the Warsaw Pact community was said to be based on the purportedly common values, interests, and attitudes of the "brother nations." The term "brotherhood in arms" was used as a particularly strong expression of this "natural" community. It referred primarily to the relations among the allied armies, but it also served to describe the interstate/interparty network. As was typical of communist rhetoric, the term suggested an emotional, almost irrational bond between the nations in question, as the counterpart to the equally "natural" hatred directed against the class enemy. The East German NVA regarded its "brotherhood," especially with the Soviet Army, as essential to the existence of the GDR. In 1954, the Group of Soviet Troops in Germany was turned into an allied force by the official end to the state of occupation, just as the Western troops came to be regarded as "friendly" forces in the FRG after 1952. The actual behavior of the still-massive Soviet military force in East Germany looked quite different and reflected the continued state of de facto occupation. In any case, the NVA, counting on its value for Soviet strategic planning, was eager to achieve the highest possible military standards through cooperation with the Soviets.[47]

Official military relations between the GDR and its neighbors had existed since the founding of the NVA in 1956. At the political level, relations had already been in existence since 1955, when the GDR joined the Warsaw Pact. Any trustful cooperation, however, was rendered difficult on both sides by deeply rooted negative sentiments. While Poles and Czechs remembered the wartime German occupation in their countries, the East Germans felt uneasy about taking part in military exercises conducted in former German territory in Poland and Czechoslovakia. As a result, in some instances, Polish sources reporting on common exercises noted a "wrong" attitude among East German soldiers toward Poland's "historical claims" to those territories and a lack of political sensitivity. Over time, however, workable relations did develop, especially at the regional level between adjacent units of the neighboring armies.[48]

The Polish Army had been formally allied with the Soviet Army since 1943. Unlike its East German counterpart, and despite its communist ideological base, it preserved "national" traditions that by default tended to be not only anti-German but also anti-Russian. This problem was addressed by identifying the GDR and the Soviet Union as new regimes with no connection to their "evil" historical predecessors. Thus, like the NVA, though for quite different reasons, the Polish Army emphasized the value of its "brotherhood" with the Soviet Army for the survival of its state. The GDR and its army, while never popular on the Vistula, were seen as an indispensable Soviet-guided tool that helped to safeguard Poland's western border. In this way, Polish membership in the Warsaw Pact supported a foreign policy approach aimed at—to paraphrase a saying from the West—keeping the Russians in and the East Germans down. Still, at the military level, the "brotherly" relations between Polish Army and NVA units worked quite well from the 1970s onward. This smooth functioning was undoubtedly facilitated by both technological and generational change. On the whole, the political and military leaderships of both the GDR and People's Poland were united, if for different reasons, in their unambiguous loyalty to the Soviet Union.

The issue of bilateral and multilateral military relations leads one to examine also the nature and degree of loyalty between the Warsaw Pact allies. Again, starting from the claim of "brotherhood" as well as the "historically logical" path toward communism, one might imagine and even consider necessary a gradual growth of transnational connections between, at the least, the civilian and military elites of the socialist countries. Given the power asymmetry in the Warsaw Pact, in practical terms this development would look like Sovietization, but not like the early Sovietization before 1956. Though East Germany and Poland were hugely interested in the Soviet strategic arrangement, and in that sense were clearly loyal, they also wished to see a means of effective communication and coordination that would help them express and promote their national interests. Although they knew that equality with Moscow could not be achieved, they worked to convince the hegemon that an open internal exchange of views as well as a distribution of roles in the international arena would enhance the Warsaw Pact's standing and efficiency.[49] In this way, they could seek a larger role for themselves without risking the loss of Soviet protection.

During the 1980s, some Western scholars thought that they observed a process of unification in the military sector similar to the amalgamation of ethnic groups within the Soviet Army.[50] These scholars adduced the fact that thousands of non-Soviet staff officers, with the exception of the Romanians, were gaining their final qualification for the highest posts in their respective national armies by attending Soviet military academies. Such preparation was viewed as an intensive schooling, both military and political, for the future military leaders on whom the Soviet Army would rely for the defense of the Eastern bloc.[51] Current research sheds light upon the effectiveness of this approach in political and ideological terms. Although many generals and staff officers seem to have built lasting transnational relationships, lower-ranking officers generally were excluded from these privileged circles,[52] and like ordinary soldiers they often reported ambiguous relations with their Soviet peers. In addition, some East German officers who attended Soviet military academies and thus did belong to the "chosen few" reported restrictions of personal contacts among students from different countries and only limited access to the latest products of the Soviet arms industry.[53] The latter phenomenon was also visible from the fact that the non-Soviet armies, despite their general need for compatible materiel and communications technology, almost never received the newest weaponry from their Soviet partners.

Rivalry and Cooperation in the Polish–East German Neighborhood, 1970–80

After 1970, both countries underwent a generational change of leadership, which was partly the result of a Soviet interest in calming intra-pact relations. In Poland, Władysław Gomułka, a proponent of "national communism," was removed from the post of PZPR first secretary in 1970. The immediate cause of his ouster was the bloodshed by the army and police during a clampdown on workers' protests in several coastal cities. His successor, Edward Gierek, focused on consumer interests in order to win popular support. Because the ideological basis of the PZPR had been weak ever since 1956, the communists sought to retain control by accommodating the noncommunist forces, notably the Catholic Church and moderate intellectuals, on the basis of a "national understanding." This approach mostly took the "positive" form of emphasizing common postwar achievements and the merits of the party in that context. At the same time, Polish relations with both German states began to improve and anti-German resentment slowly began to lose strength. As had been true under Gomułka and despite Gierek's own pragmatism, the policy of "national understanding" nonetheless allowed for at least occasional references to nationalist thought in basically the same way that had worked since 1944 to unite noncommunist groups in society.[54] Gierek's complex approach to domestic trust-building worked reasonably well for a long time. In the end, it was less political contradiction than economic difficulties that eroded the legitimacy of communist rule in the eyes of ordinary citizens. But all the while, stabilizing the Soviet alliance remained the primary goal of Polish foreign policy.

In the international area, Poland was a staunch supporter of the Conference on Security and Cooperation in Europe process because it hoped to benefit the most from the acknowledgment of its postwar borders and from increased economic and cultural cooperation. At the same time, it was less afraid than, say, the GDR of human rights issues and cross-border contacts. If successful, the process promised a permanent improvement in the European security environment and a reduction of Poland's dependence on the Soviet Union and East Germany for protection of its western borders.[55]

In the GDR, in 1971 Erich Honecker succeeded Walter Ulbricht, whose obstinacy, especially where Poland was concerned, had become a nuisance for the Kremlin. Honecker also pursued a policy favoring consumers, although it did not depart from the theoretical ground of Marxism-Leninism. Having lost any chance of reuniting Germany on communist terms, the ruling SED made a gradual turnaround and eventually came to endorse a "socialist nation" of the GDR in the 1970s. The change was embodied in two constitutional reforms, one in 1968 and the other in 1974. To promote this development, the SED was ready to invest all its wealth to stabilize the Warsaw Pact as a permanent, integrated structure. Critical to the SED's readiness to trust its allies was the question of whether they, too, were ready to subordinate their national interests to the "common cause." The SED would judge their reliability and trustworthiness very much in these terms. At this point, differences among the allies were easy to identify because few shared the SED's extreme "postnational" views, least of all the Poles. In this respect, however, the GDR actually behaved similarly to Poland. To preserve itself, East Berlin needed a divided Europe. Consequently, the SED's perception of its international environment, both friends and foes, underwent several changes during the 1980s in reaction to the larger political climate.[56]

Thus, during the 1970s, East Berlin and Warsaw pursued a similar foreign policy based on self-interest and good relations with the Soviet Union and with West Germany. With the latter, both countries maintained "special relations," in large part because they became increasingly worried about the

Soviet ability to maintain its external empire, especially by the end of the 1970s after Moscow's decision to reduce exports of commodities at favorable prices to its allies. Both countries exploited West Germany's sense of responsibility toward the East Germans as fellow citizens and toward the Poles as victims of the Second World War. In the long run, however, the assumption of West German chancellor Willy Brandt and his advisers that rapprochement and temporary concessions would serve to soften and ultimately split up the Eastern community would prove correct. In addition, Władysław Gomułka, Poland's leader in the 1960s, also prophesied correctly that the GDR, by driving intra-German cooperation, was digging its own grave.[57]

East Germany and Poland in the Crises of 1980–85: Common Fate, Divergent Goals

When the arms race entered a phase of renewed intensity after 1977, Poland was already burdened with an internal crisis that had started in 1976, after Gierek's policy of deficit spending led to bankruptcy. The dual strain made Poland regard itself as particularly vulnerable to the effects of the strategic conflict, and it was critical of any Soviet measures that were likely to increase tensions. Accordingly, the regime supported attempts on both sides aimed at cooling the political climate. In the next, prolonged, crisis of 1980–81, surrounding the Polish trade union movement Solidarność (Solidarity), the Polish leadership again found itself exposed to multilateral pressure not only from its allies—notably the Soviet Union and East Germany—but also from the West. The ruling PZPR was internally split over how to deal with the challenge posed by Solidarność and the mounting pressure from abroad, and it displayed growing confusion.[58] It sought to buffer foreign influences as much as possible, while domestically it appealed to the opposition for "national unity," invoking the threat of foreign intervention. At the same time, the civilian and military leaders remained in close contact with their allies.

For the East German leadership, the pressure exerted on the Polish regime was an expression of ideological enmity toward Solidarność, but it was equally motivated by a fear of economic loss, especially from commodities like coal, and the threat of losing its geographical connection with the Soviet Union in case Poland should "fall." The East Germans wished to eliminate the Polish troubles as a contributing cause of their own difficulties, instability in the Eastern bloc, and Western interference. Thus, a fundamental interest in maintaining the status quo and mitigating international tensions influenced the policy of both East Germany and Poland.

To the East German leaders, moreover, it seemed that the crisis, while mainly attributable to Poland's economic problems, was aggravated by the

Polish comrades' long tolerance of nonsocialist forces. This stance was at variance with the SED's own totalitarian principle that divergent attitudes must be eliminated. Therefore, the East German leadership pressed Warsaw to take harsh measures against the Polish opposition but retained severe doubts about their comrades' motives and determination. In September and November 1980, studies made by the SED's Central Committee had diagnosed in its Polish counterpart a neglect of Marxist positions and a prevalence of a nationalistic perspective, which made it difficult for the regime to react to a "national" opposition and would effectively make it revert eventually to "revisionist" positions. According to the SED Politburo, the developments not only were a "betrayal of internationalism" but also "called into question the vitally important alliance of People's Poland with the Soviet Union and the countries of the socialist community."[59]

During the crisis of 1980–81, both then–First Secretary Stanisław Kania and the "orthodox" Politburo members such as Stefan Olszowski sought contact with and advice from the SED. The SED was aghast at the PZPR's passivity in the face of Solidarność's efforts to undermine it, a development that increased the danger of political "contagion" for Poland's neighbors. In November 1980, Olszowski told Erich Honecker that the PZPR was losing trust among the population. At the same time, he emphasized its determination to justify the trust placed in it by the Warsaw Pact allies. Honecker confirmed that the GDR would continue to support the "healthy" forces in Poland, but at the same time he gave his Polish guest to understand that it would have harmed the "friendship" between the neighbors if "[the Polish] troubles had spread to [the GDR]."[60]

Apart from these political problems, the GDR faced detrimental economic side effects from the Polish crisis. Accordingly, Erich Honecker complained repeatedly to the Soviets that the GDR had been providing substantial support to Poland but was suffering from the decrease in coal and oil deliveries from Poland and the Soviet Union. This situation caused him to urge the Soviet Union to find a solution backed by the Warsaw Pact. Honecker neither favored nor ruled out a military intervention but pressed for the use of force by the Polish regime as the best option available.[61]

The NVA leadership, using intelligence sources in the Polish Army, arrived at similar conclusions. A November 1980 report from the NVA's own military intelligence service stated that the decision to base "patriotic education" solely on the inflated grounds of "victorious traditions and successes in the building of socialism" in the Polish Army had made the soldiers incapable of recognizing the "dangerous nature of the counterrevolutionary groups."[62] By June 1981, the NVA had ceased to believe that the Polish regime, which after all was led by the NVA's Polish Army comrades, would be able and willing to give the necessary orders.[63] Similarly, the omnipresent Stasi, the Ministry for State Security, had little faith in the new Polish leader Wojciech Jaruzelski's ability to save the regime, though it identified his stronghold, the Polish Army, as the only reliable force in the country and approved of the purges taking place within the army's ranks in 1981 and 1982.[64]

After October 1981, Jaruzelski held the triple positions of prime minister, defense minister, and PZPR first secretary. He pursued a policy of unambiguous loyalty to the Soviet Union, and as one expression of this loyalty his government repeatedly considered in 1980 and 1981 the possible forms of pressure that could be exerted by the "brother countries" and did not entirely rule out a military intervention, despite his later claims to the contrary.[65] However, he singled out the East German NVA by insisting that it should not take part in such a move, claiming that it would be unacceptable for the population.[66] Given Jaruzelski's complicity in the planning, this claim probably meant that he feared that East German participation might jeopardize public readiness in Poland to accept such a measure. West Germany, hesitating to be too severe toward the "war victim" Poland and wishing to maintain the state of relations achieved with East Germany and Poland during the 1970s, supported the Polish leadership's course of "stabilization" and "normalization." Jaruzelski nonetheless displayed a degree of paranoia regarding West German territorial claims. His mistrust of both German states was due less to rational reflection than to an irrational reflex deriving from his and his fellow generals' experience in the Second World War. They had begun their careers in 1943 by fighting Nazi Germany in the ranks of the Soviet-supported Polish army led by Zygmunt Berling, and they had never managed to overcome their anti-German attitude.

But there was agreement between the Polish leadership and their Warsaw Pact comrades about the need to assume a collective threatening posture against Solidarność. This consensus is illustrated by information that Marshal Victor Kulikov, supreme commander of the Unified Armed Forces of the Warsaw Pact, gave to East German deputy defense minister Heinz Kessler and NVA chief of staff Fritz Streletz during the pact's Military Council meeting in Sofia on April 24, 1981. Kulikov told them that Jaruzelski and Kania had requested that a joint command center for the Unified Armed Forces be installed in Legnica, the headquarters of the Soviet Northern Group of Troops in Poland. Jaruzelski and Kania allegedly believed that the presence of Soviet, East German, and Czech military there "would help the Polish party and leadership with their work."[67]

It appears nonetheless that Soviet trust in the Polish comrades was limited, because a short time later, on June 13, 1981, Kulikov met with East German and Czech army members in the headquarters of the Soviet 1st Guards Tank Army in Dresden to discuss future cooperation with the Polish Army. Kulikov had chosen the place expressly to avoid Polish eavesdropping. After some flattering remarks about the "orderly" situation in East Germany, which he contrasted with the "chaos" and growing anti-Soviet attitudes in Poland, Kulikov stated that the Polish Army, despite uncertainty on the part of some officers, was the only reliable state organ left in Poland, while the civilian leadership appeared clueless. He then mapped out measures to improve cooperation. There, he put the main emphasis on a more intense participation of Polish military in meetings and common maneuvers. Of particular importance was to be cooperation between the NVA and the Polish Army. East German officers were to take part in all Warsaw Pact exercises in Poland, "in order to force a meeting with their Polish partners." The officers were to aim *"for a thorough study of the leading cadres of the Polish Army and for a realistic assessment of whom we can trust and where caution is advisable."* In any case, the Soviet Army and Baltic Fleet and the NVA were to closely coordinate their reconnaissance for an eventual crossing into Poland, while remaining constantly in touch.[68]

Obviously, the Soviet hegemon, cooperating with the Polish leadership but aware of its potential unreliability, sought to install "safety measures" by using the more "reliable" East Germans and Czechs as "supporters." When martial law was implemented on December 13, 1981, by the Polish Army, acting without "external help," East German and Soviet institutions expressed their satisfaction and reverted to a supportive attitude toward Warsaw.

In those days of the so-called Second Cold War, the West was eager to assess the political and military reliability of the non-Soviet countries in the Eastern bloc. For lack of real insight, or so it appears, into the military effectiveness of the Warsaw Pact, Western analysts focused largely on the perceived political interests of Moscow's allies. For example, in 1981, the RAND Corporation presented a study that was probably among the best of its kind. It plausibly stated that there were significant differences between the East German, Polish, and Czechoslovak officer corps with respect to traditions, social prestige, and political training. The Soviet military leaders were said to view their German comrades as tougher and more powerful than the Czechs and Slovaks and, at the same time, as less inhibited by anti-Russian nationalism than the Poles. In the event of war, the Germans and Poles, if for different reasons, were both considered to be more reliable than the Czechs. The latter surmise, however, was limited to the short-term perspective of a blitzkrieg in which the Soviet First Front would simply carry the German and Polish units along.[69] Beyond that point, any real prediction was virtually impossible.

Rupture: East German and Polish Neighbors
in the Cold War's Final Phase, 1985–90

Mikhail Gorbachev's rise to power in 1985 changed crucial parameters of both intrabloc and interbloc relations. Initially, the Soviet Union was broadly concerned with domestic reform efforts and attempts at finding a common language with the United States. However, when Moscow started to rethink its positions in Central Europe and indicated that it might relinquish its external empire, the GDR was thrown into an existential crisis. It reacted by adopting the role of sole guardian of communism, defending the postwar status quo even against the Soviet Union,[70] as well as against its "fellow liberals," the Poles. This reaction became especially noticeable in 1987 when the Warsaw Pact, under the guidance of the Soviet General Staff, adopted a new, more defensive military doctrine and announced unilateral arms reductions. Though this move effectively reduced the danger of destruction for East Germany, it was received with great reservation there. The NVA's Main Staff[71] assembled a group to draft the GDR's own national military doctrine, an unheard-of and wholly unrealistic step that essentially was meant to send a strong political signal to Moscow. In a similar vein, in November 1988, for the first time ever the GDR's National Defense Council questioned the existing legal framework for the presence of Soviet troops on East German soil.[72] This action did not aim at the departure of Soviet troops from East Germany, but represented instead an act of angry defiance on part of the German communists, who came to fundamentally question the sincerity and reliability of their Soviet "friends" and to relive their old nightmare of being traded for strategic peace.

In contrast, in Poland, the new Soviet course provided a framework for a gradual exit from the political deadlock and the dependence on East Germany that had resulted from the imposition of martial law. After martial law was lifted in July 1983, Poland began to receive political help from the Soviet Union and economic help from the West. It became evident that the possibility of Poland's return to "true" Marxism-Leninism was now finally dead. In response, East Germany increasingly applied strict economic parameters to its cooperation with Poland that left little room for "socialist friendship." After 1986, a rapprochement between the Polish government and the opposition, based on goals of gradual modernization and a common path toward regime change, became possible.

Though the West German government and public were, like Poland, positive about Gorbachev, Poland's attitude toward West Germany remained ambiguous. One explanation for this may have been the consideration that a continued rapprochement would in the long term mean "real" Westernization rather than the selective, fairly conservative concept of a "national consensus" that the regime favored. Jaruzelski shared the aim of Gorbachev's reformist policies to create a "renewed socialism" rather than a Western-style democracy.[73] Nonetheless, after 1980 the image of West Germany improved in the eyes of the Polish public. In contrast, opinions of East Germany tended to be very critical and colored by negative stereotypes, just as the German communists employed anti-Polish stereotypes in their fight against Solidarność. Certainly, the SED's attempts to rescue "socialism" were seen as a threat; yet interestingly, some Poles interpreted the GDR's moderate policy toward the FRG as the sign of a "conspiracy" aiming at reunification. Thus, the East Germans were called unreliable with respect to their obligations under the Warsaw Pact.[74] Apart from the fact that from the GDR's point of view such an idea was wholly absurd, these Polish voices were biased and inconsistent, in view of Poland's own endeavor to profit from its Western contacts. Time and again, Polish politicians and scholars resorted to nationalist arguments that aimed to challenge the East Germans' right to define their own collective memory. They tried specifically to censor a "national revival" that took place in the GDR in the 1980s, when the SED sought to reconcile certain elements of German, notably Prussian, history that helped to create a historical identity and formed part of an intellectual competition with the FRG.[75] Moreover, the Polish criticisms were fairly hypocritical, as the Poles themselves felt free to draw, with little self-criticism, on their own national past.

In the second half of the 1980s, a number of incidents between East Germany and Poland indicated dissent and distrust. Examples included the dispute over the delineation of the sea shelf border in the Pomeranian Bay and East Germany's repeated requests for the repatriation of valuable collections of the Berlin State Library. The collections, which included manuscripts of Goethe, Beethoven, and others, had been stored in Silesia during the war to protect them from Allied air raids on the German capital. In 1945, they had been captured by the Poles and were afterwards kept at the Jagiellonian Library in Kraków, where they remain today. Such conflicts between East Germany and Poland were likely an expression of growing national assertiveness by the East Germans, whose trust in any "internationalist" attitude on the part of the Poles had faded away and who finally decided to start talking in their own "national" language.[76]

A point about security that deserves emphasis is that during those critical last years, the East German and Polish armies apparently continued to cooperate without significant problems or disagreements.[77] Interestingly, in 1988, late in the day of "real socialism," a joint publication by the two countries' military history institutes highlighted the "common revolutionary military traditions of the National People's Army of the GDR and the Polish Army."[78]

The authors made a tantalizing effort to identify, or invent, such common traditions. Despite presenting a lot of interesting facts, the artificial and imbalanced result reflected the uneasy combination of East German internationalism and Polish nationalism. In any case, the genuine stabilizing factors were more likely to have been, on the one hand, professionalism and, on the other, a military routine that promoted an instinctive course of stabilization during times of political uncertainty. These factors can be considered to have represented a specific instance of trust at a very crucial level of intrabloc cooperation, and they likely offer one reason why the unified command structures of the Warsaw Pact remained functional right to the very end in 1990.

Conclusion

The search for trust as a resource for the coherence of the Warsaw Pact, and in particular for the East German–Polish neighborhood as a crucial subunit of the "socialist community," can at the moment lead to only limited conclusions. One reason for this seems to be that the then-allies rarely used the term "trust" to describe their mutual relationships. Their silence may in turn be explained by the communists' claim of a predetermined identity of interests and corresponding harmony of political action, which did not require any trust-building. As an element of "classical," presocialist diplomacy, trust-building was necessary—and at the same time was practically unachievable—only for capitalist countries that needed to domesticate their "natural aggressiveness." The sole exception was the Warsaw Pact's use of "peaceful coexistence" as a tactical measure in the struggle for global primacy in the nuclear age. To faithful Marxists, trust would not make too much sense as a political principle or value. But then, Marxism was certainly not the only and often not even the main force shaping relations within the "socialist community." Even the shock-like introduction of Soviet-style "socialism" after 1945—and Sovietization in all the countries concerned was a mixture of violence, political seduction, and a lack of alternatives—could not overcome the powerful tradition of nationalism, or at least national specificity.

The triangular relations between the two uneasy neighbors and the Soviet hegemon were based on the fact that Poland and East Germany—

- formed the western main strategic direction of the Soviet war plan and, as a result, the main deployment and supply routes ran across their territories, so that they required direct or indirect Soviet control;[79]
- had the largest and most advanced economies, along with Czechoslovakia, in the Soviet zone of influence;

- engaged in a competition for second place under the preeminent Soviet Union; and
- owing to their historical enmity, to some extent could be played by the Soviets against each other, beginning with the 1945 "westward shift" of Poland at the territorial expense of Germany.

Indeed, Stalin himself had led and won the Second World War not least by appealing to "Soviet patriotism." This patriotism and their own homegrown nationalist heritage represented two factors that made the Polish communists turn after 1956 to "national communism" as the only viable way to secure the alliance with Moscow in the face of a starkly anticommunist population. The Soviets quickly came to understand this fact because their own mindset, after all, was not so different. The East German SED for its part did not follow a similar path of national exceptionalism after its original idea of getting all of Germany under its control had failed by the mid-1950s. Seeing its fate as exclusively dependent on the Soviet connection, it then sought to exploit Soviet nationalist/imperialist politics for achieving a position of indispensability within the "bloc," in the same way that Lenin after 1917 had invoked German intellectual leadership for the sake of world revolution. This effort by the SED entailed two major goals: maintaining and strengthening the Warsaw Pact and the other organizations that tied the socialist countries together, and at the same time establishing within the common institutions, as far as possible, the SED's own views on how to do things. Here, however, Soviet distrust, or rather jealousy, set narrow limits to the East Germans' ambitions. The Soviets' attitude toward "their" Germans stemmed not only from the war but also from more distant historical experiences: it always displayed an awkward love-hate polarity. In case of doubt, the Soviets were always ready to demonstrate their power and remind the Germans of their junior-partner status.

The Poles, with their more pragmatic and limited view of the Warsaw Pact, were not very supportive of East German policy, especially because an actual evolution toward some degree of communist transnationalism might further enhance the role of the East Germans, who never hesitated to display their "supreme" knowledge of Marxism and of pretty much everything else. As a practical matter, People's Poland's larger size and population was outbalanced by the GDR's more advanced technological and industrial heritage and the fact that the GDR had had a "real," historical proletariat in 1945. Poland, despite its efforts in the interwar period, underwent industrialization and urbanization only after 1945. This background, plus the fervent ambition of the rulers in East Berlin and Warsaw, fueled an almost forty-year rivalry. "Trust" between Poles and East Germans could work only so long as their interests left both of them in need of the Soviet connection. This situation prevailed until the mid-1980s. Meanwhile, "brotherly" confrontations did occur but were rarer than might be assumed and never called the alliance into question; contrary to certain legends, Polish "national communism" was actually never of an anti-Soviet character and was fairly consistent with the East German orthodox Marxist position. This situation endured until the Soviet change of interbloc policy under Gorbachev allowed the Poles to adopt a more flexible approach based on the belief that "Polish socialism," an amalgamation of authoritarian social reformism, nationalism, and pragmatism, could be maintained even within a post-bloc European security arrangement. In contrast, the SED knew that the end of the Cold War and a Soviet withdrawal from Central Europe would mean its own demise.

The Soviet Union, for its part, did not aim to withdraw completely, but when it had to do so it weathered the historical sea change by turning principally into a renewed Russia, in which many substantial elements of the past are working again today. One of these historical aspects is the conviction that its western neighbors can be exploited but not trusted, because as long as they wish to remain independent, their national interests are incompatible with the Russian one. As in earlier days, the only alternative for them appears to either join Russia or be treated as her enemies—but for the first time, the German and Polish positions on this issue seem to coincide.

Notes

1. The German Democratic Republic (GDR) had already left the alliance in September 1990.

2. For a classic East German account of this concept, see, e.g., Siegmar Quilitzsch and Joachim Krüger, eds., *Sozialistische Staatengemeinschaft: die Entwicklung der Zusammenarbeit und der Friedenspolitik der sozialistischen Staaten* [Socialist community of states: The development of cooperation and of the peace policies of the socialist states] (Berlin: Staatsverlag der DDR, 1972).

3. Here, I deliberately borrow terminology established principally by the European Union in the field of its Common Foreign and Security Policy; for a concise introduction see Dieter Mahncke, "The Need for a Common Foreign Policy," in *European Foreign Policy. From Rhetoric to Reality?*, ed. Dieter Mahncke, Alicia Ambos, and Christopher Reynolds (Brussels: Peter Lang, 2004), 27–42. Indeed, the phenomenon of supranationality is studied by scholars, using in particular the example of the European Union as the most advanced regional interstate association of our time, to which other regions are compared in terms of purpose, institutions, and policies. See Sergio Fabbrini, ed., *Democracy and Federalism in the European Union and the United States: Exploring Post-National Governance* (London: Routledge, 2005).

4. See Arnd Bauerkämper and Constantin Iordachi, "The Collectivization of Agriculture in Eastern Europe: Entanglements and Transnational Cooperation," in

The Collectivization of Agriculture in Communist Eastern Europe: Comparison and Entanglements, ed. Arnd Bauerkämper and Constantin Iordachi (Budapest: Central European University Press, 2014), 3–48.

5. All quotations in the preceding paragraph are from a semiofficial presentation on the principles of communist foreign policy coordination, in *DDR-VRP: Bündnis und Zusammenarbeit* [GDR-PPR: Alliance and cooperation] (Berlin-Warsaw: Staatsverlag der Deutschen Demokratischen Republik and Polski Instytut Spraw Międzynarodowych, 1974), 238–9 (translated from German).

6. On this process in general, see Norman Naimark, "The Sovietization of Eastern Europe," in *The Cambridge History of the Cold War*, Vol. 1: *Origins*, ed. Melvyn P. Leffler and Odd Arne Westad (Cambridge, UK: Cambridge University Press, 2010), 175–97.

7. See Deborah Welch Larson, *Anatomy of Mistrust: U.S.-Soviet Relations during the Cold War* (Ithaca, NY: Cornell University Press, 1997), 16–17.

8. See Dominik Trutkowski, *Der geteilte Ostblock: Die Grenzen der SBZ/DDR zu Polen und der Tschechoslowakei* [The divided Eastern Bloc: The SOZ/GDR boundaries with Poland and Czechoslovakia], Zeithistorische Studien, Bd. 49 (Cologne/Weimar/Vienna: Böhlau, 2011), 47.

9. See Winfried Heinemann, "Einleitung" [Introduction], in *Der Warschauer Pakt von der Gründung bis zum Zusammenbruch 1955–1991* [The Warsaw Pact from its founding to its collapse, 1955–1991], ed., Torsten Diedrich, Winfried Heinemann, and Christian F. Ostermann, eds., (Berlin: Ch. Links Verlag, 2009), 1–8.

10. Still useful for essential information is Alexander Uschakow and Dietrich Frenzke, *Der Warschauer Pakt und seine bilateralen Bündnisverträge: Analyse und Texte* [The Warsaw Pact and its bilateral alliance treaties: Analysis and texts] (Berlin: Berlin Verlag, 1987).

11. Memorandum concerning the Warsaw Pact and the development plan for the Armed Forces of the Polish People's Republic, with a cover letter by General J. Bordziłowski to First Secretary of the Central Committee of the Polish United Workers' Party Władysław Gomułka, November 7, 1956, Archive of New Acts (AAN) [Warsaw], Central Committee of the Polish United Workers' Party (KC PZPR), XIA/102, in Wanda Jarząbek, *PRL w politycznych strukturach Układu Warszawskiego w latach 1955–1980* [The PPR in the political structures of the Warsaw Pact, 1955–1980] (Warsaw: ISP PAN, 2008), Doc. 1, 103–9.

12. Ibid., 21–24.

13. This judgment generally can be derived from the account rendered, for example, by Andrew Michta, *Red Eagle: The Army in Polish Politics, 1944–1988* (Stanford, CA: Hoover Institution Press, 1990).

14. Document No. 34: Polish Proposals for Reform of the Warsaw Pact, January 21 and 26, 1966, b) Proposal by the Polish Defense Ministry, January 26, 1966, in *A Cardboard Castle? An Inside History of the Warsaw Pact, 1955–1991*, ed. Vojtech Mastny and Malcolm Byrne (Budapest: Central European University Press, 2005), 204.

15. See Otto Wenzel, *Kriegsbereit: Der Nationale Verteidigungsrat der DDR 1960 bis 1989* [Ready for war: The National Defense Council of the GDR, 1960–1989] (Cologne: Verlag Wissenschaft und Politik, 1995). The complete session protocols of this institution have been digitalized and put online by the German Federal Archives (Bundesarchiv), available at "Die Sitzungsprotokolle des NVR der DDR von 1960–1989," accessed February 26, 2015, http://www.nationaler-verteidigungsrat.de.

16. See Torsten Diedrich and Walter Süss, "Einleitung" [Introduction], in *Militär und Staatssicherheit im Sicherheitskonzept der Warschauer-Pakt-Staaten* [Military and state security in the security concept of the Warsaw Pact countries], ed. Torsten Diedrich and Walter Süss (Berlin: Ch. Links Verlag, 2010), 1–28. From a more theoretical perspective, see Patricia Clavin, "Defining Transnationalism," *Contemporary European History* 14, no. 4 (2005): 421–39; and Bogdan C. Iacob, "Is It Transnational? A New Perspective in the Study of Communism," *East Central Europe* 40, no. 1–2 (2013): 1–26.

17. For an introduction to this concept, see Ute Frevert, "Does Trust Have a History?" (Max Weber Lecture Series 2009-01, European University Institute, Florence, 2009), http://cadmus.eui.eu/bitstream/handle/1814/11258/MWP_LS_2009_01.pdf.

18. Piotr Sztompka, "Trust, Distrust and Two Paradoxes of Democracy," *European Journal of Social Theory* 1, no. 1 (1998), 25–26.

19. See, e.g., Jan C. Behrends, "Soll und Haben: Freundschaftsdiskurs und Vertrauensressourcen in der staatssozialistischen Diktatur" [Debit and credit: Friendship discourse and trust resources in the state socialist dictatorship], in *Vertrauen: Historische Annäherungen* [Trust: Historical approaches], ed. Ute Frevert (Göttingen: Vandenhoeck & Ruprecht, 2003), 336–64.

20. As one of many voices from the 1980s, see Peer Lange, "Militärische Macht als Herrschaftsinstrument in Osteuropa" [Military power as an instrument of power in Eastern Europe], in *Die Sowjetunion als Militärmacht*, ed. Hannes Adomeit, Hans-Herrmann Höhmann, and Günther Wagenlehner (Stuttgart et al.: Kohlhammer, 1987), 236–51, here 236.

21. Ken Booth and Nicholas J. Wheeler, *The Security Dilemma* (Houndmills, UK: Palgrave Macmillan, 2008), 243–4.

22. See, e.g., the review by Bernd Bonwetsch, "Die Stalin-Note 1952 – kein Ende der Debatte" [The Stalin Note 1952: Not the end of the debate], *Jahrbuch für Historische Kommunismusforschung* (2008), 106–13.

23. See Andrzej Ajnenkiel, "Die Armee im stalinistischen, abhängigen Staat" [The army in the Stalinist, dependent state], in *Das internationale Krisenjahr 1956: Polen, Ungarn, Suez* [The international crisis year of 1956: Poland, Hungary, Suez], ed. Winfried Heinemann and Norbert Wiggershaus (Munich: Oldenbourg, 1999), 3–25.

24. For a general account of nationalistic legitimization patterns of communist rule in Poland, see Marcin Zaremba, *Im nationalen Gewande: Strategien kommunistischer Herrschaftslegitimation in Polen 1944–1980* [In national dress: Strategies of communist rule legitimation in Poland, 1944–1980] (Osnabrück: fibre, 2011).

25. See Jan C. Behrends, *Die erfundene Freundschaft: Propaganda für die Sowjetunion in Polen und in der DDR* [The invented friendship: Propaganda for the Soviet Union in Poland and the GDR] (Cologne: Böhlau, 2006), 263; and Sylwester Fertacz, "Von Brüdern und Schwestern: Das Allslawische Komitee in Moskau 1941–1947," [Of brothers and sisters: The Panslavic Committee in Moscow, 1941–1947], in *Gemeinsam einsam: Die slawische Idee nach dem Panslawismus* [Lonely together: The Slavic idea after Panslavism], ed. Agnieszka Gąsior et al., special issue of *Osteuropa* 59, no. 12 (2009): 139–52.

26. Sheldon Anderson, *A Cold War in the Soviet Bloc: Polish-East German Relations 1945–1962* (Boulder, CO: Westview Press, 2001), 10.

27. Ibid., 52.

28. See Trutkowski, *Der geteilte Ostblock*, 49.

29. For an account of the rather similar challenges stemming from forced resettlements to the GDR and Poland, see Philipp Ther, *Deutsche und polnische Vertriebene. Gesellschaft und Vertriebenenpolitik in der SBZ/DDR und in Polen 1945–56* [German and Polish expellees: Society and displaced persons policy in the SOZ/GDR and in Poland, 1945–56] (Göttingen: Vandenhoeck und Ruprecht, 1998).

30. See Behrends, *Die erfundene Freundschaft*.

31. See the essays in Basil Kerski, Andrzej Kotula, and Kazimierz Wóycicki, eds., *Zwangsverordnete Freundschaft? Die Beziehungen zwischen der DDR und Polen 1949–1990* [A forcefully imposed friendship? The relations between the GDR and Poland, 1949–1990] (Osnabrück: fibre, 2003).

32. Behrends, *Die erfundene Freundschaft*, 264–71; and Anderson, *A Cold War*, 56–59. Also see Trutkowski, *Der geteilte Ostblock*, 17.

33. Anderson, *A Cold War*, 53.

34. See Ludwig Mehlhorn, "Zwangsverordnete Freundschaft? Zur Entwicklung der Beziehungen zwischen der DDR und Polen" [A forcefully imposed friendship? On the development of relations between the GDR and Poland], in Kerski, Kotula, and Wóycicki, *Zwangsverordnete Freundschaft?*, 36–7.

35. See DDR-VRP, 172–3.

36. On fundamental differences between East German and Polish historiography and widely failed efforts to forge a common view, see Stefan Guth, "Erzwungene Verständigung? Die Kommission der Historiker der DDR und der Volksrepublik Polen 1956–1990" [An enforced understanding? The Commission of Historians of the GDR and the People's Republic of Poland, 1956–1990], *Vierteljahreshefte für Zeitgeschichte 4* (2009): 497–542.

37. Quote from Anderson, *A Cold War*, 56; for the opinion, see Vojtech Mastny, "The Warsaw Pact as History," in Mastny and Byrne, *A Cardboard Castle?*, 1–74, here 42.

38. See Booth and Wheeler, *Security Dilemma*, 233.

39. See Trutkowski, *Der geteilte Ostblock*, 80–1.

40. See Mastny, "The Warsaw Pact as History," 34–39; and Douglas A. MacGregor, "Uncertain Allies? East European Forces in the Warsaw Pact," *Soviet Studies* 38, no. 2 (1986): 227–47.

41. See Burkhard Olschowsky, "Die staatlichen Beziehungen zwischen der DDR und Polen" [Interstate relations between the GDR and Poland], in Kerski, Kotula, and Wóycicki, *Zwangsverordnete Freundschaft?*, 44–45.

42. See Mastny, "The Warsaw Pact as History," 26.

43. Document No. 69: East German Evaluation of Polish Proposal for a European Security Treaty, November 13, 1969 (Source: G-A 556, 161–68, MfAA [GDR Foreign Ministry]), in Mastny and Byrne, *A Cardboard Castle?*, 354–55; for the context, see Wanda Jarząbek, "Polish Reactions to the West German Ostpolitik and East-West Détente, 1966–1978," in *Perforating the Iron Curtain: European Détente, Transatlantic Relations, and the Cold War, 1965–1985*, ed. Poul Villaume and Odd Arne Westad (Copenhagen: Museum Tusculanum Press, 2010), 35–56.

44. See Olschowsky, "Die staatlichen Beziehungen zwischen der DDR und Polen," 47; and Mastny, "The Warsaw Pact as History," 25–26.

45. DDR-VRP 49, 172.

46. See Burkhard Olschowsky, *Einvernehmen und Konflikt: Das Verhältnis zwischen der DDR und der Volksrepublik Polen 1980–1989* [Consensus and conflict: Relations

between the GDR and the People's Republic of Poland, 1980–1989] (Osnabrück: fibre, 2005), 427.

47. See Rüdiger Wenzke, "'Sozialistische Waffenbrüder?' Über die Beziehungen der Nationalen Volksarmee zu den anderen Warschauer-Pakt-Armeen" ["Socialist comrades in arms?": On the relationship between the National People's Army and the other Warsaw Pact armies], in Diedrich, Heinemann, and Ostermann, *Der Warschauer Pakt*, 85–118.

48. See Document No. 65: Polish Army Report on East German Misbehavior During the "Oder-Neisse-69" Exercise, October 22, 1969 (Source: Dept. I, Spis 28/74, Wiązka 6, AMSZ), in Mastny and Byrne, *A Cardboard Castle?*, 339–41; and Wenzke, "Sozialistische Waffenbrüder?," 103–6.

49. See Jordan Baev, "Die blockinterne Koordination des Warschauer Pakts und die DDR" [The intrabloc coordination of the Warsaw Pact and the GDR], in *Die beiden deutschen Staaten in ihren beiden Bündnissen 1970 bis 1990* [The two German states in their respective alliances, 1970–1990], ed. Oliver Bange and Bernd Lemke (Munich: Oldenbourg, 2013), 183–202.

50. See Teresa Rakowska-Harmstone et al., *Warsaw Pact: The Question of Cohesion. Phase II, Vol. I.: The Greater Socialist Army: Integration and Reliability* (ORAE Extramural paper No. 29, Ottawa, February 1984); quoted after Lange, *Militärische Macht*, 244.

51. See Rüdiger Wenzke, "Generale und Admirale im DDR-Militär: Eine Einführung" [Generals and admirals in the GDR military: An introduction], in *Die Generale und Admirale der NVA: Ein biographisches Handbuch* [The generals and admirals of the NVA: A biographical handbook], ed. Klaus Froh and Rüdiger Wenzke (Berlin: Ch. Links Verlag, 2000), 1–66, here 18–20.

52. This information is supported by talks that the author has had with several former Polish officers.

53. See Sabine Collmer, Georg-Maria Meyer, and Hanne Isabell Schaffer, *"Begegnungen": Deutsch-sowjetische Beziehungen im Spiegel der Wahrnehmungen von Offizieren der ehemaligen NVA* ["Encounters": German-Soviet relations reflected in the perceptions of officers of the former NVA], SOWI-Arbeitspapier Nr. 68 (Munich: Bundeswehr Institute for Social Research, 1992), 9–10.

54. It should be generally noted that in Poland, "regime nationalism" and "opposition nationalism," which informed a significant part of Solidarność ideology, shared many essential features; see Jie-Hyun Lim, "The Nationalist Message in Socialist Code: On the Court Historiography in People's Poland and North Korea," in *Making Sense of Global History: The 19th International Congress of Historical Sciences Commemorative Volume*, ed. Sølvi Sogner (Oslo: Universitetsforlaget, 2001), 373–80.

55. See Wanda Jarząbek, *Hope and Reality: Poland and the Conference on Security and Cooperation in Europe, 1964–1989*, Cold War International History Project Working Paper No. 56 (Washington, DC: Woodrow Wilson International Center for Scholars, 2008).

56. For periodization, see Hermann Wentker, "Öffnung als Risiko: Bedrohungsvorstellungen der DDR-Führung infolge der Ost-West-Entspannung" [Opening-up as a risk: Perceptions of threat on part of the GDR leadership as a result of East-West détente], in *Militär und Staatssicherheit im Sicherheitskonzept der Warschauer-Pakt-Staaten*

[Military and state security in the safety concept of the Warsaw Pact countries], ed. Torsten Diedrich and Walter Süss (Berlin: Ch. Links Verlag, 2010), 297–318.

57. See Oliver Bange, "Ostpolitik – the Hidden Agenda" (open paper delivered at the London School of Economics, February 26, 2003), http://www.ostpolitik.net /ostpolitik/publications/download/article3.pdf.

58. Out of an abundance of related literature on this topic, see, e.g., the recent account by Andrzej Friszke, *Rewolucja Solidarności* [The Solidarity revolution] (Warsaw: Wydawnictwo Znak, 2014). In English, still valuable is Timothy G. Ash, *The Polish Revolution: Solidarity*, 3rd ed. (London: Penguin Books, 1999).

59. "[Es] wird nicht nur der Internationalismus preisgegeben, sondern das lebenswichtige Bündnis Volkspolens mit der Sowjetunion und den Ländern der sozialistischen Gemeinschaft in Frage gestellt." See the analysis in "The Development in the People's Republic of Poland Since the VI Party Congress of the PZPR," presented to the SED's Politburo on September 30, 1980, in *"Hart und kompromisslos durchgreifen": Die SED contra Polen 1980/81* ["Crack down in a hard and uncompromising manner": The SED versus Poland, 1980–81], ed. Michael Kubina and Manfred Wilke (Berlin: Akademie-Verlag, 1995), No. 6, 74–89. A similar remark was made by Erich Honecker during his Crimea talks with Leonid Brezhnev on August 3, 1981; see *Risse im Bruderbund: die Gespräche Honecker – Breshnew 1974 bis 1982* [Cracks in the brotherhood: The Honecker-Brezhnev talks, 1974–1982], ed. Hans-Hermann Hertle and Konrad Hugo Jarausch (Berlin: Links, 2006), 218.

60. "Wir hätten unserer Freundschaft keinen guten Dienst erwiesen, wenn sich Eure Schwierigkeiten auf uns übertragen hätten." Protocol No. 47/80 of Politburo meeting on November 25, 1980, source: SAPMO-BArch ZPA, J IV 2/2/A-2363, quoted by Kubina and Wilke, *"Hart und kompromisslos durchgreifen,"* No. 11, 101–14.

61. See Honecker's account of dangers for the GDR stemming from the Polish crisis in "Memorandum Regarding the Meeting Between Comrade Leonid Ilyich Brezhnev, Erich Honecker, and Gustav Husak in the Kremlin," May 16, 1981, History and Public Policy Program Digital Archive, SAPMO-BArch ZPA, vorl.SED 41559 http:// digitalarchive.wilsoncenter.org/document/112630; see also the talk of Erich Honecker with Secretary of the CPSU Central Committee Konstantin Rusakov on October 21, 1981, in Kubina and Wilke, *"Hart und kompromisslos durchgreifen,"* No. 86, 377–83.

62. See NVA Hauptstab/Verwaltung Aufklärung, Information on the Situation in Poland No. 17/80 of November 22, 1980, German Military Archives (BA-MA), Sign. DVH 32/32674c, f. 79.

63. See the speech by GDR Minister of National Defense General Heinz Hoffmann on June 3, 1981, before officers of the Military Reconnaissance Department (Verwaltung Aufklärung), German Military Archives (BA-MA), Sign. DVW 1/44073.

64. See Włodzimierz Borodziej, Jerzy Kochanowski, and Bernd Schäfer, *Grenzen der Freundschaft: Zur Kooperation der Sicherheitsorgane der DDR und der Volksrepublik Polen zwischen 1956 und 1989* [Limits of friendship: On the cooperation of the security organs of the GDR and the People's Republic of Poland, 1956–1989] (Dresden: Hannah-Arendt-Institut für Totalitarismusforschung, 2000), 29–30.

65. See Mark Kramer, "The Soviet Union, the Warsaw Pact, and the Polish Crisis of 1980–1981," in *The Solidarity Movement and Perspectives on the Last Decade of the Cold War*, ed. Lee Trepanier, Spasimir Domaradzki, and Jaclyn Stanke (Kraków: Krakow Society for Education-AFM Publishing House, 2010), 27–66.

66. See Wojciech Jaruzelski, *Mein Leben für Polen. Erinnerungen* [My life for Poland: Memoirs] (Munich: Piper, 1993), 235.

67. Document No. 90 b): East German Report of the Military Council Meeting in Sofia, April 24, 1981 (AZN, 32641, BA-MA), in Mastny and Byrne, *A Cardboard Castle?*, 445.

68. Document No. 91: Report on Conversation between Marshal Kulikov and Senior East German Military Officials, June 13, 1981 (BStU, Zentralarchiv, AIM 17164/81, Part II, Vol. I, 79–88), in Mastny and Byrne, *A Cardboard Castle?*, 446–48 (emphasis added).

69. See A. Ross Johnson, Robert W. Dean, and Alexander Alexiev, *Die Streitkräfte des Warschauer Pakts in Mitteleuropa: DDR, Polen und CSSR* (Stuttgart: Seewald, 1982), 197–203 [original version: A. Ross Johnson, Robert W. Dean, and Alexander Alexiev, *East European Military Establishments: The Warsaw Pact Northern Tier* (New York: Crane Russak, 1982)].

70. One "famous" incident here was the East German government's ban of the reformist Soviet youth periodical *Sputnik* in November 1988. See Gunter Holzweissig, *Die schärfste Waffe der Partei. Eine Mediengeschichte der DDR* [The most effective weapon of the Party: A media history of the GDR] (Cologne: Böhlau, 2002), 147–56.

71. The NVA was the only Warsaw Pact army that was not allowed to use the term "General Staff" for its central planning body. The Soviet hegemon gave no official reason for its refusal to permit such use; see Wenzke, "Generale und Admirale," 11. This policy was perceived and undoubtedly intended as a form of second-class treatment, although (or perhaps because) the Prussian-German General Staff had been the role model for most other armies, including the Soviet one, from the nineteenth century until 1945.

72. See the protocol of the 77th session of the National Defense Council on November, 25, 1988, German Federal Archives Berlin, DVW 1/39538, esp. appendix 2.2, "Conclusions."

73. Vojtech Mastny, "Did Gorbachev Liberate Eastern Europe?," in *The Last Decade of the Cold War: From Conflict Escalation to Conflict Transformation*, ed. Olav Njølstad (London: Frank Cass, 2004), 405.

74. For example, in an exemplary report of the GDR's embassy in Warsaw from 1987; see Olschowsky, *Einvernehmen und Konflikt*, 306–7.

75. Ibid., 308–12.

76. Ibid., 426–7.

77. Cf. Rüdiger Wenzke, "Die NVA und die Polnische Armee als Koalitionsstreitkräfte auf dem europäischen Kriegsschauplatz in den 1980er Jahren" [The NVA and the Polish Army as coalition forces in the European theater of war in the 1980s], in *Die Streitkräfte der DDR und Polens in der Operationsplanung des Warschauer Paktes* [The armed forces of the German Democratic Republic and Poland in the operational planning of the Warsaw Pact], ed. Rüdiger Wenzke (Potsdam: Militärgeschichtliches Forschungsamt, 2010), 115.

78. *Klassenbrüder – Waffenbrüder. Gemeinsame revolutionäre militärische Traditionen der Nationalen Volksarmee der DDR und der Polnischen Armee* [Class brothers – brothers in arms: Joint revolutionary military traditions of the National People's Army of the GDR and the Polish Army], by a team of authors from the "Wanda Wasilewska" Militärhistorisches Institut der Polnischen Armee (WIH, Wojskowy

Institut Historyczny) and the Militärgeschichtliches Institut der DDR (MGI) (Berlin: Militärverlag der Deutschen Demokratischen Republik, 1988).

79. For the strategic situation in the 1980s, see the informed (if somewhat affirmative) account by former NVA staff officer Siegfried Lautsch, *Kriegsschauplatz Deutschland: Erfahrungen und Erkenntnisse eines NVA-Offiziers* [Theater of war Germany: The experience and knowledge of an NVA officer] (Potsdam: Zentrum für Militärgeschichte und Sozialwissenschaften der Bundeswehr, 2013), 111–32.

9. Institutionalizing Trust? Regular Summitry (G7s and European Councils) from the Mid-1970s until the Mid-1980s

Noël Bonhomme and Emmanuel Mourlon-Druol

"In parting, Giscard commented that 'in diplomacy mistrust is deep-rooted' and hoped that we could work together to deal with such mistrust by full and frank exchanges."[1] This conversation took place in July 1973, when Valéry Giscard d'Estaing was still French finance minister. More than two years before the November 1975 Rambouillet summit that brought together the American, British, French, Italian, Japanese, and West German leaders as the Group of Six, Giscard's reflection highlights how deep-rooted the search for "full and frank" exchanges among top-level officials was in the mid-1970s. The role of trust in international relations is widely studied; so too is the role of institutional arrangements fostering trust. Yet the emergence of summitry from the mid-1970s onward is not taken into account as a subject of enquiry in its own right. For instance, Aaron M. Hoffman briefly mentions the creation of the European Council in 1974, but does not delve into its wider meaning in European politics.[2] The Group of Seven (G7) is largely absent from Andrew H. Kydd's analysis of trust and mistrust in international relations.[3] Conversely, if the literature on the two summits offers some development of the theme of trust in these gatherings, its analysis of it is not systematic.[4] The classic entente between French president Valéry Giscard d'Estaing and West German chancellor Helmut Schmidt is of course mentioned. But the fact that the G7 and the European Council encouraged cooperation without trust has not really been explored.

By contrast, this chapter will focus on this dimension. It aims at analyzing the relationship between trust and the emergence of regular, frequent, and increasingly "banal" heads of government meetings.[5] By nature, trust is impermanent, and can be built or destroyed. Quite obviously, trust between individuals such as heads of government is not a given. One defining feature of the mid-1970s was the attempt at creating permanent fora of discussion between these heads of government. Two such fora emerged: the European Council (the meeting of the European Economic Community's [EEC] heads of government, three times a year and whenever else necessary), created in 1974, and the G6/G7 (the meeting of the heads of state or government of the most industrialized countries), which first met in 1975. Interestingly, an important underlying motivation in both cases was the need to create a structure that could maintain and foster trust among Western leaders in times of turmoil. This idea was widely shared by a generation of political leaders who created and developed these summits during the mid-1970s (Valéry Giscard d'Estaing, Helmut Schmidt, James Callaghan, and Gerald Ford and Jimmy Carter), and remained central for their successors who inherited institutionalized summits in the late 1970s and early 1980s (Margaret Thatcher, Ronald Reagan, François Mitterrand, Helmut Kohl, Bettino Craxi, and Nobuhiko Nakasone). This framework for international cooperation was thus institutionalized and stabilized with a view to create trust both at personal and collective levels.

Based on extensive archival research in British, French, German, and some American archives, this chapter examines how these institutionalized summits served as a tool to foster trust during the Cold War. It argues that these summits tried to foster trust both "internally" and "externally": summitry aimed at developing not only trust among the leaders, but also crucially trust with regard to the Western (economic) system. These two ambitions—interpersonal and systemic—represented a vital transformation, albeit one imperfectly fulfilled, of the international system in the 1970s and 1980s.

Trust between the Leaders

A first important motivation behind the creation of the European Council and the G7 was to foster trust between the leaders involved in the meetings. Trust was not only a foundation of the summits, but also—even more important—a value that they nurtured.

Trust as a Foundation for the Summits

Trust is of course not the only reason why the G7 and the European Council were created in the mid-1970s. In each case, different issues were at stake. The G7 was not immediately thought of as a permanent institution; it only

199

became clear that the G7 would be an annual gathering in 1976/1977. More important, the European Council was part of a functioning political system, the EEC, while the G7's influence over the international system was less clear. Yet the two summits were created by the same heads of government (Helmut Schmidt and Valéry Giscard d'Estaing, and to a lesser extent British prime minister Harold Wilson), who shared the same vision of international cooperation. All three heads of government had identified that regular, frequent, and relatively informal gatherings at the top level were lacking from European and international diplomacy. In the case of the EEC, they were needed to orient the future endeavors of European integration and try to find a solution to problems which could not have been solved at a ministerial level. In the case of the G7, Giscard and Schmidt considered that "technicians" or "experts" had for too long been the only ones involved in economic and monetary discussions, and that directly elected heads of government should have a greater say in the process. Harold Wilson shared this skepticism toward the multiplication of "international bodies,"[6] and so did Gerald Ford and his secretary of state, Henry Kissinger, who criticized the inability of bureaucracies to shape innovative policies.[7] In that sense, it could be said that the heads of government's willingness to gather among themselves was rooted in their mistrust of their own national administrations, or even international ones.

The Giscard-Schmidt entente or, to put it differently, the great Franco-German trust of that period provided the necessary background for the initiatives leading to the creation of the G7 and the European Council. This trust was all the more salient in the case of the creation of the European Council (figure 9.1). Indeed, the French initiative for regular and frequent meetings between EEC heads of government did not fail to recall earlier Gaullist ideas, in particular a preference for intergovernmentalism over supranationalism. These meetings had been widely considered as an attempt to denature the integration process, and to introduce ever more intergovernmentalism into the EEC. By contrast, the French government proposal of 1974 was not received that way. True, the emergence of such an intergovernmental forum aroused skepticism and fears on behalf of the smaller member states. Yet importantly, the trust placed in Giscard and also in Schmidt, and the fact that it was well perceived that Giscard did not have Gaullist ambitions toward the EEC, helped smooth out differences of opinion. The informal dinner in Paris between the EEC heads of government and the European Commission on September 14, 1974, was instrumental here. Its main purposes had been to create an atmosphere of greater mutual trust, and to show by example the type of informal meetings that the French government wished to institutionalize.[8] In short, it served to overcome potential misunderstandings. Similarly, the first meeting

Figure 9.1. General view of The Hague European Council meeting, November 30, 1976.

Source: EC – Audiovisual Service. Photo credit: Jean-Louis Debaize. Reproduced with permission.

of the G7 in Rambouillet owed much to interpersonal relations. It was during a quadripartite meeting, on the margins of the Helsinki conference on July 31, 1975, that Giscard, Schmidt, Wilson, and US president Gerald Ford first envisaged such a summit.[9] The good trust that Giscard and Schmidt shared allowed Schmidt to modify Giscard's initial proposal without harming it. Giscard initially had suggested a monetary conference, which would have had little appeal for the participants; Schmidt transformed the idea into that of an economic summit, a more interesting prospect for all.[10]

Simply put, the summit was an opportunity for heads of government to meet. Until the mid-1970s, surprisingly enough, heads of state rarely used to gather in multilateral frameworks. Their meetings were bilateral, trilateral, or even quadripartite, but seldom involved more participants and certainly not on a regular, frequent basis.[11] By contrast, ministers themselves met more regularly and more often, as in the EEC Council of Ministers (to take but one European example) or in the G5 (to take but one Western example, which involved Britain, France, Japan, the United Kingdom, and the United States). The North Atlantic Treaty Organization (NATO) had had annual meetings of the Atlantic Council, but until the mid-1970s summit meetings were exceptions rather than the rule. Before then, there had been only three such summits in twenty-five years; the repeated NATO summits in 1974, 1975, 1977, and 1978—precisely when the European Council and G7 summits were created—structurally changed the diplomatic practices of the organization. Indeed, institutionalized (or nearly institutionalized) heads of government summits were an occasion to foster interpersonal trust among Western leaders. Yet the reverse was also true. As Raymond Barre (Giscard's personal adviser—also known as a "sherpa"[12]—at Rambouillet) retrospective comment underlines, if summits were an occasion to develop trust among leaders, this trust-building potential was highly contingent: "le courant passe, ou non."[13] Crucially, therefore, summits allowed cooperation *without* trust, precisely because cooperation was per force regular and frequent. Trust thus helped regular summitry to emerge—and it was precisely this regularity that was meant to nurture trust among its participants.

Trust as a Value to Be Nurtured by the Summits
The issue of trust was frequently referred to in the official discourse. To take but one example, Giscard announced "a new era of mutual trust among the seven" after the Bonn G7 meeting in 1978.[14] He echoed the initial message of the G7, whose first summit in 1975 had highlighted a "spirit of Rambouillet, made of international cooperation and responsibilities"—a formula that Giscard himself had inspired.[15] The recurrence of this semantics in official declarations helped "depersonalize" the establishment of trust among leaders. Institutionalized summits, however, were (and are) certainly by no means a panacea. As remarked above, one key feature of institutionalized summitry is that it allows cooperation without trust. At summits, regardless of the quality of the working relationship of heads of government, their administrations have to cooperate. This cooperation may not lead to groundbreaking joint actions, but it may still improve the mutual understanding of two administrations, avoid (further) misunderstandings, and over the long run prove a better option than not meeting at all—even in the absence of concrete apparent results.[16] For instance, distrust between Jimmy Carter and Helmut Schmidt did not prevent them from reaching an agreement on international macroeconomic cooperation at the Bonn G7 meeting in 1978.[17] Trust, therefore, was both a reason to hold summits and a value to be nurtured by holding summits. This is one of the reasons why summitry was institutionalized: to ease and improve cooperation in times of crisis. Importantly, the existence of regular summitry could help overcome some nascent misunderstandings. For instance, in the 1981 Ottawa G7 meeting, as well as the European Councils in that year, the head

of government summits helped newly elected leaders (France's François Mitterrand and the United States' Ronald Reagan) and their administrations get acquainted with each other and with their fellow participants. Regular summits offer a continuum of cooperation beyond changes of political majority. In addition, as Robert Putnam and Nicholas Bayne have noted, while heads of government do not necessarily share great mutual trust, the senior officials involved in the preparations often did.[18] This fact underlines once more that the central dimension is the institutionalization of summitry: regular and frequent heads of government summits have encouraged the development of habits of cooperation.

In analyzing how trust relationships are fostered, Aaron Hoffman identifies three key elements: learning, identity, and institutions. Though regular summitry is most obviously linked to the last element, it lies at the crossroads of all three. The role of institutions is arguably the role that calls first for analysis. This line of thinking "focuses on the importance of institutions and locates the problem of trust in the character of the environment in which states interact."[19] The institutional environment must "desensitiz[e] actors to the costs of opportunism. . . . Overcoming trust, therefore, involves introducing rules, norms, and decision-making procedures that effectively eliminate the possibility that an actor will be eliminated by a counterpart's treachery."[20] This description fits well with both the G7 and the European Council—though again, each case deserves some nuance. The G7 smoothed international economic discussions, while the European Council offered a forum where EEC leaders could, at the very least, discuss various issues in an EEC setting, and thereby stressed the need not to develop measures harmful to the development of European integration. Both the G7 and the European Council set a framework of largely informal rules of coordination in order to allow cooperation with—or, more important, without—trust. Eurosceptic or Europhile, all had to attend European Councils. Supporters and opponents of globalization had to confront international issues at a G7. This requirement was already making a significant difference in the second half of the 1970s, most famously in the case of strong interpersonal relationships as that between Giscard and Schmidt.[21] The opposite case is also interesting to mention. Throughout the second half of the 1970s, British prime ministers retained little enthusiasm for European cooperation, but they still had to come and share their thoughts with their European partners in an EEC framework. Similarly, the German and Japanese governments were not keen on reflating their economies in 1977 and 1978 for both political and financial reasons, but nevertheless they took limited steps in that direction, partly because G7 participation made it plain that they needed to make some concessions on this issue.

A second element identified by Hoffman is "learning." This hypothesis "suggests that actors establish their trustworthiness through their behavior toward others. Those with a demonstrated record of reliability and rectitude are worthy of trust in the future."[22] Hoffman explains that incremental processes—like the case of "step-by-step" diplomacy—help overcome distrust.[23] Institutionalized summitry, with its socialization of leaders and senior officials, is close to such an incremental process. European Councils and G7s were a good opportunity for heads of governments to meet together on a regular basis—an opportunity that had not really been present before the mid-1970s. Ad hoc summits existed, but they were infrequent and did not involve many more than two, three, or four heads of government. Until the mid-1970s, virtually all other government officials had a setting where they could meet on a regular basis, whether in the International Monetary Fund, the Bank for International Settlements, the various EEC institutions, NATO, or the Organization for Economic Cooperation and Development. Heads of government, however, were missing such a setting.

Changes in political leadership arguably give a further example of the importance of such fora as the G7 and European Council. From 1979 to 1982, many changes in political leadership occurred in Western European countries and the United States. In about three years, virtually all members of the G7 changed leaders, and often changed political orientation. Even more important, those who had been at the origin of the G7 had left the international political scene: in Ottawa in 1981, only Helmut Schmidt and Canadian prime minister Pierre Trudeau remained. Margaret Thatcher, François Mitterrand, and Ronald Reagan had all been elected. Even though one could not predict how long these politicians would remain in power, the French case stands out: Mitterrand had a seven-year mandate, which meant that he would be a central figure in summits for quite a long time. None of his counterparts could enjoy such political stability. The institution, very little codified, now had as such a life of its own. New leaders arrived, and they confirmed the options taken by their predecessors, and supported this type of meetings. Thatcher, for instance, took from the beginning the same critical stance toward G7 summits that Giscard, Schmidt, or Callaghan had had about its "bureaucratization," the length of its public declaration, or the excessive pressure from mass media during the meetings. Thatcher nevertheless praised the personal and informal discussions that such opportunities provided. A habit of cooperation had been created—in itself a factor of trust—that maintained the basic purpose of regular summitry: personal knowledge and understanding among political leaders mattered as much as the formal or informal "decisions" that could be made. This aspect also underlines the socialization function of these summits.

A small elite of persons who were used to participating to these meetings— and were not limited to heads of government—was slowly emerging. Japanese prime minister Masayoshi Ohira, who organized the Tokyo summit in 1979, had been present in Rambouillet four years earlier. At that time, he was finance minister. Such a situation naturally would repeat itself in the future and provide familiarity among political leaders even for governments suffering from chronic instability. Giulio Andreotti, for instance, became a regular summiteer for 15 years through different positions, first as head of the Italian coalition government (1977–79), then as foreign minister (1984–89), and finally as prime minister (1990–91).

This socialization has two main features: the process by which new entrants become full members; and the result, namely the new entrants' adoption of preexisting rules. As Putnam and Bayne put it, summits tend to "educate leaders."[24] Summits were indeed an opportunity for many participants to familiarize themselves with international issues. The Tokyo G7 summit of 1979 was the first time in its history that the Japanese government had organized a major international meeting. This was crucial with respect to the idea of belonging to a (Western) group, and certainly was a stepping-stone in learning a specific diplomatic practice. It can also be noted that Mitterrand, who was elected in May 1981, had had little previous international experience, and the Ottawa summit was his first important international meeting since winning the election. Also important, Mitterrand had just appointed four communist ministers to his government: the G7 in Ottawa was the first and best opportunity to explain why he had done so and to reassure his partners about his intentions— in short, to overcome potential mistrust. By contrast to the 1980 Venice or the 1987 Louvre summits, which decided important joint actions on energy and monetary issues, the 1980 Ottawa summit is not usually remembered for having yielded great results. Yet it is often dubbed an "exploratory summit": it offered the occasion for new political personnel to get together, for the first time, in an international forum. This exploration, in turn, fostered trust, or helped to overcome initial misunderstandings. The result of this socialization is also important. Be it in European Councils or in G7s, new entrants were able to learn the language, the initial ambitions of these summits. The new entrants adapted themselves to the existing institution and learned how it functioned. In this spirit, Jacques Attali, Mitterrand's sherpa, tellingly has written in his memoirs that he "discovered the ceremony of European Councils" in Luxembourg in June 1981, and similarly has explained that he "discovered the ritual of these meetings" in Ottawa the same year.[25] As a result, even if some of the participants had originally criticized the summit discourse as being pointless, they soon adopted the same discourse as their predecessors: the need to foster

Figure 9.2. Formal dinner during the G7 economic summit at the Imperial Palace in Tokyo, Japan, May 6, 1986.

L to R: Jacques Delors, Rudolphus Lubbers, Bettino Craxi, Anna Maria Moncini Craxi (seated), Margaret Thatcher, Ronald Reagan, Nancy Reagan (seated), Emperor Hirohito, François Mitterrand, Helmut Kohl, Hannelore Kohl (seated), Brian Mulroney, Jacques Chirac, Mila Mulroney (seated), Yasuhiro Nakasone, Tsutako Nakasone (seated).
Source: Ronald Reagan Presidential Library and Museum. Reproduced with permission.

trust within the West, the importance of cooperating (with or without trust), the need for solidarity (of the West or of the EEC), and the restricted character of the club. In the case of the European Council, participants other than heads of government had to be limited to only those who were strictly necessary; in the case of the G7, the admission of new countries was avoided.

The third and last feature identified by Hoffman is "identity." This feature suggests that "actors trust those with whom they share membership in a social group or groups."[26] This description also fits well the case of the two summits studied. The G7 was composed of the seven most industrialized countries in the world, all belonging to the "West." The European Council was made up of the heads of government of each EEC member state—also part of the "West"—thereby giving to these meetings the feeling of a club. It can also be noted that the name often given in the press to the pictures taken at the end of such meetings—"family pictures"—is not devoid of meaning, as it suggests that the participants share a common identity, or at least that they want to show a common public face (see figure 9.2). Taken together, Hoffman's three elements—institutions, learning, and identity—help underline how important regular summitry was in order not only to build or maintain trust, but also to overcome mistrust.

Trust with Regard to the Western System

The creation of the European Council and the G7 aimed also at fostering trust in the Western system. The economic and monetary crises of the mid-1970s called into question the liberal capitalist system, and hence the governance of the West and the EEC, in the context of the Cold War competition. The emergence of summitry was part of a need to reassert trust in these systems, or at least to overcome the growing mistrust in them, by showing the public a collective answer to the crisis at the highest level.

Restoring Trust in the Western System

From the late 1960s and early 1970s onward, the increasing globalization of financial markets, highly sensitive to irrational reactions, added a strong psychological dimension to international economic and monetary coopera-tion.[27] One of the goals of G7 summits as such was to smooth out the distress caused by the crisis in industrialized countries, to iron out the potential con-tradictions of their individual policies. Within less than three years from 1973, the Bretton Woods international monetary system had collapsed, the energy crisis had occurred, and a global recession had taken hold. Owing to these economic problems, Western leaders feared the development of mistrust in Western industrialized societies, as Giscard explained on July 31, 1975: "The current economic and financial crisis deeply affects the Western world. . . . On top of all this comes along an ideological conflict which remains very active. It is impossible that M. Brejnev [Brezhnev] does not bet on the worsening of the economic and social disorders and on the rise of unemployment. In that respect, the apparent inability, to face this crisis where we stand, is for the West a very serious element of weakness. . . . Therefore we must show that we can exercise our collective responsibility."[28] The same year, a Trilateral Commission report noted a pessimism widely shared in the West, and con-cluded that Western democracies needed stronger leadership at both national and international levels.[29] Many intellectual, economic, and political person-alities shared this idea of a global crisis of liberal democracies. This fear was fed by the memory of the 1930s. The crux of the interwar period had been the "dual crisis": the simultaneous collapse of the international economic system and the international political system.[30] Whether or not they were mistaken in their assessment of the situation, in the 1970s many leaders—Schmidt, Gis-card, Ford, Wilson, and Japanese prime minister Takeo Fukuda, to name but a few—feared that the same would happen again. Fukuda thus explained during the 1977 London summit that he recalled his time in London between 1930 and 1933, and "thought that there was now [in 1977] a better chance of inter-national cooperation."[31]

Since the 1970s economic crisis created mistrust, which "could create dangerous tensions in the social fabric of the industrial democracies,"[32] the real purpose of the G7 was to reinforce confidence in the West as a whole. The Italian sherpa Sergio Berlinguer explained in 1982 that summit participants not only shared common interests but "the same basic goal: to demonstrate the superiority of the industrial societies' development model and, in the final analysis, to defend the values of Western civilization."[33] G7 summits and European Councils were an occasion to reassert the commitment of Western countries and the EEC to public freedom, open trade, human rights, and democracy. Hence the European Council of July 1975, celebrating the thirtieth anniversary of the United Nations, reaffirmed its commitment to democracy and human rights.[34] The declaration that ended each G7 meeting became longer and longer about specific economic topics, but its purpose was always to emphasize liberal values as an ideological system linking "democratic society, individual liberty and social advancement."[35] During each G7 summit, the writing of the declaration was harshly negotiated, but the declaration reflected less the reality of discussions between leaders than the message they personally wished to broadcast. Helmut Schmidt, for example, stressed the psychological importance of summitry: "If we can create the impression we intend to work together and coordinate our policies, that will be enough."[36] Hartmut Soell, one of Schmidt's biographers, even wonders whether the economic summit was not just a *Seelenmassage*—a massage of the soul.[37]

Leaders and diplomats were very conscious of the limits of economic summitry. Henri Froment-Meurice, head of the Directorate of Economic and Financial Affairs at the Quai d'Orsay, wrote in September 1977 that the Rambouillet, Puerto Rico, and London summits had only "[settled] at the margins a few problems between the big states," whereas the only remedy to economic crisis might be the confidence of consumers and investors.[38] "I have shaken hands with Helmut [Schmidt] and the New York stock exchange has immediately risen," joked Jimmy Carter during the Bonn G7 summit.[39] In the same way, the 1979 Tokyo and 1980 Venice summits reacted to the second oil shock of 1979 by defining some ceilings on oil imports. These ceilings were never actually reached, but they stressed the Western will to limit its oil dependence in order to reassure consumers and economic actors.

Staging Unity: Collective Leadership and National Strategies
Leaders who participated in international summits faced a dilemma vis-à-vis the media. They used their participation to demonstrate publicly their solidarity, such as through declarations and "family pictures." Yet G7 summits were

Figure 9.3. Ronald Reagan having a bilateral meeting with François Mitterrand during the G7 economic summit in Williamsburg, Virginia, May 28, 1983.

Source: Ronald Reagan Presidential Library and Museum. Reproduced with permission.

also conceived as informal meetings whose discussions dealt with political divergences (see figure 9.3). Initially kept at a distance, the media became more and more "embedded" with the gradual institutionalization of the G7, as it was a better way to control the media's coverage of the summits. The case of France is particularly interesting. In 1975, Giscard did not want any journalists in Rambouillet; he provided a press room in Paris. Though he underlined the psychological importance of summits, he did not regard relationships with the press as a priority. According to his former advisers[40] and the presidential archives, there were few contacts with the media during the summit itself, and neither Giscard's sherpa nor his economic advisers dealt directly with the press. This situation changed with François Mitterrand. At the 1981 Ottawa summit, his administration discovered that the United States was using media pressure to reach its objectives; the US administration had briefed the press for months about the topics of the summit, and informed American journalists during the discussions in its own conference center. Jacques Attali (Mitterrand's sherpa from 1981) concluded that "making the summit a success is first being successful in the relationship with the media."[41] At the 1982 Versailles summit, Attali organized, to that end, various thematic, general, formal, and informal meetings with a number of personalities of the French delegation (including ministers, senior officials, and Mitterrand's own advisers)[42] in order to feed the press across three days with the facts and pictures that France expected would be echoed by the national and international press.

Studying the role of the media, however, does not really demonstrate whether the G7 did or did not generate trust in Western societies. Scholars can hardly evaluate the reception of political declarations. Still, the G7 meetings and the European Councils became a kind of ritual for public opinion, and summitry was actually a useful tool for a global public diplomacy using international media networks.[43] The structure and outcomes of G7s were strongly criticized from the early 1980s by leaders themselves, but the existence of the G7 itself was never called into question, as breaking with this ritual probably would have been interpreted by public opinion as a proof of distrust. Furthermore, G7s melded international and domestic issues into an intermestic approach, as the leaders always perceived summits as a way to highlight their personal role and to improve their political legitimacy. Leaders facing domestic problems could use summitry for support. For instance, the Italian government initially was not invited to Rambouillet in 1975, but then it requested a seat for the next summit meeting, arguing that its absence at such a conference might weaken its governing position.[44] Social troubles caused by the international economic situation aroused fears of a high vote for the Italian Communist Party in Italy's June 1976 general election. Consequently, one of the "major objectives" of the 1976 Puerto Rico summit was to support Aldo Moro's Christian Democratic government.[45] Some leaders also used G7 summits to improve their domestic popularity before elections. The American press underlined that Gerald Ford had hastily organized the Puerto Rico summit because he wanted to appear an international statesman in advance of the 1976 Republican presidential convention. Giscard later said that he went to the Puerto Rico summit "just out of politeness."[46] The domestic dimension was particularly important for the leader who organized the summit. As a result, the host generally succeeded in reaching a minimal agreement between the participants, ensuring at least media success for the summit.

Nevertheless, leaders faced two different and sometimes contradictory imperatives: they had to reach a consensus in order to build a trusting relationship with the other leaders, but they also had to defend their perceived national interests. Concessions could have domestic costs, and decision makers could either use this "two-level game"[47] or be made vulnerable by it. In Puerto Rico in 1976, Italian prime minister Aldo Moro's fellow leaders asked him for a commitment not to govern with the communists, but the G7 as a whole could not endorse this decision, which would have broken Italian sovereignty. Giscard, Ford, Schmidt, and Callaghan secretly agreed that this commitment would be a condition of Western financial support to Italy. Yet Schmidt revealed this decision publicly in order to maintain the pressure on Italy's Christian Democrats. In doing so, he provoked reactions in Italy, forced

Moro to explain himself in the Italian parliament, and as a result may have hastened Moro's replacement by Giulio Andreotti in July.[48]

The link between international and national imperatives of trust can explain the form and the timing of the concessions made by G7 participants. Before the 1978 Bonn summit, the United States asked Germany to take strong measures of economic reflation in order to pull the West out of the recession. After strong resistance, Helmut Schmidt made specific commitments, which he presented as a political risk for him: "I can't give the detailed measures for domestic policy reasons. I intend to gather the majority's leaders together a week after our summit in order to examine these measures with them. . . . I seriously risk failure if I lead tactlessly."[49] Actually, inside the German federal government, the governing coalition of Liberals (supporting financial orthodoxy) and Social Democrats disagreed. As Schmidt could not openly disagree with the Liberals, he "let himself be pushed into a policy that he probably favored on domestic grounds, but would have found costly and perhaps impossible to pursue without the 'tail wind' provided by the summit."[50] Thus, Schmidt could keep his political partners' trust by explaining that concessions to Germany's allies were necessary, while at the same time presenting to other leaders his commitment as a proof of trust made in spite of domestic pressures. The media declarations before the summit, as much as the dramatization of disagreements during the meeting and the common declarations after it, were part of the negotiations rather than real proof of mistrust.

In fact, each leader created a specific combination between domestic expectations and international pressure. Whereas the United States regarded the G7 as an institution that served its leadership, France regarded the G7 as a forum where its leaders could both cooperate and express their national specificity within the Western world without having to endorse Washington's policy.

Summitry and the Cold War: The Limits of an Institutional Tool

Often compared with the nineteenth-century Concert of Europe because of its oligarchic character, the G7 was hardly accepted by those who were not members. Other Western states and organizations contested the legitimacy of these "new aristocrats"[51] to speak in the name of the West as a whole. Trust created by the G7 among the main Western powers could thus create distrust within the West. The EEC members that were not invited, as well as the president of the EEC Commission, protested from 1975 onward against the emergence of a restricted and permanent directorate in charge of governing the West. Yet Giscard and Schmidt saw the European Commission as a bureaucratic structure, one that was not legitimate for dealing with issues—especially foreign affairs issues—at a political level. This battle stirred up the mistrust that always existed inside the EEC between the "small" and "big" states.[52]

In addition, the internal organization of the G7 could create distrust among its own members. Italy had joined the group in 1975 and Canada in 1976, but both were excluded from the political discussions relating to the Cold War. Japan was a necessary partner on economic matters, but not strategic ones. Small-group discussions on political issues were organized among the French, American, German, and British leaders in Puerto Rico in 1976 and London in 1977. These four-state meetings were presented as a political summit separate from the G7 itself, and theoretically justified by the fact that it discussed "Berlin issues." The Guadeloupe summit, organized by Giscard in January 1979, raised protests from the Italians and Japanese for being conceived on exactly the same model as the G7 but with a political agenda (strategic issues, especially the Euromissile crisis and Soviet policy) and only four participants. Quadripartite meetings were organized more discreetly in Bonn in 1978 and Tokyo in 1979, but in 1980 Italy (which hosted the G7 summit in Venice) made it clear that a four-power meeting on the margin of the summit was excluded; yet even though the formal preparation was enlarged to include all seven countries, the political discussions of the meeting were prepared by a semiclandestine quadripartite group.[53] Nevertheless, the rise of political topics in the agenda of the G7 summits justified Italian claims—subtly supported by Canada and Japan—and made it impossible to maintain quadripartite side-meetings inside the G7. This informal hierarchy remained in the background, but the debate about the legitimacy of the four-power meetings lost its strength under the Reagan administration, when the meetings ceased to be held.[54] This evolution demonstrated the G7's ability to evolve in order to maintain trust among its members.

However, the G7 never became a governing structure. It remained instead a tool used by governments according to circumstances, as Cold War issues underline. From the beginning, there were political side-discussions at the G7, and these increased from the early 1980s. During the 1980 Venice summit, the Soviet Union announced that it would withdraw some troops from Afghanistan. This declaration was aimed at dividing Western leaders while they had to show their unity in Venice. They were thus led to reach an agreement that smoothed out their divergences: namely, Giscard and Schmidt still cared about saving détente, whereas Carter and Thatcher wished to maintain a harder line. From 1980 onward, the Cold War became a recurrent topic. The G7 remained, however, an "economic summit," and a framework that staged Western solidarity rather than an active structure in the Cold War. Indeed, economic relationships with Eastern countries were regularly discussed, and there were cooperation agreements about specific topics—for instance, an agreement about Poland in 1980, both in the G7 and the European Council. But in 1981–82, the Reagan administration failed to impose the idea of an economic Cold War in the framework of the G7, because the European countries and Japan had divergent economic interests. In the same way, Reagan wanted to publish at the 1983 Williamsburg summit a "declaration on security," which would define a common Western position toward the strategic negotiations with the Soviet Union. However, he again met with opposition from Mitterrand, who feared for French nuclear independence and saw in the American project a kind of "global super-NATO."[55] Once again, the G7 did not become the Western strategic institution that had been imagined. Regarding economic topics as well as political ones, the G7 was complementary but not equivalent to classic multilateral organizations. In fact, the distrust caused by the creation of the G7 progressively disappeared as its institutionalization demonstrated that the summits worked as a framework for cooperation but did not marginalize the other Western institutions. For instance, the president of the European Commission was admitted to the G7 from 1977 onward. And even if the "smaller" members of the EEC continued to rhetorically denounce the G7, relations with the EEC had been normalized.

Conclusion

The problematic definition of "trust" leads to two interpretations of the role of summitry: one purporting that it was successful in "oiling" the international system; the other arguing it was more about posture than deeds. If summitry did not institutionalize trust, it crucially facilitated cooperation *without* trust. The minimalist/maximalist interpretation underlined throughout this chapter highlights the central paradox of the relationship between trust and summitry. One is talking about the institutionalization—as if it could make it more secure—of what is, by essence, transient (namely an emotion). This is to be compared with another oxymoron that also lies at the center of the whole summitry idea: the institutionalization of informality (see figure 9.4). In the mid-1970s, Valéry Giscard d'Estaing, Helmut Schmidt, and Harold Wilson shared a preference for the "fireside chat" and were willing to reproduce it at the European and international level and regularize it. In other words, they were willing to formalize informality.

Far from a success story, the study of regular summitry in the 1970s and 1980s emphasizes that institutionalizing trust was from the beginning a utopia. Yet it remained a constant idea for Western leaders. This was because summitry had a real usefulness for the Western world in fulfilling twin functions: creating trust at the individual and collective levels, and encouraging Western cooperation, even without trust.

Figure 9.4. Ronald Reagan and G7 leaders viewing a colonial craft display in Williamsburg, Virginia, May 29, 1983.

L to R: Ronald Reagan, Helmut Kohl, Amintore Fanfani, Yasuhiro Nakasone, Gaston Thorn, Margaret Thatcher, François Mitterrand, Pierre Trudeau
Source: Ronald Reagan Presidential Library and Museum. Reproduced with permission.

Notes

1. Telegram from the Embassy in France to the Department of State, July 27, 1973, in *Foreign Relations of the United States (FRUS), 1969–1976*, Vol. XXXI, *Foreign Economic Policy, 1973–1976* (Washington, DC: US Government Printing Office, 2009), doc. 48, 182–83.

2. Aaron M. Hoffman, *Building Trust: Overcoming Suspicion in International Conflict* (Albany: State University of New York Press, 2006).

3. Andrew H. Kydd, *Trust and Mistrust in International Relations* (Ithaca, NY: Cornell University Press, 2005).

4. See, e.g., Robert Putnam and Nicholas Bayne, *Hanging Together: Cooperation and Conflict in the Seven-Power Summits* (London: Sage, 1987); Harold James, *Rambouillet, 15. November 1975: Die Globalisierung der Wirtschaft* [Rambouillet, 15 November 1975: The globalization of the economy] (Munich: Deutscher Taschenbuch Verlag, 1997); Emmanuel Mourlon-Druol, "Filling the EEC Leadership Vacuum? The Creation of the European Council in 1974," *Cold War History* 10, no. 3 (2010): 315–39; and Enrico Böhm, *Die Sicherheit des Westens: Entstehung und Funktion der G7-Gipfel, 1975–1981* [The security of the West: The origin and role of the G7 summit, 1975–1981] (Munich: Oldenbourg Verlag, 2013).

5. On the notion of increasingly regular summits in international relations, see Emmanuel Mourlon-Druol, "'Managing from the Top': Globalisation and the Rise of Regular Summitry, Mid-1970s—early 1980s," *Diplomacy & Statecraft* 23, no. 4 (2012): 679–703.

6. "Existing bodies concerned with the subjects on the agenda at Rambouillet" memorandum, n.d., PREM 16/358, The National Archives, UK (hereafter TNA); and Nigel Wicks to Harold Wilson, "Economic summit" note, November 10, 1975, PREM 16/358, TNA.

7. Mario Del Pero, *The Eccentric Realist: Henry Kissinger and the Shaping of American Foreign Policy* (Ithaca, NY: Cornell University Press, 2010), 70–71; Böhm, *Die Sicherheit des Westens*, 272–77.

8. Mourlon-Druol, "Filling the EEC Leadership Vacuum?," 321.

9. French record of Helsinki Quadripartite Lunch (proposal for a "Sommet Moni-taire"), August 28, 1975, Margaret Thatcher Archive, http://www.margaretthatcher.org /document/110973.

10. Memorandum from Secretary of the Treasury Simon to President Ford, July 26, 1975, in *FRUS, 1969–1976*, Vol. XXXI, doc. 93, 303–4. See also Elizabeth Benning, "Economic Power and Political Leadership: The Federal Republic, the West and the Re-shaping of the International Economic System, 1972–1976" (PhD diss., London School of Economics, 2011); and Elizabeth Benning, "The Road to Rambouillet and the Creation of the Group of Five," in *International Summitry and Global Governance: The Rise of the G7 and the European Council, 1974–1991*, ed., Emmanuel Mourlon-Druol and Federico Romero (Abingdon, UK: Routledge, 2014), 39–63.

11. See, e.g., Michael Butler, *Europe: More Than a Continent* (London: Heinemann, 1986).

12. For an overview of the sherpas' background, see Emmanuel Mourlon-Druol, "Less Than a Permanent Secretariat, More Than an Ad-hoc Preparatory Group: A Prosopography of the G7s Personal Representatives, 1975–1991," in Mourlon-Druol and Romero, *International Summitry and Global Governance*, 64–91.

13. Raymond Barre, *L'expérience du pouvoir: Conversations avec Jean Bothorel* [The experience of power: Conversations with Jean Bothorel] (Paris: Fayard, 2007), 73.

14. Putnam and Bayne, *Hanging Together*, 87.

15. Giscard's handwritten notes on the Rambouillet declaration, 5AG3/886, Archives nationales, Paris (hereafter, AN), author's translation.

16. Emmanuel Mourlon-Druol, "Assessing the Role of G7/8/20 Meetings in Global Governance: Processes, Outcomes, and Counterfactuals," in *Summits and Regional Governance: The Americas in Comparative Perspective*, ed., Gordon Mace, Jean-Philippe Thérien, Diana Tussie, and Olivier Dabène (Abingdon, UK: Routledge, 2016), 177–92.

17. See, e.g., Johannes von Karczewski, *"Weltwirtschaft ist unser Schicksal": Helmut Schmidt und die Schaffung der Weltwirtschaftsgipfel* ["World economy is our destiny": Helmut Schmidt and the creation of the World Economic Summit] (Bonn: Dietz Verlag, 2008), chapter 5; see also Klaus Wiegrefe, *Das Zerwürfnis: Helmut Schmidt, Jimmy Carter und die Krise der deutsch-amerikanischen Beziehungen* [The disagreement: Helmut Schmidt, Jimmy Carter, and the crisis in German-American relations] (Berlin: Propyläen Verlag, 2005).

18. Putnam and Bayne, *Hanging Together*, 90.

19. Hoffman, *Building Trust*, 37.

20. Ibid., 43.

21. See, e.g., Haig Simonian, *The Privileged Partnership: Franco-German Relations in the European Community, 1969–1984* (Oxford: Clarendon, 1985).

22. Hoffman, *Building Trust*, 37.

23. Ibid., 40.

24. Putnam and Bayne, *Hanging Together*, 257.

25. Jacques Attali, *Verbatim, Vol. I* (Paris: Fayard, 1993), 48 and 59 (authors' translation).

26. Hoffman, *Building Trust*, 37.

27. Niall Ferguson, Charles S. Maier, Erez Manela, and Daniel J. Sargent, eds., *The Shock of the Global: The 1970s in Perspective* (Cambridge, MA: Harvard University Press, 2011), especially Charles Maier, "'Malaise': The Crisis of Capitalism in the 1970s," 25–48.

28. Extract from discussion at a quadripartite lunch (CSCE Helsinki), prepared by Sauvagnargues' cabinet, 5AG3/885, AN.

29. Michel J. Crozier, Samuel P. Huntington, and Joji Watanaki, *The Crisis of Democracy: Report on the Governability of the Democracies to the Trilateral Commission* (New York: New York University Press, 1975), 166–67.

30. Robert Boyce, *The Great Interwar Crisis and the Collapse of Globalization* (Basingstoke, UK: Palgrave Macmillan, 2009).

31. Note of the first session of the Downing Street summit conference, May 7, 1977, PREM 16/1223, TNA; Federico Romero, "Refashioning the West to Dispel Its Fears: The Early G7 Summits," in Romero and Mourlon-Druol, *International Summitry and Global Governance*, 117–37.

32. Letter from Sergio Berlinguer to Jacques Attali, February 11, 1982, 5AG4/PM64, AN.

33. Ibid.

34. Communiqué of the European Council, Brussels, July 16–17, 1975, European Council, http://www.consilium.europa.eu/en/european-council/conclusions/pdf-1992-1975/BRUSSELS-EUROPEAN-COUNCIL,-16-AND-17-JULY-1975/.

35. Declaration of Rambouillet, November 17, 1975, Margaret Thatcher Archive, http://www.margaretthatcher.org/document/110957.

36. Memoranda of Conversation, Box 14. Secret, Bonn, July 27, 1975, Gerald R. Ford Presidential Library, Ann Arbor, Michigan.

37. See Hartmut Soell, *Helmut Schmidt, 1969 bis heute, Macht und Verantwortung* [Helmut Schmidt: 1969 to today, power and responsibility] (Deutsche Verlags-Anstalt: München, 2008), 415; "Weltwirtschaftsgipfel als Seelenmassage?"

38. Henri Froment-Meurice, *Vu du Quai. Mémoires, 1945–1983* [Seen from the Quai: Memoirs, 1945–1983] (Paris: Fayard, 1998), 495–96.

39. Transcription of the first session of the Bonn summit by Jean-Pierre Dutet, July 16, 1978, 5AG3/893, AN.

40. Guy de Panafieu, interview by Noël Bonhomme, April 7, 2011; Henri Froment-Meurice, interview by Noël Bonhomme, April 19, 2011; Patrick Leclercq, interview by Noël Bonhomme, April 29, 2011; and Gabriel Robin, interview by Noël Bonhomme, June 15, 2011.

41. Note from Attali to Mitterrand, September 28, 1981, 5AG4/PM63, AN.

42. Note of Jacques Attali, May 27, 1982, 5AG4/PM62, AN.

43. Noël Bonhomme, "Between Political Messages and Public Expectations: G7 Summits in French and US Public Opinions, 1975–1985," in Mourlon-Druol and Romero, *International Summitry and Global Governance*, 92–113; on the US-USSR

summits, see, e.g., Robert S. Fortner, *Public Diplomacy and International Politics: The Symbolic Constructs of Summits and International Radio News* (Westport, CT: Praeger, 1994).

44. Note n°222/CE, August 15, 1975, CE-956, Archives du Ministère des Affaires étrangères, France.

45. Letter from Ford to Giscard, June 2, 1976, 5AG3/887, AN.

46. Meeting Giscard – Mondale, January 28, 1977, 5AG3/984, AN.

47. Robert D. Putnam, "Diplomacy and Domestic Politics: the Logic of Two-Level Game," *International Organization* 42, no. 3 (1988): 427–60.

48. See Antonio Varsori, "Puerto Rico (1976): le potenze occidentali e il problema comunista in Italia" [Puerto Rico (1976): The Western powers and the communist problem in Italy], *Ventunesimo Secolo* 16 (2008): 89–121; and Frédéric Heurtebize, *Le péril rouge. Washington face à l'eurocommunisme* [The red peril: Washington faces Eurocommunism] (Paris: PUF, 2014), 148–57.

49. First session of the Bonn summit, July 16, 1978, 5AG3/893, AN.

50. Putnam and Bayne, *Hanging Together*, 79; for a more detailed study, see Robert Putnam and C. Randall Henning, "The Bonn Summit of 1978: A Case Study in Coordination," in *Can Nations Agree?: Issues in International Economic Cooperation*, ed. Richard N. Cooper, Barry Eichengreen, Gerald Holtham, Robert D. Putnam, and C. Randall Henning (Washington, DC: Brookings Institution Press, 1989).

51. Bertrand Badie, *La diplomatie de la connivence: les dérives oligarchiques du système international* [The diplomacy of connivance: Oligarchic excesses of the international system] (Paris: La Découverte, 2011), 105–7.

52. See Giuliano Garavini, "The Battle for the Participation of the European Community in the G7 (1975–1977)," *Journal of European Integration History* 12, no. 1 (2006):141–57.

53. "Political discussion at Venice," note from Michael Palliser to Douglas Alexander, June 6, 1980, PREM 19/188, TNA.

54. Piers Ludlow, "Creating the Expectation of a Collective Response: The Impact of Summitry on Transatlantic Relations," in Mourlon-Druol and Romero, *International Summitry and Global Governance*, 145.

55. Hubert Védrine, *Les mondes de François Mitterrand: À l'Elysée, 1981–1995* [The worlds of François Mitterrand: At the Elysée, 1981–1995] (Fayard: Paris, 1996), 246. See also Jacques Attali, *Verbatim I* (Robert Laffont: Paris, 2011), 538–43.

10. Trust through Familiarity: Transatlantic Relations and Public Diplomacy in the 1980s

Reinhild Kreis

When Jonathan Dean, a former US Foreign Service officer, was interviewed about his years in Germany from 1968 to 1972, he pointed out the latent distrust inherent in German-American relations as they had emerged after the Second World War. On the one hand, there was "the continuing German malaise about American . . . protection vis-à-vis the Soviet Union. . . . Can you really trust another country with final responsibility for your own security?" On the other hand, Dean continued, there was the question of "German neutralism or whether Germany would be a reliable ally or not. . . . These two factors . . . were the two main factors in the German-American relationship."[1]

Building up and maintaining trust in an asymmetric relationship such as the one between the Federal Republic of Germany (FRG) and the United States during the Cold War was certainly no easy task. West Germany's security depended heavily on US military protection, yet due to the division of Germany the FRG's interests, fears, and aims sometimes ran contrary to those of its allies, repeatedly resulting in mutual distrust. Likewise, the economic interdependence of the United States and Europe led not only to cooperation but also to suspicions about the other side's motives and intentions.[2] To reduce both latent and current tensions, and to increase support for their own standpoints, both countries employed public diplomacy—"an international actor's attempt to conduct its foreign policy by engaging with foreign publics"—usually in the form of government-to-people contacts.[3] By spreading information about a state's policies or its society, disseminating cultural practices, or offering exchange programs, these international actors tried to win over and attract a foreign public.[4] In the United States, the newly created United States Information Agency (USIA) took over the country's public diplomacy in 1953.[5] The USIA directed its efforts not only toward the Eastern bloc and neutral states but also toward US allies. Throughout the Cold War, successive administrations felt that it was an important goal to convince societies friendly to the United States of the positive nature of American aims, values, and polices in order to ensure their allegiance. West Germany took up a more cautious stance toward public diplomacy. After the Second World War, several independent West German agencies conducted programs abroad, yet they carefully tried to avoid any reminiscing about the German "cultural imperialism" of previous decades.[6]

Public diplomacy is a tool of what Joseph Nye has deemed soft power, namely "the ability to get what you want through attraction rather than through coercion or payments."[7] Power, Nye has argued, rests not only on hard power such as military strength; countries also succeed because others feel attracted by their values, institutions, ideals, and lifestyles, and want to follow them. Therefore, shaping the preferences of other societies according to one's own preferences helps produce desired results.[8] From this perspective, states are well-advised to apply soft power strategies and aim to establish this kind of values congruence in order to gain legitimacy, acceptance, and prestige—and, therefore, power.

An aspect that has been neglected so far in studies on both soft power and public diplomacy is the meaning of trust. Systematically including this concept, however, will lead to a more comprehensive understanding of how soft power works. This chapter argues that public diplomacy is a means of building trust and credibility, and therefore it is a precondition for soft power to work. Both public diplomacy and soft power aim at producing resemblance and similarities between societies, and therefore emphasize aspects that are essential to trusting relationships. The wordplay in the ambiguous title of Liping Bu's book on US cultural expansion, *Making the World Like Us*, hints at this connection.[9] The world was to become like the United States, and at the same time to like the "American way." Admittedly, familiarity with a country's policies, culture, and society does not necessarily lead to affection; it can also evoke contempt.[10] Yet generally speaking, familiarity makes it easier to trust, and evoking familiarity was the exact aim of public diplomacy. It was thought to be a means of helping bridge the trust gap that Jonathan Dean had identified as an ongoing problem in German-American relations.

Public diplomacy programs—including cultural centers, broadcasting, and exchange programs—were directed not at political leaders or decision makers but at a broader public, in particular at opinion makers. Public diplomacy did

219

not aim at producing definite actions in specific situations, but rather sought to influence basic attitudes on a far more general level. Therefore, approaches that have been developed for studies on trust and mistrust in government-to-government contacts or between heads of state apply only partly when it comes to public diplomacy.[11] The focus of public diplomacy is not on immediate decisions or on definable relations between identifiable subjects but rather on attempts to influence the attitudes and opinions of foreign publics so they would understand another country's goals and ideas, and regard it a trustworthy ally. Public diplomacy thus aimed at arousing and stimulating collective attitudes in a more general sense.

Throughout the Cold War, it was of the utmost importance for both superpowers to influence public discourses and foreign societies, not only with regard to hostile or neutral states but equally toward friends and allies.[12] Whereas research on public diplomacy usually focuses on the institutional settings or on programs with respect to specific challenges, this chapter concentrates on the strategy of creating familiarity as an important characteristic of public diplomacy programs directed at the societies of friendly states. This strategy has always been an important element of public diplomacy, but the early 1980s are particularly suited for investigating attempts into building trust by creating a sense of familiarity. By the late 1970s, the latent distrust as identified by Jonathan Dean and many others turned into a substantial debate about the state of transatlantic relations. Both US and West German representatives concluded that German-American relations had worsened considerably and might threaten the cohesion of the Atlantic alliance, and therefore they made substantial efforts to reinforce the sense of togetherness in both countries. As a period of intensified public diplomacy efforts, the late 1970s and early 1980s show how states and actors close to the state used public diplomacy to generate on a societal level a sense of trust through familiarity, generated by interaction and shared experiences, similar to that built by interpersonal contacts.

None of these developments was restricted to German-American relations. Politicians, academics, and media in other Western countries voiced similar concerns about the state of the alliance. Nevertheless, it seems reasonable to concentrate on German-American relations for two reasons: first, because of the closeness and importance of this relationship during the Cold War, and second, because of its specific genesis after the Second World War. It had made Germany a crucial but also a very young ally of the United States, and, due to its division, it was an ally with interests that were partially different from those of other North Atlantic Treaty Organization (NATO) members.

The challenge lay in convincing the target audiences in both countries that Germany and the United States were trustworthy allies who should work together closely. The United States had to prove that it was still a strong leader that took West Germany's interests to heart. In 1982, the USIA therefore defined one of its most important goals as showing "the Strength and Vitality of American Society: In view of the erosion of Germans' belief in the will, wisdom, and search for excellence in American society, and in view of the importance to the ongoing bilateral relationship that this belief is resuscitated and sustained, it is [our] first long-range task to adduce evidence that the United States is indeed a strong, cohesive, creative and vital society."[13] Germany, by contrast, still had to prove to the West it was a reliable ally. Michael Stürmer, a prominent conservative historian and political adviser to Chancellor Helmut Kohl during the 1980s, stated in a talk in 1985 that West Germany's allies still wondered "how predictable the Germans were [and] how stable their liberal and democratic lifestyle [was]. . . . 40 years after the war, trust is still a scarce good which Germans can't claim for themselves to the extent they usually think they can." West German policy during the previous decade had "called into question again Germany's predictability and reliability."[14]

New Challenges for Public Diplomacy

By the early 1970s, US public diplomacy in West Germany faced difficulties quite different from those of the immediate postwar years, when the main task had been to promote and guide German democratization. The Vietnam War had severely damaged America's image and caused disillusionment, especially among younger generations, both at home and abroad.[15] Young Germans considered the United States no longer as a model democratic society but rather as an imperialist power, power-crazed and inhumane. It was difficult to make American values or policy attractive to these critics. The country's declining image also affected the institutions that transferred information on the United States. In 1973, for example, students in Munich labeled the local American cultural center, the Amerikahaus, an "outpost of US imperialism," claiming that it only served to "burnish the ugly face of the system," and demanded its closure.[16] Throughout the 1970s and 1980s, one of the key goals of US public diplomacy was to win back the younger generation. Yet the Vietnam War and the Watergate scandal of 1974 only added a moral component to an existing image of decline and loss of power. Of course, the United States undisputedly remained a superpower. But it lost some of its overwhelming military and economic advantage, while other countries within the alliance as well as the Soviet Union seemed to gain ground.[17] In the United States and abroad, people worried whether America would be able to fulfill its role as the leader of the Western world in future.

Meanwhile, Germany's strengthened economic and political position gave rise to increased self-confidence, as manifested for example in Willy Brandt's Ostpolitik toward the Eastern bloc.[18] As the USIA put it in 1974: "The US . . . , once mentor for the FRG's democratic development, no longer is a model for the Germans, although more wish to have good relations with the US than with any other nation. Attitudes toward the US today are more differentiated, and the propensity toward criticism of the US is considerably higher than it was ten years ago."[19] Ted Achilles, a high-ranking former diplomat, put it even more plainly in January 1981 when, in a letter to the *New York Times*, he described a "decline in our pre-eminent leadership position—economically, militarily, morally, and politically—in our own eyes and in those of our friends and of our adversaries."[20] This development had to be overcome for the sake of both the American nation and the Western alliance.

At the same time, American attitudes toward West Germany and Western Europe also underwent transitions. Accusations of an "ungrateful" Germany and Europe, of "self-Finlandization"—that is, deliberately adapting one's political policies to appease a more powerful neighboring country, in Finland's case the Soviet Union—and neutralist tendencies led to increased claims in Congress and from the American public to withdraw from Western Europe.[21] In her brief outline of changing American perceptions of Europe in the 1980s, Catherine McArdle Kelleher identified three major positions prevalent in US public opinion: the older and the younger generations of Atlanticists who adhered to the Atlantic alliance, and a separate group of "Non-Atlanticists" which, according to Kelleher, had grown to considerable size in the preceding years. Kelleher labeled this last group "disappointed Atlanticists" who complained about "the 'softness' of the Europeans" and who saw "the United States as being taken advantage of, that the present alliance bargain [was] of far greater benefit to the Europeans." This "attitude of disappointment" admitted "only limited hope for positive change in the future," she concluded.[22]

Growing political and economic tensions between the United States and West Germany further aggravated the situation from the late 1970s onward. The bad relationship between West German chancellor Helmut Schmidt and US president Jimmy Carter was almost legendary.[23] Deteriorating relations between the Eastern and Western blocs caused new difficulties at the turn of the 1980s. The Soviet invasion of Afghanistan in December 1979, the crisis in Poland from August 1980 onward, and the NATO double-track decision to station medium-range nuclear weapons in several Western European countries all led to severe tensions about how to react toward the Eastern bloc. Among the allies, distrust rose. While US politicians and media started to wonder whether the FRG was still a loyal and reliable ally with a clear pro-Western stance, doubts rose among West Germans as to whether US policies were still in their interest at all.

Americans were not the only ones who feared a deterioration of their country's image abroad. Starting in the late 1970s, German politicians, scholars, and media increasingly started to worry about how West Germany was perceived by Americans, and demanded efforts to improve the image of their country. In particular, American plans to establish a memorial to the victims of the Holocaust—later the United States Holocaust Memorial Museum in Washington, D.C.—led to immense fears that Germany would be identified only with the Holocaust. In this view, Germany's history would be reduced to the years between 1933 and 1945, while the achievement of having established a stable and prospering democracy, one of which the Germans were so proud, would be forgotten.[24] After Ronald Reagan's accession to office in 1981, fears of a deteriorating image of Germany in the United States grew. Reagan's confrontational course toward the Soviet Union left no room for any form of détente—a policy supported by large parts of the West German population—and he strongly disapproved of any dissenting attitude or policy on the matter.

A flood of publications further fueled the debate. Throughout the 1980s, Americans and Germans alike published widely on the changing state of German-American and European-American relations. The publications covered the full range of opinions on the subject. Critics of the United States stressed their "fear of the friends," as West German Social Democratic Party politician Oskar Lafontaine titled his 1983 book.[25] Other journalists and diplomats bewailed deteriorating German-American relations in a concerned fashion.[26] A third group, mainly scholars of different fields, focused instead on the changing nature of German-American relations without loading the topic morally or trying to alarm the public.[27]

Taken together, the alliance had to deal with uncertainties about mutual perceptions and about the distribution of roles, causing demands for the renegotiation of German-American relations. Rethinking public diplomacy strategies was an important part of this process. Whereas the FRG aimed at presenting itself as a prospering democracy, a truly Western country, and a reliable partner, American priorities focused on winning back the younger generations lost during the second half of the 1960s and the 1970s, ending détente, and reestablishing an image of the United States as a strong and trustworthy leader. Public diplomacy was supposed to help convince West Germans and Europeans "that America is still the generous, reliable, believable, peace-loving country that gave [them] CARE packages, the Marshall Plan and the Berlin airlift, and saved them from the Russians."[28]

223

Widening Gaps

One thought in particular came up when Americans, Germans, and other West Europeans reflected on the changing and, as many perceived it, deteriorating state of transatlantic relations. This thought was the notion of a younger generation who either held unfavorable and distorted opinions about their transatlantic allies or took the Atlantic alliance for granted and therefore did not pay too much attention to it. This so-called "successor generation" was considered to consist of those up to roughly forty years of age who would soon take over leading positions in both the United States and Western Europe. If this group did not start to take the Soviet threat more seriously and think of the transatlantic relationship as the guarantor of a powerful West, the fear was that the Atlantic alliance would "drift apart" and lose its strength.[29]

In the late 1970s, the USIA became one of the first institutions to take up the generation question. As early as 1978, the USIA Office of Research compiled a compendium on the "successor generation" in Western Europe, which focused on the FRG in particular.[30] Soon others also got in on the subject, and at the turn of the decade several newly founded working groups took up work on similar subjects. In 1979, the Atlantic Council of the United States (ACUS), a Washington-based think tank, established a "Working Group on the Successor Generation" which consisted of about sixty renowned representatives of politics, universities, think tanks, and foundations. Also in 1979, the North Atlantic Assembly (NAA), an informal interparliamentary organization of NATO member states, established a committee on the successor generation, as did the Atlantic Treaty Association (ATA), an umbrella organization of groups devoted to the promotion of NATO.[31] These groups shared the goals of increasing knowledge about and appreciation of their Western allies, creating awareness of the threat posed by the Soviet Union, and establishing programs dedicated to strengthening transatlantic ties.

In West Germany, there was no counterpart to these working groups on the institutional level. Yet the question raised considerable interest among German politicians of nearly all parties (with the exception of the Greens, whose majority called for the FRG's resignation from NATO), think tanks, foundations, the media, and private persons. They shared the fears of a "drifting apart," of loosening ties between the two countries, and of Anti-Americanism. These fears and aspirations, shared by both Americans and Germans, led to the US and West German governments establishing coordinators for German-American relations in 1981. Chancellor Helmut Schmidt appointed Minister of State Hildegard Hamm-Brücher of the Free Democratic Party as coordinator, and President Ronald Reagan assigned his Undersecretary of State for Political Affairs Lawrence Eagleburger.[32] The topic also played an important role at the newly established Arbeitsgruppe USA (Working Group on the USA), formed at the German Federal Foreign Office in 1982. According to these groups, the younger generations' lack of interest in the Western alliance also involved a lack of appreciation for the values that the older generations held in high esteem. In 1983, the ACUS working group discerned "a disturbing uncertainty, and confusion, about the traditional values of Western democracy in the countries of the Atlantic community" and accordingly addressed in its second working paper the questions of how to define and to transmit these values to succeeding generations.[33] Youth seemed to not be ready to fully appreciate and therefore defend what was sometimes referred to simply as "Western values" or, more specifically, democracy and freedom. The reports adapted Ronald Inglehart's terminology of the importance of the "formative years" and an intergenerational shift from "materialist" to "post-materialist" value sets, as Inglehart had established in his 1977 study *The Silent Revolution: Changing Values and Political Styles among Western Publics*. This choice of terminology further strengthened the diagnosis of fundamental differences between the generations.[34]

At the turn of the decade, debates revolved around two gaps that seemed to threaten the Atlantic alliance: a gap between the United States and Western Europe, and a gap between the older and younger generations. To highlight the seriousness of the matter, the newly founded working groups contrasted the recent situation with the 1950s, which they portrayed as the golden age of the Western alliance and of German-American relations. Reports, speeches, and articles praised the common efforts of building the alliance after the war, extolling the comradeship, shared experiences, trusting relations, and a sense of togetherness that all seemed to have been lost by the late 1970s and early 1980s.[35]

Many of those who made the question of the "successor generation" a topic and who pushed initiatives to overcome the perceived threat were dyed-in-the-wool Atlanticists, such as Ted Achilles, James Huntley (cofounder of numerous nongovernmental organizations and initiatives on behalf of NATO), and former US High Commissioner for Germany John McCloy on the American side; Hildegard Hamm-Brücher and German ambassador to the United States Peter Hermes in West Germany; and personalities like US Foreign Service officer Hans N. Tuch, who had truly German-American biographies. All of them had shaped or at least experienced the establishment of the Western alliance and of close German-American relations, and belonged to the "ancestors" of the so-called "successor generation."[36] Their efforts, however, were not only an attempt to restrengthen the alliance, but also attempts to secure their own political heritage.

Closing the Gaps: Regaining Trust in the Late 1970s and 1980s

In this atmosphere of perceived threats of a "drifting apart" between the two countries and of insecurity about each other's political intentions, the institutionalization of contact persons such as the coordinators or the working groups (as within the ACUS, ATA, and NAA) was only a first step. To an extent inconceivable only a few years earlier, Germans and Americans established new transatlantic programs or expanded existing ones. Based on public, private, or mixed initiatives, these programs aimed at bridging both the transatlantic and the generational gaps.[37]

Foreign exchanges experienced a revival. The flagship program was the Congress-Bundestag Youth Exchange Program. Established in 1983 and jointly funded by both countries, the program allowed each member of Congress and the Bundestag to send one teenage student to the United States or West Germany for one year. Although the focus of most exchange programs was clearly on teenagers and young adults, the spectrum also included exchange of parliamentarians, staffers, media representatives, and scholars.[38] International conferences on the topic and meetings of "young leaders" aimed at discussing the topic of a "successor generation"; developing solutions for the perceived crisis in German-American relations; fostering exchange of both opinions and individuals; and, not least, convincing the young that the alliance was worth keeping alive.[39] After a twenty-year break, the German-American Schoolbook Commission met in 1979 and developed recommendations concerning the adequate treatment of Germany and the United States in both countries' history textbooks.[40] To name just a few more activities, the FRG opened up five new Goethe-Institute locations between 1982 and 1986, aimed at establishing media programs to bring Americans in contact with German culture and politics, and promoted the idea of a textbook on German postwar history (an area of history that was felt to be less well studied).[41]

Three aspects of these public diplomacy campaigns are of particular interest in the question of building trust. First, public diplomacy brought together people of all societies concerned, whether on the purely German-American level as with the Congress-Bundestag Youth Exchange Program, or on a broader level as with Ronald Reagan's Youth Exchange Initiative, which was announced at the G7 states' Versailles economic summit in 1982. The focus on exchange of persons aimed at restrengthening personal ties and, most important, familiarizing the participants with their allies' countries and societies. Personal familiarity and closeness, it was hoped, would translate into closer and more trusting political relations in the future.

Second, public diplomacy created many opportunities to perform symbolic acts and thus to stage closeness and transatlantic trust. The 1983 Tricentennial, a celebration of 300 years of German immigration to America, provided an opportunity to launch new programs and to demonstrate German-American bonds at both a rhetorical and visual level, for example at the launch of the Congress-Bundestag Exchange Program or the opening of the German-American Friendship Garden in Washington, D.C. Prominent representatives from the fields of politics, economy, culture, and society lent their reputation to the cause of transatlantic relations by attending ceremonies, donating money, giving speeches, and initiating new campaigns.

Third, public diplomacy allowed participants to tell a story that interlinked the past, present, and future of Americans, Germans, and Europeans to a broader public, and deduce instructions for future action from that. When talking about the Western alliance, the advocates of the "successor generation" theory did not restrict themselves to the postwar period, but placed NATO in a much broader context. To an unprecedented extent, they frequently stressed the "common heritage" and the "shared values" of Americans and West Europeans as democratic societies that were rooted in traditions going back as far as Greek and Roman times.[42] For West Germany in particular, this narrative (which encompassed more than 2,000 years) was very appealing, since it allowed the country to be integrated into "the West" despite its belligerent and nondemocratic recent past. All of a sudden, references to the past enjoyed a positive rather than negative connotation.

References to past experiences were supposed to evoke a feeling of security and trust for the present and the future. The narrative depicted the NATO states, particularly the United States and its allies in Western Europe, as a group of countries with the same roots, sharing a common past as well as visions for the future. Past strains over political, military, economic, and cultural disagreements had little place in this narrative, despite the many and sometimes fundamental controversies during the previous decades and until now. According to USIA, ACUS, NAA, ATA, and other organizations or individuals engaged in the debate, the United States and Germany shared the same values and faced the same problems, and therefore were natural allies in tackling them.

In this perspective, the situation of the early 1980s was simply a variation of the enduring efforts to defend "Western values" against external threats. Therefore, future cooperation was not a risky venture, but rather was the logical extension into the future of a successful, long-standing tradition. The ACUS working group, too, was very clear about the commitment that arose from the common heritage: "The civic values nurtured in the history of the Western world can inspire individual and national loyalty and a willingness to sacrifice some measure of personal and national interest. Those values are so fundamental that they must stand above immediate political issues."[43] In a way, this narrative can be seen as an attempt to invent a common past and in doing so create a common transatlantic identity.

It is important to note that the efforts to restore these "common values, common causes"—as the West German embassy's public policy department put it—and to rebuild the alliance had a strong domestic dimension.[44] The "real task," Hildegard Hamm-Brücher stated in 1981, was "to convince the citizens of our countries, and above all the young people, of the vital importance of our common intellectual and political principles and our alliance."[45] Many actors such as NAA and ACUS working groups devoted a substantial share of their activities to the education not only of foreign students but of their own youth.[46]

Although the narrative of a "successor generation" aroused considerable interest as well as money and support among political and private actors, the efforts to overcome the perceived threat also engendered skepticism. At times, representatives of media and academia would deny that there was a crisis at all, definitely none that was more dangerous than previous disagreements.[47] Others critics, such as West Germany's Green Party, not only opposed the measures taken to improve the transatlantic relationship but also, as mentioned, voted for West Germany to leave NATO. Still others agreed that the Western alliance indeed faced major challenges in the "drifting apart" of its member states, but as a 1983 *New York Times* article put it, "If Mr. Reagan thinks propaganda and agents will turn the tide, he is out of date. It requires more than stirring or seductive words now. It takes demonstrable, consistent good sense and 'a decent respect for the opinions of mankind.'"[48] Likewise, German newspapers such as the *Deutsches Allgemeines Sonntagsblatt* questioned whether "Uncle Sam and the German Michel will really shake hands just because some undersecretaries have drawn up a piece of paper."[49]

Skeptical statements along these lines demanded "costly concessions" rather than words. To critics, companionship and an alliance based on a sense of togetherness and trust required deeds, not words.[50] Yet the narrative of the "successor generation" was more than just a declaration of intent. It united actors across countries and spheres in common action, since it proved to be compatible with different concerns. It also provided an emotional language and common terminology that allowed for common action on the international level but also for the winning of domestic support. The terminology of generations and values proved to be particularly successful in this regard, as it combined fears of a crumbling alliance with reservations about the younger generations, which were frequently identified with the 1968 generation. USIA, for example, lamented "teachers, who, as a product of the sixties, are frequently hostile to American capitalism" and therefore conveyed a distorted and stereotype image of the United States to their students.[51] The rejection of "1968" and the social and cultural changes attributed to the members of this generation helped unite persons from different backgrounds. At the same time, the narrative of the successor generation allowed them to evoke positive images of friendship, trust, and togetherness.

Taken together, the "successor generation" narrative helped create an atmosphere in which public diplomacy was seen as a solution to the problem of seemingly estranged allies. Within only a few years, public and private actors started new activities and programs to an extent that no one would have expected before. This surge in interest was not necessarily anticipated, as for different reasons public diplomacy had not enjoyed a strong US or West German lobby in previous years. Legitimizing programs aimed at allies, in particular, was quite difficult. The number and extent of newly launched programs in the early 1980s do not, of course, say anything about their success.[52] As is always the case with public diplomacy, it is hard if not impossible to attribute mindsets or shifts of opinion to such programs, and it is equally difficult to determine if these programs generated trust. Nor did the programs provide a quick solution for the short-term political conflicts; these concerns did not go away. What can be observed, however, is the attempt to (re-)familiarize societies with one another in order to (re-)establish an alliance based on mutual trust about the other's intentions and policy. Paradoxically, these efforts were based on mistrust: mistrust toward change and toward a generation that was feared to be either incapable of or reluctant to tell friends from foes or to take the alliance's interest to heart. Therefore, the expanded or newly established programs aimed to produce affinities, as a prerequisite for trust, between the United States and West Germany and between the older and the younger generations.

Conclusion

Promoting the idea of mutual efforts to generate "new trust" between the transatlantic partners, Hildegard Hamm-Brücher called these attempts the "moral armament" of the alliance.[53] Her figure of speech highlights the meaning of trust as a sort of necessary capital that must be deliberately produced. This chapter, however, does not argue that NATO or any other alliance would not be able to exist without the trust of the population of its member states. Successful cooperation does not necessarily need trust, and depending on how trust is defined it remains controversial to what extent trust in governments, institutions, or large collectivities is possible at all.[54] Yet it has become clear that there was a certain desire to evoke a feeling of trust toward the United

States, Germany, and NATO among the Western societies. Representatives of all states concerned wanted to show that German-American, or European-American, relations were more than an alliance of convenience: they were an alliance that jointly followed higher purposes and was held together by values and trust as much as by military and economic necessity.

Both the United States and West Germany supported this approach, although they considered the situation from different angles. Under Ronald Reagan, the United States aimed to regain its lost strength and reputation and to enforce its leadership within the alliance, whereas the Federal Republic sought to hold onto American protection and further establish the image of West Germany as a truly democratic Western society. Public diplomacy aimed at bridging the imbalance in power between the two states by developing narratives that familiarized both societies with each other and synchronized, at least on the narrative level, their pasts, presents, and futures, as well as their overall goals and values. This narrative, while focused on togetherness, at the same time was broad enough to leave room for interpretations compatible with the demands of each society.

Notes

1. Jonathan Dean, interview by Charles Stuart Kennedy, July 8, 1997, Frontline Diplomacy: The Foreign Affairs Oral History Collection of the Association for Diplomatic Studies and Training (Washington, DC: Library of Congress), http://www.loc.gov/item/mfdipbib000279

2. John Pinder, "Interdependence, Problem or Solution," in *The Troubled Alliance: Atlantic Relations in the 1980s*, ed. Lawrence Freedman (New York: St. Martin's Press, 1983), 67–87; and Reinhild Kreis, ed., *Diplomatie mit Gefühl. Vertrauen, Misstrauen und die Außenbeziehungen der Bundesrepublik Deutschland* [Diplomacy with emotion: Trust, mistrust, and the foreign relations of the Federal Republic of Germany] (Munich: De Gruyter Oldenbourg, 2015).

3. Nicholas Cull, *The Cold War and the United States Information Agency: American Propaganda and Public Diplomacy, 1945–1989* (Cambridge, UK: Cambridge University Press, 2008), xv; and Joseph S. Nye Jr., "Public Diplomacy and Soft Power," *The Annals of the American Academy of Political and Social Science* 616 (2008): 94–109.

4. On the different components of public diplomacy see Cull, *The Cold War*, x.

5. Cull, *The Cold War*.

6. Eckard Michels, *Von der Deutschen Akademie zum Goethe-Institut: Sprach- und auswärtige Kulturpolitik 1923–1960* [From the German Academy to the Goethe Institute: The promotion of German abroad and foreign cultural policy, 1923–1960] (Munich: Oldenbourg, 2005), 219.

7. Joseph S. Nye Jr., *Soft Power: The Means to Success in World Politics* (New York: Public Affairs, 2004), x. For the combination of hard and soft power that Nye

thinks is the best strategy in foreign policy, he invented the term "smart power." For a brief summary of the current discussion of the concept of soft power, see Craig Hayden, *The Rhetoric of Soft Power: Public Diplomacy in Global Contexts* (Lanham, MD: Lexington Books, 2012), 4–9, 27–75.

8. Nye, *Soft Power*, 5–6.

9. Liping Bu, *Making the World Like Us: Education, Cultural Expansion, and the American Century* (Westport, CT: Praeger, 2003).

10. Martin Klimke, *The Other Alliance: Student Protest in West Germany and the United States in the Global Sixties* (Princeton, NJ: Princeton University Press, 2010); and Philip M. Taylor, "Public Diplomacy and the Information War on Terror," in *Soft Power and US Foreign Policy: Theoretical, Historical and Contemporary Perspectives*, ed. Inderjeet Parmar and Michael Cox (London: Routledge, 2010), 163.

11. Deborah Welch Larson, *Anatomy of Mistrust: U.S.-Soviet Relations during the Cold War* (Ithaca, NY: Cornell University Press, 1997); Aaron M. Hoffman, *Building Trust: Overcoming Suspicion in International Conflict* (Albany: State University of New York Press, 2006); and Andrew H. Kydd, *Trust and Mistrust in International Relations* (Princeton, NJ: Princeton University Press, 2007).

12. Michael Hochgeschwender, "Westernisierung und Amerikanisierung im Kalten Krieg" [Westernization and Americanization during the Cold War], *Geschichte, Politik und ihre Didaktik* 34, nos. 3/4 (2006): 290. See also Jan C. Behrends, "Agitation, Organization, Mobilization: The League for Polish-Soviet Friendship in Stalinist Poland," in *The Sovietization of Eastern Europe: New Perspectives on the Postwar Period*, ed. Balázs Apor, Péter Apor, and E. A. Rees (Washington, DC: New Academia Publishing, 2008), 181–200; and Jens Gieseke's chapter in this volume.

13. USIA, Country Plan for West Germany 1982, E6/799, box 676, Stadtarchiv Nuremberg (StadtAN). Under President Jimmy Carter, the USIA had been renamed the United States International Communication Agency (USICA), but it regained its old name again soon after Ronald Reagan came into office.

14. Michael Stürmer, "Die Deutschen in Europa – Chancen und Grenzen der Deutschlandpolitik" [The Germans in Europe: Opportunities and limits of policy toward Germany] (lecture given on June 14, 1985, B 32, Ref. 204, no. 135191, Zwischenarchiv, Politisches Archiv des Auswärtigen Amtes (PAAA), Berlin), author's translation. Although Stürmer's lecture focused on Europe rather than the United States, the quote reflects general thoughts on the FRG's foreign policy.

15. Klimke, *The Other Alliance*.

16. Leaflet "Warum findet ein Vietnam-Festival im Amerikahaus statt?" [Why is a Vietnam Festival taking place in the Amerikahaus?], 1973, Polizeidirektion München nach 1945, no. 17023, Staatsarchiv Munich (StAM) (author's translation).

17. James T. Patterson, *Grand Expectations: The United States, 1945–1974* (New York: Oxford University Press, 1997), 782–83.

18. Judith Michel, *Willy Brandts Amerikabild und -politik 1933–1992* [Willy Brandt's America image and policy, 1933–1992] (Göttingen: Vandenhoeck & Ruprecht, 2010), 299–306 and 340–43.

19. USIS Bonn, Country Plan 1974/75, E 418, no. 126, Stadtarchiv Tübingen (StadtAT).

20. Achilles to New York Times, January 1, 1981, ACUS, box 14, Hoover Institution Archives, Stanford, California.

21. For a contemporary overview, see Laurence Radway, "Let Europe Be Europe," *World Policy Journal* 1, no. 1 (1983): 23–43; and Alan Wolfe, "American Domestic Politics and the Atlantic Alliance: Crisis and Controversy," in *Dealignment: A New Foreign Policy Perspective*, ed. Mary Kaldor and Richard Falk (Oxford: Blackwell, 1987), 65–81.

22. Catherine McArdle Kelleher, "America Looks at Europe," in Freedman, *The Troubled Alliance*, 63.

23. Jimmy Carter, *White House Diary* (New York: Farrar, Straus and Giroux, 2010), 172–73, 439–40, and 485; and Klaus Wiegrefe, *Das Zerwürfnis: Helmut Schmidt, Jimmy Carter und die Krise der deutsch-amerikanischen Beziehungen* [The disagreement: Helmut Schmidt, Jimmy Carter, and the crisis in German-American relations] (Berlin: Propyläen, 2005).

24. Jacob S. Eder, *Holocaust Angst: The Federal Republic of Germany and American Holocaust Memory since the 1970s* (Oxford: Oxford University Press, forthcoming 2016).

25. Oskar Lafontaine, *Angst vor den Freunden: Die Atomwaffenstrategie der Supermächte zerstört die Bündnisse* [Fear of the friends: The nuclear strategy of the superpowers destroys the alliances] (Hamburg: Rowohlt, 1983). Lafontaine was referring to both superpowers' relations with their allies and did not concentrate solely on the United States. Yet such an approach might have been regarded as even less favorable in the United States.

26. To name but a few: Stephen F. Szabo, ed., *The Successor Generation: International Perspectives of Postwar Europeans* (London: Butterworths, 1983); Klaus Harpprecht, *Amerikaner: Freunde, Fremde, ferne Nachbarn* [Americans: Friends, strangers, distant neighbors] (Munich: DTV, 1986); Hans N. Tuch, ed., *Arthur Burns and the Successor Generation: Selected Writings of and about Arthur Burns* (Lanham, MD: University Press of America, 1988); Arnulf Baring, *Unser neuer Größenwahn: Deutschland zwischen Ost und West* [Our new megalomania: Germany between East and West] (Stuttgart: DVA, 1988).

27. See, e.g., Joyce M. Mushaben, "Anti-Politics and Successor Generations: The Role of Youth in the West and East German Peace Movements," *Journal of Political and Military Sociology* 12, no. 1 (1984): 171–90; Stanley Hoffman, "Cries and Whimpers: Thoughts on West European–American Relations in the 1980s," *Daedalus* 113, no. 3 (1984): 221–52; William K. Domke, Richard C. Eichenberg, and Catherine M. Kelleher, "Consensus Lost? Domestic Politics and the 'Crisis' in NATO," *World Politics: A Quarterly Journal of International Relations* 39, no. 3 (1987): 382–407; Harald Mueller and Thomas Risse-Kappen, "Origins of Estrangement: The Peace Movement and the Changed Image of America in West Germany," *International Security* 12, no. 1 (1987): 52–88; and Hans Rattinger, "Change versus Continuity in West German Public Attitudes on National Security and Nuclear Weapons in the Early 1980s," *Public Opinion Quarterly* 51, no. 4 (1987): 495–521.

28. Flora Lewis, "Foreign Affairs: Alas For Plausibility," *New York Times*, April 8, 1983.

29. Peter Hermes, "Is the Alliance Drifting Apart?" (speech given at Yale University, December 1, 1981), in *Statements and Speeches*, Vol. IV-21, ed. German Information Center (New York: German Information Center, [1981]); Dell Pendergast, "Comment," in *The Successor Generation: Its Challenges and Responsibilities* (Washington, DC: The Atlantic Council of the United States [ACUS], 1981), 24; Otto Graf Lambsdorff, "Are we drifting apart? German-American relations today" (speech

given at the American Council on Germany, February 23, 1982), in *Statements and Speeches*, Vol. V-6, ed. German Information Center (New York: German Information Center, [1982]); and Martin J. Hillenbrand, *Germany in an Era of Transition* (Paris: Atlantic Institute for International Affairs, 1983), 44. On earlier debates about a "successor generation" during the 1960s, see Valérie Aubourg, "Problems of Transmission: The Atlantic Community and the Successor Generation as Seen by US Philanthropy, 1960s and 1970s," in *Atlantic, Euratlantic, or Europe-America?*, ed. Giles Scott Smith and Valérie Aubourg (Paris: Soleb, 2010).

30. RG 306, Office of Research, S-Reports, box 18, US National Archives and Records Administration (NARA). In the following years, USIA continued to frequently conduct polls on the topic. See RG 306, Office of Research, S-Reports, boxes 18–22, NARA.

31. North Atlantic Assembly (NAA), Committee on Education, Cultural Affairs & Information, Introductory Report for the Working Group on the Successor Generation, May 1980, ACUS, box 253, Hoover Institution Archives; Harned to Pellegrino, July 31, 1979, ibid.; and Achilles, Memorandum, September 9, 1980, ibid.

32. Reinhild Kreis, "Bündnis ohne Nachwuchs? Die 'Nachfolgegeneration' und die deutsch-amerikanischen Beziehungen in den 1980er Jahren" [Alliance without offspring? The "successor generation" and German-American relations in the 1980s], *Archiv für Sozialgeschichte* 52 (2012): 607–31.

33. ACUS, *The Teaching of Values and the Successor Generation* (Washington, DC: ACUS, 1983), 9.

34. Inglehart later became a member of the ACUS Working Group on the Successor Generation himself. For the widespread use of Inglehart's terminology in both the United States and West Germany see, e.g., USIA, "A Compendium of Research Evidence on the Successor Generation in Europe," April 1978, RG 306, Office of Research, S-Reports, box 18, NARA; Federal Foreign Office, Ref. 204 to Genscher, November 8, 1981, B32, Ref. 204, no. 123313, PAAA; and Kenneth P. Adler, "The Successor Generation: Why, Who and How," in Szabo, *The Successor Generation*, 4–16.

35. Pendergast, "Comment"; Hamm-Brücher, Opening statement at symposion at Harvard, November 5, 1981, B32, no. 123314, PAAA; Berndt von Staden, "Deutsche und Amerikaner – Irritationen" [Germans and Americans: Irritations], *Außenpolitik* 35, no. 1 (1984): 44–53; and Tuch, *Arthur Burns*, 16.

36. Kreis, *Bündnis ohne Nachwuchs*, 618–19. Some contemporaries, including former US ambassador to Germany Martin J. Hillenbrand, had already hinted at this; see, e.g., Hillenbrand, *Germany*, 43.

37. On the full range of activities, see the publication series *Austausch über den Atlantik* [Exchanges across the Atlantic], later *Brücken über den Atlantik* [Bridges across the Atlantic], published by the West German Federal Foreign Office (Auswärtiges Amt) from 1983 onward. See also Kreis, *Bündnis ohne Nachwuchs*. At the European level, see, e.g., Giles Scott-Smith, "Searching for the Successor Generations: Exchange Programs, Networks of Influence, and US Foreign Policy towards Western Europe in the 1980s," in *The United States and Public Diplomacy: New Directions in Cultural and International History*, ed. Ken Osgood and Brian Etheridge (Leiden: Nijhoff, 2010); and Giles Scott-Smith, "Reviving the Transatlantic Community? The Successor Generation Concept in U.S. Foreign Affairs, 1960s–1980s," in *European Integration and the Atlantic Community in the 1980s*, ed. Kiran Klaus Patel and Kenneth Weisbrode (Cambridge, UK: Cambridge University Press, 2013), 201–25.

38. Kreis, *Bündnis ohne Nachwuchs*.

39. Alan Platt, ed., *The Atlantic Alliance: Perspectives from the Successor Generation* (Santa Monica, CA: Rand Corporation, 1983); ACUS, Report on Student Conference, December 3, 1981, ACUS, box 253, Hoover Institution Archives; and AAPYL Seminar "The Successor Generation" in Oxford, preliminary program, July 4–6, 1981, ACUS, box 253, Hoover Institution Archives.

40. *Recent History of the Federal Republic of Germany and the United States: Recommendations for Treatment in Textbooks* (Boulder, CO: Westview Press, 1985).

41. Elsaesser, Politische Öffentlichkeits- und Kulturarbeit, March 1982, B32-204, no. 135189, PAAA. Goethe-Institut, *Jahrbuch 1982/83* [Yearbook 1982–83] (Munich, 1983); Goethe-Institut, *Jahrbuch 1985/86* [Yearbook 1985–86] (Munich, 1986); German Embassy/Washington, D.C. to Auswärtiges Amt, December 17, 1981, B 32, Ref. 204, no. 135176, PAAA.

42. Achilles, Memo on "The problem of Value Transmittal," April 23, 1979, ACUS, box 253/11, Hoover Institution Archives; NAA, Minutes of the Working Group on the Successor Generation, February 26/27, 1980, box 253/10, Hoover Institution Archives; Hildegard Hamm-Brücher, Memorandum, November 25, 1981, B 32, Ref. 205, no. 123313, PAAA; Jacomet to Achilles, March 17, 1982, James R. Huntley Papers, box 50, Hoover Institution Archives; and ACUS, *The Teaching of Values*, 10.

43. ACUS, *The Teaching of Values*, 14.

44. German Information Center, ed., *Common Values, Common Cause: German Statesmen in the United States, American Statesmen in Germany 1953–1983: Statements and Speeches* (Washington, DC: German Information Center, 1983).

45. Speech given by Hamm-Brücher, Press Luncheon in Washington, D.C., November 2, 1981, B 32, box 123313, PAAA.

46. In the United States, efforts focused on the overlapping but distinct fields of strengthening the appreciation of the Western Alliance and "citizen education" with its emphasis on educating American citizens. ACUS, Subcommittee on Contacts, First Preliminary Report, February 2, 1980, James R. Huntley Papers, box 50, Hoover Institution Archives; ACUS, *The Teaching of Values*; and NAA, Introductory Report for the Working Group on the Successor Generation, May 1980, ACUS, box 253, Hoover Institution Archives.

47. Daniel Yergin, "Unequal Partners," *New York Times*, December 18, 1983; and Derek Leebaert, "Letter to the Editor," *New York Times*, February 5, 1986.

48. Lewis, "Foreign Affairs."

49. Jochen Stumm, "Dünnbrettbohrer" [Lightweights], *Deutsches Allgemeines Sonntagsblatt*, November 15, 1981.

50. Larson, *Anatomy of Mistrust*, 27–28.

51. USIA, USIS Germany, Country Plan Financial Year 1983, E 6/799, no. 754, StadtAN. See also Ronald Reagan's remarks during a talk with Helmut Schmidt. Well to Genscher, May 21, 1981, in *Akten zur Auswärtigen Politik der Bundesrepublik Deutschland 1981* [Foreign policy documents of the Federal Republic of Germany, 1982], Vol. 2 (Munich: Oldenbourg, 2012), no. 146.

52. Public diplomacy programs of the 1980s have not yet been analyzed in detail. For first insights, see Scott-Smith, "Searching for the Successor Generations," and Scott-Smith, "Reviving the Transatlantic Community?"

53. Hamm-Brücher, opening statement at symposium at Harvard University, November 5, 1981, B32, box 123314, PAAA (author's translation).

54. Karen S. Cook, Russell Hardin, and Margaret Levi, *Cooperation Without Trust?* (New York: Russell Sage Foundation, 2007), 1–5.

IV. On the Sidelines or in the Middle? Small and Neutral States

11. "Footnotes" as an Expression of Distrust? The United States and the NATO "Flanks" in the Last Two Decades of the Cold War

Effie G. H. Pedaliu

The Christmas of 1979 is etched in collective memory because of the Soviet invasion of Afghanistan. For many Western Europeans, this dramatic event was preceded by another shock that winter—the North Atlantic Treaty Organization (NATO) double-track decision on December 12, 1979. On this date, at a special meeting, NATO foreign and defense ministers agreed to modernize the alliance's nuclear arsenal and its capabilities through the deployment on European soil of 572 long-range theater nuclear forces (TNF) that would be able to strike the Soviet Union directly. The decision also was linked to a NATO offer to the Soviet Union to hold immediate negotiations on arms limitations on TNF, with the explicit understanding that the new missiles would be installed within four years if an agreement had not been reached.[1] The United States was to provide the new weapons, but it had not been the sole initiator of the upgrading process. The primary instigation came from its European NATO allies, who had become alarmed by the deployment of Soviet SS-20 medium-range missiles in Eastern Europe. Many Western European leaders, especially West German chancellor Helmut Schmidt, saw the Soviet deployment of the SS-20s as a deliberate design to upset the military balance between NATO and the Warsaw Pact and thereby increase the vulnerability of the NATO area and, more especially, of West Germany.[2]

The double-track decision was to lead to the deeply divisive "Euromissile" crisis of the early 1980s, which rattled the social stability of many European societies and also affected transatlantic relations.[3] NATO's troublesome experiences during the 1980s also came to be known as its "footnote era": a period in which transatlantic relations were typified by the recourse, far

237

more frequently than usual, to "footnotes" by member states to official NATO documents to express disagreement with policy relating to nuclear issues. The most regular "offenders" were Denmark and Greece, two small states that had very little in common apart from their location at NATO's "flanks." Their geographical position, away from the "Central Front" along the inter-German border and in the exposed NATO flanks, led public opinion in both countries to assume that within the heavy militarization of the Cold War, the collapse of détente—even in the comatose state it was in at this point in time—would increase their vulnerability to Soviet attack much more than the SS-20s.[4] Denmark and Greece drew this common conclusion even though they faced different local security environments. Denmark existed within a desecuritized local environment, the Norden, which was based on the close socioeconomic and political cooperation of the Nordic countries.[5] In contrast, Greece was located in a heavily militarized, complex, and adversarial environment, where from the mid-1970s on its communist enemies appeared to be less threatening than its ostensible NATO ally, Turkey.[6]

Two historiographical views attempt to explain "footnoting." One view suggests that footnoting stemmed from long-standing, deeply embedded hostility in both countries to nuclear weapons, as shown by Denmark's policy of refusing to station nuclear weapons and Greece's refusal to station intermediate-range ballistic missiles in 1959.[7] The other position holds the view that footnoting was the result of domestic upheavals. In the case of Denmark, its practice of footnoting has been explained by reference to Danish responses to the rhetoric of the Reagan administration and onset of the heightened tensions of the Second Cold War in the late 1970s and early 1980s, as well as to the Danish political system's propensity toward fragmentation, which at this time produced shifting parliamentary majorities on foreign policy matters.[8] In the case of Greece, the debate about footnoting has focused on the difficult relationship that the mercurial socialist leader Andreas Papandreou had with NATO and the United States in the 1980s.[9]

This chapter does not disagree with the views above, but will argue that the origins of "footnoting" had a longer gestation period, one that can be traced back to the 1960s and 1970s when an accretion of distrust and diffidence, felt by many Danes and Greeks, was directed toward the United States and NATO. It was during this period that the political and social systems of both countries were affected by key international events. These events included a sense of increasing risk-taking by the United States in its relations with the Soviet Union through an exclusive superpower détente, the Americanization of the Vietnam conflict, and the corrosive impact on both Greece and Denmark of the Greek dictatorship of 1967–74. These events helped to create, by the early 1980s, a volatile body of intermestic issues in the two countries that affected their notions of how best to maintain their national security.[10] The strident anti-Soviet rhetoric of the Reagan administration clashed with Greek and Danish public opinion, which was not ready to accept the formal end of détente, and in the 1980s the governments of Greece and Denmark chose to soothe their electorates by raising objections to NATO policy through the use of footnotes. Footnoting embarrassed America, creating palpable tensions, but it neither invalidated nor threatened to unravel the alliance, because neither Denmark[11] nor Greece,[12] ultimately, was prepared to leave it. Footnoting was a trying but essentially conformist mode of dissent. Both Denmark and Greece kept within established dissent practice in NATO, and they did not raise the "unanimity and common accord" rule of the North Atlantic Council (NAC) decision-making process.

Background

In the early 1980s, the domestic affairs of both Greece and Denmark were going through a period of turbulence. The failure of the Danish government to deal with the country's economy, which had been hit hard by recessions in 1974–75 and 1980–81, undermined the popularity of the pro-NATO Social Democratic governments of the 1970s.[13] Anker Jørgensen's Social Democratic–dominated government that emerged after the December 1981 elections was short-lived, as it could not resolve Denmark's economic problems. In September 1982, it was succeeded by a four-party coalition, known as the "four-leaf clover" government, that was led by Poul Schülter and comprised the Conservative People's Party, the Venstre, the Centre Democrats, and the Christian People's Party. Schülter's government was Denmark's first Conservative-dominated administration since 1894. With a deepening economic crisis and rising unemployment that threatened social cohesion, Schülter needed to have a free hand in order to achieve his program of domestic and economic reform and tackle galloping public distrust.[14] To achieve this, he had to avoid no-confidence votes in a finely balanced Folketing. The radicals adopted the role of a "swing party" when voting on matters of defense and foreign policy and, as a consequence, the outcome was an ad hoc "alternative majority" in parliament. This grouping consisted of the left wing of the Social Democrats, the Social Liberals, the Socialist People's Party, and other smaller left wing parties. From 1982 to 1988, the radical-led alternative majority was able to pass twenty-three parliamentary resolutions that were contrary to NATO policy.[15]

The shifting parliamentary majorities reflected the complex demands of Danish public opinion, but throughout this period support for NATO within

Denmark remained high, peaking at 69 percent during the summer of 1983. At the same time, however, 58 percent of those polled were against the deployment of missiles, as against only 24 percent in favor. By 1985, 42 percent favored the establishment of a Nordic nuclear-free zone, while 37 percent were against the idea.[16] In a Gallup survey, 56 percent of Danish respondents replied that they had either no "great confidence" or "no confidence at all" in the Reagan administration's ability to handle the problems of the world.[17] Schülter's government was forced to suppress its own pro-NATO convictions and resort to dissenting footnotes in order to abide by the parliamentary resolutions of the "alternative majority."[18] Relations between Denmark and the United States suffered. US secretary of state George Shultz told his Danish counterpart Uffe Ellemann-Jensen that "if all the countries in Europe acted like Denmark, we wouldn't have an alliance."[19] Similarly, Joseph M. A. H. Luns, NATO's fifth secretary-general, under whose watch the footnoting drama broke out, was reported as saying that the members of the alliance deplored the actions of the Danish parliament.[20] As a pro-NATO politician, Ellemann-Jensen became a resentful hostage of circumstances and had to carry out the task of footnoting at the NAC level, despite his better judgment. Subsequently, he was to describe the practice as "a virtual appeasement of the USSR."[21]

In Greece in October 1981, the Panhellenic Socialist Movement (PASOK) won a landslide electoral victory on the back of strongly worded anti-Western rhetoric, underpinned by promises to take the country out of NATO permanently. Since the 1970s, PASOK leader Andreas Papandreou had adopted a populist and adversarial approach toward the United States and NATO, cashing in on a growing anti-Americanism that had followed the collapse of the military dictatorship and the invasion of Cyprus by Turkey in 1974.[22] According to his latest biographer, Papandreou was a man who "left in his wake no clear-cut answer to the question of who he was and what he stood for."[23] His foreign policy was often expressed in slogans such as "Greece belongs to the Greeks"[24] or in paying lip service to the idea of nonalignment.[25] Yet the Cold War and Greece's regional vulnerabilities limited Papandreou's actions. Despite his inflammatory anti-Western rhetoric and his blistering preelection criticisms of the Haig-Davos Agreement of 1978[26] and the Rogers proposal of 1980[27] that enabled Greece to return to NATO—after its temporary withdrawal from NATO's integrated military structure following the second Turkish invasion of Cyprus in August 1974—Papandreou was mindful of not upsetting the delicate regional balance on which the security of Greece hung.[28] He realized that leaving NATO was suicidal, and although relations with the Reagan administration were bad, he exercised brinkmanship but was not seeking to cut the umbilical cord.[29] Papandreou's realism, however, needed to be presented in such a way so as to avoid punishment at the ballot box from Greeks who were convinced that a NATO exit would benefit the country.[30] PASOK adopted footnotes as a means of balancing domestic distrust toward NATO and the United States, and this policy was typified by incessant footnoting.[31]

It has been said that the foreign policy of small states is more responsive to international conditions than to domestic ones because their relative weakness leads them to amplify the immediacy of external threats and to focus primarily on national security.[32] However, during the "footnote era," in the case of Greek and Danish foreign policy over nuclear issues and relations with the United States and NATO, this hypothesis only partially holds. Closer scrutiny shows that in both countries, foreign and domestic policy issues fused together, and foreign policy came to be conditioned by both international and domestic factors. Such developments brought deep change in the foreign policy–making process of both countries. It led to a collision between domestic and foreign policy realms, and resulted in a dispersal of input into the foreign policy–making process from sections of society outside those groups who traditionally had made foreign policy their preserve.

The question then arises of how this intermestic dynamic came about and to what extent it was the product of declining Danish and Greek trust in NATO's ability and willingness to protect their national interests. The *Oxford English Dictionary* defines trust (as a noun) as "confidence, strong belief in the goodness, strength, reliability of something or somebody" or as "responsibility." It also defines trust (as a verb) as "having trust in" or to "believe in the honesty and reliability of someone of something," "have confidence in," or "earnestly hope." On the basis of this definition, the flourishing of trust in alliances such as NATO was based, according to Deborah Welch Larson, on the estimation that the "hegemon" (the United States) would do "the right thing at the right time."[33] NATO's raison d'être "was to deter the Soviet threat," and the foundations for the emergence of trust in such an alliance were to be based on belief, obligation, responsibility, reliability, and consistency. It was, in a few words, the expectation of commitment that would not allow scope for doubt. Jan Ruzicka and Nicholas Wheeler have defined a trusting relationship as one which actors enter into knowingly and as a consequence increase their vulnerability to other actors whose behavior they do not control, with potentially negative consequences for themselves.[34] In the NATO framework, smaller allies like Denmark and Greece put their trust in US nuclear superiority for their defense, and their own "willingness of taking risks" was concomitant to the "expectation that others [would] honor particular obligations."[35] NATO was about deterrence and assurance. Indeed, if Piotr Sztompka is right when he states that "trust is a bet about the future contingent actions of others,"[36] the whole essence of the inclusion of Article 5 (the principle of collective defense) in the NATO treaty was to minimize elements of unpredictability and gambling. This explains why levels of trust were at their highest during the period of "massive retaliation" and plummeted during the eras of "flexible response" and "détente."

At the same time, although NATO was by its very nature a hegemonic alliance *par excellence* where American dominance was taken for granted, it had not been fashioned on the Athenian-Melian model, where "the strong do what they have the power to do and the weak accept what they have to accept."[37] The alliance was based on the shared values held by its core members, as outlined in NATO's preamble. Some commentators have tended to dismiss these stated values as mere "niceties," but most European NATO member states were deeply committed to defending the Western liberal democratic principles that the preamble embodied.[38] Many had suffered appalling abuses of human rights during World War II, so the text of the preamble was of seminal importance to their reconstruction as liberal democracies.[39] Above all, however, it was "the ability of the US to project trustworthiness" that enabled the European NATO allies to reconcile and build a Western European identity.[40] NATO thus was structured around deeply held ideological and moral tenets operating under a regime of a "culture of trust." This was exemplified by the close, behind-the-scenes cooperation of the permanent representatives and also by the NAC ministerial meetings. It was a "security community" that was able to contain many of the disagreements that arose among its members and even mitigate, to a degree, a perceived "consultation deficit" within the alliance.[41] Lord Carrington, NATO's sixth secretary-general, put it thus: "we may not always as an alliance sing in unison, we nearly always manage to sing in harmony."[42]

Deepening Concerns

From its formation, the limited military resources of the alliance meant that the degree of trust of each member had correlated closely to its geography. Joining NATO entailed a high level of risk, and the proffered trust was not "blind trust" but was based on "encapsulated interests"—namely, containing and deterring the Soviet Union.[43] Both Greece and Denmark were located well away from the primary battlefield of the Cold War. The primacy of the Central Front in NATO strategy and the potential expendability of Greece and Denmark as "flank states" meant that both developed an acute existential awareness of their own vulnerability.[44] As a result, both put high value on the trustworthiness of the Americans and their nuclear guarantee along with the ability of NATO to project overwhelming strength. Such a guarantee provided post–World War II Denmark with security from a Soviet invasion and an assurance that Germany would remain harnessed, and gave it the scope to build on its policies of liberalism and humanitarian internationalism.[45] The Danes needed to be sure that their allies would understand and act upon Prime Minister Hans Hedtoft's words that "Denmark wants to be defended, not liberated."[46] Yet, in the early years of the Cold War, NATO's strategy for the defense of its northern flank had been based on the premise that "the loss of these countries [Norway and Denmark] would not make the defence of Western Europe impossible."[47] This scenario allowed for the unthinkable: the capture of Danish territory by Soviet forces. As far as Greece was concerned, there was a strong sense that the country was one of the most vulnerable in the Western world.[48] It put its trust in NATO and the United States to afford it security from the danger from the "North" and also against internal subversion. This fostered an absolute dependence on the United States. The defense of Greece, however, even after its entry into NATO, centered on the alliance's need to defend Crete and the facilities available to the US Sixth Fleet at Souda Bay. Greece's own ability to mount an effective conventional defense was compromised because its security forces were small and had been designed primarily to prevent internal subversion rather than defend the country's northern borders.[49]

Bipolarity did indeed reduce tensions that could arise from the "alliance security dilemma."[50] In both Greece and Denmark, the question of whether borders could be defended preoccupied their governments deeply, but whatever NATO's shortcomings, there was no other credible security alternative. There was no scope for either dealignment or realignment, and any concerns that both countries harbored were mitigated by their perception of the high trustworthiness of the United States. In the late 1940s and throughout the1950s, the hegemonic power proved to be as good as its word. The Marshall Plan, NATO, "sword and shield," and "massive retaliation" addressed their insecurities; both countries came to assess the "not knowing for sure aspect" in their relationship with the United States as being minimal. However, as insurance, both countries tried to keep American attention focused on their security needs.[51]

In the post-Sputnik era, however, with the advent of Soviet intercontinental ballistic missiles and the retirement of the "massive retaliation" strategy, insecurities began to grow. As the 1960s unfolded, the tensions arising from the American handling of the Cuban missile crisis, the challenge to NATO's military structure posed by French president Charles de Gaulle, and US president John F. Kennedy's adoption of "flexible response" increased the

243

European NATO allies' sense of vulnerability. Later, the Vietnam War and superpower détente would highlight tensions within the depths of NATO arising from differing and evolving interpretations over the nature of the alliance, with the Europeans seeing it as based on balance-of-threat considerations and the United States adopting a balance-of-power view.[52] The United States thus found itself having to maintain the trust of its European allies in an increasingly suspicious environment, where those same allies judged its global aspirations for "a free world" to be detrimental to their own security. In this new environment, America's ability to maintain the credibility of extended deterrence would determine the harmony of intra-alliance relations.[53] In fact, American preoccupation with the Vietnam War convinced its already nonplussed NATO allies that flexible response not only was an inadequate safeguard for Western European security, but also made the flanks feel more vulnerable.[54]

The debate about flexible response within NATO was paralleled by a Soviet thrust to augment its naval power in the Mediterranean and the Arctic. The Soviet naval buildup highlighted what Glenn Snyder has called the two "bads" of the alliance security dilemma: abandonment and entrapment.[55] Fears of both surfaced with a vengeance in the 1960s in both Denmark and Greece. There were suggestions that the possibility for an opportunistic, non-nuclear "limited war" against Thrace or Norway was likelier than war over Berlin.[56] By the time that NATO adopted the Harmel Report in 1967, both flanks had become profoundly concerned about the hegemon's ability to maintain extended deterrence and also about what they perceived to be American inattention.[57] The augmented Soviet presence in the "northern cap"—the Kola Peninsula and the Barents Sea—could now chip away at the delicate balance of Nordic defense,[58] which by this time comprised "a trade-off between considerations of deterrence and reassurance."[59] The rapid decline of the British Royal Navy as a result of Denis Healey's and Roy Mason's Defense Reviews in 1965–68 and 1974–75, respectively, was also a serious blow, since the defense of the northern flank was based on timely naval reinforcement. The Soviets also began to upgrade their naval base at Kola. In the age of Polaris, Kola offered the Soviet Navy the only ice-free exit to the Atlantic that was not blocked by a NATO-controlled choke point such as at the Dardanelles or Gibraltar. Yet despite the importance of the northern flank in NATO's security structure, up until 1969 no reprioritization of strategy had taken place. The United States was taking increased risks, moving toward superpower détente with the Soviet Union and bypassing NATO, which accentuated negative feelings among the European NATO allies. Even the Danes, who had long advocated détente, felt that the type and timing of US détente with the Soviet Union were a problem.[60] During the 1970s, the security situation at the northern flank deteriorated even further as consecutive Danish governments, in their attempts to deal with a weak economy, cut back on defense spending. During the Nixon years, relations between the two countries suffered to such an extent that in the Oval Office, derogatory comments such as "who are the Danes" had become quite acceptable.[61] By the early 1980s, the Kola Peninsula came to be considered "the most valuable piece of real-estate on earth,"[62] and yet the countries of the northern flank continued to regard their region as the "forgotten flank."[63]

In the Mediterranean, meanwhile, decolonization in North Africa and the dearth of robust security arrangements in the Mediterranean South dented the favorable position that Truman and Eisenhower had bequeathed to the region. In time, the perception that the southern flank was the "neglected flank"[64] increased, especially when the Soviet Union attempted to destabilize the region by exploiting the tensions created by the Arab-Israeli conflict.[65] Both the flexible response strategy and superpower détente were particularly troubling for Greece, as NATO's priority for its defense remained focused on Crete.[66] Traditionally, Athens viewed any relaxation in superpower tensions with suspicion. Détente was seen as endangering the security of the country, and such fears within Greek ultra-right wing paramilitary circles played a part in the "colonels' coup" and the establishment of a military dictatorship on April 21, 1967.[67] A policy of superpower rapprochement, therefore, seemed even more dangerous as regional insecurity in the Mediterranean increased, especially after June 1967, when the Soviet Union gained enhanced access to Egyptian facilities after the Six-Day War. By 1971, the Soviets had established a naval base in Tartus, Syria.[68]

Dissenting Voices

With such gloomy conjectures and amid amplified fears of entrapment, the high levels of trust in the United States began to erode on both the northern and southern flanks. Successive Danish governments had held the belief that any decrease of US troops from the Central Front would embolden the Soviet Union to hasten its naval buildup in the North Sea.[69] The war in Vietnam drew American troops away from Europe, and as early as 1964 the Danish government advised the United States to "open unconditional peace negotiations" in Vietnam.[70] The Vietnam War and the coup in Greece raised questions over NATO's shared values and, ultimately, of the American commitment to NATO itself. Both points of criticism came at a time when Denmark was undergoing political and social change; from the mid-1960s, sections of Danish society started to encroach on the stronghold of its foreign policy–making elites.[71] There was popular agitation for a referendum to be held over Danish NATO membership by the decade's end, and Copenhagen experienced unprecedented violent political street protests that further eroded trust in both government and politicians.[72] By 1967, the Danish government began to think that American involvement in Vietnam was weakening "the West" in terms of legitimacy, firepower, and popular appeal, while in Denmark in general the coverage of the war was promoting distrust in politicians, raising fears of entrapment, and undermining the "national wellbeing."[73] The coup in Greece, which led to human rights violations against the junta's political opponents, also proved to be intolerable to a country like Denmark that had based its foreign policy on humanitarianism. NATO's choice to prioritize the stability of its southeastern flank over the violation of the democratic process in Greece[74] put prime ministers from both sides of the Danish political divide on the spot, especially in light of the frequent parliamentary resolutions demanding that the matter of the Greek dictators be taken to NATO.[75] Foreign Minister Poul Hartling warned that tolerating the dictators within the alliance was giving impetus to all those who sought a referendum and a "grand debate" on Denmark's continued membership.[76]

The Greek dictatorship spread distrust in NATO to the European South as well. The logic and practice of superpower détente compelled the superpowers to strive to control events in volatile regions by tolerating and even supporting dictatorships. This logic helped the Greek military regime to remain in place until 1974, when a near-war with its NATO ally Turkey over Cyprus dislodged it.[77] As a result of the dictatorship and the events in Cyprus, anti-Americanism, anti-NATO-ism, and suspicion and emotions of betrayal and distrust grew dramatically in Greece across the entire political spectrum. National reconciliation and democratization were to be effected eventually, though only by fostering a "collective amnesia" where all that had gone wrong for Greece from the end of World War II up to the Turkish invasion of Cyprus was blamed on the foreign factor—the United States and NATO. The first postdictatorship prime minister, Konstantinos Karamanlis, had to reposition Greek defense strategy so as to tackle the threat from Turkey. He sought to cultivate the European Economic Community to help preserve a pro-Western orientation for Greece,[78] and at the same time he tried to promote détente with Greece's communist northern neighbors and even visited the Soviet Union in 1979 to seek out markets and to lessen threats to Greek security.[79] Karamanlis also made sure that even though Greece was still estranged from NATO's military aspect, it remained embedded in NATO structures, and he paved the way for its full return to the alliance just before his New Democracy party was defeated at the polls in 1981 by Andreas Papandreou's PASOK.[80] Karamanlis' revised defense dogma created its own new dynamic. As the new decade began and détente expired, Greece now had a vital stake in détente's continuation, since it could not effectively defend both its northern and Turkish borders at the same time. In these circumstances, the policies of the first Reagan administration and the renewed Cold War were interpreted as imperiling Greek national security. In PASOK's hands, therefore, the "footnoting" of NATO communiqués would become a useful means for keeping Greek public opinion sweet and keeping NATO and the United States on their toes.[81]

America's acceptance of the Conference on Security and Cooperation in Europe (CSCE) process came too late to repair the damage to its public image, even though the CSCE's agenda was close to Danish and Greek desires.[82] The euphoria that followed President Gerald Ford's signing of the Helsinki Act in 1975 was short-lived, since both he and his successor, Jimmy Carter, could not keep détente alive under pressure from the US Congress and the weight of international developments. Carter's vacillation regarding NATO nuclear politics had decreased confidence and increased insecurities and distrust to such a degree that American participation in the Helsinki process could not reverse them.[83] The experience of the CSCE negotiations and the realization that more weapons did not really provide more security led majority opinion in both Denmark and Greece to reject an intensified Cold War—or, as Hans Morgenthau put it, "the primitive spectacle of two giants eyeing each other with watchful suspicion."[84] These views found a voice in both countries through the rejuvenation of popular movements that had once opposed the Vietnam War and the Greek dictatorship. These dissenting voices left their governments with the dilemma of how to bring the views of their electorates to the attention of the United States and NATO without impairing their national security at a time when the Cold War was heating up. It was in this climate of compromised trust that in December 1979, despite strong misgivings from grassroots supporters and their coalition partner, the Danish Social Democrats voted along with their NATO allies in favor of the double-track decision, conferring on it the legitimacy of unanimity.[85] By 1982, the Social Democrats had performed an about-face on this unpopular issue, but they still could not hold on to power.[86]

The new Danish government was forced to continue to communicate various parliamentary resolutions by inserting dissenting footnotes into NAC,[87] Defense Planning Committee[88] and Nuclear Planning Group communiqués[89] on matters such as intermediate-range nuclear forces (INF) and defense and space systems (such as the US Strategic Defense Initiative). These shackles would be removed only in late 1987 after the signing of the INF treaty in December of that year.[90] Greece's distrust was much deeper than Denmark's, and in the Greek case the footnoting was not undertaken by an unwilling government. The difference between the two cases is also reflected in the fact that Greece proved to be a more assiduous footnoter than Denmark.[91]

Footnotes therefore provided a low-key means of protest for both countries, which enabled them to dissent while still having the security of knowing that NATO would tolerate this behavior in the interest of alliance cohesion. As Danish defense minister Bernt Johan Collet said in 1988, "The footnotes were all needle pricks."[92] However, footnoting did have important consequences. By manifesting traits of distrust, footnoting undermined the effective working of NATO, so that NAC meetings often became fora for dissent rather than cooperation among allies. Footnoting also contributed to the instability of the northern and southern flanks and became a tool for expressing anti-Americanism.

Conclusion

With the advent of the Soviet threat after World War II, the Danes and the Greeks had placed their trust—both emotionally and rationally—in the United States. They suspended any niggling suspicions that they may have harbored over possible abandonment and entrapment, and did so for as long as the United States was able to maintain the credibility of its strategy of extended deterrence and its focus on Western Europe. In the 1960s and 1970s, a series of American decisions connected to its global aspirations challenged the Danish and Greek agendas, as well as their security preconceptions and their domestic well-being. The American decisions also tampered with Denmark's deeply held humanitarian principles and Greece's aspirations and dreams of stability and security. By the end of the decade, both countries had come to consider that American actions over Vietnam, the Greek dictatorship, and superpower détente had impaired US credibility and reliability, and not even America's participation in the CSCE process could rectify this damage. During the Carter years, Denmark and Greece also grew to doubt the predictability of US actions. However, even though NATO seemed to be in a permanent state of crisis during the bipolar conflict, it remained an essentially stable alliance. Furthermore, bipolarity acted as a centripetal force to keep the United States and its European allies together.[93] Neither Denmark nor Greece lost sight of the fact that the United States was the only protector they could rely on to defend their territory—whatever their own behavior—since it was in American interests to do so. Although they eventually saw that Soviet actions did contain a defensive element, they never entertained ideas of investing their trust in the Soviet Union. It was within this framework of a stable alliance on the one hand and compromised trust on the other that the policies of the

Reagan administration encountered the habitual "footnoting" of the 1980s. Distrust as expressed in footnotes was about assertion, rather than defection. It was a policy of dissent that had its roots in social change, popular insecurities, and disillusionment with the United States and NATO that had been growing in both countries throughout the 1960s and 1970s.[94]

Epilogue

Subsequent reactions to this period have been starkly different in Denmark and Greece. The current NATO secretary-general Anders Fogh Rasmussen, a Danish Liberal politician and former prime minister whose early political career was forged in this peculiar environment, has characterized the period of footnoting as "despicable" and on a par "with the period of collaboration with the Nazi occupiers of World War II."[95] Between the 1990s and mid-2000s, four reports were commissioned by Danish governments to determine how the Danish political system had produced and tolerated such behavior or, in the words of the doyen of Danish international relations, Nikolaj Petersen, to get to the "right truth."[96] No such report has been commissioned by any Greek government, and so far no mainstream Greek politician has expressed similar critical condemnation of Greece's contribution to the "footnote era."

Notes

1. "Special Meeting of Foreign and Defense Ministers, Brussels," December 12, 1979, Ministerial Communiqués, NATO Online Library, http://www.nato.int/docu /comm/49-95/c791212a.htm; and "Final Communiqué," December 6–7, 1983, Defense Planning Committee, NATO Online Library, http://www.nato.int/docu/comm/49-95 /c831207a.htm.

2. "Special Meeting of Foreign and Defense Ministers (The 'Double-Track' Decision in Theatre Nuclear Forces)," December 12, 1979, NATO Online Library, http://www.nato.int/cps/en/natolive/official_texts_27040.htm; Strobe Talbott, "The Road to Zero," *Time*, December 14, 1987, http://www.time.com/time/magazine /article/0,9171,966263,00.html; William Burr, "A Question of Confidence: Theater Nuclear Forces, US Policy toward Germany, and the Origins of the Euromissile Crisis, 1975–1976," in *The Euromissile Crisis and the End of the Cold War*, ed. Leopoldo Nuti, Frédéric Bozo, Marie-Pierre Rey, and Bernd Rother (Washington, DC: Woodrow Wilson Center Press; Stanford, CA: Stanford University Press, 2015), 123–39; Kristina Spohr, "Conflict and Cooperation in Intra-Alliance Nuclear Politics: Western Europe, the United States, and the Genesis of NATO's Dual-Track Decision, 1977–1979," *Journal of Cold War Studies* 13, no. 2 (2011): 39–89; Jeffrey Herf, *War by Other Means: Soviet Power, West German Resistance and the Battle of the Euromissiles* (New York: Free Press, 1991), 113–44; Joachim Scholtyseck, "The United States, Europe, and the Dual Track Decision," in *The Strained Alliance: U.S.-European*

Relations from Nixon to Carter, ed. Mathias Schulz and Thomas A. Schwartz (New York: Cambridge University Press, 2010), 101–23; and Hans-Henrik Holm and Niko-laj Petersen, eds., *The European Missiles Crisis: Nuclear Weapons and Security Policy* (London: Pinter, 1983).

3. Richard C. Eichenberg, "Dual Track and Double Trouble: The Two Levels of Politics of INF," in *Double-edged Diplomacy: International Bargaining and Domestic Politics*, ed. Peter B. Evans, Harold K. Jacobson, and Robert D. Putnam (Berkeley: University of California Press, 1993), 45–76; Leopoldo Nuti, ed., *Reheating the Cold War: From Vietnam to Gorbachev, 1975–1985* (London: Routledge, 2008); Lawrence Wittner, *Toward Nuclear Abolition: A History of the World Nuclear Disarmament Movement, 1971 to the Present*, Vol. 3, *The Struggle Against the Bomb* (Stanford, CA: Stanford University Press, 2003); Diana Johnstone, *The Politics of Euromissiles: Europe's Role in America's World* (London: Verso, 1984); Maria Eleonora Guasconi, "Public Opinion and the Euromissile Crisis," in Nuti, Bozo, Rey, and Rother, *The Euro-missile Crisis and the End of the Cold War*, 271–90; and Simon Lunn, "INF and Politi-cal Cohesion in NATO," in Holm and Petersen, *The European Missiles Crisis*, 215.

4. Bernd Lemke, ed., *Periphery or Contact Zone? The NATO Flanks, 1961 to 2013* (Freiburg: Rombach Verlag, 2015), 17–42, 69–134.

5. Christine Ingebritsen, *The Nordic States and European Unity* (Ithaca, NY: Cor-nell University Press, 2000); Christine Ingebritsen, *Scandinavia in World Politics* (Lan-ham, MD: Rowman & Littlefield, 2006); and Franz Wendt, *Cooperation in the Nordic Countries: Achievements and Obstacles* (Stockholm: Almqvist & Wiksell, 1981).

6. John O. Iatrides, "Failed Rampart: NATO's Balkan Front," in *NATO and the Warsaw Pact: Intrabloc Conflicts*, ed. Mary Ann Heiss and S. Victor Papacosma (Kent, OH: Kent State University Press, 2008), 58–74; Eirini Karamouzi, "Managing the 'Helsinki Spirit' in the Balkans: Greece's Initiative for Balkan Cooperation, 1975–1976," *Diplomacy & Statecraft* 24, no. 4 (2013): 587–618; and Lykourgos Kourkouve-las, "Détente as a Strategy: Greece and the Communist World, 1974–9," *International History Review* 35, no. 3 (2013): 58–74.

7. See the 1959 telegrams discussing the initial stationing of US missiles on Greek soil in *Foreign Relations of the United States (FRUS), 1958–1960*, Vol. X, Part 2: *Eastern Europe; Finland; Greece; Turkey* (Washington, DC: US Government Printing Office, 1993), docs. 261–62 and 265–66.

8. Fredrik Doeser, "Domestic Politics and Foreign Policy Change in Small States: The Fall of the Danish Footnote Policy," *Cooperation and Conflict* 46, no. 2 (2011): 222–41; Nikolaj Petersen, "Footnoting as a Political Instrument: Denmark's NATO Policy in the 1980s," *Cold War History* 12, no. 2, (2012): 295–317; and Danish Insti-tute for International Studies, *Danmark under den kolde krig: Den sikkerhedspolitiske situation 1945–1991* [Denmark during the Cold War: The security situation 1945–1991] (Copenhagen: Danish Institute for International Studies, 2005), http://www .diis.dk/publikationer/danmark-kolde-krig.

9. S. Victor Papacosma, "Greece and NATO: A Nettlesome Relationship," in *A History of NATO: The First Fifty Years*, ed. Gustav Schmidt (New York: Palgrave, 2001), 3:359–374; John Iatrides, "Beneath the Sound and the Fury: U.S. Relations with the PASOK Government," in *Greece, 1981–1989: The Populist Decade*, ed. Richard Clogg (New York: St. Martin's, 1993), 153–66; and Theodore Couloumbis, "PASOK's Foreign Policies 1981–89: Continuity or Change?," in Clogg, *Greece, 1981–1989*, 113–30.

10. John P. D. Dunbabin, *The Cold War: The Great Powers and Their Allies* (London, Routledge, 1994), 69; and Effie G. H. Pedaliu, "Transatlantic Relations at a Time When 'More Flags' Meant 'No European Flags': The United States' War in South-East Asia and Its European Allies, 1964–68," *International History Review* 35, no. 3 (2013): 556–75.

11. Knud J. V. Jespersen, *A History of Denmark* (London: Palgrave Macmillan, 2011), 31; Hans-Henrik Holm, "A Democratic Revolt? Stability and Change in Danish Security Policy, 1979–1989," *Cooperation and Conflict* 24, no. 3 (1989): 179–97; and Richard A. Bitzinder, *Denmark, Norway and NATO: Constraints and Challenges*, RAND Note N-3001-RC (Santa Monica, CA: RAND Corporation, November 1989), 10, http://www.rand.org/content/dam/rand/pubs/notes/2009/N3001.pdf.

12. David T. Jones, interview by Charles Stuart Kennedy, March 16, 1999, The Association for Diplomatic Studies and Training, Foreign Affairs, Oral History Project (Washington, DC: Library of Congress), 75–76 and 79–80, http://www.adst.org/OH%20TOCs/Jones,%20David%20T.toc.pdf; and Nathan Gardels, "Europe Turns Left [interview with Andreas Papandreou]," *New Perspectives Quarterly* 11, no. 1 (1994): 50–53.

13. "Green IT: Denmark: Key Developer of Climate Solutions," *Mandag Morgen* Special Edition (Copenhagen: Ministry of Foreign Affairs of Denmark, November 2008); and Raymond L. Garthoff, *Détente and Confrontation: American-Soviet Relations from Nixon to Reagan* (Washington, DC: Brookings Institution Press, 1985), 524, 701, 708, 713–14.

14. Carsten Holbraad, *Danish Neutrality: A Study in the Foreign Policy of a Small State* (New York: Oxford University Press, 1991), 155; J. D. Hagan, *Political Opposition and Foreign Policy in Comparative Perspective* (Boulder, CO: Lynne Rienner, 1993); and Jeffrey W. Knopf, "Domestic Sources of Preferences for Arms Cooperation: The Impact of Protest," *Journal of Peace Research* 35, no. 6 (1998): 677–95.

15. Poul Villaume, "Denmark and NATO through 50 Years," in *Danish Foreign Policy Yearbook 1999*, ed. Bertel Heurlin and Hans Mouritzen (Copenhagen: Danish Institute for International Studies, 2000): 29–61; Karoliina Honkanen, *The Influence of Small States on NATO Decision Making: The Membership Experiences of Denmark, Norway, Hungary and the Czech Republic* (Stockholm: Swedish Defence Research Agency, 2002), 35, and 53–4; and Ingemar Dörfer, "Scandinavia and NATO: á la carte," *Washington Quarterly* 9 (Winter 1986): 15–30.

16. Doeser, "Domestic Politics," 222–41; and Petersen, "Footnoting," 295–317.

17. Danish Institute for International Studies, *Danmark under den kolde krig*, Vol. 3, *1979–1991*, 191, http://pure.diis.dk/ws/files/27986/KKBind3.pdf.

18. Doeser, "Domestic politics," 222–41.

19. "The Ally Who's Come in from the Cold," *Copenhagen Post*, February 21, 2012, http://cphpost.dk/news/international/ally-who%E2%80%99s-come-cold.

20. "NATO Affirms '83 Missile Deployment," *New York Times*, June 3, 1983.

21. Uffe Ellemann-Jensen, *Fodfejl: da Danmark svigtede under den Kolde Krig* [Stepping in it: When Denmark failed during the Cold War] (Copenhagen: Gyldendal, 2004), 133.

22. Konstantina E. Botsiou, "The Interface between Politics and Culture in Greece," in *The Americanization of Europe: Culture, Diplomacy, and Anti-Americanism after 1945*, ed. Alexander Stephan (New York: Berghahn Books, 2007), 279–306; Konstantina E. Botsiou, "Anti-Americanism in Greece," in *Anti-Americanism: History, Causes, and Themes*, Vol. 3, *Comparative Perspectives*, ed. Brendon O'Connor

(Oxford: Greenwood World Publishing, 2007), 213–34; Ioannis D. Stefanidis, *Stirring the Greek Nation: Political Culture, Irredentism and Anti-Americanism in Post-War Greece, 1945–1967* (Aldershot, UK: Ashgate, 2007), 104; and Richard Clogg, *Parties and Elections in Greece* (London: Hurst, 1987).

23. Stan Draenos, *Andreas Papandreou: The Making of a Greek Democrat and Political Maverick* (London: I. B. Tauris, 2012).

24. Andreas Papandreou, *He Hellada stous Hellenes* [Greece belongs to the Greeks] (Athens: Karanassis, 1976).

25. Nicholas Gage, "Opposition Leader in Athens of Two Minds about U.S.," *New York Times*, May 23, 1978.

26. See the Carter administration memoranda, telegrams, and other papers on this agreement in *FRUS, 1977–1980*, Vol. XXI, *Cyprus; Turkey; Greece* (Washington, DC: US Government Printing Office, 2004), docs. 171, 176, 177, 184, 186, 189, 191, 192, 198, 199, and 206.

27. See the Carter administration memoranda, telegrams, and other papers on this proposal in *FRUS, 1977–1980*, Vol. XXI, docs. 157, 196, 198, 200, 201, 202, 208, and 211.

28. Dionysios Chourchoulis and Lykourgos Kourkouvelas, "Greek Perceptions of NATO during the Cold War," *Southeast European and Black Sea Studies* 12, no. 4 (2012), 508–10; and Couloumbis, "PASOK's Foreign Policies," 113–30.

29. Akis Kalaitzidis and Nikolaos Zahariadis, "Papandreou's NATO Policy: Continuity or Change?," *Journal of Hellenic Diaspora* 23, no. 1 (1997), 106; Richard Hass, "Managing NATO's Weakest Flank: The United States, Greece, and Turkey," *Orbis* 30 (1986): 457–73; John Iatrides, "Beneath the Sound and the Fury: U.S. Relations with the PASOK Government," in Clogg, *Greece 1981–1989*, 153–66; James Petras, "The Contradictions of Greek Socialism," *New Left Review* 163 (1987): 3–25; and Robert Pranger, "U.S.-Greek Relations Under PASOK," in *Greece Under Socialism: A NATO Ally Adrift*, ed. Nikolaos Stavrou (New Rochelle, NY: Orpheous, 1988), 251–79.

30. Richard Clogg, "Obituary: Andreas Papandreou," *Independent* (London), June 23, 1996; and Fotini Bellou, "The Political Scene: Consolidating Democracy," in *Greece in the Twentieth Century*, ed. Theodore A. Couloumbis, Theodore Kariotis, and Fotini Bellou (London: Frank Cass Publishers, 2003), 155–169.

31. Papacosma, "Greece and NATO," in Schmidt, *A History of NATO*, 3:364; and Van Coufoudakis, "PASOK and Greek-Turkish Relations," in Clogg, *Greece 1981–1989*, 167–80.

32. Annette B. Fox, *The Power of Small States: Diplomacy in World War II* (Chicago: University of Chicago Press, 1959); Arnold Wolfers, *Discord and Collaboration: Essays on International Politics* (Baltimore: Johns Hopkins University Press, 1962); James N. Rosenau, "Pre-theories and Theories of International Politics," in *Approaches to Comparative and International Politics*, ed. R. B. Farrell (Evanston, IL: Northwestern University Press, 1966); Kenneth N. Waltz, *Theory of International Politics* (Reading, MA: Addison-Wesley, 1979); Stephen Walt, *The Origins of Alliances* (Ithaca, NY: Cornell University Press, 1987); and John Mearsheimer, *The Tragedy of Great Power Politics* (New York: Norton, 2001).

33. Deborah Welch Larson, *Anatomy of Mistrust: U.S.-Soviet Relations During the Cold War* (Ithaca, NY: Cornell University Press, 1997), 6, 19.

34. Jan Ruzicka and Nicholas J. Wheeler, "The Puzzle of Trusting Relationships in the Nuclear Non-Proliferation Treaty," *International Affairs* 86, no. 1 (2010), 72, and

69–85; and Jan Ruzicka and Nicholas J. Wheeler, "Decisions to Trust: Maintaining the Nuclear Non-Proliferation Regime," *RUSI Journal* 155, no. 2 (2010): 20–25.

35. Aaron Hoffman, "A Conceptualisation of Trust in International Relations," *European Journal of International Relations* 8, no. 3 (2002), 376, and 375–401.

36. Piotr Sztompka, "Trust, Distrust and the Two Paradoxes of Democracy," *European Journal of Social Theory* 1, no. 1 (1998): 19–32.

37. Thucydides, *History of the Peloponnesian War*, trans. Rex Warner (London: Penguin Books, 1972), 402.

38. "NATO Treaty: April 4, 1949," The Avalon Project, Yale Law School, http://www.yale.edu/lawweb/avalon/nato.htm; and "Details of Treaty No. 001: Statue of the Council of Europe," May 5, 1949, Council of Europe Treaty Office, http://conventions.coe.int/treaty/en/Treaties/Html/001.htm.

39. CM (48)72, memorandum by Bevin, March 3, 1948, CAB 129/25, The National Archives, UK (hereafter, TNA); Paper, no. CE(PREP)P3, March 28, 1949, FO 371/7 9944/ZW25/1072/170, TNA; Recommendations of the European Movement to the Conference of Ambassadors for the Establishment of a Council of Europe, April 6, 1949, FO 371/79944/ZW 112/1072/170, TNA; despatch, no. 248, Victor Mallet, British Ambassador, Rome to Attlee, July 29, 1949, FO 371/79965/ZW1356/1072/170, TNA; A. W. Brian Simpson, *Human Rights and the End of Empire: Britain and the Genesis of the European Convention* (Oxford: Oxford University Press, 2001), 337, 347–8, 429, 543–5, 623–6, and 630–6; and Effie G. H. Pedaliu, *Britain, Italy and the Origins of the Cold War* (London: Palgrave Macmillan, 2003), 151–54.

40. Andrew H. Kydd, *Trust and Mistrust in International Relations* (Princeton, NJ: Princeton University Press, 2005), 5.

41. Brief, 3, NATO Ministerial Discussions, April 9, 1965, FO 371/184376, TNA; John Ikenberry, *After Victory: Institutions, Strategic Restraint, and the Rebuilding of Order after Major Wars* (Princeton, NJ: Princeton University Press, 2001); Andreas Wenger, Christian Nuenlist, and Anna Locher, eds., *Transforming NATO in the Cold War: Challenges beyond Deterrence in the 1960s* (London: Routledge, 2006); Lawrence S. Kaplan, *NATO Divided, NATO United: The Evolution of an Alliance* (Westport, CT: Praeger, 2004); and Andreas Wenger, "Crisis and Opportunity: NATO's Transformation and the Multilateralization of Détente, 1966–1968," *Journal of Cold War Studies* 6, no. 1 (2004): 22–74.

42. "Remarks on Presenting the Presidential Medal of Freedom to Lord Peter Carrington," May 10, 1988, Ronald Reagan Presidential Library and Museum, University of Texas at Austin, http://www.reagan.utexas.edu/archives/speeches/1988/051088a.htm.

43. Annette Baier, *Moral Prejudices: Essays on Ethics* (Cambridge, MA: Harvard University Press, 1994), 98–99; and Annette Baier, "Trust and Antitrust," *Ethics* 96, no. 2 (1986): 231–60.

44. John J. Mearsheimer, "Maneuver, Mobile Defense, and the NATO Central Front," *International Security* 6, no 3 (1982): 104–22; Rolf Tamnes and Kristine Offerdal, eds., *Geopolitics and Security in the Arctic: Regional Dynamics in a Global World* (London: Routledge, 2014); and Nikolaj Petersen, "The Dilemmas of Alliance: Denmark's First Fifty Years," in Schmidt, *A History of NATO*, 3:275–94.

45. Rolf Tamnes, *The United States and the Cold War in the High North* (Aldershot, UK: Dartmouth Publications, 1991), 87, 145, and 155; and Helle Malmvig, "Denmark: Between Clumsy Hans and Thumbelina?," in *Northern Europe and the Making of the*

EU's Mediterranean and Middle East Policies, ed. Timo Behr and Teija Tiilikainen (Farnham, UK: Ashgate, 2015), 110–13.

46. Gunnar Skogmar, "The Attitudes of Denmark and Norway towards Western German Rearmament and the EDC (1950–1954)," in *La Communauté Européenne de Défense, leçons pour demain? | The European Defence Community: Lessons for the Future?*, ed. Michel Dumoulin (Brussels: Peter Lang, 2000), 237.

47. "North Atlantic Defense Committee Decision on D.C. 13: A Report by the Military Committee on North Atlantic Treaty Organization Medium Term Plan," April 1, 1950, in *NATO Strategy Documents 1949–1969*, ed. Gregory W. Pedlow, NATO Archives, May 1999, http://www.nato.int/docu/stratdoc/eng/a500328d.pdf; and Olav Riste, "NATO, the Northern Flank, and the Neutrals," in Schmidt, *A History of NATO*, 3:241–43.

48. Evanthis Hatzivassiliou, *Greece and the Cold War: Front Line State, 1952–1967* (London: Routledge, 2006); Evanthis Hatzivassiliou, "Propaganda, Internal Security and Alliance Politics: Greek Proposals to NATO in the 1950s," *Intelligence and National Security* 30, no. 1 (2015): 137–58; and James E. Miller, *The United States and the Making of Modern Greece* (Chapel Hill: University of North Carolina Press, 2009).

49. Dionysios Chourchoulis, *The Southern Flank of NATO, 1951–1959: Military Strategy or Political Stabilization* (Lanham, MD: Lexington Books, 2014), xvi–xxi.

50. Glenn H. Snyder, "The Security Dilemma in Alliance Politics," *World Politics* 36, no. 4 (1984): 461–96.

51. Nikolaj Petersen, *Denmark and NATO, 1949–1987* (Oslo, Forsvarshistorisk Forskningssenter, 1987), 26–30; and Hatzivassiliou, *Greece and the Cold War*.

52. Waltz, *Theory of International Politics*, 38, and 151–58; and Walt, *The Origins of Alliances*, 5, 9, 22–23, 171–72, and 263–65.

53. Memo, "Plan for political/psychological activities in connection with the NATO crisis," 5 May 1966, box 1, E5157, RG 59, NARA.

54. Speech by Dean Rusk and NAC, May 14, 1964, Box 18, E5376, RG 59, US National Archives and Records Administration, College Park, Maryland (hereafter, NARA); "Anti-Americanism," February 8, 1969, Box 2361, E1613, RG 59, NARA; *FRUS, 1964–1968*, Vol. I, *Vietnam, 1964* (Washington, DC: US Government Printing Office, 1992), docs. 41, 283, and 442; Thomas Alan Schwartz, *Lyndon Johnson and Europe: In the Shadow of Vietnam* (Cambridge, MA: Harvard University Press, 2003), 87; Lawrence S. Kaplan, "The Vietnam War and Europe," in *La guerre du Vietnam et l'Europe, 1963–1973* [The Vietnam War and Europe, 1963–73], ed. Christopher E. Goscha and Maurice Vaisse (Brussels: Bruylant, 2003), 90–102; and Tamnes, *The United States and the Cold War in the High North*, 185–86.

55. Snyder, "The Security Dilemma in Alliance Politics," 466.

56. Department of Defense, Vol. 3, May 31, 1965, National Security Files, Lyndon Baines Johnson Library, University of Texas at Austin.

57. *Documents on British Policy Overseas*, series 3, vol. 5, *The Southern Flank in Crisis, 1973–1976* (London: Routledge, 2006), Appendix II, doc. 44; Memo, "Plan for political/psychological activities in connection with the NATO crisis," May 5, 1966, box 1, E5157, RG 59, NARA; and Ute Frevert, "Does Trust Have a History?" (Max Weber Lecture Series 2009-01, European University Institute, Florence, 2009), 3, http://cadmus.eui.eu/bitstream/handle/1814/11258/MWP_LS_2009_01.pdf.

58. Brief, 1, Prime Minister's visit to Copenhagen, June 9, 1972, PREM 15/795, TNA; Anders C. Sjaastad, "Security Problems on the Northern Flank," *The World*

Today 35, no. 4 (1979): 137–49; Tom Kristiansen, ed., *Navies in Northern Waters* (London: Routledge, 2004); Johan Jørgen Holst, "Norwegian Security Policy for the 1980s," *Cooperation and Conflict* 17, no. 3 (1982): 207–36; Pavel Podvig, "The Window of Vulnerability That Wasn't: Soviet Military Buildup in the 1970s: A Research Note," *International Security* 33, no. 1 (2008): 118–38; and Marian Kirsch Leighton, *The Soviet Threat to NATO's Northern Flank* (New York: National Strategy Information Centre, 1979), 80.

59. Johan Jørgen Holst, "The Pattern of Nordic Security," *Daedalus* 113, no. 2 (1984): 195–225.

60. Mitchell Lerner, "'Trying to Find the Guy Who Invited Them': Lyndon Johnson, Bridge Building, and the End of the Prague Spring," *Diplomatic History* 32, no. 1(2008): 77–103; James V. R. Ellison, *The United States, Britain and the Transatlantic Crisis: Rising to the Gaullist Challenge, 1963–68* (London: Palgrave Macmillan, 2007), 97; Schwartz, *Lyndon Johnson and Europe*, 226; Birnbaum, "The Nordic Countries and European Security," *Cooperation and Conflict* 3, no. 1 (1968), 10; and Jonathan Søborg Agger, "Striving for Détente: Denmark and NATO, 1966–67," in Wenger, Nuenlist, and Locher, *Transforming NATO in the Cold War*, 183–97.

61. Oval Office, 25/3/1971, no. 473–10, White House Tapes, Nixon Presidential Materials Staff, NARA. For an edited version of this document, see Editorial Note, *FRUS, 1969–1976*, Vol. XXIX, *Eastern Europe; Eastern Mediterranean, 1969–1972* (Washington, DC: US Government Printing Office, 2008), doc. 309.

62. Peter de Leon, "Emerging Security Considerations for NATO's Northern Flank," *RUSI* 130, no. 2 (1985), 34 and 36.

63. National Security Council Report, April 6, 1960, in *FRUS, 1958–1960*, Vol. VII, Part 2, *Western Europe* (Washington, DC: US Government Printing Office, 1993), doc. 300; and Jonathan Søborg Agger and Trine Engeholm Mishelsen, "How Strong Was the 'Weakest Link'?: Danish Security Policy Reconsidered," in *War Plans and Alliances in the Cold War: Threat Perceptions in the East and West*, ed. Vojtech Mastny, Sven S. Holtsmark, and Andreas Wenger (London: Routledge, 2006), 240–65.

64. Elena Calandri, "The 'Neglected Flank'?: NATO in the Mediterranean, 1945–56," in *Securing Peace in Europe, 1945–62: Thoughts for the Post-Cold War Era*, ed. Beatrice Heuser and Robert John O'Neill (London: Macmillan, 1991), 173–95; Edward A. Kolodziej, "The Southern Flank: Nato's Neglected Front," *American Enterprise Institute Foreign Policy and Defense Review* 6, no. 2 (1986): 45–57; Ray S. Cline, James A, Miller and Roger E. Kanet, eds., *Western Europe in Soviet Global Strategy* (Boulder, CO: Westview, 1987); and John Chipman, *NATO's Southern Allies: Internal and External Challenges* (London: Routledge,1988), 3.

65. National Intelligence Estimate, March 5, 1970, in *FRUS, 1969–1976*, Vol. XII, *Soviet Union, January 1969–October 1970* (Washington, DC: US Government Printing Office, 2006), doc. 138.

66. Off-the-Record Remarks by President Nixon, September 16, 1970, in *FRUS, 1969–1976*, Vol. I, *Foundations of Foreign Policy, 1969–1972* (Washington, DC: US Government Printing Office, 2003), doc. 71; National Intelligence Estimate, March 5, 1970, *FRUS, 1969–1976*, Vol. XII, doc. 138; Effie G. H. Pedaliu, "Truman, Eisenhower and the Mediterranean Cold War, 1947–57," *The Maghreb Review* 31, no. 1/2 (2006): 15–18; Salim Yaqub, *Containing Arab Nationalism: The Eisenhower Doctrine and the Middle East* (Chapel Hill: University of North Carolina Press, 2004); Ray Takeyh, *The Origins of the Eisenhower Doctrine: The United States, Britain and*

Nasser's Egypt, 1953–57 (New York: St Martin's Press, 2000); Effie G. H. Pedaliu, "'A Sea of Confusion': The Mediterranean and Détente, 1969–1974," *Diplomatic History* 33, no. 4 (2009), 741; and David Winkler, *Cold War at Sea: High-Seas Confrontation between the United States and the Soviet Union* (Annapolis, MD: Naval Institute Press, 2000).

67. Effie G. H. Pedaliu, "Human Rights and Foreign Policy: Wilson and the Greek Dictators, 1967–1970," *Diplomacy and Statecraft* 18, no. 1 (2007): 185–214; and Effie G. H. Pedaliu, "'A Discordant Note': NATO and the Greek Junta, 1967–74," *Diplomacy and Statecraft* 22, no. 1 (2011): 101–20.

68. Deputy Director of Central Intelligence, *Soviet Policies in the Middle East and Mediterranean Area*, March 5, 1970, Central Intelligence Agency, Doc. SE 00445, Digital National Security Archive (ProQuest), http://search.proquest.com/docview/16 79138836?accountid=29118; and Pedaliu, "Sea of Confusion," 740–41.

69. Brief, 1, for Prime Minister's visit to Copenhagen, June 9, 1972, PREM 15/795, TNA; Tamnes, *The United States and the Cold War in the High North*, 185–6; Sjaastad, "Security Problems," 137–49; Tom Kristiansen, ed., *Navies in Northern Waters, 1721–2000* (London: Routledge, 2004); Holst, "Norwegian Security Policy for the 1980s"; and Podvig, "The Window of Vulnerability That Wasn't."

70. C-VR(65)51, NAC meeting, December 14, 1965, NATO Archives.

71. Ole Borre and Jørgen Goul Andersen, *Voting and Political Attitudes in Denmark: A Study of the 1994 Election* (Aarhus: Aarhus University Press, 1997), 11–19; and Erik Allardt et al., eds., *Nordic Democracy: Ideas, Issues, and Institutions in the Politics, Economy, Education, Social and Cultural Affairs of Denmark, Finland, Iceland, Norway, and Sweden* (Copenhagen: Det Danske Selskab, 1981), 73–75.

72. Brief, 3, Prime Minister's visit to Copenhagen, May 30, 1972, PREM 15/795, TNA; telegram, Rome to FO, April 3, 1965, PREM 13/416, TNA; Petersen, *Denmark and NATO*, 5–30; James Godbolt, Chris H. Larson, and Søren H. Rasmussen, "The Vietnam War: The Danish and Norwegian Experience, 1964–75," *Scandinavian Journal of History* 33, no. 4 (2008): 397; Ole Borre, "Critical Issues and Political Alienation in Denmark," *Scandinavian Political Studies* 23, no. 4 (2000): 285–309; Ole Borre, "The Danish Protest Election of December 1973," *Scandinavian Political Studies* 9 (1974): 197–204; and Fredrik Logevall, "The American Effort to Draw European States into the War," in Goscha and Vaisse, *La guerre du Vietnam et l'Europe, 1963–1973*, 3–16.

73. Francis Fukuyama, *Trust: The Social Virtues and the Creation of Prosperity* (New York: The Free Press, 1995), 5; Leopoldo Nuti, "Italy and the Battle of the Euromissiles: The Deployment of the US BGM-109 G 'Gryphon,' 1979–83," in *The Last Decade of the Cold War: From Conflict Escalation to Conflict Transformation*, ed. Olav Njolstad (London: Frank Cass, 2004), 332–59; and Leopoldo Nuti, ed., *The Crisis of Détente in Europe: From Helsinki to Gorbachev, 1975–1991* (London: Routledge, 2009).

74. Record of conversation between Brown and Pierre Harmel, Belgian Foreign Minister, January 29, 1968, PREM 13/2140,TNA; Telegram no. 1356, Washington to FO, April 25, 1967, FCO 9/124, TNA; Telegram no. 153, UK Delegation, NATO to FO, April 25, 1967, FCO 9/124, TNA; Telegram no. 350, Athens to FO, April 25, 1967, FCO 9/124, TNA; Telegram no. 703, Frank K. Roberts (Bonn) to FO, May 2, 1967, FCO 9/125, TNA; Telegram no. 196, UK Delegation, NATO to FO, May 11, 1967, FCO 9/126, TNA; Telegram no. 200, FO to Rome, January 13, 1968, FCO

9/148, TNA; Telegram no. 12, January 12, 1968, FCO 9/148, TNA; Letter, B. Burrows (NATO) to Peter Garson, The Hague, January 25, 1968, FCO 9/148, TNA; Letter, British Embassy (Oslo) to FCO, February 2, 1970, FCO 9/148, TNA; Telegram no. 60, UKDEL NATO to FCO, February 3, 1970, FCO 41/652, TNA; Amnesty International, *Torture in Greece: The First Torturers Trial, 1975* (London: Amnesty International Publications, 1977), 6–7; Konstantina Maragkou, "Favouritism in NATO's South-Eastern Flank: The Case of the Greek Colonels, 1967–74," *Cold War History* 9, no. 3 (2009): 347–66; James E. Miller, *The United States and the Making of Modern Greece: History and Power, 1950–1974* (Chapel Hill: University of North Carolina Press, 2009), 111–201; and Pedaliu, "A Discordant Note," 101–20.

75. Nikolaj Petersen, "Danish Security Policy in the Seventies: Continuity or Change?," *Cooperation and Conflict* 7, no. 1 (1972): 7–38.

76. Telegram no. 302, FCO to UKDEL, NATO, August 27, 1970, FCO 41/654, TNA; and Telegram no. 330, British Embassy (Copenhagen) to FCO, September 4, 1970, ibid.

77. Record of FO meeting, May 3, 1967, FO 800/968, TNA; FO brief, Wilson's visit to Washington, January 3, 1970, FCO 9/1215, TNA; memorandum: Policy towards Greece, FCO9/885, TNA; record of a FCO meeting, December 17, 1969, FCO8/871, TNA; Maragkou, "Favouritism," 347–66; Miller, *The United States*, 157–75; and Pedaliu, "A Discordant Note," 101–20.

78. Eirini Karamouzi, *Greece, the EEC and the Cold War 1974–1979: The Second Enlargement* (London: Palgrave Macmillan, 2014).

79. Karamouzi, "Managing the 'Helsinki Spirit,'" 587–618; and Kourkouvelas, "Détente as a Strategy," 58–74.

80. John O. Iatrides, "Challenging the Limitations of the Atlantic Community: Konstantinos Karamanlis and NATO," in *Konstantinos Karamanlis in the 20th Century*, ed. Konstantinos Svolopoulos, Konstantina Botsiou, and Evanthis Hatzivassiliou (Athens: Karamanlis Foundation, 2008), 17–36.

81. Papacosma, "Greece and NATO," in Schmidt, *A History of NATO*, 3:364; and Coufoudakis, "PASOK and Greek-Turkish Relations," in Clogg, *Greece 1981–1989*, 167–80.

82. Letter, Nixon to Heath, May 8, 1972, PREM 15/1281, TNA; Angela Romano, *From Détente in Europe to European Détente: How the West Shaped the Helsinki CSCE* (Brussels/Bern: PIE/Peter Lang, 2009); and Matthias Schulz and Thomas Schwartz, eds., *The Strained Alliance: U.S.-European Relations from Nixon to Carter* (Cambridge, UK: Cambridge University Press, 2009).

83. Sherri Wasserman, *The Neutron Bomb Controversy: A Study in Alliance Politics* (New York: Praeger Publishers, 1983); Jussi Hanhimäki, *The Rise and Fall of Détente: American Foreign Policy and the Transformation of the Cold War* (Washington, DC: Potomac Books, 2013); and Kristina Spohr, "NATO's Nuclear Politics and the Schmidt-Carter Rift," in Nuti, Bozo, Rey, and Rother, *The Euromissile Crisis and the End of the Cold War*, 139–57.

84. Hans J. Morgenthau, *Politics among Nations: The Struggle for Power and Peace.*, 7th ed. (New York: McGraw-Hill Higher Education, 1978).

85. Holm, "A Democratic Revolt?," 184.

86. Nikolaj Petersen, "The Scandilux Experiment: Towards a Transnational Social Democratic Security Perspective?," *Cooperation and Conflict* 20, no. 1 (1985): 1–22; Michael A. Krasner and Nikolaj Petersen, "Movement and Its Impact on National

Security Policy," *Journal of Peace Research* 23, no. 2 (1986): 155–73; and Nikolaj Petersen, "The Security Policies of Small NATO Countries: Factors of Change," *Cooperation and Conflict* 23, no. 2 (1988): 145–62.

87. For example, Denmark dissented on INF deployment statements made in final NAC communiqués in December 1983, May 1984, and June and December 1985; all available at "Ministerial Communiques 1980s," NATO Online Library, http://www.nato.int/docu/comm.htm.

88. For example, Denmark dissented on INF deployment statements made in final Defense Planning Committee communiqués in December 1983 and May and December 1985; all available at "Ministerial Communiques 1980s," NATO Online Library, http://www.nato.int/docu/comm.htm.

89. For example, Denmark dissented on INF deployment statements made in final Nuclear Planning Group communiqués in October 1985 and March and October 1986; all available at "Ministerial Communiques 1980s," NATO Online Library, http://www.nato.int/docu/comm.htm.

90. K. C. Pedersen, "Denmark and the European Security and Defense Policy," in *The Nordic Countries and the European Security and Defense Policy*, ed. A. J. K. Bailes, G. Herolf and B. Sundelius (Oxford: Oxford University Press, 2006), 42; Villaume, "Denmark and NATO through 50 years," in Heurlin and Mouritzen, *Danish Foreign Policy Yearbook 1999*, 42–45; Carsten Holbraad, *Danish Neutrality: A Study in the Foreign Policy of a Small State* (Oxford: Clarendon Press, 1991); and Carsten Due-Nielsen and Nikolaj Petersen, eds., *Adaptation and Activism: The Foreign Policy of Denmark 1967–1993* (Copenhagen: Jurist- og Økonomforbundets Forlag, 1995).

91. Greece issued dissenting footnotes on a number of issues, including the NATO response to martial law in Poland (see "Documents on Events in Poland," January 11, 1982) and INF deployment statements made in final communiqués on NAC meetings (see May and December 1982; June, October, and December 1983; May 1984; June and December 1985; and December 1986); final communiqués on Defense Planning Committee meetings (see June 1982, December 1983, May and December 1985, and May 1986); and final communiqués on Nuclear Planning Group meetings (see April 1984, October 1985, and March and October 1986); all available at "Ministerial Communiques 1980s," NATO Online Library, http://www.nato.int/docu/comm.htm.

92. Serge Schmemann, "Danes Divided on Nuclear Resolution," *New York Times*, April 26, 1988.

93. Snyder, "Security Dilemma," 483.

94. Bruce Russett and Donald Delucca, "Theatre Nuclear Forces: Public Opinion in Western Europe," *Political Science Quarterly* 8, no. 2 (1983): 179–96.

95. Petersen, "Footnoting," 2.

96. Ibid.

12. Switzerland and Détente: A Revised Foreign Policy Characterized by Distrust

Sandra Bott and Janick Marina Schaufelbuehl

At the beginning of the 1970s, a general redefinition of the scope of Swiss foreign policy took place. The Swiss government could not ignore the shifting international context of détente and was forced to rethink certain aspects of the position it had taken in the global arena since the beginning of the Cold War. During these two-and-a-half decades, its international outlook had been firmly oriented toward the United States and Western Europe and essentially was guided by economic interests, although officially Switzerland claimed to be strictly neutral. In the face of East-West rapprochement, the fear of growing isolation and international distrust in the country's diplomatic position if Switzerland kept on clinging to its traditional stance of neutrality prompted a reorientation. There was also new awareness of the disadvantages of having resisted the trend toward multilateralism and supranational integration. Switzerland had not participated in the process of European unification and was the only neutral state that was not a member of the United Nations (UN). As of 1969, the Swiss government began to analyze the transformed international situation and define a fresh foreign policy line. However, this analysis also brought to light fundamental distrust within Switzerland's Federal Political Department—in charge of the country's foreign policy—for the process of détente.[1]

The Swiss government developed a double strategy between 1969 and 1975. On the one hand, it maintained and even strengthened its traditional Cold War policies of armed defense, neutrality, and solidarity. Reinforcement

The authors would like to thank Marc Perrenoud for his precious advice.

259

of the army, intensive surveillance of the Swiss population, and a new extensive national security policy were the components of this approach. On the other hand, the Swiss government reluctantly engaged in more active and outward-looking diplomatic relations. Given Switzerland's strong attachment to the West since the beginning of the Cold War and the newly independent African and Asian countries' growing importance in the international arena, this reorientation was aimed at gaining international goodwill and trust in Swiss neutrality. It came about not so much as the result of direct pressure from the outside, but from an awareness that a proactive attitude was called for in the new global context. The Federal Political Department thus pushed for participation in the Conference on Security and Cooperation in Europe (CSCE), for UN membership, for the expansion of aid to developing countries, and for recognition of the few remaining communist states with which Switzerland had not yet established official diplomatic relations. This overhaul took place within the Swiss Federal Council (the collective head of state) and was largely inspired by the Federal Political Department. A government public relations effort to communicate this new international orientation to the Swiss population did not entirely succeed. Criticism came in particular from a significant xenophobic and somewhat isolationist movement that was gaining momentum in the Swiss political landscape. It is noteworthy that it was only thirty years later, in 2002, and after much reluctance, that the Swiss population agreed in a popular vote to join the UN.

This chapter analyzes leading Swiss policymakers' perception of the changing international context during the period of détente, and aims to determine the influence this perception had on the remodeling of foreign policy.[2] Its focus is thus on the Federal Council and especially on the members of the Federal Political Department and their attempts to remodel key components of the Swiss approach to international relations after critically assessing the changes taking place in the global arena. It briefly presents Switzerland's Cold War policies from 1947 through the beginning of détente, then discusses the Federal Political Department's appraisal of the transformed international situation, and finally addresses the double strategy put into place as a result of this analysis in domestic and foreign policy matters.

Switzerland and the Cold War, 1947–1969:
A Selective Approach to Neutrality

Switzerland's foreign policy during the first two decades of the Cold War was very much influenced by its geopolitical situation at the end of World War II. The country had found itself in a difficult position in the new postwar order because of the close economic ties its industrial and financial circles had maintained with the Axis powers throughout the conflict. Neutrality had a very difficult stance after the war, since the Allies felt that the neutral European countries had profited economically from the conflict but had not contributed to the liberation of Europe. International law experts were of the opinion that proclamations of neutrality were no longer justifiable, as they went against the idea of collective security.[3]

To counter this widespread suspicion toward neutrality and avoid international isolation, the nature of Switzerland's international positioning had to be thought over afresh. It was in the process of this redefinition that the concepts of solidarity and universality were added to the traditional Swiss maxim of neutrality, in the framework of the Petitpierre and the Bindschedler doctrines.[4] Solidarity was meant to promote policies of "good offices"[5] and humanitarian activities, while universality implied the diplomatic recognition of all states, regardless of their political systems. Both maxims were aimed at regaining global confidence in Switzerland, especially from the United States. However, as a number of historians have pointed out, the actual implementation of these three dimensions of Swiss foreign policy in the 1950s and 1960s was highly problematical.[6]

On the one hand, the position of official neutrality was greatly weakened by concessions made to the Western bloc—in particular Switzerland's secret participation in CoCom (the Coordinating Committee for Multilateral Export Controls, a program that prevented arms sales to Eastern bloc countries) in 1951[7]—and the highly selective interpretation of what Switzerland's neutral status implied. The choices made regarding neutrality policy largely overlapped with the economic interests of Swiss industry and banks, which overwhelmingly were tied to Western Europe and the United States.[8] Swiss authorities distinguished between political and "technical" organizations. Political organizations, such as the North Atlantic Treaty Organization (NATO), could not be joined for reasons of maintaining neutrality. In contrast, adherence to "technical" organizations, such as the Organisation for European Economic Cooperation (OEEC), or UN specialized agencies and ancillary organs, such as the United Nations Conference on Trade and Development, was not considered contrary to neutrality. This relatively artificial distinction allowed for a pick-and-choose policy of neutrality that was guided by specific political and economic interests. Furthermore, the maxim of solidarity was put into perspective by the fact that the cooperative and developmental measures implemented by the Swiss federal government often seemed to be linked to commercial benefits, and development aid was relatively modest: Switzerland has never dedicated as important a part of its gross national product to development aid as, for instance, Sweden has.[9] Finally, the principle of universality was also compromised by the Swiss government's refusal to recognize North Vietnam until 1971, East Germany until 1973, and North Korea until 1974.

The Swiss Government's Suspicious Assessment of Détente and Domestic Protest

When reassessing the main lines of Switzerland's foreign policy in May 1968, the federal government reaffirmed the timeliness of neutrality, solidarity, and universality as major guiding principles.[10] However, over the following years, Swiss authorities engaged in a process of evaluating this approach to international relations with respect to détente on the one hand and the global protest movements that had gained momentum after 1968 on the other. Willy Spühler, the social democratic foreign minister (and head of the Federal Political Department) from January 1966 to January 1970, considered these two developments to be the essential challenges that Switzerland and the world were facing.[11]

If a general statement can be made regarding the Swiss government's assessment of détente, one could say that it was marked by increasing distrust. Threat perception was an important factor during the Cold War era. For a country like Switzerland, whose politics and economy were so closely linked to the Western bloc and whose ideological position was largely convergent with the United States on anticommunism and the ideals of liberalism and the free-market economy,[12] the assessment of whether or not Washington could be trusted to maintain international stability during the process of détente was decisive and determined the government's views on how to participate in this process. A question at the heart of the Federal Political Department's discussions during this era was thus to ascertain if the superpowers were truly capable of "civilizing their relations."[13]

In 1969, Foreign Minister Willy Spühler evaluated the changing international situation. To him, the Soviet Union was a real source of danger for world peace, especially because of the regime's backward relationship to technological innovation and its incapacity to keep its domestic situation under control. Other than this, he thought that the United States could be trusted to hold back in international confrontation and to find solutions for the instability within its own borders.[14] Yet Spühler's successor as foreign minister, Pierre Graber (February 1970–January 1978), who also was a social democrat, began to see the US role in much more circumspect fashion.

At the very beginning of 1973, Graber declared that "the years 1972 to 1973 will be remembered by historians as a time of profound change in world history,"[15] due to China's growing importance on the international scene and the deepening of the Sino-Soviet split. In Graber's view, China's expanding role in the international arena "put an end to a long era of stability in bipolar relations."[16] His main worry, however, concerned the US government's capacity to protect Western Europe against a potential attack from the Soviet army and to enforce a united and structured Europe.[17] For Graber, détente implied a risk that the US government would feel less concerned about other important issues of global stability, given its particular role in the newly formed triangle of superpowers: "In this situation, Washington can contemplate the clash between the two communist empires at a distance and with serenity. . . . Steering clear of this conflict, seeking neither to alleviate nor to shelter it—which would be illusory anyway—or to take sides with one or the other of the antagonists, America (which this conflict does not directly affect) can temporize, and, strengthened by its huge military and economic power, benefit from [the conflict] in various ways."[18] This concern that the US government had become somewhat less involved in global stability also influenced Graber's impression of the encounter between US president Richard Nixon and Soviet leader Leonid Brezhnev in June 1973.[19] He felt that, from a European perspective, skepticism was called for regarding the evolution of the international balance of power: "1973, the year of Europe, is mostly the year of concern and uncertainties for Europe."[20] In Graber's eyes, the fact that Washington manifested its reluctance to use the atomic bomb against the Soviet Union also meant that it would be less likely to defend Western Europe in case of a Soviet attack. Moreover, Graber viewed the probable withdrawal of US troops as a premonitory sign of a military vacuum in Western Europe. He perceived Nixon's foreign policy to be growing more hesitant as the Watergate scandal deepened at home. At the same time, in his eyes Brezhnev's position had been reinforced domestically and also on a global level by the economic development that was taking place, with Western help, in the context of détente.[21] As Graber considered the Soviets a real source of danger for world peace, Nixon's difficulties in Washington caused worry and distrust. To illustrate this concern, Graber quoted a report from Jean de Stoutz, the Swiss ambassador in Moscow, who had stated that "the atmosphere of détente that the USSR is determined to promote will probably create more favorable conditions for a communist penetration of free countries."[22] Graber's sense of mistrust was still vivid in October 1974 when he declared in a meeting with West German foreign minister Hans-Dietrich Genscher that "détente is an ambiguous word that should be used with caution, especially regarding public opinion. For our part, we are somewhat disillusioned about détente."[23] The Federal Political Department and the Federal Council in general were very much influenced by this feeling of disillusionment regarding East-West rapprochement, and

Graber's personal position on the question thus played an instrumental role in the Swiss government's attempts at reorientation in world politics.

This feeling of general distrust toward détente also had an impact on the Swiss government's perception of the existence of a significant potential domestic threat and on the measures that it believed would be necessary to counter such a threat. A polyvalent protest movement, which had developed in Switzerland after 1968, criticized in particular the Swiss state's foreign policy of the past few decades as a policy guided by economic interest, very much on the side of the United States but hiding behind a position of official neutrality. The government's conservative and anticommunist domestic policy, characterized by the Cold War climate, was equally targeted in these protests.[24] Reacting to these accusations, the Swiss federal police intensified its surveillance system. As was brought to light in 1989,[25] throughout the Cold War the federal police established files on more than 700,000 Swiss citizens and organizations. Although this activity had started well before the protest movements of 1968 and initially had targeted foreigners and members of the communist Swiss Party of Labour, it was scaled up at the beginning of the 1970s and increasingly focused on proponents of the New Left. At this point, the federal police had a secret file on more than one in ten Swiss citizens. This level of surveillance shows that the Swiss government intensely distrusted large segments of the Swiss population and saw them as a "threat from within" to Swiss society, in the words of Pierre Graber.[26] Of course, state surveillance was a widespread phenomenon in Cold War societies, yet the extent of the spying that the Swiss government put into place was outstanding, especially so for a country that was following a position of official neutrality.[27] But besides this domestic response of intensified surveillance, the protest movements partly inspired the general reorientation of foreign policy.

A Fresh Assessment of Foreign and Security Policies

The Swiss government's observation of shifting international power relations led it to establish new structures to revise Swiss foreign policy. One of these structures was an expert committee in the Federal Military Department, created in September 1970 and assigned the task of developing Switzerland's first global security policy.[28] Nine drafts were prepared before the report was finalized and presented to the Federal Assembly on June 27, 1973. The report started by describing the contrasting global tendencies present at the time: on the one hand, the trend toward more international collaboration, détente, and disarmament; on the other, persisting political, social, and ideological tensions between states and attempts at subversion within European societies.[29] The experts recommended facing this dual situation with a double-track strategy: Switzerland should participate in the global preservation of peace and crisis management through good offices and peace initiatives, while also investing in defense readiness, centered on a strong dissuasive army.

The dual policy line proposed by experts thus had an outward-looking, active component, one oriented toward peace-building and participation in transnational structures. The keywords used in the report to defend this new positive approach were those of "hope" in the process of the CSCE and in détente, "confidence" that should be strengthened in the potential of peaceful solutions to conflicts, and finally the need for "courage" in foreign policy. This part of the guidelines therefore was motivated by a general attitude of confidence in the superpowers and their ongoing process of rapprochement. It also required fresh trust in transnational institutions, notably in the UN, and in the fact that these global players would allow Switzerland to assume an acceptable place in their midst.

Yet the security policy paper also advocated a defensive approach to the changed international context. The possibility of a military attack on Switzerland was seen as real. In the paper, Moscow was not explicitly named, but it was clear that what was feared was an assault by the Soviet army. Thus, senator and future federal councillor Hans Hürlimann, who presented the paper to the Swiss parliament, pointed out where the danger lay: in the significant quantitative superiority of troops and tanks on the side of the Warsaw Pact countries compared with those of the Western forces.[30] Besides this threat of Soviet soldiers crushing NATO defenses and therefore menacing Swiss autonomy, the experts also worried about "indirect war," which in earlier versions of the policy paper was called "subversive-revolutionary war." This threat was said to come from guerrilla or terrorist movements that either "act for the benefit of a foreign State to which they are tied ideologically or are animated by anarchist motives."[31] Again, the culprit was not openly identified, but in the context of 1973 it is clear that the experts felt that the threat of this type of "indirect war" came from liberation movements in the Middle East or in newly independent African and Asian countries and certain components of Western protest organizations.[32] Even though the report was not explicit about the exact nature of the threat to Switzerland, it stated that in the worst case scenario, such an indirect war would "impose a foreign political and ideological system on us."[33] The armed forces were therefore to be strengthened and prepared for this eventuality.

At the heart of Switzerland's first global security policy, elaborated between 1970 and 1973 and approved by parliament in June 1973, there was an antagonism between trust toward détente and transnational institutions

265

and distrust toward the Soviet Union and liberation movements abroad or dissident political forces in Western societies. From the beginning, it was clear that the defensive aspects of the new policy outweighed the dimension of peace-building. As the report was being presented to parliament, Senator Pierre Aubert pointed out that it gave a clear definition of the military defense that should be developed but was vague on how a more active foreign policy was to be implemented.[34] During the following two decades, it was indeed the defensive element of this two-sided strategy that was consolidated by the Swiss government, while the more active foreign policy component was implemented with a great deal of hesitation.[35]

Parallel to the development of a new security policy, the Federal Political Department had also put into place a committee of experts to come up with a new foreign policy line: the study group on foreign policy.[36] This step caused quite a stir in parliament, as several delegates resented the Federal Council's top-down approach in the matter and feared competition with the already existing parliamentary group in charge of foreign affairs. As a result of this criticism, the members of parliament who had initially intended to participate in the committee ultimately abstained from joining it.[37] The study group on foreign policy, under the leadership of Pierre Graber, brought together Swiss diplomatic, academic, military, journalistic, business, and trade union leaders, and met sixteen times. Its main objective was to analyze the principles that had guided Swiss foreign policy since the end of World War II and to evaluate if those principles were still adequate to defend Switzerland's sovereignty as well as its economic interests, given the new dynamics in international relations.[38] Several members of the group readily admitted that the main components of Swiss foreign policy since 1945 had simply been the product of a judicious adaptation to international circumstances.[39] Thus, the expert consideration was aimed at adjusting Swiss policies to four major external factors of global change: the superpowers' rapprochement, European integration, developments in Africa, Asia, and the Middle East, and what was seen as "the crisis of society."[40] What role and influence could a small and neutral country have in a "perpetually changing world"? How could Swiss neutrality emerge from this process in a positive way?

The study group on foreign policy wished to avoid two possible pitfalls in regard to the country's international position: "isolation and satellization."[41] The members of the group agreed that a more active and outward-looking foreign policy would avoid these problems. The main element of this reorientation should be to collaborate with other nations in fields where neutrality could be useful: by formulating a stronger and more clearly defined policy toward developing countries, by actively participating in the superpowers' negotiations on armament and defense (notably in the CSCE),[42] by becoming a member of the UN, and by reflecting on Switzerland's relations with the European common market. Yet as Switzerland engaged in this new direction, the study group pointed out, it was important to maintain some autonomy from the United States and to systematically favor an open-minded policy in the direction of the communist states.[43]

Timid Steps toward a More Active Foreign Policy

The expert commissions put into place by the Swiss government in 1970 and 1971 had both arrived at the same conclusion: they called for a more active, outward-looking attitude in the country's diplomatic relations in order to adapt to the transformed global relations. One of the main challenges would be for Bern to stay informed of the progress in East-West negotiations and to regularly assess how Switzerland might participate in order to avoid isolation.[44] The aim was to take part in the process of détente, but still adopt measures of "caution." This new formula was applied to three areas in particular: Swiss participation in the CSCE, Swiss government efforts to join the UN, and formal recognition of several communist states.

The sheer magnitude of the CSCE as the biggest European multilateral gathering since World War II, with thirty-five participating nations, made it the expression of a "new kind of Europe, one no longer exclusively dominated by East-West rivalries."[45] This global dimension to the conference led to the decision that Switzerland should not be the only European country besides Albania not to take part. However, from the beginning, the Federal Political Department adopted a very skeptical and distrustful attitude toward the CSCE.[46]

After the Budapest appeal of March 1969, in which the Warsaw Pact states called for a conference on security in Europe, and the subsequent Finnish offer to host such a conference, Bern was expected to clarify its position. At this point, Pierre Graber considered the chances of the conference actually seeing the light of day as "slim." He furthermore suspected that "each country had particular hidden agendas."[47] Still, the Swiss government officially announced its interest in participating, on the condition that the United States and Canada would be invited to join. From 1969 to 1972, the Federal Political Department temporized without taking any further official steps. It did set up a special working group, under the direction of legal expert Rudolf Bindschedler, to evaluate the proposed security conference. As Thomas Fischer points out, the group's attitude "was mainly characterized by distrust."[48] Bindschedler in particular considered the suggestions for greater East-West rapprochement to be just so much hot air that would leave the real problems unresolved. Specifically, he distrusted the Soviet Union's intentions. Moscow had expressed its support for Swiss participation in the CSCE.[49] Leading Swiss policy experts agreed with Bindschedler that the conference was just a means for the Soviets to slow down Western European integration in order to secure the status quo and make deeper inroads into the West on an ideological and maybe even military level. In their eyes, détente was based on too much optimism concerning the Soviet regime.[50]

But despite this skepticism, the Swiss government decided to participate in the multilateral process of the CSCE, which would help it avoid the "isolation that threatens the European non-aligned and Neutrals at a time of pacific confrontation of the two blocs' security theses" and show "that Switzerland's European policy was not exclusively addressed to the West but also to Europe as a whole."[51] With the objective of actively contributing to the discussions on the content of the conference agenda, in close collaboration with the other neutrals[52] and notably regarding peaceful settlement mechanisms,[53] a Swiss delegation took part in the talks that began in November 1972 at the Dipoli conference center near Helsinki, continued in Geneva, and ended with a summit in Helsinki in July 1975. Even though, as Fischer shows, the role of the neutral states in the conference tended to gradually narrow,[54] overall Swiss participation in the CSCE process brought it numerous advantages, in particular a strengthening of Geneva's role as a crossroads for international diplomatic negotiations, rapprochement with fellow neutral states Sweden and Austria as well as with the nonaligned states of Europe with which Switzerland came to act in close coordination, multilateral integration toward the East and even closer bilateral ties to the United States, and the anchoring of the right to neutrality in the Helsinki Accords. In the context of the Swiss government's desire to engage in a more outward-looking foreign policy, Switzerland's participation in the CSCE talks can as such be considered successful.

The second dimension of the renewal in its international outlook was the Swiss government's decision to engage in a process that might lead to Switzerland joining the UN. Although the government issued a first report in June 1969 that concluded that the time was not yet ripe for Swiss adherence—since it was uncertain whether its status of neutrality was compatible with membership—a second report issued in November 1971 was more clearly influenced by détente, the admission of the People's Republic of China to the UN, and the UN's much more universal character following the entry of newly independent Asian, African, and Caribbean states.[55] It was again mainly the fear of being isolated and losing the trust of the global community that drove the Federal Council to contemplate UN membership. As the 1971 report stated, if Switzerland remained the only state that voluntarily chose not to join the UN, "We can't conceal to ourselves the fact that we would in this case risk isolation of our country, which would not only bring negative consequences to our international relations as such, but could also bring moral disadvantages, if the international community would not understand our attitude under these new circumstances."[56] The government thus intended to put the decision of UN membership before the Swiss population "soon."

The third area to which the government's new foreign policy formula was applied was that of recognition of the communist parts of Vietnam, Germany, and Korea. In fact, Switzerland had established official relations with the noncommunist part of these divided states years before it even considered recognizing the other part: with West Germany in 1951, with South Vietnam in 1958, and with South Korea in 1962.[57] Concerning its nonrelations with the other halves of these nations—which contradicted its official maxim of universality—the Swiss government saw no need to overhaul its pragmatic policy based on "national interest," even after Sweden recognized North Vietnam in January 1969.[58] It was only in the context of détente and its new foreign policy orientation that Bern reconsidered its position. The question was discussed in September 1970 at a meeting of leading diplomats.[59] It was decided that recognition of the German Democratic Republic (GDR) should be treated separately, owing to Switzerland's special economic and cultural relations with West Germany, and that "the taking up of regular relations with North Korea should be postponed as long as possible," since "we must pay tribute to our relatively important economic interests in South Korea."[60] In the case of Vietnam, neither the north nor the south had any economic importance for Switzerland. However, the Swiss ambassador to Washington thought that recognition could give more international confidence in Swiss neutrality, on condition that such a diplomatic step would be presented as a purely humanitarian action and not a political one.

The Federal Political Department prepared a first draft for official recognition of North Vietnam in December 1970, but it decided not to act on it, subjecting itself to Saigon's insistence that it did not wish to see Switzerland establish diplomatic relations with North Vietnam "now or in a foreseeable future": Switzerland should at least wait until autumn 1971, after the South Vietnamese elections.[61] After the publication of the Pentagon Papers in the summer of 1971 and the rapprochement of President Nixon and Chinese leader Mao Zedong, Bern started to interpret the situation in Vietnam differently. It no longer wished to wait for the South Vietnamese elections, but thought it important to profit from the present situation and the prospect of a foreseeable end of the conflict in order to be among the first Western countries to establish official relations with Hanoi. This decision would speak well for its policy of universality and its humanitarian approach, and would allow Switzerland to participate in Vietnam's reconstruction.[62] On September 1, 1971, Bern unilaterally recognized North Vietnam.

At the same time, the situation relating to the GDR had also begun to shift. Bern had avoided official recognition of the GDR, fearing that doing so would rebuff its number-one commercial partner, the Federal Republic of Germany (FRG).[63] But it was not only economic interests that were at play; as a Federal Political Department official pointed out in April 1971, "Both the ruling circles and the population in West Germany are close to Switzerland on the level of ideas and on a personal level," and thus Switzerland was inclined "on a psychological level" not to recognize the GDR.[64] In the framework of the general foreign policy overhaul, and following the signing of the Basic Treaty (Grundvertrag) between the GDR and the FRG in December 1972 (which normalized intra-German relations), the Federal Council established official relations with the GDR in January 1973.[65] Even though Bern had thus taken the plunge regarding North Vietnam and East Germany, it postponed recognition of North Korea until 1974. In addition to the commercial benefits of its relationship with South Korea, the Swiss government did not want to jeopardize Seoul's trust in the Swiss diplomats' role in the Neutral Nations Supervisory Committee in Korea.

Public Skepticism toward the Government's New Foreign Policy Line

At the same time as Graber had created the study group on foreign policy in March 1971, he had set up a group of journalistic experts to consider how to sell the new outlook in Switzerland's international policies to the general public. It was especially in three problematic areas that the government felt it urgent to bridge the distance between its own perspectives and those of the "masses of citizens": more intense public cooperation with developing countries, attitudes toward European integration, and lastly possible UN membership.[66] Graber's concerns were related to the recent strengthening of a nationalistic movement in the country under the leadership of the politician James Schwarzenbach, whose xenophobic federal popular initiative (a petition signed by 100,000 registered voters, which forces an automatic public vote on the topic of the petition) proposing a limit on the number of foreigners in Switzerland—the so-called Überfremdungs-Initiative, a law against excessive "foreignization"—had been supported by just under half of all participants in a national popular vote the summer before. However, faced with press and parliamentary criticism that accused him of wanting to install a "governmentalist" propaganda group, Graber was obliged to downscale the journalist group's role and to abstain from any permanent participation of journalists and media representatives in Swiss foreign policy debates.[67]

The government's aim to build up public trust in its foreign policy reform was not entirely successful. Large portions of the Swiss population remained skeptical, as was for example shown in a public debate that took place at the University of Geneva in December 1972. According to the press, the main conclusion of the different speakers was that "the Swiss government gave the impression of trying to do too much too fast with its policy of international opening. All at once it [was] active in the Security Conference in Helsinki, [was] preparing Switzerland's entry into the UN, and at the same time recognize[d] the existence of certain states."[68] As a consequence of this widespread skepticism, the government's intention to build up financial aid to developing countries met with major parliamentary and extraparliamentary resistance. Although the new law on international cooperation and development finally passed after three years of intense parliamentary debate and accusations of wastage of public resources, the proposed $200 million support for the International Development Association was blocked by a public vote initiated by the xenophobic movement, National Action.[69]

When it came to the government's project of Swiss membership in the UN, opposition was even stronger. Resistance from the public and the parliament put off a decision on the matter for more than a decade. When the question was finally put to popular vote in 1986, a massive majority refused membership. As Carlo Moos has analyzed, the political campaign of those opposing it had been focused on distrust. This attitude was well summed up in one of the anti-UN group's main campaign posters: "UN membership? Less neutrality, less independence, less security, more costs, more federal officers. For the sake of Switzerland: NO."[70] It was only after the end of the Cold War that Switzerland at last joined the UN, in 2002.

Defense Preferred to Détente: Switzerland's Missed Opportunities

Deborah Welch Larson has shown that "U.S. and Soviet leaders passed up opportunities to cooperate on arms control and on Germany largely because of mutual mistrust, based on ideological differences, historical baggage, and intuitive mental biases. These diplomatic failures were wasteful, tragic, self-defeating, and often, if not always, avoidable."[71] Was the Swiss government also a victim of such missed opportunities during the process of détente? As we have seen, the general attitude of the Swiss government toward the shifting international constellations between 1969 and 1975 was one of basic and

271

constant distrust. There was distrust in the United States' willingness to offer military protection to Western Europe despite the process of rapprochement with the Eastern bloc. The Soviet Union's participation in détente was met with general and deeply rooted suspicion. The top leaders of Swiss foreign policy were at first skeptical of the CSCE, participating only reluctantly in these transnational negotiations even though they were aware of the indirect benefits that their cooperation could imply for the international standing of neutrality. Switzerland's population was deeply distrusted by the government, which spied on it intensely, and the Swiss population in turn distrusted the political openings that the Federal Council wished to initiate toward the UN and the European Economic Community. For the authorities responsible for the country's foreign affairs, the problem of defense continued to be central to foreign policy after 1969. As Pierre Graber put it in August 1973, speaking about the CSCE: "At the heart of the matter it is [Switzerland's and Western Europe's] security that is at stake and it should be completely clear for everybody that détente sheds a new light on the problems of defense. Defense becomes artificial . . . if it is accompanied by such a flagrant imbalance of forces that the most disadvantaged would actually be condemned to live in fear and to be consoled only by words."[72] The perspective of military threat and defense that had played such a profound and structuring role in Switzerland's Cold War policies since 1947 thus continued to influence foreign relations during détente, despite the hesitant steps made toward a more open-minded conception of diplomatic relations. This skeptical attitude, combined with the ever-present influence of economic interests abroad, may have prevented Switzerland from embracing a more proactive and upbeat role in détente.

Notes

1. The Federal Political Department was renamed in 1979 to the Federal Department of Foreign Affairs.

2. Certain aspects of Switzerland's foreign policy during détente have already been dealt with, notably by Thomas Fischer, *Die Grenzen der Neutralität. Schweizerisches KSZE-Engagement und gescheiterte UNO-Beitrittspolitik im kalten Krieg 1969–1986* [The boundaries of neutrality: Swiss CSCE commitment and failed UN membership policy during the Cold War, 1969–1986] (Zurich: Chronos, 2004).

3. On the United States' and the Soviet Union's attitude toward neutrality after 1945, see Jürg Martin Gabriel, *The American Conception of Neutrality After 1941* (Basingstoke, UK: Palgrave Macmillan, 2002); Vladislav M. Zubok, "The Soviet Attitude towards the European Neutrals during the Cold War" in *Die Neutralen und die europäische Integration 1945–1995* [The neutrals and European integration, 1945–1995], ed. Michael Gehler and Rolf Steininger (Vienna: Böhlau, 2000), 29–43; and, more recently, Marco Wyss, Jussi M. Hanhimäki, Sandra Bott, and Janick Marina

Schaufelbuehl, "Introduction: A Tightrope Walk—Neutrality and Neutralism in the Global Cold War," in *Neutrality and Neutralism in the Global Cold War. Between or Within the Blocs?*, ed. Sandra Bott, Jussi M. Hanhimäki, Janick Marina Schaufelbuehl and Marco Wyss (London: Routledge, 2016), 1–14.

4. Referring to Max Petitpierre, Swiss foreign minister from 1945 to 1961, and Rudolf L. Bindschedler, who had drawn up a guiding document on the consequences of neutrality for Switzerland's international relations.

5. Switzerland's "good offices," which designate diplomatic or legal measures aimed at reducing international tensions, are notably discussed in Raymond Probst, "The 'Good Offices' of Switzerland and Her Role as Protecting Power," in *Diplomacy under a Foreign Flag: When Nations Break Relations*, ed. D. D. Newsom (Washington, DC: Georgetown University Institute for the Study of Diplomacy, Georgetown University, 1990), 18–31.

6. See, e.g., Marco Wyss, *Arms Transfers, Neutrality and Britain's Role in the Cold War: Anglo-Swiss Relations 1945–1958* (Leiden: Brill, 2012); Daniel Trachsler, *Bundesrat Max Petitpierre. Schweizerische Aussenpolitik im Kalten Krieg 1945–1961* [Federal Councillor Max Petitpierre: Swiss foreign policy in the Cold War, 1945–1961] (Zurich: NZZ, 2011); and Hans Ulrich Jost, "Switzerland's Atlantic Perspectives," in *Swiss Neutrality and Security: Armed Forces, National Defence, and Foreign Policy*, ed. Marko Milivojević and Pierre Maurer (New York: Berg, 1990), 110–21.

7. On this point, see André Schaller, *Schweizer Neutralität im West-Ost-Handel. Das Hotz-Linder Agreement vom 23. Juli 1951* [Swiss neutrality in East-West trade: The Hotz-Linder Agreement of July 23, 1951] (Bern: Verlag P. Haupt, 1987).

8. See, e.g., Jost, "Switzerland's Atlantic Perspectives"; and Janick Marina Schaufelbuehl and Mario König, "Les relations entre la Suisse et les Etats-Unis pendant la guerre froide" [Relations between Switzerland and the United States during the Cold War], *Traverse* 2 (2009): 15–22.

9. Marc Perrenoud, "Les relations de la Suisse avec l'Afrique lors de la décolonisation et des débuts de la coopération au développement" [Switzerland's relationship with Africa during decolonization and the beginnings of development cooperation], *Revue internationale de politique de développement* 1 (2010): 81–98.

10. *Rapport du Conseil fédéral concernant les grandes lignes de la politique gouvernementale pendant la législature 1968–1971* [Federal Council report on the main lines of government policy during the 1968–1971 legislative term], May 15, 1968, *Feuille Fédérale* [Federal Gazette] 1/22, 1221–64.

11. Spühler also mentioned a third challenge: technology and innovation. See Botschaftertagung, Referat von Dr. W. Spühler, *Die drei Herausforderungen unserer Zeit* [The three challenges of our time], September 3, 1969, Diplomatic Documents of Switzerland, 1848 ff., Swiss Federal Archives (SFA), Bern, Online Database Dodis: dodis.ch/30860.

12. On Switzerland's role in transnational anticommunism, see Luc Van Dongen, Stéphanie Roulin, and Giles Scott-Smith, eds., *Transnational Communism and the Cold War: Agents, Activities, and Networks* (Basingstoke, UK: Palgrave Macmillan, 2014); and Luc Van Dongen, "La Suisse dans les rets de l'anticommunisme transnational durant la guerre froide: réflexions et jalons" [Switzerland in the net of transnational anticommunism during the Cold War: Reflections and milestones], in *Itinera, Die internationale Schweiz in der Zeit des Kalten Krieges / Relations internationales de la Suisse durant la Guerre froide* [Itinera: Swiss international relations during the

Cold War], ed. Sandra Bott, Janick Marina Schaufelbuehl, and Sacha Zala (Basel: Schwabe Verlag, 2011), 30:17–30.

13. See, e.g., Swiss ambassador in Washington Felix Schnyder's intervention, Protokoll der Botschaftertagung, September 3–5, 1969, 43, dodis.ch/30859.

14. *Die drei Herausforderungen*, September 3, 1969, 14, dodis.ch/30860. (All citations in German or French have been translated by the authors.)

15. See Graber's "overview," Annex 1 to the minutes of the Commission of Foreign Affairs of the National Council, January 29, 1973, E 2004 1979/31/2, SFA, 1.

16. Ibid.

17. See Graber's "overview," sent to the Commissioners of the National Council in preparation for their session of May 21, 1973, E 2004 1979/31/2, SFA, 9.

18. See Graber's "overview," Annex 1, E 2004 1979/31/2, SFA, 3–4.

19. See Graber's confidential report, annex to the 14 August 1974 session of the Foreign Affairs Committee of the Council of States, E 2004 1979/31/2, SFA, 2.

20. Ibid.

21. See Graber's "overview," sent to the Commissioners of the National Council in preparation for their session of May 21, 1973, E 2004 1979/31/2, SFA, 8.

22. Ibid.

23. See the confidential report of the meetings between the Federal Councillor Pierre Graber and the West German foreign minister Hans-Dietrich Genscher, Bonn, Foreign Affairs Committee of the Council of States, October 17, 1974, E 2004 1979/31/2, SFA, 20.

24. On the 1968 movement in Switzerland, see in particular Brigitte Studer and Janick Marina Schaufelbuehl, "Die 68er Bewegung und ihre Auswirkungen in der Schweiz – Einleitung" [The '68 movement and its impact in Switzerland: Introduction] in *1968–1978. Ein bewegtes Jahrzehnt in der Schweiz. Une décennie mouvementée en Suisse* [1968–1978: An eventful decade in Switzerland], ed. Janick Marina Schaufelbuehl (Zurich: Chronos, 2009), 9–33; Nicole Peter, "Switzerland," in *1968 in Europe. A History of Protest and Activism, 1956–1977*, ed. Martin Klimke and Joachim Scharloth (New York: Palgrave, 2008), 229–38; and Damir Skenderovic and Christina Späti, *Die 1968er-Jahre in der Schweiz. Aufbruch in Politik und Kultur* [1968 in Switzerland: Awakening in politics and culture] (Baden: Hier + Jetzt, 2012).

25. On the scandal of the uncovering of these files, see ed. Georg Kreis, *Staatsschutz in der Schweiz: Die Entwicklung von 1935–1990: eine multidisziplinäre Untersuchung im Auftrage des schweizerischen Bundesrates* [State protection in Switzerland: The development of 1935–1990: A multidisciplinary study on behalf of the Swiss Federal Council] (Bern: Haupt, 1993).

26. Presentation of Pierre Graber to the Commission of Foreign Affairs of the National Council, on *Ideological Questions: The Crisis of Youth*, August 20, 1971, E 2004 (B) 1979/31/1, SFA.

27. See Kreis, *Staatsschutz in der Schweiz*; and Jakob Tanner, Jürg Frischknecht, and Paul Rechsteiner, eds., *Schnüffelstaat Schweiz: Hundert Jahre sind genug* [Switzerland as a snooping state: A hundred years is enough] (Zurich: Limmat Verlag, 1990).

28. It was to be based on the earlier report of the Study Commission on Strategic Issues. See Christoph Breitenmoser, *Strategie ohne Aussenpolitik. Zur Entwicklung der schweizerischen Sicherheitspolitik im Kalten Krieg* [Strategy without foreign policy: On the development of Swiss security policy during the Cold War] (Bern: Peter

Lang, 2002), 179–88; and Mauro Mantovani, *Schweizerische Sicherheitspolitik im Kalten Krieg 1947–1963: Zwischen angelsächsischem Containment und Neutralitäts-Doktrin* [Swiss security policy in the Cold War, 1947–1963: Between Anglo-Saxon containment and the neutrality doctrine] (Zurich: Orell Füssli, 1999).

29. "La politique de la sécurité de la Suisse (Conception de la défense générale)" [Swiss security policy (concept of general defense)], June 27, 1973, *Bulletin officiel de l'Assemblée fédérale* IV/06, 105–47, at 105.

30. "Politique de sécurité. Rapport du Conseil fédéral" [Security policy: Report of the Federal Council], June 27, 1973, *Bulletin official de l'Assemblée fédérale* [Official bulletin of the Federal Assembly] IV/06, 714.

31. "La politique de la sécurité de la Suisse," 111.

32. See Aviva Guttmann, "Une coallition antiterroriste sous l'égide d'un pays neutre: la réponse suisse au terrorisme palestinien, 1969–1970"[An antiterrorist coalition under the auspices of a neutral country: The Swiss answer to Palestinian terrorism, 1969–1970], special issue "Suisse et Guerre froide dans le tiers-monde" [Switzerland and the Cold War in the Third World], *Relations Internationales* 163 (2015), 95–110; and Nuno Pereira, "Anti-impérialisme et nouvelle gauche radicale dans la Suisse des années 68" [Anti-imperialism and radical new left in Switzerland during the 1968 movements] (unpublished PhD thesis, University of Lausanne, 2015).

33. "La politique de la sécurité de la Suisse," 114.

34. "Politique de sécurité. Rapport du Conseil fédéral," 719.

35. This is the conclusion of Kurt R. Spillmann, Andreas Wenger, Christoph Breitenmoser, and Marcel Gerber, *Schweizer Sicherheitspolitik seit 1945: Zwischen Autonomie und Kooperation* [Swiss security policy since 1945: Between autonomy and cooperation] (Zurich: NZZ, 2001), 117.

36. See Fischer, *Die Grenzen der Neutralität*, 78–80.

37. See *Interpellation Baechtold-Lausanne. Groupes d'étude du Département politique. Postulat Hofstetter. Groupes d'étude de politique étrangère* [Baechtold-Lausanne Inquiry: Political Department study groups: Postulat Hofstetter: Foreign policy study groups], June 14, 1971, *Feuille fédérale* 4 (1971), 674–83.

38. See Federal Council's communiqué, March 8, 1971, E 2812 1985/204/3, SFA.

39. See, for example, the intervention of the President of the Federation of the Swiss Watch Industry, Gerard Bauer, minutes of the Study Group on Foreign Policy, February 14, 1972, FPD, February 25, 1972, E 2812 1985/204/3, SFA. 21.

40. See the intervention of the Swiss ambassador in Beijing, Albert Natural, minutes of the Study Group on Foreign Policy, February 1, 1972, FPD, February 14, 1972, E 2812 1985/204/3, SFA.

41. See Gerard Bauer's intervention, President of the Federation of Swiss Watch Industry, minutes of the Study Group on Foreign Policy, March 16, 1973, FPD, April 16, 1973, E 2812 1985/204/3, SFA, 4.

42. See Graber's intervention, minutes of the Study Group on Foreign Policy, May 12, 1973, FPD, May 21, 1973, E 2812 1985/204/3, SFA, 8.

43. Regarding this point, see Bauer's intervention, minutes of the Study Group on Foreign Policy, 16 March 1973, FPD, April 16, 1973, E 2812 1985/204/3, SFA, 5.

44. On this aspect, see for example the confidential report of the FPD, signed by Graber, to the Federal Council titled *Switzerland and the CSCE Conference*, November 1, 1972, E 7001 (c) 1984/200/12, SFA, 13.

45. Jussi M. Hanhimäki, "Détente in Europe," in *The Cambridge History of the Cold War*, ed. Melvyn P. Leffler and Odd Arne Westad (Cambridge, UK: Cambridge University Press, 2010), 198–218, 213.

46. On Switzerland and the CSCE process, see Fischer, *Die Grenzen der Neutralität*, 81–95, 140–58, and 210–24; Thomas Fischer, *Neutral Power in the CSCE. The N+N States and the Making of the Helsinki Accords 1975* (Baden-Baden: Nomos, 2009); Philipp Rosin, "Annäherung im Zeichen von multilateraler Entspannungspolitik und Menschenrechtskampagne. Der KSZE-Prozess und die Entwicklung der schweizerisch-amerikanischen Beziehungen von Helsinki bis Madrid, 1972–1983" [Approaching the mark of multilateral détente and the human rights campaign: The CSCE process and the development of the Swiss-American relations from Helsinki to Madrid, 1972–1983], in Schaufelbuehl and König, *Schweiz-USA im Kalten Krieg*, 85–98; and Christoph Breitenmoser, *Sicherheit für Europa. Die KSZE-Politik der Schweiz bis zur Unterzeichnung der Helsinki-Schlussakte zwischen Skepsis und aktivem Engagement* [Security for Europe: Swiss CSCE policy until the signing of the Helsinki Final Act: Between skepticism and active engagement] (Zurich: ETH, 1996).

47. Bundesratsprotokoll, *Conférence européenne de Sécurité* [European security conference], July 9, 1969, www.dodis.ch/1180.

48. Fischer, *Die Grenzen der Neutralität*, 86–87.

49. *Aufzeichnung über die Vorsprache des sowjetischen Botschafters, A.S. Chistakov, bei Bundesrat Pierre Graber* [Record of the conversation between Soviet ambassador A. S. Chistakov and Federal Councillor Pierre Graber], February 29, 1972, SFA E 2001 (E) 1982/58/475.

50. This was notably the position of the expert group called "Historische Standortbestimmung" (Historic Positioning), whose main aim was to deal with Switzerland's role in European integration; see Fischer, *Die Grenzen der Neutralität*, 87. See also Commission on Foreign Affairs of the Council of States, minutes of the meeting of November 23, 1971, November 30, 1971, E 2004 (B) 1979/31/1, SFA, 11.

51. Confidential report, *Switzerland and the CSCE Conference*, from the FAD to the Federal Council, November 1, 1972, SFA E 7001 (c) 1984/200/12, 13.

52. This was considered fundamental by Graber; see his report on "Disarmament and Security" presented to the Commission on Foreign Affairs of the National Council, September 6, 1971, E 2004B 1979/31/1, SFA, 12.

53. Confidential report of the FPD, signed by Graber, to the Federal Council, *Switzerland and the CSCE Conference*, November 1, 1972, E 7001 (c) 1984/200/12, SFA, 15–18.

54. Thomas Fischer, "Bridging the Gap between East and West. The N+N as Catalysts of the CSCE Process, 1972–1983," in *Perforating the Iron Curtain: European Détente, Transatlantic Relations, and the Cold War, 1965–1985*, ed. Poul Villaume and Odd Arne Westad (Copenhagen: Museum Tusculanum Press, 2010), 143–78.

55. On the question of this reconsideration of Swiss UN membership, see Fischer, *Die Grenzen der Neutralität*, 96–114, as well as Carlo Moos, *Ja zum Völkerbund – Nein zur UNO, Die Volksabstimmungen von 1920 und 1986 in der Schweiz* [Yes to the League of Nations–No to the United Nations: The Swiss referendums of 1920 and 1986] (Lausanne/Zurich: Payot/Chronos, 2001); and Daniel Möckli, "The Long Road to Membership: Switzerland and the United Nations," in Gabriel and Fischer, *Swiss Foreign Policy*, 46–73.

56. *Rapport du Conseil fédéral à l'Assemblée fédérale sur les relations de la Suisse avec l'Organisation des Nations Unies et des institutions spécialisées de 1969 à 1971* [Federal Council report to the Federal Assembly on Swiss relations with the United Nations and specialized institutions, 1969–1971], November 17, 1971, *Feuille fédérale* 1 (1972), 52.

57. On this question, see Janick Marina Schaufelbuehl, Marco Wyss, and Sandra Bott, "Choosing Sides in the Global Cold War: Switzerland, Neutrality, and the Divided States of Korea and Vietnam," *International History Review* 37, no. 5 (2015): 1014–36. On the legal aspects of Switzerland's recognition policy, see Heinz Klarer, *Schweizerische Praxis der völkerrechtlichen Anerkennung* [Swiss practice of international recognition] (Zurich: Schulthess Polygraphischer Verlag, 1981); and Urban Kaufmann, "'Nicht die ersten sein, aber vor den letzten handeln': Grundsätze und Praxis der Anerkennung von Staaten und Regierungen durch die Schweiz (1945–1961)" ["Do not be the first, but act before the last": Principles and practice of recognition of states and governments in Switzerland (1945–1961)], in *Die Schweiz und Deutschland 1945–1961* [Switzerland and Germany, 1945–1961], ed. Antoine Fleury; Horst Möller; and Hans-Peter Schwarz (München: Oldenburg, 2004), 70–72.

58. *Rapport du Conseil fédéral concernant les grandes lignes de la politique gouvernementale pendant la législature 1968–1971*, May 15, 1968, *Feuille Fédérale* 1/22, 1225; on the question of Swiss recognition of South and North Vietnam, see David Gaffino, *Autorités et entreprises suisses face à la guerre du Viêt Nam, 1960–1975* [Swiss authorities and companies face the Vietnam War, 1960–1975] (Neuchâtel: Éditions Alphil, 2006), 174–90.

59. Minutes of a meeting with the Swiss Ambassador to Washington Felix Schnyder, Delegate for Commercial Agreements Raymond Probst, the Swiss Ambassador to China Oscar Rossetti, the Swiss Ambassador to Thailand, Rudolf Hartmann, and a member of the Political Affairs Section of the FPD, September 7, 1970, E 2001 (E) 1980/83/400, SFA.

60. Ibid., 4, 5.

61. Gaffino, *Autorités et entreprises suisses*, 181.

62. Commission des affaires étrangères du Conseil national, Minutes of the special meeting of August 26, 1971, August 27, 1971, E 2004 (B) 1979/31/1, SFA.

63. On the relations between Switzerland and the German Democratic Republic, see Thérèse Gerber, *Das Kreuz mit Hammer, Zirkel, Ährenkranz. Die Beziehungen zwischen der Schweiz und der DDR in den Jahren 1949–1972* [The cross with the hammer, compass, and wreath of rye: Relations between Switzerland and the GDR, 1949–1972] (Berlin: Berling Verlag Arno Spitz, 2002).

64. Heinrich Reimann, Official at the FPD, to Hans Miesch, Minister, head of the "Eastern Section" of the FPD, *Zum Thema der Beziehungen der Schweiz zu den geteilten Staaten* [On the subject of Swiss relations with divided states], April 16, 1971, E 2001 (E) 1982/58/233, SFA.

65. *Commission des affaires étrangères du Conseil des Etats*, minutes of the meeting of January 29, 1973, February 8, 1971, 2, E 2004 (B) 1979/31/1, SFA; see also minutes of a meeting between Italian and Swiss delegates, December 11, 1972, December 22, 1972, E 2001 (E) 1982/58/233, SFA.

66. See Graber's presentation in the meeting of the Commission on Foreign Affairs of the Council of States, minutes of the meeting of April 21, 1971, May 25, 1971, E 2004 (B) 1979/31/1, SFA, 21–22.

67. J.-S. Eggly, "Création de deux groupes d'études au DPF. Composition problématique" [Creation of two study groups in the FPD: Problematic composition], *Journal de Genève*, March 9, 1971; and "Les soucis de M. Graber. Une concession aux députés" [The concerns of M. Graber: A concession to parliament], *Journal de Genève*, May 14, 1971.

68. V. S., "Bon débat à l'Aula de l'Université. La Suisse s'ouvre au monde: avec trop de précipitation?" [Good debate in the university hall—Switzerland opens up to the world: Too hastily?], *Journal de Genève*, December 18, 1972.

69. See "Pierre Graber," in *Die Schweizer Bundesräte. Ein biographisches Lexikon* [The Swiss Federal Council: A biographical dictionary], ed. Urs Altermatt (Zurich: Artemis & Winkler, 1991), 528–33.

70. Reproduced in Moos, *Ja zum Völkerbund – Nein zur UNO*, 119.

71. Deborah Welch Larson, *Anatomy of Mistrust: U.S.-Soviet Relations during the Cold War* (Ithaca, NY: Cornell University Press, 1997), 5.

72. Pierre Graber, minutes of the Commission of the National Council and the Council of States on Foreign Affairs, August 27, 1973, confidential, Secrétariat de l'Assemblée fédérale, September 19, 1973, SFA E 2004 1979/31/2.

Conclusion

Deborah Welch Larson

Trust and mistrust, while intangible and subjective, deeply affect relations among allies, adversaries, and neutrals by influencing perceptions and beliefs. The chapters in the book explore trust as a goal, strategy, process, and emotion. Although trust and mistrust are usually conceived of as interpersonal constructs, as the chapters in this book illustrate, they may be studied at the individual, societal, and alliance levels. Perhaps the best way to explore the importance of trust is to examine the impact of mistrust as a baseline.

As the editors highlight in the introduction, mistrust is not merely the opposite of trust. Mistrust is a psychological state based on beliefs and information. Mistrust, if deeply entrenched, may be virtually impossible to mitigate owing to psychological processes. Conciliatory gestures such as offers to negotiate are dismissed as tricks, posturing, or propaganda. Efforts to reinforce deterrence are viewed as evidence of aggressive intent. In a telling anecdote, Sergey Radchenko (chapter 1) relates how a Chinese telephone operator fulminated against the Soviets when Soviet premier Alexei Kosygin attempted to make a phone call to Mao Zedong or Zhou Enlai to defuse tensions after the March 1969 Sino-Soviet border clashes. Even after he found out about Kosygin's outreach efforts, Zhou ruled out direct Sino-Soviet conversations, which he thought would be inappropriate because of the poor state of their relations. In light of Soviet troop movements around Zhenbao Island, Zhou believed that Kosygin's conciliation was merely "posturing." When Zhou and Kosygin actually did meet at the Beijing airport on the way back from Ho Chi Minh's funeral in September 1969, each gave good reasons to the other for why their country did not want war. Kosygin proposed renewing relations and consultations; Zhou suggested a pullback of forces from the border. But the Soviets perceived Zhou's caution and circumspection as evidence of arrogance and deceitfulness, reinforcing their image of the Chinese as untrustworthy. Chinese officials suspected that Kosygin did not have the support of the rest of the Politburo. When the situation on the border calmed down, Chinese leaders believed that the Soviets were preparing for a surprise attack against China, similar to Pearl Harbor, and that Soviet diplomatic approaches were a "smoke screen" for a possible blitzkrieg.

Perhaps more consistent Soviet policies toward China would have been more effective in reassuring the Chinese that the Soviets wanted to avoid war. Soviet overtures to China were dismissed because of the Soviets' veiled nuclear threats and the buildup of military forces at the border. To convey trustworthiness, a state must be consistent and predictable. The Soviets were in turn constrained by fear that the Chinese would take advantage of any pullback of forces or relaxation of pressure by occupying the disputed territory.

The inability of states to understand how they are perceived by others—the security dilemma—is a major obstacle to overcoming mistrust. According to Radchenko, Mao initially approved the March 2, 1969, ambush against Soviet border guards at Zhenbao/Damanskii Island in order to deter the Soviet Union and perhaps encourage revolutionary spirit around the world, including within China. Mao assumed that the Soviets knew that China was not able to fight a war because of its focus on domestic affairs and weak nuclear deterrent. According to Mao, "The Soviets know that we will not invade their country as it is so cold there."[1] When the Soviets struck back on March 15 and 17, Mao was perplexed. Not understanding how the Soviets might view his previous provocative behavior as irrational, dangerous, and threatening, Mao inferred that the Soviets must be trying to get "face" by counterattacking. Mao assumed that the Soviet response must be motivated by internal difficulties rather than by fear of China. Mao's inability to understand how his actions were viewed by others made it impossible for him to understand the level of mistrust, much less take action to overcome it.

In contrast, Mikhail Gorbachev gradually came to understand how US perceptions of threat prevented the Reagan administration from reciprocating his arms control concessions. Partly due to the "New Thinking" in the Soviet Union, which borrowed the concept of mutual security from the Europeans, and partly due to his interactions with Reagan, Gorbachev realized that he would have to change Western images of the Soviet Union and reassure Western publics about Soviet intentions in order to get the United States to make agreements on arms control and allow more technology transfers.[2]

Trust is necessary for agreements between adversaries because of ineluctable uncertainty. Even if the other side currently intends to keep the agreement, its intentions could change due to a change in leadership or circumstances. Yet the attempt to increase trust by acquiring more information about the adversary can contribute paradoxically to greater mistrust, as Simon Rofe shows in chapter 3. Trust is based on calculation, but it also includes an emotional component, a willingness to make a leap of faith.[3] President George H. W. Bush, with his cautious nature, tried to garner as much information as possible to determine whether he could trust Gorbachev. But ultimately, the gap could not be bridged with intelligence and expertise alone. Even if Gorbachev himself was sincere, no one knew how long the Soviet system would survive or how long Gorbachev could cling to power before being replaced by a hard-liner. As the editors indicate, trust is an open-ended process. Trust can only be demonstrated over time by observing whether the other side keeps the agreement, a factor that contributed to President Bush's innate predisposition to a cautious policy. Bush was immobilized by the need for greater certainty, and as a result he may have missed opportunities to strengthen Gorbachev domestically by providing more financial and political support.

Establishing certainty as a criterion for arms control verification ultimately also led to greater mistrust. No verification system can eliminate the need for trust, because there is always some probability that the other side may be able to cheat and that the language of the treaty may allow for different interpretations. According to Arvid Schors (chapter 4), during the SALT I negotiations the US government tried to build domestic support for arms control by arguing that agreements with the Soviets were not based on trust; instead, US verification capabilities would detect any violations. When inevitable compliance issues arose, there was a domestic backlash in the United States against Soviet cheating, which undermined the prospects for the ratification of SALT II. Setting up the artificial standard of absolute certainty created the basis for subsequent mistrust. Although the short-term consequences were negative for US-Soviet relations, Schors concludes that the realization that SALT verification would inevitably entail ambiguities, and that the gray areas helped undermine the strict lines drawn between the United States and the Soviet Union, contributed to a reconceptualization of the Cold War relationship that outlasted détente.

Trust requires accepting vulnerability to loss due to the other's violation of trust. While it is usually assumed that vulnerability refers to the risk of being attacked, vulnerability can also mean the possibility of shame, humiliation, or loss of prestige. This is one of the themes of chapter 2: Sarah Snyder's discussion of Reagan's efforts to persuade Gorbachev to release dissidents and other Soviet citizens who wished to emigrate. Snyder argues that Reagan's promise not to "crow" publicly over Soviet human rights concessions was important in inducing Gorbachev to accept the risk of domestic criticism and international loss of face. In chapter 6, Nicholas Wheeler, Joshua Baker, and Laura Considine explore different sources of vulnerability. For example, some Soviet officials were concerned that onsite inspection would be a cover for US espionage. Gorbachev's acceptance of onsite inspection in the Stockholm agreement was therefore a major concession and a sign of his increased trust in Reagan. Thus, rather than verification leading to trust, trust was required for verification. Gorbachev also assumed the risk that the Reagan administration might take advantage of his arms control concessions. Consistent with Snyder's findings, Wheeler, Baker, and Considine argue that the Reagan administration's policy of rhetorical restraint—that is, not taking credit publicly for Soviet concessions—was important in winning Gorbachev's trust.

Trust-building may also be a strategy aimed at achieving other goals rather than an intrinsic goal. In chapter 2, Snyder indicates that Gorbachev initially wished to induce greater trust in the West of Soviet intentions so that he could obtain arms control agreements, advanced technology, and trade that could help improve the Soviet economy. Partly as a result of Reagan's numerous personal appeals, Gorbachev eventually realized that the Soviet Union would have to carry out the Helsinki Final Act provisions on human rights to prove Soviet good faith and reliability. Similarly, Michael Cotey Morgan's analysis of the Conference on Security and Cooperation in Europe (CSCE) negotiations (chapter 5) suggests that Eastern and Western states did not perceive their efforts as aimed at building greater trust between the two blocs but as a means to achieve concrete objectives. The Soviet Union wanted to achieve international recognition of existing borders in Europe, while the Western European countries wished to induce the Soviet government to allow more contacts between citizens in Eastern and Western Europe and to show greater respect for individual human rights.

One shared insight emerging from both chapters 2 and 5 is the linkage between domestic and international trust. During the CSCE negotiations, according to Morgan, the Western countries justified the inclusion of human rights on the grounds that governments that did not respect their citizens were unlikely to respect their neighbors. Similarly, Snyder reports that the Reagan administration linked Soviet respect for human rights obligations to the United States' ability to trust Soviet international commitments.

States may use their reputation for trustworthiness as a bargaining asset, as Morgan found in his analysis of the CSCE negotiations, where the neutral countries were able to exercise more influence than could have been predicted based on their material power. The reverse holds true as well. Henry Kissinger tried, and failed, to exploit the mutual confidence of the NATO alliance in order to get the other Western European countries to accept Soviet positions on human rights, but trust in the United States did not translate into trust for him personally.

Personal relations between leaders mattered in building trust. This was particularly evident in the relations between Ronald Reagan and Mikhail Gorbachev. According to Wheeler, Baker, and Considine, strong emotions of elation followed by disappointment were evoked by the October 1986 Reykjavik meeting, when Reagan and Gorbachev came very close to agreeing to the abolition of nuclear weapons. Having gone through the emotional disappointment together, they developed an intuitive sense that the other was serious about ending the Cold War. One of the problems with interpersonal trust, however, is that it may not survive a change in leadership.

Whereas we usually think of personal trust as existing between individual leaders, in chapter 7 Jens Gieseke presents evidence that the East German public trusted in the good intentions of Willy Brandt more so than in those of his successor Helmut Schmidt. Brandt was very good at making symbolic gestures, such as visiting Erfurt in East Germany and allowing the East German crowd to glimpse him at the hotel window, showing the importance of communication of trust, as the editors suggest. Even the Stasi observed—with disappointment—the strong trust that linked the East German population with the Brandt administration. Brandt's resignation in 1974 removed much of the emotional component of the trust that the East Germans bore for West Germany.

The task of building trust is affected by the environment and political context. It was much easier to build trust in the 1970s before the renewal of Cold War with the Soviet invasion of Afghanistan in 1979 and the early years of the Reagan administration. In the détente period, there were popular expectations of increased cooperation, openness, and reduced tension. During the 1970s, in addition to the emotional bond that East German people developed for Brandt, the East Germans had high expectations for increased trade and travel between East and West Germany, increased liberalization of the German Democratic Republic (GDR), and even reunification, according to the evidence surveyed by Gieseke.

In contrast, efforts to build trust between the superpowers led to greater mistrust within each bloc. Smaller countries within each alliance seemingly feared that the superpowers might make a deal at their expense. As Morgan shows in chapter 5, this was the case for the CSCE negotiations, where the Western countries did not trust the United States to look after their interests. The Helsinki Final Act represented a calculated judgment that it was preferable to trust than to mistrust the other bloc in order to achieve each side's interests. During the détente years, Effie Pedaliu argues in chapter 11, both Denmark and Greece were increasingly concerned about their security against a Soviet attack. Although the decline in North Atlantic Treaty Organization (NATO) solidarity should not have affected Switzerland, a neutral state, it was also increasingly distrustful of the West as a result of détente, as Sandra Bott and Janick Marina Schaufelbuehl demonstrate in chapter 12. Switzerland's approach to trust-building took the form of greater engagement in international diplomacy such as the CSCE to improve the Swiss image and therefore increase the probability that it would be defended in the event of war.

Denmark's and Greece's mistrust of US protection, Pedaliu argues, may be traced back to the 1960s, when the United States became involved in the Vietnam War and supported the Greek junta (1967–74). This mistrust was structural in origin. As the leader of the NATO alliance and a superpower, the United States had interests in global stability that the smaller members did not share. In contrast to West Germany, which was part of the NATO Central Front that would be defended at all costs, Denmark and Greece were on the flanks of the alliance and conceivably would be considered dispensable in the event of war with the Soviet Union. Pedaliu relates how in the early 1980s, this distrust was expressed in the form of "footnotes" in official NATO documents that expressed disagreement on nuclear issues, a singularly ineffective but symbolic form of protest. In the end, security concerns took precedence over both states' distrust of the United States and the populations' anti-American sentiments.

In the case of the Warsaw Pact, as Jens Boysen shows in chapter 8, cooperation between East Germany and Poland was based not on mutual trust or ideological solidarity but on a combination of coercion and leadership by the Soviet Union. Mistrust between East Germany and Poland was based in part on the history of German occupation, and in part on conflicting territorial interests, following the Soviet grant of substantial German territory to Poland at the end of World War II. Because of their lack of domestic legitimacy, the Polish communists emphasized to their population the need for Soviet protection against German revanchism and radical nationalism. Also without much domestic support, the GDR regarded alignment with the Soviet Union as necessary for its regime's continued existence. When Gorbachev hinted that the Soviet Union might consider giving up its external empire, the GDR tried to defend the status quo even against the Soviet Union as well as the Poles. The East German National People's Army general staff was highly suspicious of Gorbachev's defensive military doctrine, even though it would have reduced destruction to East Germany. Poland's image of West Germany improved, while the Polish leadership became more suspicious of East Germany for trying to defend socialism while secretly aiming at reunification.

More research needs to be done on the mechanisms underlying the development of trust. According to Morgan in chapter 5, in the CSCE negotiations,

Western and Eastern countries had different approaches to building trust. The West believed that transparency and openness would create greater trust between blocs; the East argued that firmer borders and more predictable interactions could lead to trust. In this case, the West mostly won the argument because the Soviets were willing to allow somewhat more openness in order to obtain Western recognition of borders established at the end of World War II and of their sphere of influence in Eastern Europe.

Trust can also be created through institutionalized exchanges, according to Noël Bonhomme and Emmanuel Mourlon-Druol's discussion of the Group of Seven (G7) and the Council of Europe in chapter 9. Thomas Schelling has theorized that trust is often created by the expectation of future profitable exchanges whose value outweighs the momentary gain from cheating and which will be lost if trust is violated.[4] The Council of Europe and the G7 were venues for the first regular summits between leaders since the beginning of the Cold War. Indeed, regular exchanges may be a substitute for lack of trust, because leaders who know that they will have to meet their counterparts have an incentive to reach agreement and to observe their obligations.[5] The institutionalization of such meetings also compensated for changes in leadership, helping to bridge differences when interpersonal trust was no longer available. Through regular meetings, the leaders were "socialized" to accept the rules and norms of the G7 as well as the content of international issues. The G7 summitry also aimed to create trust in the Western financial system— "system trust," in sociologist Niklas Luhmann's terms, whereby people can have confidence in the predictability and reliability of institutions affecting their everyday lives.[6] Increasing globalization of financial markets and the resulting instability created the need for an institution to coordinate policy and manage periodic crises.

Trust was enhanced by the evolution of a group identity for members of the G7. According to social identity theory in social psychology, the creation of a superordinate identity is one means for groups to view each other more positively.[7] Another approach to creating a broader shared identity was public diplomacy between the United States and West Germany in the 1980s, which promulgated a narrative of a common identity between Americans and the Germans based on their shared heritage of Western values going back to the Greeks and Romans, as Reinhild Kreis discusses in chapter 10. Public diplomacy between the United States and West Germany also tried to increase mutual familiarity as a basis for greater trust through such mechanisms as exchange programs, working groups, conferences, and cultural institutes. Familiarity enhances predictability, a component of trust.[8] It was hoped that greater familiarity on the interpersonal level would promote greater trust at the international level. Public diplomacy received government support and attention because officials on both sides feared that the successor generation of West Germans would decline to support the transatlantic alliance, since they had only memories of US involvement in the Vietnam War rather than of the more benevolent origins of NATO and the Berlin airlift. Whereas many West Germans were concerned that the United States no longer had the moral stature to lead the Western alliance, the Americans were worried about the risk of German neutralism. Reports, speeches, and articles by West Germans and Americans, many of whom had participated in the birth of the NATO alliance, sought to educate the public on the golden age of alliance-building and the sense of common effort, shared enterprise, and sacrifice.

For relations between adversaries, creating a superordinate identity—which would allow each to view the other as a member of the in-group—is not feasible. Instead, the primary means of building trust seems to be acceptance of vulnerability through the mechanism of costly concessions. Snyder (chapter 2) and Wheeler, Baker, and Considine (chapter 6) argue that costly concessions by Gorbachev in the field of human rights and arms control verification, as well as Reagan's restraint in publicizing these concessions or taking advantage of the Soviet Union, were the basis of greater US-Soviet trust.

Can trust be built between adversaries through means other than costly concessions? Can symbolism substitute in some manner for material concessions? Do regularized summit meetings between adversaries increase mutual trust, or at least cooperation? Other questions for future research relate to alliance management in the context of détente and cooperation. How can the alliance leader reassure smaller allies about the credibility of its commitment to defend them while at the same time cooperating with the adversary? These problems are perennial, as shown in recent US negotiations that have tried to secure a rapprochement with Iran while preserving Washington's ties to traditional allies in the Middle East.[9] The process of trust-building is complex and multidimensional, with wide-ranging consequences for international peace and cooperation.

Notes

1. Cited in Chen Jian and David Wilson, "All Under the Heaven Is Great Chaos: Beijing, the Sino-Soviet Border Clashes, and the Turn Toward Sino-American Rapprochement, 1968–69," *Cold War International History Project Bulletin* 11 (Winter 1998), 162.

2. See Nicholas Wheeler, Joshua Baker, and Laura Considine's chapter in this volume.

3. J. David Lewis and Andrew Weigert, "Trust as a Social Reality," *Social Forces* 63, no. 4 (June 1985), 970.

4. Thomas C. Schelling, *The Strategy of Conflict* (Cambridge, MA: Harvard University Press, 1960), 45–46.

5. Robert Keohane, *After Hegemony: Cooperation and Discord in the World Political Economy* (Princeton, NJ: Princeton University Press, 1984).

6. Niklas Luhmann, *Trust and Power: Two Works* (New York: Wiley, 1979).

7. Mathias Blanz, Amélie Mummendey, Rosemarie Mielke, and Andreas Klink, "Responding to Negative Social Identity: A Taxonomy of Identity Management Strategies," *European Journal of Social Psychology* 28, no. 5 (1998): 697–729; and John F. Dovidio, Samuel L. Gaertner, and Tamar Saguy, "Commonality and the Complexity of 'We': Social Attitudes and Social Change," *Personality and Social Psychology Review* 13, no. 1 (2009): 3–20.

8. "Introduction," in Deborah Welch Larson, *Anatomy of Mistrust: U.S.-Soviet Relations during the Cold War* (Ithaca, NY: Cornell University Press, 1997), 19.

9. Roula Khalaf, "The Real Cost of the Iran Deal," *Financial Times*, August 31, 2015, 7.

Contributors

Joshua Baker is an Economic and Social Research Council–funded doctoral researcher in the Department of Political Science and International Studies and the Institute for Conflict, Cooperation and Security at the University of Birmingham, United Kingdom.

Noël Bonhomme is a high school teacher (professeur agrégé) and lecturer at the Institut d'études politiques, University of Strasbourg and the University of Paris I. Under the supervision of Éric Bussière, he is finishing his doctorate at the University of Paris IV–Sorbonne on "Le complexe du directoire: la politique française et les sommets du G7 (1975–1991)" [The complex of directorate: French politics and the G7 summits (1975–1991)]. His research areas of interest include the history of diplomatic practices, the Cold War, European integration, economic globalization, and international organizations.

Sandra Bott is a research associate at the University of Lausanne, Switzerland, and is currently in Singapore, pursuing her research project on the political and economic role of neutral nations in the Cold War. Notably, she has published *La Suisse et l'Afrique du Sud, 1945–1990: commerce, finance et achats d'or durant l'apartheid* [Switzerland and South Africa, 1945–1990: Trade, finance, and gold purchases during apartheid] (Chronos, 2013). She holds a PhD in history from the University of Lausanne.

Jens Boysen is a historian and political scientist specializing in civil-military relations, most notably in Central Europe. Since 2010, he has been a research fellow at the German Historical Institute Warsaw. Previously, he worked for the College of Europe in Bruges, the Simon Dubnow Institute at Leipzig, and the University of Leipzig. He received his doctorate from the University of Tübingen in 2008. Currently, he is finalizing a postdoctoral thesis on the societal role of armies in communist Poland and East Germany.

Laura Considine is a lecturer in international relations at the University of Leeds. She received her doctorate from Aberystwyth University in 2014.

Jens Gieseke is head of the "Communism and Society" department at the Centre for Contemporary History, Potsdam. His major publications include *The Silent Majority in Communist and Post-Communist States: Opinion Polling in Eastern and South-Eastern Europe*, edited with Klaus Bachmann (Peter Lang, 2016); *The History of the Stasi: East Germany's Secret Police, 1945– 1990* (Berghahn, 2014); *Soziale Ungleichheit im Staatssozialismus* [Social inequality in state socialism], special issue of *Zeithistorische Forschungen* 10 (2013), edited with Klaus Gestwa and Jan-Holger Kirsch; *Die Geschichte der SED. Eine Bestandsaufnahme* [The history of the SED: An appraisal], edited with Hermann Wentker (Metropol, 2011); and *Die hauptamtlichen Mitarbeiter der Staatssicherheit. Personalstruktur und Lebenswelt 1950–1989/90* [The full-time employees of state security: Personnel structure and environment, 1950–1989/90] (Ch. Links, 2000).

Martin Klimke is associate dean of humanities and associate professor of history at New York University Abu Dhabi, as well as an associated faculty member of the NYU History Department. He is the author of *The Other Alliance: Student Protest in West Germany and the United States in the Global Sixties, 1962–1972* (Princeton University Press, 2010) and coauthor, with Maria Höhn, of *A Breath of Freedom: The Civil Rights Struggle, African-American GIs, and Germany* (Palgrave Macmillan, 2010). He is coeditor of the Protest, Culture and Society series from Berghahn Books and of several volumes on various aspects of transatlantic and transnational history, protest movements and cultures, as well as the Cold War, most recently *Nuclear Threats, Nuclear Fear and the Cold War of the 1980s* (Cambridge University Press, 2016), edited with Eckart Conze and Jeremy Varon.

Reinhild Kreis is assistant professor at the University of Mannheim. Her research focuses on the history of consumption, diplomatic history, German-American relations, protest history, and the history of emotions. Her publications include *Orte für Amerika. Deutsch-Amerikanische Institute und Amerikahäuser in der Bundesrepublik seit den 1960er Jahren* [Places for America: The German-American Institute and America Houses in the Federal Republic since the 1960s] (Franz Steiner, 2012) and the edited volume *Diplomatie mit Gefühl. Vertrauen, Misstrauen und die Außenpolitik der Bundesrepublik Deutschland* [Diplomacy with feeling: Trust, mistrust, and the foreign policy of the Federal Republic of Germany] (De Gruyter Oldenbourg, 2015).

Her current project is on "Making Things Oneself in an Age of Consumption: Values, Social Order, and Practices from the Late 19th Century to the 1980s."

Deborah Welch Larson is professor of political science at the University of California, Los Angeles. Her book *Anatomy of Mistrust: U.S.-Soviet Relations during the Cold War* (Cornell University Press, 2000) uses social psychology to explain missed opportunities for US-Soviet cooperation. Larson's articles have appeared in *International Organization, International Security*, and *International Studies Quarterly*. She is currently doing research with Alexei Shevchenko on how status-seeking affects the foreign policy of China and Russia, using social identity theory in social psychology. Her most recent book is *Status in World Politics*, edited with T. V. Paul and William C. Wohlforth (Cambridge University Press, 2014).

Michael Cotey Morgan is assistant professor of history at the University of North Carolina at Chapel Hill. He is the author of a forthcoming book on the origins of the Helsinki Final Act.

Emmanuel Mourlon-Druol is Lord Kelvin Adam Smith Fellow in the Adam Smith Business School, University of Glasgow, and visiting professor at the Université Libre de Bruxelles. Educated at the European University Institute, he was previously Pinto Postdoctoral Fellow at London School of Economics. He is the author of *A Europe Made of Money: The Emergence of the European Monetary System* (Cornell University Press, 2012), and co-editor, with Federico Romero, of *International Summitry and Global Governance: The Rise of the G7 and the European Council, 1974–1991* (Routledge, 2014). He has published in journals such as *Business History, Contemporary European History, JCMS: Journal of Common Market Studies*, and *West European Politics*.

Christian F. Ostermann is the director of the History and Public Policy Program, which includes the Cold War International History Project, at the Woodrow Wilson International Center for Scholars in Washington, D.C. His publications include *Connecting Histories: Decolonization and the Cold War in Southeast Asia, 1945–1962*, edited with Christopher E. Goscha (Woodrow Wilson Center Press and Stanford University Press, 2009), and *Uprising in East Germany 1953: The Cold War, the German Question, and the First Major Upheaval behind the Iron Curtain* (Central European University Press, 2001).

Effie G. H. Pedaliu is a fellow at LSE IDEAS. She is the author of *Britain, Italy, and the Origins of the Cold War* (Palgrave Macmillan, 2003) and coeditor, with John W. Young and Michael Kandiah, of *Britain in Global Politics: Volume 2, From Churchill to Blair* (Palgrave Macmillan, 2013). Her latest publication is "Human Rights and International Security: The International Community and the Greek Dictators," *International History Review* 3 (March 2016). She is a member of the peer review college of the Arts and Humanities Research Council, and coeditor, with John W. Young, of the Security, Conflict and Cooperation in the Contemporary World series from Palgrave Macmillan.

Sergey Radchenko is Zi Jiang Distinguished Professor at East China Normal University, Shanghai, and professor of international relations at Cardiff University. He is also a Global Fellow at the Woodrow Wilson International Center for Scholars in Washington, D.C. He is the author of, among other books, *Two Suns in the Heavens: The Sino-Soviet Struggle for Supremacy, 1962–1967* (Woodrow Wilson Center Press and Stanford University Press, 2009) and *Unwanted Visionaries: The Soviet Failure in Asia at the End of the Cold War* (Oxford University Press, 2014).

J. Simon Rofe is senior lecturer in diplomatic and international studies, program director for the master's degree in global diplomacy, and lead instructor on the Coursera "Global Diplomacy" and "Understanding Research Methods" modules at SOAS, University of London. His research interests focus on international and transnational histories of postwar planning, diplomatic practice, sport and diplomacy, and twenty-first century pedagogies. Recent books include *Global Diplomacy: Theories, Types, and Models*, with Alison Holmes (Westview Press, 2016); *International History and International Relations*, with Andrew Williams and Amelia Hadfield (Routledge, 2012); and *The Embassy in Grosvenor Square: American Ambassadors to the United Kingdom, 1938–2008*, with Alison Holmes (Palgrave Macmillan, 2012)

Janick Marina Schaufelbuehl is assistant professor of the history of international relations at the University of Lausanne. Her recent publications include *Neutrality and Neutralism in the Global Cold War: Between or Within the Blocs?*, edited with Sandra Bott, Jussi M. Hanhimäki, and Marco Wyss (Routledge, 2016).

Arvid Schors is assistant professor (Akademischer Rat auf Zeit) of modern history at the University of Freiburg. He received his doctorate from the University of Freiburg in 2015. His dissertation will be published as a monograph by Wallstein Verlag in fall 2016, under the title *Doppelter Boden. Die SALT-Verhandlungen 1963–1979* [Uncertain ground: The SALT negotiations, 1963–1979].

Sarah B. Snyder is an associate professor at the School of International Service at American University. She is a historian of US foreign relations who specializes in the history of the Cold War, human rights activism, and US human rights policy. Her book *Human Rights Activism and the End of the Cold War: A Transnational History of the Helsinki Network* (Cambridge University Press, 2011) analyzes the development of a transnational network devoted to human rights advocacy and its contributions to the end of the Cold War. She is completing her second book on US human rights activism in the long 1960s for Columbia University Press.

Nicholas J. Wheeler is professor of international relations and director of the Institute for Conflict, Cooperation and Security at the University of Birmingham. His publications include *The Security Dilemma: Fear, Cooperation, and Trust in World Politics*, with Ken Booth (Palgrave Macmillan, 2008); *National Interest and International Solidarity: Particular and Universal Ethics in International Life*, edited with Jean-Marc Coicaud (New York: United Nations University Press, 2008); and *The British Origins of Nuclear Strategy, 1945–1955*, with Ian Clark (Oxford: Oxford University Press). He has also written widely on humanitarian intervention, and is the author of *Saving Strangers: Humanitarian Intervention in International Society* (Oxford: Oxford University Press, 2000). His most recent book, *Trusting Enemies*, is under contract with Oxford University Press. He is coeditor, with Christian Reus-Smit and Evelyn Goh, of the Cambridge Studies in International Relations series from Cambridge University Press.

Index

Figures and tables are indicated by "f" and "t" respectively.

ABM. *See* Anti-Ballistic Missile (ABM) Treaty (1972)
ACDA. *See* Arms Control and Disarmament Agency
Achilles, Ted, 222, 225
ACUS (Atlantic Council of the United States), 224–25, 227, 228
Adamishin, Anatoly, 52, 53, 54
Adenauer, Konrad, 173
adequate verification, 93–94
Afghanistan, Soviet invasion of, 96, 212, 222, 237, 283
Akhromeyev, Sergey, 134
Albania: China's relationship with, 21; CSCE, nonparticipation in, 267
alliances and blocs: alliance security dilemma, 243, 244; Cold War structure of, 3, 154; divisions within, at CSCE, 105–9; emergence of trust in, 240. *See also* NATO; Warsaw Pact
Amerikahaus (Munich cultural center), 221
Anatomy of Mistrust (Larson), 28
Andreotti, Giulio, 205, 211
Andropov, Yuri, 44, 45, 136n20
anti-Americanism, 10, 224, 240, 246, 248, 284
Anti-Ballistic Missile (ABM) Treaty (1972), 90, 123
anticommunism, Reagan's, 42, 56n10

appeasement, Bush administration's views on, 69
Arab-Israeli conflict, 245
Arbeitsgruppe USA (Working Group on the USA), 225
Arctic, Soviet naval power in, 244
Arendt, Hannah, 143
arms: arms control negotiations, 47, 50–51; arms deployments in Europe, 126, 158, 160; NATO double-track decision, 8, 156–57, 157t, 222, 237, 247; sales to Eastern bloc countries, prevention of, 261. *See also* nuclear weapons; Strategic Arms Limitation Talks; verification
Arms Control and Disarmament Agency (ACDA), 87–88, 95
Asia, Soviet proposal for collective security system in, 31, 34
"Asia after Viet Nam" (Nixon), 25
asymmetric relationships, 218
Athenian-Melian model, 242
Atlantic Council (NATO), 201–2
Atlantic Council of the United States (ACUS), 224–25, 227, 228
Atlanticists, 222, 225
Atlantic Treaty Association (ATA), 224, 227
atomization theory, 143–44
Attali, Jacques, 205, 209

Aubert, Pierre, 265
Austria, Swiss rapprochement with, 268
authenticity, 125, 126, 131, 133–34, 135
authoritarianism, 145, 162, 176, 190

back-channel negotiations, at CSCE,
   105, 109, 112, 113
Bagley, Worth, 93
Bahr, Egon, 154
Baier, Annette, 124–25
Baker, James A., III: Bush and, 63, 68,
   72–73; on Bush-Gorbachev relation-
   ship, 69; Cheney, relationship with,
   74; influence of, 72; on Saddam Hus-
   sein, 69; strategies of, 7; on trust, 66
Baker, Joshua, 8, 121, 282, 283, 286
balance of threat vs. balance of power,
   244
Barents Sea, Soviet presence in, 244
Barre, Raymond, 202
Basic Treaty (Grundvertrag), 270
Basket I (CSCE issues), 108
Basket III (CSCE issues), 108, 109, 110
Bayne, Nicholas, 203, 205
Belarus, decommissioning of weapons
   of mass destruction in, 75–76
Berling, Zygmunt, 184
Berlinguer, Sergio, 208
Berlin State Library, repatriation of col-
   lections from, 187
Berlin Wall, 148, 176
Berridge, Geoff, 67
Bindschedler, Rudolf, 261, 267–68,
   273n4
bipolarity, 243, 248, 263
blocs. See alliances and blocs
Bonhomme, Noël, 9, 198, 216n40, 285
Bonner, Elena, 46
Bonn summit (1978), 208, 211, 212
Booth, Ken, 127, 132, 135n6, 172, 177
border disputes: Damanskii/Zhenbao
   Island, 18, 20, 22–29, 36–37, 280;
   East Germany–Poland, 174–75;
   Kazakh Soviet Socialist Republic,
   30; Sino-Soviet, 6, 18, 24–29, 35–36;
   Tielieketi/Zhalanashkol, 30
Bott, Sandra, 10, 259, 284
Boysen, Jens, 9, 167, 284

Brandt, Willy: East German attitudes
   toward, 8, 148–49, 153–54, 163,
   283; Ostpolitik, 147–54, 222; on rapprochement, 182; Stasi public opinion reports on, 153; trust in, 143
Brecht, Bertolt, 144
Breitenmoser, Christoph, 275n35
Breslauer, George, 132
Bretton Woods system, 207
Brezhnev, Leonid: on China, 29–30,
   31; CSCE negotiations and, 103–4,
   106–8, 113–14; on Czechoslovakia,
   invasion of, 20; economic crises and,
   207; Helsinki Final Act, signing of,
   43; human rights stance, 44; legacy
   of, 136n20; Nixon, relationship with,
   31, 263; on Pentecostals, 56n11
Britain/United Kingdom: G5 membership, 201; NATO cruise missile
   deployments in, 126; Royal Navy,
   decline of, 244; summitry of, 109,
   111–12, 113, 212
brotherhood in arms, 168, 178–80
brotherly association (Bruderbund), 177–78
Bu, Liping, 219
Buckley, William F., 93
Bulgaria, Soviet troop buildup in, 22
Bush, George H. W., 63–81; Bush triumvirate, role of, 72–74; as Cold War
   peacemaker, 76–78; conclusions on,
   64, 281; mistrust in administration
   of, 7, 74–76; overview of, 7, 63–64;
   personal diplomacy, roots of, 65–69;
   "read my lips" pledge, 64; and Soviet
   Union's demise, 69–72

Cairo, Michael, 72
Callaghan, James, 199, 204, 210
Canada, G7 membership, 212
capacity, 63, 64, 65, 70, 77, 125–26,
   127, 131, 133
Carrington, Lord, 242
Carter, Jimmy: on Bonn G7 summit,
   208; détente and, 247; Greece's
   and Denmark's reactions to, 248;
   on human rights, 43; SALT and, 7,
   92–96; Schmidt, relationship with,
   202, 222; summits, role in, 199, 212

CCP (Chinese Communist Party), 17, 20
Central Europe, nuclear-free zone for, 177
Central Intelligence Agency (CIA), 71–72, 94–95, 136n22
Central Military Commission (China), 23, 35, 36
Centre Democrats (Denmark), 239
Chamberlain, Neville, 69
Cheney, Dick, 74
Chen Yi, 27, 34
Chernenko, Konstantin, 44, 57n18, 136n20
Chernobyl nuclear accident, 52, 128–29
Chernyaev, Anatoly, 127, 128, 129–30, 132
China, 17–41; Chinese Communist Party, 17, 20; Central Military Commission, 23, 35, 36; conclusions on, 36–37; Cultural Revolution, 17, 18, 20, 27, 37; Foreign Ministry, 23, 27; General Staff, 23; Graber's evaluation of, 262–63; Great Leap Forward, 18; Kosygin in Beijing, 32–35; overview of, 17–19; Sino-Soviet border unrest, 6, 18, 24–29, 35–36; Soviet Union, relationship with, 19–24, 29–32; UN, admission to, 268
Chmykhalov family (Pentecostals), 43–45
Christian Democrats (Italy), 210–11
Christian People's Party (Denmark), 239
CIA (Central Intelligence Agency), 71–72, 89, 91, 94–95, 136n22
Clinton, Bill, 66
CoCom. See Coordinating Committee for Multilateral Export Controls
Colby, William, 91
Cold War: Bush as peacemaker in, 76–78; as competition, 143; overview of, 1–6; Second Cold War, 155–59, 185. See also alliances and blocs; Soviet Union; transformation of Cold War order; trust
collective leadership, 208–11
collective security system, 31, 34, 261
Collet, Bernt Johan, 248
colonels' coup (Greece), 245–46

"The Coming Resurgence of Russia" (Porter), 75
Commission on Security and Cooperation in Europe (US), 53, 59n62
common security, 127, 128
communication: Bush's lines of, 75; challenges of, 96; East Germany–Poland, 179; importance of, 4, 283; informal, 162; Kissinger's strategy for, 90; Nixon's lines of, 26; trust and, 5
communist regimes, 143–45, 152, 162, 267, 269. See also Warsaw Pact
compliance, to SALT, 91
concessions: costly concessions, as signal of trustworthiness, 4–5, 8, 47, 55, 286; G7 rules of coordination and, 203, 210, 211; by Gorbachev, 6, 8, 48, 130, 280, 286; Helsinki Final Act negotiations and, 103, 108, 110, 112, 113; INF Treaty negotiations and, 129–34, 139n63; NATO and, 228; Reagan's restraint in not taking public credit for, 54, 282; Soviet concessions on human rights, 46, 49, 53, 139n63, 281; Soviet concessions on on-site inspections, 47, 282; Soviets using to disguise their continued repression, 59n62; Swiss neutrality and, 261; West German-East German agreements and, 150–52, 182
conditional trust, 145–46, 157
Conference on Security and Cooperation in Europe (CSCE), 102–20; Basket I, 108; Basket III, 108, 109, 110; conclusions on, 113–14, 282, 283; East German public opinion on, 155–59; international security, clashing visions of, 103–6; Madrid review meeting, 44–46; military affairs, discussions of, 110–13; negotiations at, 106–10; overview of, 7–8, 102–3; Poland as supporter of, 181; Switzerland's participation in, 260, 267–68, 272; US acceptance of, 247, 248
confidence, as weapon, 114
confidence-building measures, 44, 103, 104, 111–13

Congress-Bundestag Youth Exchange Program, 226, 227
Conservative People's Party (Denmark), 239
Considine, Laura, 8, 121, 282, 283, 286
cooperation, 202–4, 213. *See also* alliances and blocs
Cooperative Threat Reduction Program (CTRP, P.L. 102-228), 75, 79n22
Coordinating Committee for Multilateral Export Controls (CoCom), 261
Costigliola, Frank, 68
Council of Ministers (EEC), 201
Craxi, Bettino, 199, 206*f*
crisis of trust, 65
Crooked Circle Club (Klub Krzywego Koła), 176
CSCE. *See* Conference on Security and Cooperation in Europe
CTRP (Cooperative Threat Reduction Program, P.L. 102-228), 75, 79n22
Cuban Missile Crisis, 30–31, 243
cultures of trust, 5, 242
Cyprus dispute, 240, 246
Czechoslovakia: East Germany, attitude toward, 179; German invasion of (1938), 69, 179; Soviet invasion of (1968), 20, 21, 22, 35, 176; uprisings in, 105; West Germany, attitude toward, 176

Dallin, Alexander, 48
Damanskii/Zhenbao Island border dispute, 18, 20, 22–23, 24–29, 36–37, 280
Dean, Jonathan, 218, 219, 220
Defense Planning Committee (NATO), 247, 258n88, 258n91
de Gaulle, Charles, 243
Deng Xiaoping, 20
Denmark, 10, 238–58; conclusions on, 283–84; domestic turbulence in, 239–40; footnoting era, reaction to, 249; NATO views of (footnoting), 10, 238, 247; reduced defense spending in, 245; security concerns, 245–46; Soviet attacks, fear of, 238;

United States, relations with, 240, 248; vulnerability in NATO, 242–43
de Stoutz, Jean, 263
détente: during Cold War, 86; East German expectations of, 148; impact on NATO and Warsaw Pact, 168; public criticism of in US, 110; SALT, comparison with, 97; of superpowers, NATO tensions and, 244–46, 248. *See also* Switzerland
deterrence theory, 89
Deutsches Allgemeines Sonntagsblatt (newspaper), 228
development aid, from Switzerland, 261–62, 271
dilemma of interpretation, 172
diplomacy: diplomatic assurances, 4; Giscard on mistrust in, 198; personal (private) diplomacy, 44, 65–69, 73; public diplomacy, 48, 218–23, 226–29; quiet diplomacy, 6, 42, 46, 48, 60; step-by-step diplomacy, 204; triangular diplomacy, 28, 34, 37
Directorate of Intelligence (CIA), report on Gorbachev, 71–72
dissent, footnoting as, 239
distrust: definition of, 3; as fundamental of international relations, 1; Reagan on, 3; Switzerland and, 262–64, 266, 267–68, 272; in West, of G7, 211. *See also* East Germany and Poland, mutual dependency and distrust in; mistrust
Dobrynin, Anatoly, 31, 44, 56n12, 97n6, 103, 130
domestic politics: influence on foreign policy, 70–71; summitry and, 210–11
domestic trust, linkage with international trust, 282
double-track decision. *See* Europe, arms deployments in; Intermediate-Range Nuclear Forces (INF) Treaty; NATO; nuclear weapons
dovorey no provorey ("trust, but verify") slogan (Reagan), 4, 42, 54, 121, 134
Dubček, Alexander, 20, 35

Eagleburger, Lawrence, 224
Eastern bloc. *See* Warsaw Pact
Eastern treaties, Infratest survey on, 149–50, 149*t*
Eastern Turkestan, Uyghurs and, 35
East Germany (German Democratic Republic, GDR), 143–66; Basic Treaty, signing of, 270; Cold War as subject of popular opinion in, 146–47; conclusions on, 162–63; at CSCE, 106; and Czechoslovakia, invasion of, 176; foreign policy (1970s), 181–82; international influences on, 8–9, 159–62; national revival, 187; overview of, 143–46; prodemocracy movement in, 161; public's trust relationship with West Germany, 147–54, 283; Soviet influence on, 171–73, 178–89; superpowers, mistrust of, 155–59; Switzerland's recognition of, 262, 269–70; uprisings in, 105; West Germany, relations with, 8, 159, 162, 177. *See also* East Germany and Poland, mutual dependency and distrust in
East Germany and Poland, mutual dependency and distrust in, 167–97; during Cold War's final phase, 186–88; conclusions on, 284; crises in (1980–1985), 182–85; as forced allies, 174–78; historical legacies, impact of, 172–74; military cooperation between, 178–80; overview of, 9; rivalry and cooperation, 180–82; trust as factor in Warsaw Pact intrabloc relations, 167–72
economic sanctions, of US against China, 28
economic summits, limitations of, 208. *See also* European Councils; G7
Eisenhower, Dwight, 111, 245
elite power in communist regimes, 145, 167, 179
Ellemann-Jensen, Uffe, 240
emigration visas, for Soviet Pentecostal families, 42

encapsulated interests, 242
energy crisis, 207
Engel, Jeffrey, 68, 76, 77
English, Robert, 52, 132
Euromissile crisis, 212, 237. *See also* Intermediate-Range Nuclear Forces (INF) Treaty; NATO; nuclear weapons
Europe: arms deployments in, 126, 156, 157, 158, 160; changing American perceptions of (1980s), 222; conventional weapons imbalance in, 110; European Commission president, at G7 meetings, 213; European Economic Community, 199–200, 212, 246; European Security Conference, 177; European Union, 190n3. *See also* Conference on Security and Cooperation in Europe; *names of individual countries*
European Councils: conclusions on, 285; creation of, 200; identity in, 206; institutionalization of, 203, 204; meetings of, 199, 201*f*; purpose of, 208; as rituals, 210

familiarity, as aim of public diplomacy, 219–20, 229
"family pictures" (at summits), 206, 208
family reunification in Soviet Union, 49, 50
Far East, Soviet troop buildup in, 22, 27–28
FDP. *See* Freie Demokratische Partei
Federal Political Department (Switzerland), 262, 266, 269, 270, 272n1
Federal Republic of Germany (FRG). *See* West Germany
financial markets, globalization of, 207
Finland: CSCE negotiations, participation in, 109; Reagan speech in, 54; "self-Finlandization," 222
Fischer, Thomas, 267–68
flexible response, NATO debate over, 244
footnote era (NATO): conclusions on, 284; description of, 10, 238; gestation period of, 238–39;

footnote era (NATO) (*continued*) overview of, 237–38. *See also* United States, NATO flanks and

Ford, Gerald: CSCE negotiations, participation in, 110; Helsinki Act, signing of, 247; international crisis, fears of, 207; Italy, secret support for, 210; Kissinger's memo to, 91; on multiplication of international bodies, 200; Reagan's criticisms of, 43; SALT compliance and, 91, 92; summits, role in, 199, 201, 210

Foreign Affairs (journal), Nixon article in, 25

foreign exchange programs, West Germany–US, 226

foreign policy. *See under individual countries*

formalization of informality, 9, 213

four-leaf clover government, 239

France: CSCE negotiations, participation in, 108; G5 membership, 201; G7, views on, 211; on media at summits, 209; at Puerto Rico and London summits, 212

free movement (of individuals), 104, 106, 107–9, 111

Freie Demokratische Partei (FDP, Liberal Party, West Germany), 150, 211

Frevert, Ute, 5, 102

FRG (Federal Republic of Germany). *See* West Germany

friendship, Baker on, 69

Froment-Meurice, Henri, 208

Fukuda, Takeo, 207

G5, 201

G6/G7, 199

G7: conclusions on, 285; creation of, 199–200; identity in, 206; institutionalization of, 203, 204; limitations of, 211–13; purpose of, 208; regular meetings of, 198–99; summits of, 202, 210

GDR (German Democratic Republic). *See* East Germany

Geneva summit (CSCE, 1973–75), 103, 105, 108–10, 112, 268

Geneva summit (US-Soviet, 1985), 3, 4, 6, 42, 46–50, 51, 136n22, 128, 156, 157

Genscher, Hans-Dietrich, 263

George H. W.Bush Presidential Library, 64

German-American Friendship Garden (Washington, DC), 227

German-American Schoolbook Commission, 226

German Democratic Republic (GDR). *See* East Germany

German-German traffic treaty (1972), 152

Gierek, Edward, 180–81

Gieseke, Jens, 8, 143, 283

Giscard d'Estaing, Valéry: on economic crises, 207; European Commission, views of, 211–12; informality, preference for, 213; international crisis, fears of, 207; Italy, secret support for, 210; on media at summits, 209; on mistrust in diplomacy, 198; on Puerto Rico summit, 210; Schmidt, relationship with, 9, 198, 200, 203; summits, role in, 199, 200, 201, 212; on trust, 202

Glaspie, April, 68

Goethe-Institute, 226

Goldfarb, David and Cecilia, 56n9

Gomułka, Władysław, 9, 169, 176, 180, 182

good offices (Switzerland), 261, 265, 273n5

Gorbachev, Mikhail: Bush, relationship with, 64, 65, 69, 281; conclusions on, 280, 281–82; influences on, 137n33; INF treaty and, 4, 121, 130–34; Poland, influence on, 9; Reagan, relationship with, 42, 46–50, 55n1, 126, 134; Reagan's trustworthiness, changing perceptions of, 8, 126–30; Reagan's vs. Bush's understanding of, 67; at Reykjavik summit, 51–52; Soviet reform culture and, 46–47; Soviet-US deadlock, breaking of, 124; on trust, 3; at Vienna CSCE Review Meeting, 53–55;

Warsaw Pact countries, impact on, 186, 190; Yeltsin as challenge to, 70–72, 74–75. *See also* concessions

"The Gorbachev Succession" (Directorate of Intelligence, CIA), 71–72

Graber, Pierre, 262–64, 266, 267, 270–71, 272

Grachev, Andrei, 130

graduated and reciprocated initiatives in tension reduction. *See* GRIT

Graybeal, Sidney, 91

"Greatest Generation," 67, 77, 78n13

Greece, 10, 238–58; conclusions on, 283–84; détente, views of, 245; dictatorship in, 245–46, 248; footnoting era, reaction to, 249; NATO views of (footnoting), 10, 238, 247–48, 258n91; Soviet attacks, fear of, 238; United States, relations with, 248; vulnerability in NATO, 242–43

Green Party (West Germany), 224, 228

Grinevsky, Oleg, 129, 134

Grishin, Victor, 132

GRIT (graduated and reciprocated initiatives in tension reduction), 29

Gromyko, Andrei, 45, 53, 109, 112, 127

Group of Five. See G5

Group of Six/Seven. See G6/G7

Group of Seven. *See* G7

Grundvertrag (Basic Treaty), 270

Guadeloupe summit (1979), 212

Haig, Alexander, 45

Haig-Davos Agreement (1978), 240

Hamm-Brücher, Hildegard, 224, 228, 229

Hammer, Armand, 56n9

Hanhimäki, Jussi, 85–86

Hansen, Lynn, 134

Harmel Report (1967), 244

Hartling, Poul, 246

Hartman, Arthur, 53

Hartmann, Martin, 4

Healey, Denis, 244

healthy suspicion, mistrust as, 3

Hedtoft, Hans, 243

hegemony in NATO, 242

Helms, Richard, 89

helplessness, East Germans' self-perception of, 156

Helsinki Final Act (1975): absence of trust and, 7; character of, 103; compromises in, 113; conclusions on, 282, 283; contents of, 110; East German public opinion on, 155–56; Reagan on, 43, 47, 54; signing of, 43, 247; source of, 102; Soviet Union's upholding of, 52

Helsinki summit. *See* Conference on Security and Cooperation in Europe (CSCE), Helsinki Final Act

Hermes, Peter, 225

Hewitt, Ed, 71

Hill, Edward, 22

historical legacies, impact on East Germany–Poland relations, 172–74

historical materialism, Warsaw Pact and, 168–69

historiography, role of emotions in, 5

"Historische Standortbestimmung" (Historic Positioning) group, 276n50

history of trust, 171

Hitler, Adolf, 34, 69, 79n21, 174

Ho Chi Minh, 32, 279

Hoffman, Aaron M., 124, 198, 203, 204, 206

Holocaust Memorial Museum (US), 223

Home Army (Poland), 174

Honecker, Erich, 150, 152–53, 159, 181, 183, 195n59, 195n61

horizontal trust, 9, 146, 160, 163

Hoyer, Steny, 53

human rights, 42, 43, 46–49, 51, 105

Hungary, uprisings in, 105

Huntley, James, 225

Hürlimann, Hans, 265

identity: collective identity of Warsaw Pact members, 171, 176; G7 group identity, 285; political identity of West, 167; role in trust relationships, 50, 188, 206; shared, 285

ideological fundamentalism, 127, 135n6

incremental processes, benefits of, 204

independent peace movement in East Germany, 9, 161–62

indirect (subversive-revolutionary) war, 265
informality, institutionalization of, 213
information asymmetry, 98n6
Infratest (opinion research institute, West Germany): Eastern treaties, survey on, 149–50, 149*t*; public opinion surveys, 147, 148, 151–54, 151*t*, 154*t*, 159, 164n14; public opinion surveys, on international issues, 155, 155–56*t*; public opinion surveys, on international peace movement, 161, 161*t*
INF Treaty. *See* Intermediate-Range Nuclear Forces (INF) Treaty
Inglehart, Ronald, 225, 233n34
institutions: institutionalized summitry, 200, 202–3, 285; role in trust relationships, 203
integrity/reliability pair, 177
Interim Agreement on Strategic Arms. *See* Strategic Arms Limitation Talks (SALT)
Intermediate-Range Nuclear Forces (INF) Treaty, 121–39; conclusions on, 134–35; Gorbachev's changing perceptions of trustworthiness, 126–30; Gorbachev's vulnerability and, 130–34; importance of verification in, 4; overview of, 8, 121–22; trust, trustworthiness, and vulnerability in, 124–26; trust and verification of, 122–24
intermesticity, 64, 143–46, 210, 239, 241
International Development Association (Switzerland), 271
international peace movement, 159–62, 161*t*
international relations: emotional dimensions of, 1; international security, clashing visions of, at CSCE, 103–6; international trust, linkage with domestic trust, 282; rarity of trust in, 102. *See also* Conference on Security and Cooperation in Europe; Warsaw Pact; *names of individual countries*
interpersonal trust, limitations of, 283
Iran, 122, 131, 139n70, 286

Iraq, 65; invasion of Kuwait, UN response to, 68–69, 72–73
isolation, Swiss desire to avoid, 266–69
Israelyan, Viktor, 123
Italy, 205, general election (1976), 210–11; at summits, 198, 208, 210, 212

Jackson-Vanik Amendment, 110
Jagiellonian Library, 187
Japan, 27, 36, 212; first international meeting organized by, 205; G5 membership, 201; summit participation, 198, 203, 205, 206*f*, 207, 212–13
Jaruzelski, Wojciech, 184, 187
Jewish refuseniks, 44–45, 52–53, 54–55
Jinmen Island, 19, 24
Jørgensen, Anker, 239

Kampelman, Max M., 44–46, 57n24, 57n26, 58n29
Kania, Stanisław, 183, 184
Karamanlis, Konstantinos, 246
Kazakh Soviet Socialist Republic border dispute, 30
Kazakhstan, decommissioning of weapons of mass destruction in, 75–76
Keating, Vincent, 125
Kelleher, Catherine McArdle, 222
Kennedy, John F., 51, 163, 243
Kessler, Heinz, 184
KGB (Soviet secret service), 110
Khrushchev, Nikita, 19, 22, 23–24, 29, 177
Kim Il Sung, 36
Kissinger, Henry: Bush and, 63, 66; conclusions on, 282–83; CSCE negotiations, participation in, 108–10, 112–14; Dobrynin and, 31, 103; on multiplication of international bodies, 200; quiet diplomacy, support for, 48; on SALT compliance and verification, 91; SALT I and, 90
Klimke, Martin, 1
Klub Krzywego Koła (Crooked Circle Club), 176
Kohl, Helmut, 63–64, 159, 163, 199, 206*f*, 214*f*
Kola Peninsula, 244, 245

Kosygin, Alexei, 26, 27, 29, 32–35, 279–80
Krass, Allan, 87, 123
Krauthammer, Charles, 77
Kreis, Reinhild, 1, 9, 218, 285
Kulikov, Victor, 184–85
Kuwait: Iraq's invasion of, 68–69, 72–73
Kydd, Andrew H., 46, 198

Lafontaine, Oskar, 223, 232n25
Lamberz, Werner, 150
language, of trust, 5
Lapidus, Gail W., 48
Larson, Deborah Welch: on basis for mistrust in international politics, 28; on Bush's actions on Gorbachev, 75; on concessions, costs of, 55; conclusions by, 10, 279–86; on consistency, 67; on individuals, importance of, 50; on lost opportunities, 271; on mistrust, 4; on trust, 44, 55n1, 66, 241
leaders, trust between, 199–206. See also names of individual leaders
learning, role in trust relationships, 203–6
Lebow, Richard Ned, 132
Lenin, Vladimir, 189
Liao Heshu, 26
liberal democracies, global crisis of, 207
Liberal Party (West Germany). See Freie Demokratische Partei
liberal values, summitry support for, 208
limited linkage (US negotiating stance), 133
Lin Biao, 17, 35
Liu Shaoqi, 20
Liu Zhinan, 35
Loeb, Nackey, 56n9
London summit (1977), 208, 212
loose nukes, fear of, 75
Lop Nor, China, nuclear facilities at, 35
Louis, Victor, 35
Louvre summit (1987), 205
loyalty: among East German elites, 145; among Warsaw Pact members, 179; Bush's loyalty to Baker, 72; of East Germany and Poland to Soviet Union, 175, 179, 184

Lublin Committee (Polish Committee of National Liberation, Polski Komitet Wyzwolenia Narodowego), 173–74, 175–76
Lugar, Richard, 75
Luhmann, Niklas, 3
Luns, Joseph M. A. H., 240

Madrid, Spain, CSCE review meeting in, 44–46, 57n17
Making the World Like Us (Bu), 219
Malta conference (1991), 69
Mansfield, Mike, 28
Mao Zedong: international situation, misjudgment of, 36–37; Khrushchev, relationship with, 23–24; Kosygin, relationship with, 32, 279; on mice, 36; at Ninth National Congress, 17; Nixon, meeting with, 269; Soviet beliefs on, 29–30; on Soviet invasion of Czechoslovakia, 21; Soviet Union, perceptions of, 6, 20, 28–29, 280; Stalin, mistrust of, 23; turn to West, historical analysis of, 18–19; United States, mistrust of, 26; Zhenbao Island clashes, response to, 24–29
Marxism, 188
Mason, Roy, 244
Massie, Suzanne, 56n9
massive retaliation strategy, 243
Matlock, Jack, 43–44, 48, 52, 53
Mazu Island, 19, 24
MBFR. See mutual and balanced force reductions
McCloy, John, 225
media, summitry and, 208–9
Mediterranean, 244, 245
MfS (Ministry for State Security, East Germany). See Stasi
military affairs, CSCE discussions of, 110–13
Ministry for State Security (MfS). See Stasi
mistrust: in Bush administration, 74–76; China-Soviet, 23; in Cold War credibility rituals, 87; in communist regimes, 145; as fundamental of international relations, 1;

mistrust (*continued*)
impact of, as baseline, 279–80;
Kydd's definition of, 46; O'Neill
on, 72; overcoming, 4; Reagan's, of
Soviet leaders, 42–43; Reagan's and
Gorbachev's use of term, 49; as result
of search for trust, 65; Reykjavik
summit reducing, 50–52; spiral of,
24, 29; successor generation and,
229. *See also* distrust
Misztal, Barbara, 125
Mitterand, François: Bush and, 63–64,
71; institutionalized summitry and,
203, 204, 206*f*, 214*f*; media and, 209;
Reagan, meeting with, 209*f*; summits, role in, 199, 205, 213
Mongolia, Soviet troop buildup in, 22, 30
monitoring, 123. *See also* verification
Moos, Carlo, 271
moral armament, public diplomacy as,
229
Morgan, Michael Cotey, 7, 102, 282,
283, 284–85
Morgenthau, Hans, 247
Moro, Aldo, 210–11
Moscow Helsinki Group, 48
Mourlon-Druol, Emmanuel, 9, 198, 285
Mulroney, Brian, 66, 70, 74–75, 76, 206*f*
multilateral preparatory talks (MPT),
106–8
mutual and balanced force reductions
(MBFR), 110–11
myths: of proletarian internationalism,
174; of Stalinist brotherhood, 174

NAA. See North Atlantic Assembly
NAC. See North Atlantic Council
Nakasone, Nobuhiko, 199, 206*f*, 214*f*
National Action (Switzerland), 271
National Defense Council (Nationaler
Verteidigungsrat, East Germany),
170, 186
National Intelligence Estimate on Soviet
domestic stresses, 136n20
National Interest (journal), 75
nationalism: opposition nationalism
(Poland), 194n54; Soviet exploitation
of, 176; in Switzerland, 270

National People's Army (Nationale
Volksarmee, NVA, East Germany),
170, 178, 183–84, 185–88, 196n71,
284
National Security Council meetings, 91
national strategies, collective leadership
and, 208–11
National Technical Means (satellite
monitoring), 94
NATO (North Atlantic Treaty Organization): Article 5, 242; Atlantic Council
summits, 201–2; Baker and disagreements over expansion of, 73; cruise
missile deployments, 126; CSCE
and, 7–8; double-track decision, 8,
156–57, 157*t*, 222, 237, 247; impact
of détente on, 168; members of, 173,
228, 246, 261; northern flank, strategy for defense of, 243; at Stockholm
Conference, 47; trust in, 241–42;
Warsaw Pact's influence on, 170. *See
also* United States, NATO flanks and
Natural, Albert, 275n40
NBC Nightly News, 94
negative reciprocation, 132–33
Netherlands, 26; CSCE negotiations,
participation in, 107–8; NATO cruise
missile deployments in, 126
neutrality: CSCE negotiations and neutral states, 114; Switzerland's selective approach to, 260–62
Neutral Nations Supervisory Committee, 270
New Thinking (Soviet Union), 280
New York, Reagan-Gorbachev meeting
in, 54
New York Times: Achilles letter to, 222;
on economic sanctions against China,
28; on Western alliance, challenges
to, 228
Nie Rongzhen, 22, 27
Nimetz, Matthew, 94
Ninth National Congress (CCP), 17
Nixon, Richard: Brezhnev, relationship
with, 31, 263; China-US rapprochement under, 6, 25–26, 28, 30, 34;
CSCE and, 106, 108–9; Denmark,
relations with, 245; Dobrynin,

agreement with, 103; *Foreign Affairs* article, 25; Mao Zedong, meeting with, 269; Nixon doctrine, 28; quiet diplomacy, support for, 48
Non-Atlanticists, 222
Norden zone, 238
North Atlantic Assembly (NAA), 224, 227, 228
North Atlantic Council (NAC), 239, 240, 242, 247, 248, 258n87, 258n91
North Atlantic Treaty Organization. *See* NATO
North Korea, Switzerland's recognition of, 262, 269, 270
North Vietnam, recognition of, 262, 269–70
Nuclear Planning Group (NATO), 247, 258n89, 258n91
nuclear weapons: Central European nuclear-free zone, 177; Denmark's and Greece's attitude toward, 238, 258nn87–89, 258n91; global double zero options, 8, 131; loose nukes, 75; Nuclear Test Ban Treaty, 87; security in nuclear age, 128; Soviet Union leadership changes and, 75; Soviet Union's assistance to China on, 19; theater nuclear forces, 237. *See also* Intermediate-Range Nuclear Forces (INF) Treaty; Strategic Arms Limitation Talks
Nudel, Ida, 45, 52–53, 57n21, 60n73
Nunn, Sam, 75
Nur Khan, Malik, 28
NVA. *See* National People's Army
Nye, Joseph, 219

Obama, Barack, 122
Oder-Neisse border, 174–75, 177
OEEC. *See* Organisation for European Economic Cooperation
official trust regimes, of communist states, 144–45
Ohira, Masayoshi, 205
Olszowski, Stefan, 183
O'Neill, Onora, 64, 65, 66, 69, 72, 78n3
on-site inspections in Soviet Union, 47, 88, 129, 134, 282

Open Skies proposal (Eisenhower), 111
Operation Desert Shield (1990), 68–69
opinion-building in small publics, 144
Order for General Mobilization in Border Provinces and Regions, 35
Organisation for European Economic Cooperation (OEEC), 261
Orlov, Yuri, 49, 56n9, 57n26
Osgood, Charles, 29
Ostermann, Christian F., 1
Ostpolitik, 8, 147–54, 222
Ottawa summit (1981), 205, 209

pacifism in East Germany, 148
Paine, Thomas, 77
Palazchenko, Pavel, 126
Palme Commission, 127
Panhellenic Socialist Movement (PASOK), 240–41, 246–47
Papandreou, Andreas, 238, 240–41, 246
paradoxes of summitry, 213
peaceful coexistence: Warsaw Pact and, 188; West's willingness for, 148, 156
Pedaliu, Effie G. H., 10, 237, 283–84
Peng Dehuai, 20
Pentagon Papers, 269
Pentecostals, 43–46, 56n11, 58n29
People's Liberation Army, Mao's reliance on, 35
People's Republic of China. *See* China
personal (private) diplomacy, 44, 65–69, 73
personal relations, importance of, 283
Petersen, Nikolaj, 249
Petitpierre Doctrine, 261, 273n4
Poland: at CSCE, 106, 181; and Czechoslovakia, invasion of, 176; East Germany, attitudes toward, 179; financial crisis, 182; foreign policy, 181–82; martial law in, 43, 185, 186, 258n91; on military cooperation within Warsaw Pact, 170; Polish People's Army, 173–74, 179, 183–84, 185, 187–88; shaping principles of politics of, 174; Solidarność (Solidarity) movement, 161, 182–84, 187; Soviet influence on, 9, 171–72, 179–80; Stalin and, 174; summit agreements on, 213;

Poland (*continued*)
uprisings in, 105; West Germany and, 176, 177. *See also* East Germany and Poland, mutual dependency and distrust in
Polish Committee of National Liberation (Polski Komitet Wyzwolenia Narodowego, Lublin Committee), 173–74, 175–76
Polish United Workers' Party (Polska Zjednoczona Partia Robotnicza, PZPR), 170, 180, 182, 183
Politburo (SED), 183
politics: of dialogue (*dialogische Politik*), 7, 85; political leadership, institutionalized summitry and changes in, 204; political organizations vs. technical organizations in Swiss foreign policy, 261; political relations, 170–71. *See also names of political parties*
Polska Zjednoczona Partia Robotnicza. *See* Polish United Workers' Party
Polski Komitet Wyzwolenia Narodowego (Polish Committee of National Liberation, Lublin Committee), 173–74, 175–76
Pomeranian Bay, territorial disputes over, 187
Porter, Bruce D., 75
positive reciprocation, 132
Prague Spring, 20
PRC (People's Republic of China). *See* China
Preston, Andrew, 74
Probst, Raymond, 277n59
protest movements, 67–68, 76, 262, 264
public mistrust in SALT, 91–92
Pueblo crisis, 31
Puerto Rico summit (1976), 208, 210, 212
Putnam, Robert, 203, 205
PZPR. *See* Polish United Workers' Party

quadripartite meetings, 212
"A Question of Trust?" (O'Neill), 65, 78n3

Radchenko, Sergey, 6, 17, 279, 280
Rafshoon, Gerald, 95–96
Rambouillet summit (1975), 198, 201, 208
RAND Corporation, 185
Rapacki, Adam, 177
Rasmussen, Anders Fogh, 249
Rawls, John, 65
Reagan, Ronald, 42–62; anticommunism, 42, 56n10; anti-Soviet rhetoric of, 239; charges of Soviet treaty violations, 123; conclusions on, 55, 280, 281–82; critiques of, 67, 228; Denmark's reaction to, 238; deteriorating image of Germany under, 223; domestic influences on, 131; East German attitude toward, 158, 163; end of quadripartite meetings under, 212; footnoting of NATO communiqués during administration of, 248–49; G7 participation, 204, 213, 214f; Gorbachev, relationship with, 6, 8, 46–50, 55n1, 58n35, 126–30, 131–34; Greece's relationship with, 240, 247; human rights, limitations of interest in, 56n8; on mistrust, 3, 58n34; Mitterand, meeting with, 209f; overview of, 6, 42–43; Pentecostals and, 43–46; public diplomacy under, 230; summits, role in, 50–55, 199, 203, 206f; "trust, but verify" slogan, 4, 42, 54, 121–22, 134; trust vs. friendship of, 61n84; Youth Exchange Initiative, 226
reconnaissance technology, 87–90. *See also* National Technical Means, verification
Reddy, William, 5
regime acceptance (US negotiating stance), 133
regimes: communist, 143–45, 152, 162, 267, 269; emotional, 5; horizontal trust regimes, 9; nationalism (Poland), 194n54; totalitarian, 162
religious dissidents. *See* Jewish refuseniks; Pentecostals
Renmin Ribao (newspaper), 26

Republic of Eastern Turkestan, 35
research, need for, 284–86
Reykjavik summit (US-Soviet, 1986), 6, 42, 50–52, 127, 129–30, 132, 133, 283
rhetorical restraint (US negotiating stance), 133
Ridgway, Rozanne, 60–61n77
risk and risk-taking, 2, 3; Bush's desire to minimize, 7, 65; cultural views of, 5; exclusive superpower détente and, 238; NATO's deterrence and assurance aspects, 241; verification and cheating, 123. *See also* vulnerability
Rofe, J. Simon, 7, 63, 281
Rogers, William P., 103
Rogers proposal (1980), 240
Romania: China's relationship with, 21; at CSCE, 106; and Czechoslovakia, invasion of, 176
Romanov, Grigory, 132
Roosevelt, Franklin Delano, 68
Rossetti, Oscar, 277n59
Rousseau, Denise, 124
Rumsfeld, Donald, 76
Rusk, Dean, 87
Russia, United States distinguishing from Soviet Union, 71
Ruzicka, Jan, 125, 240

Saddam Hussein, 65, 68–69, 78
Sakharov, Andrei, 44, 48, 49, 57n26
SALT. *See* Strategic Arms Limitation Talks
Sarotte, Mary Elise, 73
satellite reconnaissance devices, 88–90
Sauvagnargues, Jean, 109
SCC (Standing Consultative Commission), 90–91, 92
Schaufelbuehl, Janick Marina, 10, 259, 284
Schelling, Thomas, 285
Schifter, Richard, 52, 53, 54–55, 62n89
Schlesinger, James, 91, 92
Schmidt, Helmut: Carter, relationship with, 202, 222; East Germans'

attitude toward, 154, 163, 283; economic reflation, response to US request for, 211; European Commission, views of, 211–12; G7 participation, 204; Giscard d'Estaing, relationship with, 9, 198, 200, 203; informality, preference for, 213; international crisis, fears of, 207; Italy, secret support for, 210–11; MfS report on, 158–59; on Soviet missile deployment, 237; on summitry, importance of, 208; summits, role in, 199, 200, 201, 212
Schmitz, David, 73, 74
Schnyder, Felix, 277n59
Schors, Arvid, 7, 85, 281
Schülter, Poul, 239–40
Schwarzenbach, James, 270
Scowcroft, Brent: Bush and, 63, 68; influence of, 72, 73; as participant in one-on-one conversations, 79n15; on Porter article, 75; on Soviet threat, continuance of, 66; strategies of, 7; on Yeltsin, 70
SDI (Strategic Defense Initiative), 89, 129, 247
security dilemma: alliance security dilemma, 243, 244; for China and Soviet Union, 23; mistrust and, 280; new Soviet thinking on, 127; security dilemma sensibility, 127, 132; self-defeating behaviors in, 32
SED (Sozialistische Einheitspartei Deutschlands). *See* Sociality Unity Party
Seelenmassage (massage of the soul), 208
self-defeating behaviors in security dilemmas, 32
self-interest vs. trust, 90
Senate Arms Control Subcommittee, 91
Shanxi province, unrest in, 35
Shcharansky, Anatoly, 44–46, 49, 57n24, 57n26, 58n32
sherpas (personal advisors), 202, 205, 208, 209
Shevardnadze, Eduard, 53, 127, 133

Shultz, George: on Denmark, 240; Gorbachev and, 129, 130–31; on Nudel, call with, 60n73; on Pentecostals, 45–46; Reagan, memo to, 136n20; Soviet Union, influence on, 60–61n77; on US-Soviet negotiations, 54; at Vienna summit, 53

Siberia, Soviet troop buildup in, 22

Sihanouk, Norodom, 28

silent majority (East Germany), 147

The Silent Revolution: Changing Values and Political Styles among Western Publics (Inglehart), 225

Simons, Tom, 44

Six-Day War (1967), 245

Sixth Fleet (US), 243

small states: influences on foreign policy of, 240; opinion-building in, 144. *See also* United States, NATO flanks and

Smith, Gerard, 87–88

Smith, Harold P., Jr., 79n22

Snyder, Glenn, 244

Snyder, Sarah B., 6, 42, 78n12, 281–82, 286

Social Democratic Party (Denmark), 239, 247

Social Democratic Party (Sozialdemokratische Partei Deutschlands, SPD, West Germany), 148, 150, 211

social identity theory, 285

socialism, 104, 190

Socialist People's Party (Denmark), 239

Sociality Unity Party (Sozialistische Einheitspartei Deutschlands, SED, East Germany): conclusions on, 189, 190; control by, 176; independent peace movement, criminalization of, 160; MfS report on, 147; peace policy, recognition of importance of, 157; policy changes (1970s), 181; Social Democratic Party, rapprochement with, 148; socialism, attempts to rescue, 187; totalitarianism of, 183; West Germany, members' opinion on, 152

socialization, at summits, 204–5

Social Liberal Party (Denmark), 239

Soell, Hartmut, 208

Sofaer, Abraham, 133

soft power, public diplomacy as, 219

solidarity, as Swiss foreign policy goal, 261–62

Solidarność (Solidarity) movement, 161, 182–84, 187

South Korea, Switzerland's relations with, 269, 270

South Vietnam, Switzerland's relations with, 269

Sovietization, 175, 179, 188

Soviet Union: Afghanistan, invasion of, 96, 212, 222, 237, 283; China, relationship with, 6, 18, 19–24, 29–32, 279–80; Czechoslovakia, invasion of, 20, 176; Damanskii Island border conflicts, 24–29, 32–36; East German views of, 148, 150–51, 155–56; East Germany, influence on, 171–73, 178, 189; economy of, Gorbachev's interest in, 47–48; end of, 69–72; Graber's evaluation of, 263; human rights issues, 46–47, 49, 52–53; Karamanlis in, 246; leadership change in, 74–75; military buildups, 244–45; Russia as different entity, US response to, 71; SALT verification and, 97–98n6; Soviet Army, Poland and, 179; Spühler's evaluation of, 262; Swiss distrust of, 265, 268; trust and verification, views on, 123–24; United States, relations with, 30–31; US mistrust of, 43, 65–66; Warsaw Pact, domination of, 168, 176; West German cooperation treaty with, 177. *See also* Conference on Security and Cooperation in Europe; Strategic Arms Limitation Talks; Warsaw Pact

Sozialdemokratische Partei Deutschlands (SPD). *See* Social Democratic Party (Sozialdemokratische Partei Deutschlands)

Sozialistische Einheitspartei Deutschlands (SED). *See* Sociality Unity Party

Sparrow, Bartholomew, 69–70, 73, 74

SPD. *See* Social Democratic Party (Sozialdemokratische Partei Deutschlands)

Spillmann, Kurt R., 275n35

spiral of mistrust, 24, 29
Spühler, Willy, 262
Sputnik (Soviet youth periodical), 196n70
Staatssicherheit (Ministry for State Security, MfS). *See* Stasi
Stalin, Joseph, 23, 172–73, 174, 189
Standing Consultative Commission (SCC), 90–91, 92
Stasi (Staatssicherheit, Ministry for State Security, MfS): Jaruzelski, mistrust of, 184; National People's Army, control of, 170; public opinion reports, 147, 150–53, 156–59, 160, 164n14, 283
State Department (US): CSCE negotiations and, 106; working paper on verification, 88
statehood, East German vs. Polish notions of, 178
state socialist societies, 143–46, 154
Stockholm Conference on Confidence- and Security-Building Measures and Disarmament in Europe, 47, 129, 133–34
Strategic Arms Limitation Talks (SALT), 85–101; conclusions on, 96–97, 281; overview of, 7, 85–87; ratification of, 92–96; reconnaissance technology as substitute for trust, 87–90; SALT I, 123; verification technology, reliance on, 90–92
Strategic Defense Initiative (SDI), 89, 129, 247
Streletz, Fritz, 184
Study Commission on Strategic Issues (Switzerland), 274n28
study group on foreign policy (Switzerland), 266–67
Stürmer, Michael, 221
subversive-revolutionary (indirect) war, 265
successor generation, 224–25, 228–29
summitry, 198–217; Cold War and, 211–13; conclusions on, 213; leaders, trust between, 199–206; overview of, 9, 198–99; Western system, trust regarding, 207–11

Sununu, John, 79n15
superordinate identities, 285, 286
superpowers, 1–9, 24, 36, 64, 66, 75, 85–87, 92, 94, 97, 103, 105–6, 108, 114, 124, 126–27, 155–59, 221, 232n25, 238, 244–45, 246, 248, 262, 266, 283–84
supranationality, 143, 167, 169, 170, 190n3, 200, 259
Supreme Commander of the United Armed Forces (Soviet), 169
Sweden: development aid from, 262; North Vietnam, recognition of, 269; Swiss rapprochement with, 268
Switzerland: conclusions on, 284; détente and domestic protest, détente and foreign policy of, 259–78; double-track strategy, 265–67; "good offices" of, 261, 265, 273n5; government assessment of, 262–64; Federal Assembly, 264–65, 266; Federal Council, 260, 263–64, 268–69, 272; Federal Military Department, 264–65; Federal Political Department (later Federal Department of Foreign Affairs), 259–60, 262–64, 266–67, 269–70, 272n1; foreign policy, described, 259–60; fresh assessment of, 264–67; missed opportunities, 271–72; more active foreign policy, 267–70; neutrality, selective approach to, 260–62; overview of, 10, 259–60; popular initiatives, federal, 270; public skepticism toward, 270–71; surveillance of Swiss population, 264, 272; Swiss Party of Labour, 264
Sztompka, Piotr, 145, 171, 240–41

Taiwan Strait, 19, 24
Tartus, Syria, Soviet naval base in, 245
teachers' biases, 228–29
technical organizations, political organizations vs. in Swiss foreign policy, 261
Thatcher, Margaret, 52, 63–64, 199, 204, 206f, 214f, 212
theater nuclear forces. *See* nuclear weapons

threats: subjectiveness of, 29; perceptions of, during Cold War, 262
Tiananmen Square crisis, 67–68, 76
Tielieketi/Zhalanashkol border dispute, 30
Timbie, James, 95
Timerbaev, Roland, 123–24
TNF. See nuclear weapons
Tokyo summit (1979), 205, 206f, 208, 212
totalitarian (authoritarian) regimes, 143, 162, 183
transatlantic relations. See West Germany–United States relations
transformation of Cold War order: Bush and, 63–81; China, 17–41; conclusions on, 279–87; Conference on Security and Cooperation in Europe, 102–20; East Germany, 143–66; East Germany and Poland, 167–97; INF treaty, accepting vulnerability in making of, 121–39; overview of, 1–13; Reagan and, 42–62; Strategic Arms Limitation Talks, 85–101; summitry, 198–217; Switzerland, détente and foreign policy in, 259–78; United States, and NATO flanks, 237–58; West Germany–United States relations, 218–34
transparency: CSCE and, 104–5, 110–13; NATO emphasis of, 8; Stockholm Conference on Confidence- and Security-Building Measures and Disarmament in Europe and, 129; trust and, 65, 285
treaties, connection with diplomatic assurances, 4
triangular diplomacy, 28, 34, 37
Tricentennial (of German immigration to America), 226–27
Trilateral Commission, 207
Trudeau, Pierre, 204, 214f
Truman, Harry S., 245
trust: agreements in absence of, 114; Bush on, 63; as category for analysis of historical processes, 2; characteristics of, 3–4, 65–66, 199, 281; in

communist regimes, 143–44; cultures of, 5, 242; definitions of, 2–3, 46, 124–25; elements for fostering, 203; as fundamental of international relations, 1; history of, 171; as a judgment, 65; Larson on, 44, 55n1; new Ostpolitik as, 147–54; OED definition of, 240; self-interest vs., 90; as social capital, 5; Sztompka on, 145; temporality of, 4, 77; tests of, 66. See also distrust; mistrust; trustworthiness; specific alliances and treaty negotiations
trust, types of, 144–46; conditional, 157; conditional vertical, 145–46; domestic, 282; horizontal, 146, 160, 163; international, 282; interpersonal, 283; vertical, 150, 159–60, 163
"trust, but verify" (dovorey no provorey) slogan (Reagan), 4, 42, 54, 121, 134
trustworthiness: bases for, 280; costly concessions as sign of, 4–5, 8, 47, 55, 286; Gorbachev's changing perceptions of, 126–30; trust and vulnerability and, 122, 124–26
Tuch, Hans N., 225
Turkestan, 35
Turkey: Cyprus, invasion of, 240; Greece, relationship with, 238
Tygodnik Powszechny (The General Weekly) magazine, 176

Überfremdungs-Initiative, 270
Ukraine, decommissioning of weapons of mass destruction in, 75–76
Ulbricht, Walter, 9, 152–53, 173, 176, 177, 181
Unified Armed Forces of the Warsaw Pact, 184
United Kingdom. See Britain/United Kingdom
United Nations: China's admission to, 268; Iraq's invasion of Kuwait, response to, 68–69, 72–73; Switzerland's membership in, question of, 259–61, 267–69, 271; Universal Declaration of Human Rights, 47

United States: China rapprochement, 6, 25–26, 30, 34, 37; Denmark, relations with, 240; domestic arena, trust in, 64; foreign policy, 63, 65, 67, 70–71; G5 membership, 201; G7, views on, 211; Greece's dependence on, 243; human rights concerns, 45; Iran, interactions with, 122; Iraq's invasion of Kuwait, response to, 68–69; as NATO hegemon, 242; nuclear superiority, 89; public diplomacy, 218–19, 221–23; Soviet relations with, 30–31; summitry of, 48, 212; Switzerland's relations with, 262–63, 268; trust and verification, views on, 123; Vietnam War and, 21; West Germany, relationship with, 9–10, 218, 220, 226–29, 285–86. *See also* Strategic Arms Limitation Talks; West Germany-United States relations; *names of presidents*

United States, NATO flanks and, 237–58; background on, 239–42; conclusions on, 245–48; deepening concern over, 242–45; NATO, spreading mistrust in, 245–48; overview of, 10, 237–39

United States Information Agency (USIA), 219, 221–22, 224, 227–29

Universal Declaration of Human Rights (UN), 47

universality, as Swiss foreign policy goal, 261–62, 269, 270

Uyghurs, relationship with Soviet Union, 35

Vance, Cyrus, 92–93

Vashchenko family (Pentecostals), 43–45

Velikhov, Yevgeny, 128–29

Venice summit (1980), 205, 208, 212

Venstre (political party, Denmark), 239

verification: adequate, 93–94; Dobrynin on, 97n6; INF Treaty provisions on, 134–35; as risk minimization, 4; trust, relationship to, 8, 121–24, 281, 282; verification technology, 7, 86–90, 93–94, 96

Versailles summit (1982), 209, 226

vertical trust, 145–46, 150, 159–60, 163

Vest, George, 105

Vienna CSCE Review Meeting, 52–55

Vietnam War, 21, 221, 244–46, 248, 284

vulnerability: conclusions on, 281–82, 286; Gorbachev's in INF Treaty negotiations, 130–34; in trusting relationships, 240; trustworthiness and trust and, 122, 124–26

Wałęsa, Lech, 75

Walker, Martin, 136n21

Walters, Vernon, 89

Wang Ming, 20

wars: East German fear of, 156–58, 156t; indirect (subversive-revolutionary), 265; Kosygin on, 33

Warsaw, Sino-American ambassadorial talks in, 26

Warsaw Pact (Warsaw Treaty Organization): conclusions on, 284; conventional forces, superiority in, 110–11; creation of, 169; CSCE participation by members of, 7, 102, 104; foreign policy coordination, 168; military cooperation within, 169–70, 176, 178–80; military secrecy, belief in, 105; national diversity within, 169; NATO, influence on, 170; Soviet deployment of missiles in, 237; supposed basis for, 178; trust in intrabloc relations in, 167–72; unified command structures of, 188. *See also* Conference on Security and Cooperation in Europe

Watergate scandal, 221, 263

weapons. *See* arms; nuclear weapons

weapons of mass destruction, fall of Soviet Union and, 75–76

wendou (verbal struggle), 25

Wenger, Andreas, 275n35

West (Western system): East German alienation from policies of, 156, 158; on peace, 105; trust regarding, 207–11; Western values, defense of, 227. *See also* NATO; West Germany–United States relations

West Germany (Federal Republic of Germany, FRG): Basic Treaty, signing of, 270; cooperation treaties, 177; CSCE negotiations, participation in, 112; East German public's trust relationship with, 147–54; East Germany, relations with, 159, 162, 181–82; East Germany and Poland, relationship with, 172; East Germany's attitude toward, 8, 150; Federal Defense Forces, 173; Federal Foreign Office, 225; Federal Ministry for Intra-German Relations, 147; G7 participation, 203; Jaruzelski, support of, 184; NATO missile deployments in, 126; Poland, relations with, 181–82; public diplomacy, use of, 218–19; at Puerto Rico and London summits, 212; Switzerland's relations with, 269, 270

West Germany–United States relations, 218–34; conclusions on, 229–30, 285–86; overview of, 9–10, 218–21; perceived deterioration of, 224–25; public diplomacy, new challenges for, 221–23; regaining trust in, 226–29

Wheeler, Nicolas J., 121; on dilemma of interpretation, 172; on Gorbachev, concessions by, 286; on ideological fundamentalism, 135n6; on integrity/reliability pair, 177; overview of, 8; on Reagan-Gorbachev relationship, 282; on security dilemma sensibility, 127; on trusting relationships, 240

Williamsburg summit (1983), 209, 209f, 213, 214f

Wilson, Harold, 200, 201, 207, 213

Woodward, Bob, 73

"Working Group on the Successor Generation" (ACUS), 224–25, 227, 228

Working Group on the USA (Arbeitsgruppe USA), 225

A World Transformed (Bush and Scowcroft), 77–78

Xu Xiangqian, 27

Yakovlev, Alexander, 127

Yanayev, Gennady, 75

Ye Jianying, 27, 34

Yeltsin, Boris, 66, 70–71, 74–75

Youth Exchange Initiative, 226

Yudin, Pavel, 20

Zhenbao/Damanskii Island border dispute, 18, 20, 22–29, 36–37, 280

Zhivkov, Todor, 107

Zhou Enlai: in Beijing, during anticipated Soviet attack, 36; Kosygin and, 33–34; marshals' reports to, 27–28, 31–32, 34; political position of, 17; Soviet overtures, response to, 26–27, 279–80; on Soviet Union, 20–21

Zhuge Liang, 34

Zorin, Valerian, 106

Zumwalt, Elmo, 93

[*continued from p. ii*]

A Distant Front in the Cold War
The USSR in West Africa and the Congo, 1956–1964
By Sergey Mazov

Connecting Histories
Decolonization and the Cold War in Southeast Asia, 1945–1982
Edited by Christopher E. Goscha and Christian F. Ostermann

Rebellious Satellite: Poland 1956
By Paweł Machcewicz

Two Suns in the Heavens
The Sino-Soviet Struggle for Supremacy, 1962–1967
By Sergey Radchenko

The Soviet Union and the June 1967 Six-Day War
Edited by Yaacov Ro'i and Boris Morozov

Local Consequences of the Global Cold War
Edited by Jeffrey A. Engel

Behind the Bamboo Curtain
China, Vietnam, and the World beyond Asia
Edited by Priscilla Roberts

Failed Illusions
Moscow, Washington, Budapest, and the 1956 Hungarian Revolt
By Charles Gati

Kim Il Sung in the Khrushchev Era
Soviet-DPRK Relations and the Roots of North Korean Despotism, 1953–1964
By Balázs Szalontai

Confronting Vietnam
Soviet Policy toward the Indochina Conflict, 1954–1963
By Ilya V. Gaiduk

Economic Cold War
America's Embargo against China and the Sino-Soviet Alliance, 1949–1963
By Shu Guang Zhang

Brothers in Arms
The Rise and Fall of the Sino-Soviet Alliance, 1945–1963
Edited by Odd Arne Westad

WOODROW WILSON CENTER PRESS
STANFORD UNIVERSITY PRESS